# INTERNATIONAL FINANCIAL REPORTING STANDARDS DESK REFERENCE

# INTERNATIONAL FINANCIAL REPORTING STANDARDS DESK REFERENCE

## Overview, Guide, and Dictionary

**Dr. Roger Hussey**
**Dr. Audra Ong**

WILEY
John Wiley & Sons, Inc.

This book is printed on acid-free paper.



Published by John Wiley & Sons, Inc., Hoboken, New Jersey
Published simultaneously in Canada



*Library of Congress Cataloging-in-Publication Data:*

ISBN-13 978-0-471-71450-X

ISBN-10 0-471-71450-X

Printed in the United States of America

10 9 8 7 6 5 4 3 2 1

# Contents

# Foreword

The effort to achieve a single set of global accounting standards has gained significant momentum during the past three years. The logic behind the development of a single set of high-quality global accounting standards for the world's integrating capital markets has been evident for some time. The collapse of Enron and other corporate failures in the United States and elsewhere have led to the reevaluation of existing national and international accounting practices and has served as a catalyst for work being undertaken at the International Accounting Standards Board (IASB) in conjunction with national standard setters throughout the world.

Increasingly, in recognition of the integrating nature of the world's capital markets, national authorities are opting for an international approach to accounting standards. In 2005, some 92 countries throughout the world will require or permit the use of international financial reporting standards (IFRSs), as promulgated by the IASB.

Nowhere is the embrace of high-quality accounting standards possibly more significant than in Europe and Asia. Most countries, however, are beginning to experience the influence of IFRSs in their everyday business.

In Europe, a single economic market would be impossible to operate with 25 countries using 26 different methods of accounting as at present. (Only Ireland and the United Kingdom use the same accounting methods, and some countries allow either or both U.S. GAAP and international standards.)

The Asian financial crisis of the 1990s demonstrated the central role that accounting plays in globalizing capital markets and the potential devastating effects that diminished confidence in financial reporting could have in slowing economic development. The stakes of adopting a strong financial reporting infrastructure are great for emerging economies, because these economies cannot reach their full potential without participation in global markets and without continuing inflows of direct investment.

Reaching the ultimate goal of having a single set of accounting standards worldwide, however, still faces significant barriers. These include a full understanding of the terms used in their particular context and the differences in language. These are problems that the authors of this volume, Dr. Roger Hussey and Dr. Audra Ong, understand well. The IASB, located in London, sets its standards in English and considers the English language standards the official set. It is evident that jurisdictions throughout the world may wish to apply the standards translated in their own language. Without quality in translation, we will risk losing consistency in application of the standards. The IASB has worked to expand its translation resources to improve the quality of the standards provided in other languages, but there is always more work to be done.

Therefore, I welcome this important contribution from Dr. Hussey and Dr. Ong. This volume marks a significant step forward to improving access to international standards for those whose native language is not English and for English speakers. This book is written by authors who clearly understand the challenges facing all who seek to understand and apply international standards. I commend it to you.

**Sir David Tweedie**
Chair of the International
Accounting Standards Board

*London, United Kingdom*
*December 2004*

# Preface

The world of accounting and finance has been going through monumental changes in recent years. At the international level, there have been intense efforts to establish credible and transparent methods for measuring and communicating business financial results. Key factors contributing to increased scrutiny on accounting are the high-profile financial frauds and scandals that received so much media attention. Another key factor is that the increasing complexities of business in today's high-tech, global economy require new accounting approaches.

More and more companies today are doing business on an international scale, creating a need for accountants, executives, and organizations in different countries to reach agreement on accounting rules and standards. The accounting profession has responded by establishing international accounting and financial reporting standards, and substantial progress has been made toward international acceptance of these standards.

If you are a practitioner, manager, or student, or are involved in business in any way, this book will be invaluable. It provides an overview of the International Accounting Standards Board, including a guide to the standards issued as well as a comprehensive dictionary of key international accounting, reporting, and finance terms.

This book consists of three parts and two appendices. The first Part describes the growth of national accounting standards setting, the events leading to the desire for international accounting standards, and the organizational structure, funding, and operation of the IASB. It concludes with an examination of the changes that must be implemented by organizations and countries adopting international accounting standards and the implications for education and training, professional accounting bodies, regulators, and organizations.

The second Part, the Guide, describes the scope and main requirements of each current standard. International Financial Reporting Standards (IFRSs) are lengthy and complex. The Guide captures succinctly the key points of each standard.

The third section, the Dictionary, is a comprehensive reference to words and phrases used in the global business world. Definitions are included for specific terms used in the international standards and are cross-referenced to the particular standard. Appendix A consists of a list of acronyms that relate to the various terms and definitions used in the Overview, Guide, and Dictionary. In addition, a directory of national standard setters is provided as a reference in Appendix B.

It would be imprudent for any authors, particularly compilers of an international guide and dictionary, to claim that their work is the final word on a subject. The business world is complex and constantly changing, and IFRSs will be modified or developed in response to these changes. This Desk Reference is intended to provide a background on how the movement toward a common language for international accounting evolved to its present state, summarize existing standards highlighting the key issues covered, and capture those terms and phrases that are fundamental to an understanding of the common language of global business. We believe that readers will find this book an invaluable reference in helping their comprehension of this language.

**Roger Hussey**
**Audra Ong**

*Canada*
*January 2005*

# Acknowledgments

We wish to acknowledge the advice and comment we received from colleagues around the world. In particular, the following were most helpful in giving perceptive opinions on Part One of the book.

Roger Adams, FCCA, Technical Executive Director, Association of Chartered Certified Accountants (ACCA), United Kingdom

Sally Aisbitt, Ph.D., Open University Business School, England

Russell Craig, Ph.D., Australian National University, Australia

Istemi Demirag, Ph.D., Queen's University, Northern Ireland

Rob Gray, Ph.D., St. Andrew's University, Scotland

John Haverty, Ph.D., Saint Joseph's University, Philadelphia, United States

Wan Nordin Wan Hussin, Ph.D., University Utara, Malaysia

Finally, we would like to thank Andrea Steele from the Faculty of Arts and Social Sciences and Michelle Doerksen, Bree-Anne LaBute, and Alison Scratch from the Odette School of Business at the University of Windsor for their tireless efforts in preparing the manuscript for publication against tight timelines.

As always, the authors take full responsibility for any errors and omissions.

# INTERNATIONAL FINANCIAL REPORTING STANDARDS DESK REFERENCE

# Part One

# OVERVIEW: STANDARD SETTING NATIONALLY AND GLOBALLY

*"Our methods of measurement define who we are and what we value."*

Ken Alder, *The Measure of All Things.* The Free Press, 2002, page 2.

# CHAPTER 1

# The Growth of National Standards

## EARLY DEVELOPMENTS

National procedures, organizations, and regulations for accounting are currently at a watershed, due to the increasing influence of the International Accounting Standards Board (IASB). Effective April 1, 2001, the IASB had assumed standard setting responsibilities from its predecessor body, the International Accounting Standards Committee (IASC).

The national standard setting bodies are also at various stages in their response and strategies. A number of major players, for example the European Union, China, and Australia have adopted, or will soon be adopting, International Financial Reporting Standards (IFRSs) for some or all entities. The U.S. Financial Accounting Standards Board (FASB), through the Norwalk Agreement, and the IASB have given a formal commitment to convergence. More on this is discussed in Chapter 4. Other countries have also declared an intention to converge their standards with international pronouncements, and some still have not decided on their course of action.

Smaller nations generally have not had the resources and infrastructure to generate their own standards, and have either adopted or modeled their regulations on the standards of the United Kingdom or the United States. With the formation of the IASB, several countries chose to adopt international accounting standards. This was particularly true for emerging economies, where the flexibility of the standards made them easier to implement and where there was a concern that adopting the standards of one particular country would have political connotations.

Although there is some public debate concerning the number of countries that will adopt IFRSs, very few countries or organizations will remain completely unaffected by the influence of international harmonization. Business is becoming increasingly global, and accounting is changing rapidly to meet the demands placed upon it. Words and phrases originally used in one country have gained acceptance in others. Pronouncements made by the IASB have found their way, either in part or whole, into accounting practices. Anyone involved in business needs to understand the events that are taking place and how businesses are affected by them.

What is surprising, given the long history of accounting, is that these international events only commenced 30 years ago, with progress accelerating over the last few years. The following brief examination of the very slow development of accounting will help explain the changes that are now taking place.

Since the earliest times, individuals, societies, and civilizations have all experienced the need for some form of record keeping of events, transactions, and other phenomena. Images carved on cave walls illustrated records of quantities, for example, the number of cattle owned, the number of animals killed, the size of enemy forces.

The use of a medium of exchange, whether beads, shells, or coins, allowed a record to be made of economic transactions and events. However, the transactions recorded and the values placed on them possessed many great regional and local variations. It was not until the twentieth century that countries began to establish regulations for identifying the transactions and events that should be recognized and how they should be measured.

The progress over many centuries from simple local records to internationalization of accounting policies and practices has been slow, but the major influences can be identified. Some order was introduced into local practices by governments that require citizens to pay taxation. Since most early taxation systems applied only to the rich, it was clearly advantageous to claim poverty, an argument that is often used today in dealing with government demands for payments from its citizenry. It was also useful to exploit any ambiguities on how wealth should be measured, and even how best to conceal it.

Even the impact of taxation did little to establish a common system of financial record keeping. At best, the records were simple and developed to meet the immediate needs of one specific authority, whether to a tax collector or the lord of the manor. It was not until the publication of Luca Pacioli's *Summa de Arithmetica* in 1494 that a robust system for recording financial transactions, known as double entry bookkeeping, was firmly established and is now used throughout the world.

A common system of recording the financial aspects of transactions does not answer the most fundamental questions, namely:

> What constitutes an economic transaction and what aspects of it should be identified for recording purposes?
>
> What methods should be used for measuring the economic transaction?
>
> Who has the right to receive financial information on the economic transaction?
>
> For what purpose can the information be used reliably?

For individuals these questions are important, but for both profit and not-for-profit organizations, they are critical for ascertaining financial performance and stability as well as discharging disclosure responsibilities to those who have some form of interest in the organization.

## THE ADVENT OF REGULATION

With the impact of the industrial revolution and the growth of various forms of incorporated bodies in the nineteenth century, many countries tried to bring order to the variety of practices within their boundaries by either introducing legislation that set out accounting rules for businesses or providing a general framework for their conduct. An essential part of this legislation was the disclosure of financial information by organizations to various groups.

Legislation and informal consensus on accounting practices could not provide a complete answer to all accounting problems. A more flexible and comprehensive mechanism for regulating practices was required, thus the emergence of standard setting bodies. It was not until the 1970s that the term *accounting standards* came into widespread use as various bodies and committees were formed to discharge this responsibility. The Accounting Standards Steering Committee (ASSC) in the United Kingdom was established in 1970. The U.S. FASB succeeded the Accounting Principles Board (APB) on July 1, 1973, two days after the IASC was formed. The process is still continuing. The Malaysian Accounting Standards Board (MASB) came into being as recently as 1997.

Prior to standard setting boards or committees, accounting bodies issued guidance, bulletins, notes, and other documents to their members to assist them. The step to legal recognition of standards was a key factor in the influence of regulatory pronouncements on financial accounting and reporting.

The aim in developing standards is to produce financial statements that are useful, as well as conceptually and technically sound. In doing this, certain assumptions can be made about the reasons for undertaking financial accounting and communicating the results to other parties. There are two main schools of thought. One is that the purpose of financial accounting and reporting is primarily a stewardship function designed to demonstrate to owners that the business has been properly conducted. The other is that financial reporting is primarily concerned with providing information that is useful for decision makers.

The implications of these two different functions are substantial. With the stewardship function, financial statements are concerned primarily with past activities, and costs and revenues are expressed in terms of those incurred at the time of the actual transaction. With the decision-making function, financial statements are concerned with current values and growth in wealth, adjusted by changes in the value of money.

In order to address the issues concerning the purpose of publishing financial statements and their form and content, many national standard setters have produced "Conceptual Frameworks" or "Statements on the Preparation and Presentation of Financial Statements." Critics would argue that, although these have been helpful in setting standards, there are still too many ambiguities and contradictions, because existing theoretical frameworks are not sufficiently robust. In addition, it can be argued that accounting standard setting is a political process in which the flexibility to influence decisions is preferred to the fetters of theoretical constraints.

In addition, accounting standards do not reflect one strong theoretical approach, because they are issued sequentially and not simultaneously. Standards have been issued for over 30 years. There have been revisions, but standards that are 20 years old are still being applied. Present national bodies have inherited pronouncements made by predecessors with different organizational structures, ways of working, and legal powers. Establishing standards is an evolving process that is built on both strengths and weaknesses of past accounting regimes.

Initially, the demands and pressures of national environments largely formed the nature of standard setting bodies. Over the years, however, they have converged in many of their characteristics. Experiences, mistakes, and good practices have been shared and, at least as far as organizational structures and processes are concerned, there are now few significant differences. However, the contents of the standards issued by various national bodies have contained marked differences. These differences have resulted in difficulties when making international comparisons of organizational financial performance.

The next two chapters explore the drive to pursue international accounting harmonization and the present structure, funding, and operation of the IASB.

This material is followed by two chapters detailing the experiences and strategies of several countries. The penultimate chapter, "Responding to Internationalization," analyzes the potential impact of events on education and training, professional accounting bodies, national standard setters, and organizations. The final chapter is concerned specifically with the role of the accountants. The long-term impact, even in countries not adopting international accounting standards, is substantial and recommendations are given for responding to these challenges.

# CHAPTER 2

# Developing International Accounting Standards

## THE EMERGENCE OF NATIONAL SIMILARITIES

The previous chapter argues that, although early developments may differ, the move toward a national standard setting body is a common phenomenon in many countries. In recent years, national bodies have gravitated toward similar organizational structures with comparable objectives. In particular, there is some form of Oversight Board or Council that has overall responsibility for promoting and guiding standard setting. The standard setting body reports to the Oversight Board, and the committee that reports to the standard setters is referred to as either an Urgent or Emerging Issues Task Force. The Task Force responds to immediate changes that are taking place in accounting and financial reporting. Finally, there is a mechanism for providing interpretations of standards where there is ambiguity or lack of clarity. In general, this process of standard setting has some form of legal authority.

The processes and mechanisms for identifying an accounting issue that needs to be addressed by standard setters are similar among countries but the dynamics can be very different. Standard setters work within a coalition of interests including reporting organizations, shareholders, the media, political groups, and others. The powers of these interested parties differ, and the need and desire of the accounting standard setters to gain the support of particular factions also vary. For example, the United States is notable because of the considerable statutory authority of the Securities and Exchange Commission (SEC) to participate in the standard setting process and the extent to which lobbying takes place. In the United Kingdom, support is more indirect, with the legislation requiring organizations to comply with accounting standards but with little direct government influence in the development of standards.

In addition to responding to a coalition of interests, standard setters have to determine whether to strive for technically superior solutions to problems or whether to propose a more politically acceptable alternative. They also have to concern themselves with the feasibility of the solution, and the costs and benefits of attempting to resolve the problem. Understandably, standard setters would like to establish a conceptual framework, or fundamental theory of accounting, that supports their pronouncements by demonstrating that a standard has a theoretical foundation and, thus, cannot be challenged. It is equally understandable that there are others who believe either that it is impossible to achieve a conceptual framework that will deliver this intellectual support or that it is undesirable to have a technical framework controlling a sociopolitical process.

The pronouncements of governments, professional accounting bodies, and standard setters deal with a combination of accounting and reporting issues that can be grouped into four main, intertwining classifications as follows:

*Procedural matters* specify clearly how accounting records are to be kept and how transactions are to be recognized in the records. These have been most common in continental Europe and in command/socialist economies where the aim has been to establish a uniformity of accounting practices across the country.

*Recognition pronouncements* are concerned with establishing what will be accepted as an economic transaction for financial accounting and reporting purposes. For example, purchased goodwill can be recognized in the financial statements but not internal goodwill that has been generated by an organization itself.

*Measurement pronouncements* specify how revenues, expenses, gains, losses, assets, and liabilities should be measured in the financial statements. An example is the requirement to measure inventories at the lower of cost and net realizable value. Of course, the pronouncement must explain what is meant by cost and net realizable value.

*Disclosure pronouncements* are concerned with the content and presentation of information in financial statements. An example is the disclosure of accounting policies by organizations. This is possibly the most important of the four classifications because disclosure requirements have immediate impact on users. They can also be applied where there are uncertainties of recognition and measurement issues by requiring organizations to provide comprehensive information on particular matters.

## THE IMPETUS FOR GLOBAL STANDARDS

Despite similarities in organizational structures, procedures, and types of standards, there are still important differences among national standard setters in the substance of their pronouncements. This is due mainly to differences of opinion concerning recognition and measurement issues, sometimes for technical reasons but often shaped by political influences. One of the consequences is that it is possible to examine a set of financial statements from a company in one country but be unable to compare them to a similar company in another country. This is because the financial statements had been drawn up according to different accounting and reporting requirements.

In the latter half of the twentieth century, there were some highly publicized examples of very profitable companies in Europe (for example Daimler Benz) that wanted to list shares on the New York Stock Exchange (NYSE). In order to do so, the profitable company had to redraft those financial statements in accordance to U.S. Generally Accepted Accounting Principles (GAAP). In some instances, the previously declared profit for a financial year turned into a loss. Thus, a conceptual inconsistency exists, since the activities of a particular company in a specific financial period can show either a profit or loss depending on which accounting regime applies.

Plausible explanations can be found for the differences that occur. In many countries, national law has been dominant and sometimes presents the only guide to financial accounting and reporting. Often, the law has been more interested in identifying profit for tax purposes rather than revealing the financial performance and stability of an organization. In some countries, many businesses are family-owned with no outside financial interests and with little pressure to disclose financial information. In others, there are large shareholders and institutional investors with corresponding financial institutions and infrastructure to meet their needs.

The other factor that is generally agreed to be potentially very important in explaining differences in regulations is the influence of national culture. Accounting practitioners and academics have tried to explain the ways and aspects of culture that are instrumental in determining the accounting regulations adopted by a country. There may be national characteristics such as openness, morality, and prudence, as well as assumptions about the way that society should be ordered. All these issues may affect the way that financial transactions are recognized, recorded, measured, and communicated. Although our understanding of the nature of culture in the accounting context has developed, it remains a complex concept.

Although the above factors have been important in the past in explaining the different national regulations, they are now overshadowed by the needs of an increasingly globalized world. For companies, particularly multinational ones, it is expensive and complex to draw up different sets of accounts for the various countries in which they operate. A shared accounting language would enhance ease of business and credibility for the companies that conduct transactions with foreign partners. The ability to conduct international comparisons is imperative for investors, both large and small. In order for international capital markets to operate efficiently and effectively, global accounting standards are essential. All business people need to be able to communicate effectively.

Undoubtedly, there are difficulties in gaining worldwide acceptance of international accounting standards, but current events suggest that progress is being made. Increasingly, the language of accounting and the way that standards are being established have permeated all aspects of business. Even countries and companies that are not adopting international accounting standards are unable to ignore the impact of international convergence. It is, therefore, invaluable to understand the development, organization, and method of working of the international accounting standard setters, the International Accounting Standards Committee (IASC) and its successor, the International Accounting Standards Board (IASB).

## THE INTERNATIONAL ACCOUNTING STANDARDS COMMITTEE

In 1973, national accountancy bodies from Australia, Canada, France, Germany, Mexico, the Netherlands, the United Kingdom and Ireland, and the United States established the IASC. The objectives of the IASC were:

- To formulate and publish, in the public interest, accounting standards to be observed in the presentation of financial statements and to promote their worldwide acceptance and observance.
- To work generally for the improvement and harmonization of regulations, accounting standards, and procedures relating to the presentation of financial statements.

The above objectives were extremely ambitious for an organization that was resourced very modestly and had no enforcement powers. The IASC intended to achieve these objectives by:

- Ensuring that published financial statements comply with International Accounting Standards (IASs) in all material respects.
- Persuading governments and standard setting bodies that published financial statements comply with international accounting standards (IASs).

- Persuading authorities controlling securities markets and the industrial and business community that published financial statements to comply with IASs.

It is important to emphasize that the IASC was not established primarily to promote the growth of international capital markets. The reverse was the case, and it was the increasing globalization of markets and business that led to increasing pressure for international accounting standards.

It is uncertain whether the IASC had, as its long-term aim, the achievement of standardization with all accounting regimes being the same or harmonization with some differences being acceptable. In its early years, with scarce resources and little power, the IASC concentrated mainly on the harmonization of financial reporting on a worldwide basis.

It is a tribute to the effectiveness of the IASC that it received substantial support and encouragement. In 1981, IASC and the International Federation of Accountants (IFAC) agreed that IASC would have full and complete autonomy in setting international accounting standards and in publishing discussion documents on international accounting issues. At the same time, all members of IFAC became members of IASC.

Throughout the 1980s, more countries joined the IASC and in 1987, the International Organization for Securities Commissions (IOSCO) joined the Consultative Group and gave its support to the Comparability Project. In that year, the first bound volume of IASs was published.

In total, the IASC issued 41 international accounting standards that dealt with major topics of importance in the preparation and presentation of financial statements. Success was achieved at harmonizing several national standards, but many of the standards gave considerable flexibility in accounting treatments and alternative approaches. This allowed national standard setters to claim that their own standards harmonized with international standards. However, when specific regulations applied by different countries were compared, many important variations still remained. The final result was that there were substantial difficulties in comparing financial statements produced by companies in different accounting regimes.

One major factor in promoting the role of the IASC was the reaction of the emerging economies. Many were attempting to establish themselves in international trade or to move away from command economies. The IASC offered a quick and viable way for establishing an appropriate and acceptable accounting regime. The standards offered significant flexibility, which eased the process of adoption. The other benefit was they carried none of the possible political connotations from adopting the standards of one particular country.

A second factor assisting the IASC was the increased encouragement from several organizations and countries to pursue the goal of international harmonization more rapidly and effectively. For example, the European Union (EU) had for many years been seeking accounting harmonization throughout the EU by issuing Directives that were binding on all member states. In 1978, the Fourth Company Law Directive dealing with the annual accounts of companies was passed. The Seventh Directive passed in 1983 extended this to the preparation of consolidated accounts. However, progress was slow and the process cumbersome. Toward the end of the 1980s, the European Commission gave increasing support to the efforts of the IASC.

These developments encouraged the IASC to take a more proactive approach. It refined its earlier objectives and defined its role as:

- Developing robust standards to satisfy the needs of international capital markets and the international business community
- Producing and helping to implement accounting standards that satisfy financial reporting needs of developing and newly industrialized nations
- Achieving greater compatibility between national accounting requirements and international accounting standards

In 1995, the IASC embarked on an ambitious program in the next stage of its development. In an agreement with IOSCO, the IASC set out to issue a core set of standards. The "core standards" project resulted in 15 new or revised standards and was completed in 1999 with the publication of *IAS 39, Financial Instruments: Recognition and Measurement.* These core standards reduced the level of alternatives available and established benchmark treatments and permitted alternatives.

IOSCO spent a year reviewing the results of the project, releasing a report in 2000. The report recommended that IOSCO members allow multinational issuers to apply IASC standards for cross-border listings. However, it also allowed its members to require reconciliation, disclosure, and interpretation, where necessary, to address outstanding substantive issues at a national or regional level.

Although the IASC was successful in the core standards project, in retrospect, it is easy to see that the work it was attempting to undertake was impossible, because of the way that the organization was structured and resourced. The IASC recognized the problems confronting it. First, too many of its standards allowed alternative choices in accounting treatment and were open to different interpretations. Thus, companies could claim to be following international accounting standards but still draw up financial statements that were not comparable. Second, a major weakness in the operation of the IASC was that it did not have enforcement powers or mechanisms to obtain compliance. Thus, consensus could only be achieved by issuing standards that were flexible enough to obtain widespread acceptance.

Third, there were also structural and resource problems beyond the power of the IASC to remedy. The members of the IASC were from various national professional accounting bodies. Many of these had no responsibility for standard setting in their own countries, thus reducing the IASC's ability to influence and persuade national standard setters.

Finally, there was the question of how much independence the IASC needed from the professional accounting bodies to conduct its activities. The technical contribution of the professional accounting bodies was essential but was regarded by some as placing the IASC under the direct influence of one particular interest group. There were other interest groups represented, for example, analysts and academics, but professional accounting bodies were perceived as dominant. To some extent, this perceived dominance also weakened the possibility of achieving a mechanism for enforcement. Few wished to allow professional accounting bodies, however well-intentioned, to make the regulations for worldwide accounting as well as to possess the power to enforce them.

Although there was a desire to make progress, the question of whether the IASC could achieve the goals remained. Either a complete overhaul of all aspects of the IASC was required, or a new body would have to be formed. The second course of action was chosen.

CHAPTER 3

# The International Accounting Standards Board

## FORMATION OF THE IASB

The IASB was established formally in April 2001, but it took many years to arrive at that point. Although there was substantial support for the International Accounting Standards Committee (IASC), a number of organizations were looking for a more rapid and robust approach to internationalization. Discussions on how the operation of the IASC could be improved gradually moved to proposals that included the structure and funding of the IASC. One mover in these discussions was a group known as G4+1.

In 1992, the standard setters of Canada, the United Kingdom, and the United States met to discuss some of the accounting issues confronting them. A major problem was the proper treatment for provisions, and the three countries agreed to work jointly in seeking a solution. Australia later joined the working group, as did New Zealand. This was the start of the G4+1 and an invitation was given to the IASC (the +1) to join them. The reason for this inclusion was mainly political, since the original English-speaking countries did not wish to be criticized for attempting to set an international accounting agenda unilaterally.

The G4+1 addressed a number of major accounting issues from a strong conceptual basis and also became involved with discussions on the structure and effectiveness of the IASC. In the proposals that the group made on the future of the IASC, it appeared to many critics that the G4+1 would have increasing power over international accounting standards. The group denied that this was their intent, but there is no doubt of their influence in the way that international accounting standard setting has been established. In January 2001, it was agreed that the G4+1 group would disband, since the IASB was ready to take over from IASC. The G4+1 group cancelled its proposed future activities and submitted its current work to the IASB as potential future projects.

The activities of G4+1 encouraged the IASC to reflect and review its position. In 1998, a Strategy Working Party, set up by the IASC, issued a discussion paper. After extensive consultation, the IASC approved a resolution supporting a new structure. An independent organization, the IASC Foundation (IASCF), would be set up and would be responsible for four distinct bodies: the Trustees, the IASB, the Standing Interpretations Committee (SIC), and the Standards Advisory Council (SAC). Although the IASCF is the parent entity of the IASB, it is the latter body that is responsible for issuing accounting standards.

The objectives of the IASB are:

- To develop, in the public interest, a single set of high quality, understandable and enforceable global accounting standards
- To help participants in the world's capital markets and other users make economic decisions by having access to high quality, transparent, and comparable information
- To promote the use and vigorous application of those standards
- To bring about convergence of national accounting standards and international accounting standards to high quality solutions

The IASC Foundation is not merely a figurehead. It has 19 individuals who are appointed as Trustees and act under the constitution of the Foundation. They must show a firm commitment to the IASC Foundation and the IASB as a high quality global standard setter, be financially knowledgeable, and be able to meet the time commitment.

It is the responsibility of the Trustees to appoint the members of the IASB, the SIC, and the SAC. The Trustees' other duties include reviewing external events that affect accounting standards and the strategy of the IASB and its effectiveness in operation. The Foundation also approves the annual budget of the IASB and determines the basis for funding.

The resourcing of the IASB is different from that of the IASC. It is the responsibility of the Trustees to secure sufficient funding for the IASB to operate effectively and the IASB has a budget of approximately US$18 million per year. This funding greatly exceeds the modest funding of its predecessor.

The IASB and IOSCO continue to work together to resolve outstanding accounting and reporting issues and to identify areas where new standards are needed. Representatives from the International Organization for Securities Commissions (IOSCO) sit as observers on the SIC.

## STRUCTURE OF THE IASB

The IASC Foundation is an independent organization with the Trustees and the IASB, as well as the SAC and the SIC. Of the 19 Trustees, there are 6 from North America, 6 from Europe, 4 from Asia-Pacific, and 3 others from any area, as long as geographic balance is maintained. The International Federation of Accountants (IFAC) suggests candidates to fill 5 of the 19 Trustee seats. International organizations of preparers, users, and academics suggest one candidate from each group. The remaining 11 Trustees are at-large, in that they are not selected through the constituency nomination process.

In November 2004, following a year of review, the IASC published for public comment a consultative document proposing changes to its constitution. The consultative document does not alter the basic framework of the organization, and the IASB would remain responsible for standard setting (see Exhibit 3.1). The main proposals are concerned with the composition of the Trustees and the IASB and some relatively minor amendments to the operational proceedings of the IASB.

The IASB currently has 14 members (12 full-time and 2 part-time). The Board has sole responsibility for setting accounting standards. The foremost qualification for Board membership is technical expertise. The Trustees exercise their best judgment to ensure that any particular constituency or regional interest does not dominate the Board. At least five Board members have backgrounds as practicing auditors; at least three have backgrounds in the preparation of financial statements; at least three have backgrounds as users of financial statements; and at least one has an academic background.

The SAC provides a forum for further groups and individuals having diverse geographic and functional backgrounds to give advice to the Board and, at times, to advise the Trustees.

The SIC, later to become the International Financial Reporting Interpretations Committee (IFRIC), reviews accounting issues that are likely to receive divergent or unacceptable treatment in the absence of authoritative guidance, with a view to reaching consensus as to the appropriate accounting treatment. In developing interpretations, the committee works closely with similar national committees. The SIC has up to 12 voting members, with a

**Exhibit 3.1** Structure of the IASCF/IASB

non-voting chairman. Members are appointed by the Trustees. In making appointments, the Trustees aim for a reasonably broad geographical representation. Many of the members are practicing accountants with technical expertise. Membership also includes representation of accountants in industry and users of financial statements.

## FUNDING AND OPERATION OF THE IASB

One crucial element in establishing the IASB was that it would have sufficient resources to carry out the responsibilities placed upon it. The task of securing those funds rests with the Trustees. In the first year, a budget was set of approximately £12 million, and in 2001 a total of 188 corporations, associations and other institutions provided the financial support. Some of these supporters are known as underwriters and they gave five-year pledges of between US$100,000 and US$200,000 annually.

The basis of funding has not changed much over the years. Although there has been an increase in expenditure, the IASCF had managed to build up a reserve fund of £11 million by the date of the 2003 Annual Report and Accounts. It lost US$1 million through the demise of Arthur Andersen but the Trustees continue to find additional supporters.

There have been concerns expressed of the possible threat to the IASB if it is dependent on certain organizations for part of its resources. This has not, at this stage, presented a major issue, but the five-year pledges given by the underwriters will shortly come to an end. The Trustees are therefore seeking ways of funding operations that will not lead to perceptions of possible influence from fund providers and that will establish sources of funds that are regular and reliable.

A preferred model would be to require those parties who benefit from the work of the IASB to fund it. Unfortunately, this would be very difficult to apply at the international level. In addition, the national standard setters have different models for their resourcing so there is not an immediate apparent way for building on those models. For example, the FASB raises two-thirds of its operating costs from the sale of publications whereas the IASB is closer to a mere 10%.

In 2004, as part of its update on the Constitution Review, the Trustees started to explore ways of ensuring a more stable resourcing platform. At the same time, they are aware that the increasing number of countries using International Financial Reporting Standards (IFRSs) places even more demands on the resources. A large part of the work that the IASB does is already being supported by many organizations that contribute time and effort. Without this support, the Board would not be able to continue its operations at the current level.

In many respects, the process of standard setting by the IASB is little different from that of many national bodies. Board members, members of the SAC, national standard setters, securities regulators, other organizations and individuals, and the IASB staff are encouraged to submit suggestions for new topics that might be the subject of a standard.

Having established an accounting issue, there is a lengthy procedure to ensure wide consultation and full consideration of problems and alternative solutions. The IASB may decide to establish an Advisory Committee to give advice on the issues arising in the project. Consultation with the Advisory Committee and the SAC occurs throughout the project. It is also usual for the

IASB to issue Discussion Documents that are circulated widely for public response. Field tests, both in developed countries and in emerging markets, may be made as the project progresses, to ensure that proposals are practical and workable around the world.

After comments have been received and examined, and field tests have been conducted, the IASB publishes an Exposure Draft for public comment. The Exposure Draft takes the same form and content of what is expected to be the final standard, although there remains an opportunity for changes to be made. After considering comments on the Exposure Draft, the IASB issues a final International Accounting Standard (IAS).

In April 2001, the IASB announced that future accounting standards would be called "International Financial Reporting Standards" (IFRSs). Standards issued by the IASC that are still in circulation are referred to as "International Accounting Standards" (IASs).

The International Financial Reporting Interpretations Committee (IFRIC) is the successor to the SIC. It is responsible for interpreting requirements of standards that may be controversial or capable of being applied in a way other than that intended by the IASB. The Committee develops Draft Interpretations (numbered D1, D2, etc.) and releases these for public comment. When approved by IFRIC, they are sent to the IASB for review, approval, and release as Final Interpretations. Organizations cannot claim that their financial statements comply with IFRSs unless they comply both with the requirements of the standard and any interpretation that has been issued.

Meetings of the IASB, the SAC, and the IFRIC are open to public observation. However, certain discussions (primarily selection, appointment, and other personnel issues) are held in private. The IASB is investigating the greater use of technology to make it easier for interested parties, who are prevented by geographical distances, to be more involved in its procedures. The IASB has direct liaison with eight national standard setting bodies in Australia, Canada, France, Germany, Japan, New Zealand, the United Kingdom, and the United States.

## ENFORCEMENT

For standards to be effective, some form of monitoring and enforcement is required. The IASB does not have direct powers or procedures to ensure this, but some mechanisms are already available or are being created. The IASB, however, has to rely on national bodies to ensure enforcement.

The first stage of monitoring for compliance is at the internal level where control systems, including internal audit, can ensure that standards are applied. This is reinforced by external auditors who are independent and have necessary expertise. The commitment of management is also required to ensure that financial statements fairly represent the financial performance and position of the organization.

The final and critical stage is a monitoring and enforcement mechanism held by a regulator. There are models currently employed at the national level. There are security commissions, such as the SEC in the United States, stock exchanges that can de-list companies for regulatory transgressions, and other bodies that have some legal support such as the Financial Reporting Review Panel (FRRP) in the United Kingdom.

These examples are at the national level, and there is concern that differences in approach can lead to differing applications and interpretations of international standards. There are indications that effective enforcement mechanisms are beginning to appear that stretch across national boundaries. In 2003, the Committee of European Security Regulators (CESR) issued two enforcement standards that European Union national security regulators are implementing.

The first standard of CESR sets out 21 basic principles intended to be applied nationally to the financial information published by listed companies including the following measures:

- Enforcement activities to be conducted by competent independent administrative authorities in each country
- Financial statements to be selected for monitoring on the basis of risk and not on a sample basis
- A range of sanctions to be available, including public correction of misstatements where accounts are found to be deficient

The second standard from CESR aims to coordinate enforcement activities throughout the European Union. This will incorporate the exchange of information on various issues, and a database of decisions taken by national enforcers. Although the procedures laid out by CESR remain to be tested, the model is one that could be extended to an international level.

## THE PATH TO CONVERGENCE

Although the word *harmonization* was the term frequently used by the IASC, *convergence* is the term promoted by the IASB. This is not merely a case of semantics, but one suspects an attempt to signal that IFRSs are not being imposed by a global standard setter, but that nations are moving gradually toward each other in agreeing on, and establishing, the highest quality standards.

The debate is not about which country has the best standards but how the desirable elements of the alternatives can be developed into a set of rigorous standards that can achieve global acceptance. There are some who doubt this approach and argue that convergence is no more than negotiation. They claim that the outcome is not the technically best standard but a reflection of the relative negotiating powers of those involved in the process. They also argue that many countries do not participate fully in the process and that there is a considerable disparity in the balance of power among the countries attempting to influence the substance of a standard.

Another argument is that if agreement could be reached on a fundamental theory of accounting, or conceptual framework, convergence or negotiation is not required. Unless the main effort is put into developing a conceptual framework, international standards will display the same ambiguities and deficiencies as national ones.

There is some validity in these criticisms, but standard setting at both the national and international level is not only a technical process but is also a political process and is therefore concerned with what is possible. Not only is there controversy at the international level, but within countries. There are the advocates of convergence, the adherents of national standards, and those who are undecided. Agreement can be reached at the global level only if the arguments carry enough support within each country.

# CHAPTER 4

# Internationalization and the G4+1 Countries

## INTRODUCTION

The formation of an international accounting standard setting body was promoted by several countries. Of these, Australia, New Zealand, Canada, the United Kingdom, and the United States were instrumental in these developments. They met to discuss common accounting problems and possible resolutions. They also acted as a stimulus to the acceleration of international accounting harmonization and supported the emergence of the International Accounting Standards Board (IASB).

The group has now disbanded, but the countries remain highly active in the arena of international accounting. They are members of the group of eight countries with which IASB has direct liaison. They also act in combinations of two or more to address common problems and to conduct research on various accounting topics.

Given the history of the cooperation of these countries in promoting internationalization of accounting, it is somewhat surprising that they have not all responded to convergence in the same way. Australia, New Zealand, and the United Kingdom have decided to adopt International Financial Reporting Standards (IFRSs). Canada is currently debating on the issue, and the United States is committed to the principle but is less certain about the substance.

An analysis of the developments within each country helps to explain their different responses. It also highlights the difficulties and issues faced by these countries on the route to convergence and the possible solutions to some of the barriers.

## AUSTRALIA AND NEW ZEALAND

These two countries are dealt with under one heading because of the strong interconnection in the structure and processes of their standard setting. The Accounting Standard Board in New Zealand has the responsibility to maintain contact with the Australian Accounting Standards Board (AASB) with the objective of harmonizing standards between the two countries.

The Australian Accounting Research Foundation (AARF) was established originally by the Australian Society of Certified Practicing Accountants (AS-CPA) and The Institute of Chartered Accountants in Australia (ICAA). The Foundation undertakes a range of technical and research activities on behalf of the accounting profession as a whole. A major responsibility of the Foundation is the development of Statements of Accounting Concepts and Accounting Standards. The Public Sector Accounting Standards Board (PSASB) is one of the boards of the Foundation.

The Australian Securities Commission Act 1989 established the Australian Accounting Standards Board (AASB). The Board has responsibility for the development of accounting standards for application by companies and by other entities in the private sector, and for the development of Statements of Accounting Concepts. Previously, the AASB worked jointly with the accounting profession and used the services of the staff of the AARF. In 1999, the Corporate Law Economic Reform Program Act established new arrangements for standard setting, which came into effect on January 1, 2000.

There is a Financial Reporting Council (FRC) with oversight responsibility for the AASB, which is responsible for standard setting in the private and public sectors, and has its own research and administrative staff. The Council is responsible for broad oversight of the accounting standard setting process for both private and public sectors. It comprises key stakeholders from the business community, the professional accounting bodies, governments, and regulatory agencies.

Key functions of the FRC are to advise the government on the accounting standard setting process and the development of international accounting standards, and to determine the broad strategic direction of the AASB. The FRC may give the AASB directions, advice, and feedback on matters of general policy, and is responsible for approving its priorities, business plan, budget, and staffing arrangements. However, the FRC does not influence the technical deliberations of the AASB or the content of particular accounting standards.

Until December 1999, the former AASB and the PSASB developed Australian Accounting Standards Board Accounting Standards and Australian Accounting Standards (AASs), with the former applying to organizations regulated under company legislation and the latter applying to all other entities. From 2000, AASs are being phased out and AASB's Accounting Standards will apply to all types of entities.

The AASB established plans in 2003 to ensure that for-profit entities complying with AASB standards would also be complying with IASB standards. The approach is to adopt the content and wording of IFRSs except where there is a need to amend the wording to accommodate the Australian context, for example, a reference to specific legislation. However, a dilemma arises because IFRSs apply only to for-profit entities, and the AASB issues standards for all types of entities. In order to resolve this problem, additional wording will be added to meet the needs of not-for-profit entities without changing the IFRS requirements relevant to for-profit entities.

In endeavoring to ensure that Australian standards are the equivalent of IASB standards, the AASB is bound by Part 12 of the Australian Securities and Investments Commission Act 2001. In general, Part 12 states that, among other matters, accounting standards should facilitate the Australian economy by reducing the cost of capital, enabling Australian entities to compete effectively overseas and to maintain investor confidence in the Australian economy. Although it is unlikely that there will be a conflict, IASB standards do not profess to advance certain aspects of the economy in any particular country, but it is assumed that robust accounting standards will do so. However, should there be a conflict between Part 12 and a specific IFRS, it is possible for the AASB to decide that adoption of the international standard may not be in the best interests of the country.

The legal authority for accounting standards in New Zealand rests with the Accounting Standards Board that was established in 1993 as a Crown Entity. The primary role of the Board is approval of Financial Reporting Standards (FRSs) developed by other bodies or persons, thus contributing to the quality of financial accounting and reporting in both the public and private sectors.

FRSs can be submitted to the Accounting Standards Board for approval by any person or organization as long as sufficient consultation has taken place, as set out in "Release No. 6: The Role of the Accounting Standards Review Board and the Nature of Approved Financial Reporting Standards." FRSs approved by the Board may be legally applicable to a wide range of organizations, including issuers of securities to the public; companies (except small companies falling within the statutory exemption parameters); and groups of companies, the Crown, and all departments, offices of parliament, Crown Entities, and all local authorities.

The only submission of FRSs to the ASB for review and approval has been from the Financial Reporting Standards Board (FRSB). The Board comes under the auspices of the Institute of Chartered Accountants of New Zealand. The FRSB has made a commitment to the policy of international harmonization of New Zealand financial reporting standards.

## CANADA

The Accounting Standards Board in Canada (AcSB) has adopted and maintained a characteristic different from many other countries: it is not independent of the accounting profession. The Canadian Institute of Chartered Accountants (CICA) has been active, since 1946, in deliberating on accounting issues and offering guidance through an Accounting and Auditing Research Committee. The guidance was subsequently formalized into Bulletins that became the Canadian Institute of Chartered Accountants Handbook (CICA Handbook).

The dominance of the CICA was recognized in 1972, when the Canadian Securities Commission required all public firms to follow the recommendations in the Handbook. The Canadian Business Corporations Act 1975 requires the financial statements of all firms incorporated under the Act to comply with the Handbook. Subsequent legislation reinforced their position, and the CICA is responsible for accounting standard setting in Canada and has retained that authority to this day.

The present AcSB is an independent body created by the CICA. It is responsible for establishing standards of financial accounting and reporting by Canadian companies and not-for-profit organizations. Following the recommendation in May 1998 of a CICA Task Force on Standard Setting (TFOSS), the Accounting Standards Oversight Council (AcSOC) was established in 2000 to serve the public interest by overseeing and providing input to the activities of the Accounting Standards Board in Canada (AcSB). Commencing in 2003, the AcSOC also oversees and provides input to the activities of the Public Sector Accounting Board (PSAB). The PSAB is responsible for establishing accounting standards for the public sector.

The AcSOC promotes the setting of accounting standards by the AcSB and PSAB domestically, and supports and contributes to the establishment of internationally accepted standards. The AcSOC also provides opportunities for the public to comment on all aspects of accounting setting and reports to the public annually on the performance of the AcSB and PSAB. Currently, the CICA funds the AcSOC and also provides all necessary administrative and other support.

The role of the AcSB and its relationship with the CICA has been questioned, particularly by the Certified General Accountants of Canada (CGA). This has become an increasingly important issue with the advent of IFRSs and system. The FRC now has a more active role in corporate governance, compliance, auditing, and oversight of the professional accounting bodies. It also has three additional subsidiary boards reporting to it in addition to the original ASB and the Financial Reporting Review Panel (FRRP). These three new boards are:

Professional Oversight Board for Accountancy (POBA)

Auditing Practices Board (APB)

Accountancy Investigation and Discipline Board (AIDB)

Although the organizational structure of the FRC has been expanded, the subsidiary boards are independent in exercising their functions. The role and the responsibilities of the ASB remain unchanged.

Accounting standards developed by the ASB are named Financial Reporting Standards (FRSs). Soon after starting its activities, the ASB adopted the standards issued by the ASC, so that they also fall within the legal definition of accounting standards. These are designated "Statements of Standard Accounting Practice" (SSAPs). While some of the SSAPs have been superseded by FRSs, others remain in force. Accounting standards apply to all companies and to other kinds of organizations that prepare accounts that are intended to provide a true and fair view.

The embracing of IFRSs in the United Kingdom has been, to a large extent, predictable. The country had already experienced an extended period of accounting harmonization through its membership of the European Union. Although this may not have produced all the changes that were desired, it helped to create the mindset that it is possible to harmonize and that there are advantages to be gained. The main questions on convergence have been when and how, and these questions have now been answered. In 2005, the European Union adopted IFRSs for the consolidated accounts of listed companies. In the United Kingdom, unlisted companies can choose to apply IFRSs if they wish.

The plans announced by the ASB for converging with IFRSs have been based on the assumption that there is no case for the United Kingdom to retain two distinct sets of standards in the long term. Therefore, there will be a phased approach over the medium term of bringing all U.K. standards in line with IFRSs. Most of these standards are already in line with IFRSs. Thereafter, U.K. standards will be replaced by IFRSs as the projects of the IASB are completed.

It is proposed that when this process is complete, the role of the ASB will be to work with the IASB and other international bodies, communicating with its constituents, and addressing U.K. accounting issues. It has modified its role from being mainly concerned with the development of domestic standards to contributing to and influencing international accounting standard setting.

## UNITED STATES

The Securities Exchange Act of 1934 gave the Securities and Exchange Commission (SEC) the statutory authority for financial accounting and reporting standards for publicly held companies. The Commission's policy has always been to depend on the private sector for this function.

Financial accounting and reporting pronouncements were established first by the Committee on Accounting Procedure of the American Institute of Certified Public Accountants (AICPA) from 1936 to 1959 and then by the Accounting Principles Board (APB), also a part of the AICPA for the years 1959 to 1973. Pronouncements of those predecessor bodies remain in force unless amended or superseded by the Financial Accounting Standards Board (FASB).

In 1973, the FASB was established and has responsibility for establishing standards of financial accounting and reporting in the private sector. The SEC and the AICPA recognize the standards issued by FASB. The FASB is part of a structure that is independent of all other business and professional organizations but has formal arrangements with and responsibilities to other bodies and committees, particularly the Financial Accounting Foundation (FAF) and the Financial Accounting Standards Advisory Council (FASAC).

The FAF was incorporated to operate exclusively for charitable, educational, scientific, and literary activities. The FAF is separate from all other organizations. However, its Board of Trustees is made up of members from constituent organizations having an interest in financial reporting. The Trustees approve nominees from constituent organizations. There are also Trustees-at-large who are not nominated by those organizations, but are chosen by the sitting Trustees. The Foundation is responsible for selecting the members of the FASB and its advisory council, ensuring adequate funding of their activities and for exercising general oversight, with the exception of the FASB's resolution of technical issues.

Established in 1973 at the same time as FASB, the main role of FASAC is to advise FASB on issues related to projects on the Board's agenda, possible new agenda items, project priorities, and procedural matters that may require attention. FASAC is an operating arm of the FAF and selects the members, including the chairperson, and broadly oversees its operations. There are over 30 members who are appointed for a one-year term and are eligible to be reappointed for three additional one-year terms. The members of FASAC are CEOs, CFOs, senior partners of public accounting firms, executive directors of professional organizations, senior academics, and financial analysts.

The FASB develops broad accounting concepts as well as standards for financial reporting. It also provides guidance on implementation of standards.

Concepts are valuable in guiding the FASB in establishing standards and in providing a frame of reference, or conceptual framework, for resolving accounting issues. The framework assists in establishing boundaries that are reasonable in the preparation of financial information. It also aims to increase the understanding of, and confidence in, financial information on the part of users of financial reports. The framework also contributes toward public understanding of the nature and limitations of information supplied by financial reporting.

The work on both concepts and standards by the FASB is based on research aimed at gaining new insights and ideas. The activities of the FASB are open to public participation and observation under the due process mandated by formal Rules of Procedure. In addition to the work of the FASB, there are other bodies that form the accounting regulatory framework.

The Government Accounting Standards Board (GASB) was established in 1984 by the FAF to set standards of financial accounting and reporting for state and local government units. The FAF is responsible for selecting GASB's members, ensuring adequate funding, and exercising general oversight. The GASB is a successor to the National Council on Governmental Accounting, and the standards of that body are still in effect unless amended or superseded by the GASB.

More recently, the Public Company Accounting Oversights Board (PCAOB) was established as a consequence of the Sarbanes-Oxley Act of 2002. Its role is to oversee the auditors of public companies in the preparation of informative, fair and independent audit reports. The SEC must approve PCAOB rules before they take effect.

The FASB's strategy in relation to international accounting standard setting has been supportive but with caution being exercised. Currently, domestic firms that are registered with the SEC must file financial reports using U.S. GAAP. Foreign firms filing with the SEC can use U.S. GAAP, their home country GAAP, or international standards. However, if they use their home country GAAP or international standards, foreign issuers must provide reconciliation to U.S. GAAP using Form 20-F.

The burden placed on companies and regulators by these arrangements is recognized. It is acknowledged that the worldwide use of a single set of high-quality accounting standards would greatly assist both domestic and cross-border financial reporting. How those standards should be formulated has caused some controversies, but recent events have suggested a better understanding of the possible way forward.

In October 2002, the FASB and the IASB announced the issuance of a memorandum of understanding (the "Norwalk Agreement"), marking a significant step toward formalizing their commitment to the convergence of U.S. GAAP and international accounting standards. The language of the agreement is slightly guarded, since it uses the word *compatibility*, instead of *convergence*, but the expressed aims are clear. The FASB and IASB agreed to:

- Undertake a short-term project aimed at removing a variety of individual differences between U.S. Generally Accepted Accounting Principles (GAAP) and IFRSs.
- Remove other differences between IFRSs and U.S. GAAP that will remain as of January 1, 2004, by working mutually and concurrently on discrete substantial projects.
- Continue progress on current joint projects.
- Encourage their respective interpretative bodies to coordinate their activities.

There are indications that progress on convergence is taking place. In November 2004, FASB issued Statement No. 151, Inventory Costs, as part of the movement toward greater comparability with IFRSs. In discussions, the FASB and IASB had detected that both U.S. ARB 43 Chapter 4 and IAS 2 Inventories, contain the same principle that the primary basis for inventory accounting is cost. The difference in the wording of the two pronouncements, however, could lead to different applications of similar requirements. The amendment made by Statement 151 adopts language similar to IAS 2 and improves reporting in the United States.

As a result of these and other initiatives, the FASB expects to make significant progress toward international convergence in the next few years. However, due to the volume of differences and the complex nature of some issues, the FASB anticipates that many differences between the U.S. GAAP and international accounting standards would persist well beyond 2005.

Nevertheless, towards the end of 2004, the SEC announced that the requirements for financial statements prepared under IFRSs to be reconciled with U.S. GAAP may be dropped as early as 2007 and by 2010 at the latest.

# CHAPTER 5

# Different Views of Convergence

## INTRODUCTION

Chapter 4 demonstrated that the difficulties of convergence, although not insurmountable, should not be underestimated. Even countries with a long relationship and strong position in the international accounting harmonization process found themselves at different stages of convergence. This chapter examines a selection of countries where experience illustrates important issues that need to be resolved if full convergence is to be achieved.

Some of these issues are internal and depend on the availability of a robust infrastructure with which to establish change. Although countries may profess their strong intention to adopt International Financial Reporting Standards (IFRSs), implementing this policy can be very difficult. Other issues revolve around the match between the basis of IFRSs and the economic, legal, and political environment within the country.

Externally, there is the matter of the position a country adopts with respect to international relations and the strategies of its neighboring countries. The cost of adopting IFRSs for an organization may not be outweighed by the benefits if other countries within the same geographical, political, or trading set are not adopting them.

Chapter 4 highlighted the convergence issues faced by the G4+1 countries (Australia and New Zealand, Canada, United Kingdom, United States) and are taken to represent North America, Europe and Australasia. The following discussions contrast the mixture of various influences and the pressures operating on convergence in other parts of the world, mainly countries in the Asia-Pacific Basin.

Japan is illustrated, as it is currently the only country in this region with which the IASB has direct liaison. The other countries highlighted may not be in the forefront of the convergence debate to date but may be financially sophisticated (such as Taiwan) or currently experiencing great economic growth (such as the People's Republic of China). A further issue, rarely addressed in questions on convergence, is the position of Islamic countries. The specific example of Malaysia is given as well as an examination of Islamic standard setting.

## JAPAN

Japan is one of the major capital markets in the world, and it is a strong supporter of the philosophy of the IASB. Under the Commercial Code in Japan, each joint stock company has to prepare an annual report and accounts. These include an income statement, balance sheet, details of proposed profit distribution, and accompanying schedules and reports. Under the Securities and Exchange Law, companies that issue designated securities must file half-yearly and annual reports with the prime minister and with the stock exchanges where their securities are listed.

Japanese Generally Acceptable Accounting Principles (GAAP) comprise Business Accounting Principles issued by the Business Accounting Council (BAC), standards issued by the Accounting Standards Board of Japan (ASBJ), and Practical Guidelines issued by the Japanese Institute of Certified Public Accountants (JICPA). In 2001, the Financial Accounting Standards Foundation (FASF) was established, and the ASBJ was organized as an independent, private sector organization under FASF.

In recent years, Japanese accounting standards have been revised substantially to be more compatible to IFRSs, but full convergence has not yet been achieved. Some Japanese companies are listed on the European Union exchanges, and the dilemma is whether those exchanges will recognize Japanese standards as being the equivalent of IFRSs. This is a solution desired by Japan, but it is reasonable to assume that this is not possible until Japanese standards are accepted as full equivalents of IFRSs. The alternative that presents itself is that Japanese companies with a European Union listing will be required to carry out reconciliation between Japanese standards and IFRSs.

The position is further complicated by Japan's close ties with the United States and by the listing of its companies on U.S. stock exchanges. It would be very burdensome to carry out reconciliation between Japanese standards and

IFRSs for the European Union as well as Japanese standards and U.S. GAAP for the U.S. markets. One solution Japan is seeking is to bring about improvements in its own auditing practices and converging Japanese Auditing Standards with International Standards on Auditing. The hope is that, by strengthening auditing, Japanese Accounting Standards might be accepted as the equivalent of IFRSs, but it is difficult to regard this as a tenable position.

Although Japan remains supportive of the IASB, the country considers that there is an unbalanced focus on European issues, and that this is leading to deficient interpretations and applications of the Conceptual Framework. Japan is also concerned that IFRSs sometimes conflict with the accounting and economic environment in Japan and with its own commercial code. The country is currently active in convergence discussions, and it attempts to eliminate gradually as many differences as it can between its own standards and IFRSs. The emphasis is definitely on converging with the IASB as far as possible (that is, reaching a negotiated agreement on a standard rather than adopting IFRSs as they are issued).

In October 2004, the IASB and the ASBJ commenced discussions on launching a joint project to minimize differences between IFRSs and Japanese Accounting Standards. The ASBJ emphasized its enthusiasm for reducing differences between standards as much as possible.

## MALAYSIA

The Financial Reporting Act of 1997 established the Malaysian Accounting Standards Board (MASB) as an independent authority to develop and issue accounting and financial reporting standards in Malaysia. At the same time, the Financial Reporting Foundation (FRF) was established. The FRF, as a trustee body, has responsibility for the oversight of the MASB's performance, financial and funding arrangements, and provision of initial guidance for the MASB on proposed standards and pronouncements. It has no direct responsibility with respect to standard setting.

The legal status of accounting standards flows mainly from the Financial Reporting Act of 1997. This states that all financial statements required to be prepared or lodged under any law administered by the Securities Commission, the Central Bank (Bank Negara Malaysia), or the Registrar of Companies must be prepared in compliance with the MASB.

Initially, the Board adopted 24 of the extant IASs and Malaysian Accounting Standards (MASs) issued by the Malaysian professional accountancy bodies prior to the creation of the MASB. Adoption by the MASB gave these IASs and MASs the status of approved accounting standards until each of these standards is amended, rescinded, or replaced by a new MASB Standard.

The Board has principles, objectives, and concepts in their Proposed Framework for the Preparation and Presentation of Financial Statements to assist in setting standards. In addition, MASB Standards are developed with reference to the work of other national standard setters such as Australia, Canada, New Zealand, the United Kingdom, the United States, and the IASB.

The mission of the MASB is to develop and promote high quality accounting and reporting standards that are consistent with international best practices for the benefit of users, preparers, auditors, and the public in Malaysia. In a wider context, the MASB seeks to contribute directly to the international development of financial reporting for the benefit of users, preparers, and auditors of financial reports.

At the end of 2004, the MASB issued four new Exposure Drafts that are revisions to existing standards. The MASB reiterated its policy of converging with IFRSs. It intends that all future standards it publishes will be modeled closely on IFRSs and modifications will only be made if essential.

One future objective of the MASB is to promote and support research in the area of financial reporting, in particular for emerging markets and Islamic markets. This issue is not high on the agenda of the IASB, but several Islamic accounting standards have been issued, and the background to these standards is discussed at the end of this chapter.

## PEOPLE'S REPUBLIC OF CHINA

Initially, standards were developed in China to regulate the running of state-owned corporations. The main purpose of the regulatory requirements has been to generate an inventory of available assets, and, not surprisingly in a planned economy, little attention has been paid to financial performance as revealed by the income statement. The regulations were directed at production goals and financial and cost plans. This approach has been recognized as hampering a developing economy and the aspirations of China in world trade, and existing regulations are currently being phased out in favor of IFRSs.

The first stage of development was funding from the World Bank to support the Ministry of Finance (MOF) of the People's Republic of China (PRC) to produce 30 standards in a three-year period and exposure drafts were issued between 1994 and 1996. The first pronouncement was Accounting Standards for Business Enterprises. This is a conceptual framework with the same purposes and substance as the IASC's framework at that time, although there are some significant differences, particularly the emphasis on the government as a prime user of financial statements.

The original timetable of setting 30 standards for publication was not met, mainly due to the lack of infrastructure. The Ministry of Finance is the legal standard setter and, in 1998, established the China Accounting Standards Committee (CASC) to continue the development of standards. Their task is to complete the first phase of the project and to produce additional standards addressing international issues that were on the international agenda, for example interim reporting.

In 2001, the State Council issued Financial Accounting and Reporting Rules for Enterprises (FARR), and these apply to larger enterprises and those requiring external funding. Where inconsistencies exist between pronouncements issued by the MOF and FARRs, the requirements of the latter apply. In order to improve and develop its own structures and systems, China has been positioning itself to reach the level of quality found in the best international accounting practices.

This is an enormous task, and the country is now in a stage of transition. The consequence is that Chinese companies wishing to list shares on U.S. markets must prepare three sets of statements: one using PRC standards, one using international standards, and one using U.S. GAAP.

The MOF wants Chinese accounting standards to reflect the approach of IFRSs to accounting and reporting issues, but it also is compelled to take into account the existing domestic legal framework and the economic environment. State-owned enterprises still dominate the economy, and even where they have been transferred into joint stock enterprises, there remains considerable political involvement at the regional and national level. The economy is made up of partial "free" markets. The accounting and financial infrastructure, although improving, is at a rudimentary stage in some sections of the country.

## TAIWAN, REPUBLIC OF CHINA

In 1983, the Ministry of Finance in Taiwan convened a conference at which the Accounting Research and Development Foundation (the Foundation) was established. The role of the Foundation is to promote accounting knowledge and expertise and to enhance the quality of accounting and auditing practices. The development of an accounting standard setting body reflected Taiwan's increasing economic sophistication and growing international trade, particularly with the United States.

Not surprisingly, Taiwan initially based its accounting standards on those of U.S. GAAP. In 1996, however, Taiwan decided to adopt International Accounting Standards. A project has been underway since 1999 to compare the existing Taiwanese standards with IASs and to make revisions where necessary.

The process of issuing standards starts with the Financial Accounting Standards Committee (FASC) determining the accounting issue to be addressed. An ad hoc Committee is formed to write an original draft. The Securities and Futures Commission (SFC), a department of the Ministry of Finance, expresses its opinion on the appropriateness of the topic, and the FASC then writes an Exposure Draft. Their deliberations are assisted by one of the full-time researchers of the Foundation who will prepare the initial text. The Exposure Draft is issued for comment, and finally the accounting standard is issued. Contentious issues such as leases and pensions are debated through a public hearing. The whole process is consensus-driven, and normally a two-thirds voting majority is required for a standard to be issued.

The efforts for Taiwan to achieve complete comparability with IFRSs are substantial. The resources they have to invest in standard setting are limited, and consideration has to be taken of the environment. At this stage, the country has in essence three strands of influences built into its standards. There are the remnants of the FASB-based standards and the philosophy of a rules-based approach attaching to them. There are the IFRSs that have been adopted. Finally, there are the modified standards where the Ministry of Finance has determined that a proposed standard has to reflect the particular concerns and interests of Taiwan.

## ISLAMIC FINANCE AND STANDARD SETTING

Islamic finance, unlike conventional banking, is a faith-based system of financial management that derives its principles from the Shariah. The code of Shariah is based on the canon law derived from the Qur'an. The basic principle of Islamic banking is the prohibition of receiving or paying *riba*, or interest. In 1991, the Islamic banking and finance industry decided that international accounting standards were inadequate to meet its needs. The Accounting and Auditing Organization for Islamic Financial Institutions (AAOIFI), based in Bahrain, was established to prepare accounting, auditing, governance, ethics, and Shariah standards for Islamic institutions. The membership of AAOIFI consists of 110 members, representing 24 countries.

Although it has a long history, a revival of Islamic banking took place in the 1970s. Compared to conventional banking where interest rates fluctuate according to economic conditions, Islamic banking charges a fixed profit rate for the funds provided. The profit rate is determined at the beginning of the financing contract. The Islamic financial system employs the concept of participation in the enterprise, utilizing the funds on a profit-and-loss sharing basis. This does not imply that investments with financial institutions are speculative. Any such risks can be excluded by careful investment policy, diversification of risk, and prudent management by Islamic financial institutions.

The concept of profit-and-loss sharing, as a basis of financial transactions, is a progressive one as it distinguishes good performance from poor performance. Islamic banks are structured to retain a clearly differentiated status between shareholders' capital and clients' deposits in order to ensure correct profit sharing according to Islamic law.

In recent times, Islamic banks have emerged in Muslim nations such as Saudi Arabia, Egypt, and many others. These banks usually work on the basis of profit-and-loss sharing, and function without interest or usury. Although elimination of interest in all its forms is an important feature of the Islamic financial system, Islamic banking is much more. It aims to eliminate exploitation and to establish a just society by the application of the Shariah or Islamic law to the operations of banks and other financial institutions. To ensure compliance to the Shariah, Islamic banks use the services of religious boards comprised of Shariah scholars.

There is not universal agreement on certain Shariah concepts. To date, the AAOIFI has issued 56 standards on accounting, auditing, governance, ethical, and Shariah standards. These standards have been implemented in leading Islamic banking and finance centers globally, such as Bahrain, Sudan, Jordan, Malaysia, Qatar, and Saudi Arabia, where they are either mandatory or are used as a guideline by the national regulators.

Although Islamic markets and finance have seen unprecedented growth in certain parts of the world, the issue has yet to gain prominence in the agenda of the IASB. The influence of Islamic finance and accounting standard setting in Malaysia is briefly illustrated below.

The Islamic financial system in Malaysia encompasses banking, *takaful* (or insurance), money markets, and capital markets. Islamic financing has seen unprecedented growth. In Malaysia, for example, the volume traded in the Islamic inter-bank money market has reached RM340 billion to date and the Central Bank reports that the annual growth rate of Islamic banking assets is 15% to 20%.

The Islamic financial transactions in Malaysia have also seen a surge in the use of Islamic leases or *Ijarah*-based transactions. The form of *Ijarah* contracts can be compared to conventional leasing arrangements. However, although the principles of *Ijarah* and conventional leasing are operationally similar, there are fundamental differences between the two that make standards on conventional leasing inadequate under Shariah principles. To date, MASB 10 Leases explicitly excludes any forms of Islamic leases in Malaysia, and an Exposure Draft has been issued specifically for Islamic leases.

Islamic finance is also being experienced in non-Muslim environments or entities. For instance, corporations such as Nestlé have floated an Islamic bond (called a *sukuk* bond), and the Dow Jones maintains an Islamic stock index. The German state of Saxony-Anhalt is due to launch the first Islamic Eurobond, which will be listed on the Luxembourg Stock Exchange.

The foremost principle of AAOIFI is that all Islamic financial institutions should apply, either by regulatory or Shariah requirement, the standards issued by the AAOIFI if such standards are available. If there are no specific standards, the Islamic financial institution may use standards other than those issued by AAOIFI, as deemed appropriate, that do not contravene the Shariah Rules and Principles.

Should the requirements of an alternative be in conflict with Shariah Rules and Principles, and the institution be compelled to use the alternative standards, a disclosure must be made of the point of conflict while adhering to the requirements of Shariah requirements.

# CHAPTER 6

# Responding to Internationalization

## PROGRESS AND PROBLEMS

The process of convergence has encouraged more countries to follow IFRSs but simultaneously problems are also revealed. Some countries have adopted or plan to adopt IFRSs. Others have publicly expressed their commitment to internationalization, but poor infrastructure and internal influences have led to partial adoptions of IFRSs. Other countries remain undecided.

Undoubtedly, the outcome of the current discussions involving the IASB and the United States will have an impact on the decisions of some other countries. The United States has been fully involved and enthusiastic in the establishment of international harmonization from the very beginning but has expressed concerns on how this should be achieved.

At one stage, the Securities and Exchange Commission (SEC) was able to argue that international accounting standards were not as robust or comprehensive as those issued in the United States. As the IASB has improved its accounting standards and the United States has experienced financial scandals, this argument has become less convincing. What appears to be a more substantial problem has come to the surface. The IASB issues standards on what is termed a "principles-based" approach. The FASB issues standards on what is known as a "rules-based" approach.

Despite the controversy that has surrounded these two different approaches, neither has been adequately defined. A simplistic illustration is given here that can be used to describe the difference between the approaches. A principles-based approach might state that you should apply basic principles to ensure financial statements are not misleading. The burden is then put on the preparer of the financial statements and the auditors to ensure that the financial statements are not misleading. A rules-based approach would state that if you follow specific rules when issuing financial statements, they will not be misleading.

There are arguments both for and against the two approaches. The main argument against the principles-based approach is that it may not give sufficient direction to the preparer of accounts and relies too much on judgment. The argument against the rules-based approach is that it encourages preparers to find loopholes in the rules or to use accounting treatments that are not covered by the rules. The financial statements can therefore still be considered as complying with the regulations, although they may not be as transparent as they should be.

At one time, it seemed that there would be no agreement between the IASB and the FASB on these two approaches. However, a number of major financial scandals, such as the collapse of Enron and WorldCom in the United States, encouraged a review of the approach to standard setting. In 2003, it was decided to move toward a more principles-based approach. Robert H. Herz, the FASB Chairman, described it thus. "Under a principles-based approach one lays out the key objectives of good reporting in the subject area and then provides guidance explaining the objectives and relating it to some common examples. While rules are sometimes unavoidable, the intent is not to try to provide specific guidance or rules for every possible situation. Rather, if in doubt, the reader is directed back to the principles."[1]

The IASB has attempted to meet the FASB partway by holding various meetings and publicly making statements of support. Its resources, however, are beginning to look overextended. The understandable attention of the IASB on those major countries in the process of converging with international standards and its work with the FASB may divert much of the needed guidance and support for other parts of the world. The main conduit for information and influence in the Far East is the Accounting Standards Board of Japan. They have been long-term supporters of internationalization but have expressed some reservations on the focus of interest of the IASB, although at the end of 2004 there appeared to be greater rapport than previously. In the EU, the opinion has been expressed by EFRAG that more attention needs to be paid to the issues facing those countries that have decided to adopt international standards.

There are also questions on the perceived users of financial statements and their needs. The International Accounting Standards Board (IASB) has concentrated on the interests of the capital markets, and this has led to criticism

---

[1]Quoted by Linda A. MacDonald in "Right in Principle." *Accountancy U.K.*, January 2003, p. 89.

that the needs of other groups of potential users of financial statements are not being considered. The IASB's Framework for the Preparation and Presentation of Financial Statements lists several potential users of financial statements such as employees, customers, suppliers, and the public. Perhaps it is expecting too much of a general-purpose document that all the needs of these diverse users can be satisfied.

A further major difficulty that confronted the IASC also confronts the IASB: it has, by itself, no direct recourse to a statutory body to make international accounting standards mandatory. It is difficult to envisage a time when the IASB will have the powers to enforce its standards, and the Board must therefore work through other agencies to obtain compliance and enforcement. It must rely on national governments, standard setting bodies, and security regulators to require organizations to prepare financial statements in accordance with IFRSs. The support and encouragement of professional accounting bodies throughout the world undoubtedly assists in establishing the credibility of international accounting standards, but it is the cooperation of the national standard setters that ensure their adoption.

Finally, the IASB needs a funding base that is certain and transparent. The major part of its current funding comes from contributors with each of the major accounting firms donating approximately US$1 million annually. There are also approximately 200 other corporations, associations, and other institutions providing financial support. Comments have been made that the IASB may not always have the necessary independence in setting standards because of the importance of these contributions to its existence. There is also the possibility that some major contributors may cease their support either because they are unhappy with the path being taken by the IASB or for other reasons. For example, the demise of Arthur Andersen following the Enron scandal resulted in the cessation of a US$1 million contribution.

## EFFECTS AND ACTION

Globalization of business has been with us for many years and, in the main, has been managed successfully by organizations. This is because many of the problems have been concerned with practices, not policies, and working within regulations in other countries. It has not involved changes to the financial regulations affecting domestic operations. When the issue becomes one of international regulations and policies affecting domestic arrangements, the impact is much greater and pervasive.

Undoubtedly, organizations are going to be involved in a significant amount of work, but it will be gradual. However, the complete and the long-term impact on all aspects of accounting have yet to be realized. The effects can be grouped under four headings of education and training, professional accounting bodies, regulators, and companies.

### *Education and Training*

In 2000, the American Accounting Association (AAA) published the results of a joint research project with the AICPA, the Institute of Management Accountants (IMA), and a number of international accounting firms. Authored by W. Steve Albrecht and Robert J. Sack, the report makes a critical examination and analysis of accounting education in the United States. It is not surprising that these prestigious bodies were able to agree on the findings of the research. Their conclusions extend and reinforce previous studies and opinions expressed in other countries. The main message is that accounting education needs to change and it needs to change soon.

The authors of the report argue that accounting educators "have spent too much time resting on our traditions and looking into the rearview mirror when we should have been teaching for the future." To reach that conclusion, they conducted a thorough analysis of the factors that have led to that position. They also point out that improvements have taken place in some institutions and offer sound recommendations as to how further change can be brought about. With the increasing influence of international accounting standards, the present provides an opportunity for introducing and accelerating change.

Some of the fundamental issues revolve around perceptions of accounting, held by a number of accounting professors. The method of teaching has been based on the preparation of financial statements and not their use. Introductory classes concentrate on the record-keeping aspect under the mistaken belief that it is both interesting and useful. Students whose career goal is to enter the accounting profession may find this approach useful, but the majority of students earning business degrees do not share this goal. They need to be able to understand, interpret, and use financial and statistical information, as well as deal with the conceptual issues such as recognition and measurement.

The authors of the American Accounting Association report propose how this may be achieved. The main points they make are the necessity for an accounting department to:

- Assess the environment and the programs the faculty faces
- Examine rigorously every degree offered
- Challenge curricula and content from the most introductory course to the most advanced course
- Consider carefully the pedagogy in every class

The AAA report is applicable to educational institutions in many countries but it deals with the teaching of accounting per se and does not address the special needs of teaching international accounting. Such needs have been energetically debated in international circles. Conferences and workshops held by the International Association for Accounting Education and Research (IAAER) constitute a prime force for linking the activities of standard setters and professional accounting bodies with the concerns of academic institutions worldwide.

### *Professional Accounting Bodies*

Those who are not accountants find it surprising how fragmented the accounting profession is in most countries. The dictionary and list of acronyms in this book describe some of the many different bodies that exist. At one stage, professional accounting bodies attempted to secure their position and to grow by arguing a special skill and knowledge in a particular subdiscipline. Broadly speaking, this led to the division in most countries between those who claim expertise in financial accounting and those in managerial accounting. As businesses and accounting have become more complex and integrated, some accountancy bodies have established routes to specializations within a subdiscipline. For example, taxation or auditing has been considered as distinct career paths for some.

Recently, professional bodies have attempted to differentiate themselves by making geographic claims. Thus, there are claims to be the main accounting body in Europe, the largest in the world, or the fastest growing in Asia. Some, particularly the U.K. bodies, have also added international accounting as an alternative course or as a freestanding certificate or diploma in their portfolio. Such a strategy neatly fulfills a demand for knowledge and supports global ambitions.

Another strategy for growth has been to allow mutual recognition or various forms of support. Thus a member of one accounting body can be accepted as a member of another accounting body. This might require taking certain examinations, particularly taxation and regulatory requirements, when the qualification is to be used in another country.

This process of formal recognition and other working agreements has, to date, not resulted in national or international mergers. This is surprising, since the early twentieth century saw numerous mergers, often with regional bodies coming together to form a national body. The next logical stage would be for the accounting bodies in one country to combine to make it easier to achieve international presence and credibility. We would seem to be a long way from that final stage but the influence of international accounting standards is accelerating change, and interest in mergers at the national level has begun to reappear. Canada and the United Kingdom are currently the main incubators for mergers, and, if they take place, this development could accelerate further movements in other countries. To date, however, negotiations between professional accounting bodies have yet to result in mergers.

It is apparent that there have been two levels of professional accountants for many years (the general practitioner and the specialist). The specialist is someone who is a general practitioner and either through experience, study or examination, has a higher level of specific knowledge and skills. Accounting bodies have formalized this by having separate streams, interest groups, or similar divisions. In some instances, courses have to be taken with, or without, an examination. There are also examples where the specialized qualification is obtained by acceptance into another professional body. It can be anticipated that mergers or some forms of mutual recognition agreements could take place at the specialized level.

### *National Standard Setters*

The future of national accounting standard setters is uncertain as the influence of the IASB increases. It is evident that there will be a decline or a change in the focus of their powers and responsibilities. Normally, their authority comes from legislation that recognizes the accounting standards issued. If international standards are recognized as valid for the preparation and presentation of financial statements, the question arises whether national accounting standard setters are required if the IASB is doing the task.

In the foreseeable future, the response must be in the affirmative. There is the process of negotiating and managing convergence and meeting the needs of organizations, mainly small and medium-sized, which at present are not covered by international standards. The IASB currently has a project on the standards appropriate for smaller and medium-sized entities. A standard such as the U.K.'s Financial Reporting Standard for Small Entities (FRSSE) could prove a useful model.

It is probable that national standard setters will maintain their existence through various activities on several levels. First, the IASB still has to maintain an international consensus, and for this it needs national standard setting bodies. Political and interest groups are very powerful in some countries, and the IASB will have to rely on national bodies to reflect these and assist in forming opinion. Certainly, on the identification of issues for standards and emerging issues, national bodies will play a key role.

The matter of ensuring compliance has also not been addressed. The IASB does not have an appropriate mechanism whereas some national bodies have established means for monitoring financial statements. It would seem that the IASB would therefore depend on auditors, national standard setters, stock exchanges, and independent bodies to ensure compliance. In addition, the identification of problems after implementation, the operation of standards, and the need for their revision have to be monitored.

Finally, a major role for national bodies will be in the area of education and research. This may be conducted either unilaterally or by various coalitions working on common interests. The research papers produced by the G4+1 are excellent examples of the progress that can be made, and some national standard setters are now working together to seek solutions to accounting and financial reporting problems.

### *Companies and Accounting Firms*

One conclusion from the above analysis is that the main impact on harmonization of accounting standards will be best managed by companies and accounting firms. Indeed, for the latter it could be contended that a marvelous opportunity has been presented for increasing their revenues through consulting and advisory services!

The argument that these two groups will be least affected is at variance with popular thinking, which tends to concentrate on organizations that publish financial statements. The reason for this is that the most immediate, visible, and easiest impact of international harmonization that can be identified is compliance by organizations with the standards. In reality, companies have had a long history and considerable experience in dealing with new and revised accounting standards. In some countries the national accounting standard setters have issued a plethora of pronouncements and interpretations in the same year. CFOs may not have enjoyed the experience, but they have managed it successfully.

Organizations that foresee moving to an international accounting regime are advised to start making plans early. Much initial planning can be done in anticipation of regulatory changes, even if these do not finally occur. One immediate action to take is the examination and analysis of the accounting procedures and systems. This should reveal any weaknesses or areas where attention is required in the organization and, regardless of IFRSs, should improve the efficiency of the organization and its internal control system.

The next stage is to undertake a diagnostic appraisal of how IFRSs, if implemented, would affect accounting policies. The final stage is to design a plan for the transition to IFRSs. This should incorporate the following issues:

- The availability of suitably trained staff
- The adequacy of the internal control system
- The work of the internal audit department
- The knowledge of the directors and audit committee about the changes
- The likely impact on any covenants, agreements, and contracts that con-

tain key financial performance indicators, including incentive targets for employees and managers

Finally, it will be necessary to determine how to manage communications to various groups involved. There will be an impact on both the staff managing the current system and the staff needed for the new system. Training may solve many of the problems, but there may be changes in job descriptions and these will have to be handled appropriately.

As well as those handling the practical change, it must be appreciated that financial performance indicators under IFRSs will differ from those reported previously. Communication must take place with interested parties before new financial indicators are published. Not only should the immediate impact be communicated, but it is also important to clarify what may be the long-term effects on managerial incentives and compensation plans. This may require explanations of how ROI-based performance bonus and incentive plans may be affected as well as the renegotiation of agreements with external parties that are based on financial indicators.

# CHAPTER 7

# The Role of the Accountant

## THE RIPPLE EFFECT

In countries where it has been decided to adopt international financial reporting standards, accountants should be aware of and be prepared for the ripple effect that will occur. For example, all listed companies in the European Union will be required to prepare their consolidated financial statements according to IFRSs. This will directly affect approximately 2,700 companies in the United Kingdom. Should these U.K. parent companies, very reasonably, decide to require their subsidiary companies to also adopt international standards, then approximately 10 times the number of companies will be affected.

The U.K. government has also announced that unlisted companies will have the option of adopting international standards and that accounts prepared on this basis will be equally acceptable for the platform for tax calculations as those prepared using U.K. standards. It is evident that all accountants in the United Kingdom and in the entire European Union need to understand and be able to apply IFRSs.

It would be equally unwise to believe that convergence will have no impact on the work of the accountants in a country that has not adopted, or does not plan to adopt, international accounting standards. The immediate effect will be that some clients will be seeking advice on the transactions and relationships that it has with foreign organizations preparing IFRS compliant accounts. Accountants can expect to receive questions on the possible future route to convergence. Finally, even nationally generated standards are beginning to reflect some of the approaches and solutions put forward at the national level.

It is wise, therefore, for all accountants to establish some knowledge of the potential impact of the events taking place. The main guide to the effects on financial statements of changing to international standards is found in IFRS 1 First-time Adoption of International Financial Reporting Standard. This standard sets out the procedures that an entity must follow when it adopts IFRS for the first time as the basis for preparing its general-purpose financial statements. Although the standard is phrased to assist the change in the European Union, the general principles can be applied at any time.

## THE MAIN CHANGES

The most important impact is on accounting policies, and companies must apply accounting policies based on IFRSs that are in force at the end of the financial year for which accounts are being prepared. It is also essential to provide comparative information. Therefore, IFRSs in force at the end of the current year must be applied to both the current year and the previous year.

The next stage will be for the organization to eliminate assets and liabilities prepared under previous GAAP from the opening balance sheet if they do not qualify for recognition under IFRS. For many organizations, the requirements of IAS 37 Provisions, Contingent Liabilities and Contingent Assets, and IAS 38 Intangible Assets could have a dramatic and immediate impact on the balance sheet.

As well as derecognizing some assets and liabilities, organizations must recognize all assets and liabilities that are required to be recognized by IFRSs even if they were never recognized under previous GAAP. Once again, IAS 37 and IAS 38 are likely to have the most important effect.

When carrying out the above changes, it is important to remember that the general principle is to apply IFRS in measuring all recognized assets and liabilities. There are some important exceptions to this principle. Some of these are mandatory, and the requirements of IAS 39 Financial Instruments: Recognition and Measurement are particularly important. Other exceptions are optional and include the following:

- Business combinations that occurred before opening balance sheet date
- Property, plant and equipment, intangible assets, and investment property carried under the cost model
- Employee benefits with actuarial gains and losses
- Accumulated translation reserves

In addition to the measurement and recognition aspects, the appearance of the financial statements will change due to reclassification and disclosure requirements. First, the organization must reclassify previous-GAAP opening balance sheet items into the appropriate IFRS classification. There will also be disclosures that were not required under previous accounting regulations. Thus required disclosures may have to be increased.

The most significant of the disclosures at this stage are those that must be made by an organization intending to adopt IFRSs and by those that have adopted them for the first time. In the former case, certain disclosures are required in its interim financial statements prior to the year-end where the interim financial statements are intended to comply with IAS 34 Interim Financial Reporting. Explanatory information and reconciliation are required. This includes changes in accounting policies compared to those under previous regulations.

Organizations preparing their first financial statements in accordance with IFRSs must explain how the transition from previous GAAP affected the reported financial position, financial performance, and cash flows, including matters such as:

- Reconciliations of equity reported under previous GAAP to equity under IFRS
- Reconciliations of profit or loss for the last annual period reported under the previous GAAP to profit or loss under IFRS for the same period
- Explanation of material adjustments that were made to the balance sheet, income statement, and cash flow statement
- Separate disclosure of any errors in financial statements prepared under previous GAAP and discovered in the course of transition
- Disclosure of any impairment losses recognized or reversed in preparing the opening IFRS balance sheet
- Explanations of the use of any of the specific recognition and measurement exemptions permitted under IFRS 1

## THE LINK WITH CORPORATE GOVERNANCE

Internationalization of accounting is strongly linked with current concerns on corporate governance. Unless there are robust accounting standards, a process of independent assurance on financial statements and mechanisms for monitoring and ensuring compliance, financial information will lack integrity.

There is a distinct contrast between the approach of the United Kingdom to improving corporate governance and the approach of the United States. In the United Kingdom, a framework of agreed principles has been established that provides guidance but does not lay down specific rules. In the United States, the Sarbanes-Oxley Act 2002 (SOX) has taken a very strong legalistic direction. Irrespective of these differences, a brief review of a few points from the Act will illustrate the issues of concern in most countries.

The Act is the most significant change to the U.S. securities laws since the 1930s. It was enacted after the Enron and WorldCom scandals to restore investor confidence in the stock market. The fraudulent activities of these two companies resulted in US$7 trillion of market losses and thousands of lost jobs.

In summary, the Act covers items such as certification of financial reports, disclosures, internal and external audits, and annual reports on the effectiveness of internal financial controls. SOX has established a five-member Public Company Accounting Oversight Board to oversee the audit of public companies, establish audit report and rules, and inspect, investigate, and enforce compliance. Much of this section expands on these main responsibilities but also includes a direction that the SEC will report to Congress on the adoption of a principles-based accounting system by the United States.

There is a section specific to auditor independence. This includes provisions relating to performing non-audit services, and auditor rotation. The audit committee of the Board of Directors must comprise entirely of independent members (non-employees) and must have at least one member deemed to be a financial expert.

The section of the Act that gained the most publicity at the time relates to corporate responsibility. This section includes a provision that the SEC will issue rules requiring the CEO and CFO to certify in periodic financial reports, among other matters, that the report does not contain untrue statements or material omissions and the financial statements fairly present, in all material respects, the financial conditions and results of operations. CEOs and CFOs who submit a wrong certification face hefty fines and severe prison sentences.

A separate section is concerned specifically with enhanced financial disclosure. This includes a requirement that financial reports filed with the SEC will reflect all material corrective adjustments that have been identified. It also requires senior managers, directors, and principal stockholders to disclose changes in securities ownership or securities-based swap agreements within two business days. In addition, Section 404 of the Act requires top management to certify that the organization maintains an adequate system of internal controls.

In order to increase the likelihood of compliance, the SOX Act imposes wide-ranging and severe penalties. For example, the penalties for violation of the Securities Act of 1934 have been increased up to US$25 million dollars and up to 20 years in prison.

Foreign companies registered with the SEC have to comply with the Act by June 2005 if they wish to continue to be listed on the U.S. stock markets. Failure to comply could result in their eventual delisting.

It is too early to determine the extent of the success of the Sarbanes-Oxley Act and other equivalent approaches adopted in other countries. The

SOX Act and its Canadian equivalent, the Canadian Public Accountability Board, has created a need for well-qualified accountants to fill in audit and compliance-based accounting positions. It would be very naïve, however, to believe that corporate governance laws will prevent all future financial transgressions, since the history of the regulation of financial accounting and reporting has largely been a story of reacting to abuses and preventing the issuance of misleading financial statements.

## FINAL CHECK

The first step is to accept that convergence is an issue that cannot be ignored. An accountant working for a small organization operating solely in a country where there are no plans for accounting harmonization may not encounter IFRSs. Even in this case, it is unwise to believe that convergence will have no impact. Due to globalization of businesses, clients will be seeking advice on the transactions and relationships that it has with foreign organizations preparing IFRS compliant accounts. Accountants can expect to receive questions on the possible future route to convergence. Thus, for the vast majority of accountants, knowledge of convergence is essential for the work they do.

Secondly, accountants need to keep informed on the convergence issues in those countries where suppliers and clients operate. As previous chapters have demonstrated, the global picture is complex and changing rapidly. Some companies have adopted IFRSs entirely, others have recognized them for certain cases, and others are at various stages of grappling with convergence. Given that the previous year's financial figures will have to be restated, it could be argued that the more time spent on preparation, the easier the transition will be.

Thirdly, a strategy is required for dealing with convergence. At an early stage, this should incorporate an analysis of the differences between domestic standards and IFRSs. Not only will this allow discussions with clients and other parties on the potential impact on financial statements, it will also allow an assessment of the magnitude of the work required.

Finally, investigate the possible future effect of the adoption of IFRSs on financial measures. All contracts and agreements being entered into currently that are based on accounting ratios should be reviewed to determine whether a change in accounting regulations would be harmful. The guide and dictionary that comprise the rest of this book will assist in making the world of international accounting understandable and manageable.

# Bibliography

Abdullah, Nazatul Izma. "Malaysia's Vision for Islamic Finance." *Accounting & Business U.K.* (March, 2004): 21–22.

Albrecht, W. Steve, and Robert J. Sack. *Accounting Education: Charting the Course through a Perilous Future.* Accounting Education Series no. 16 American Accounting Association, 2000.

Cairns, David. "IASC's Blueprint for the Future." *Accountancy U.K.* (December 1989): 80–82.

Cairns, David, Brian Creighton, and Anne Daniels. *Applying International Accounting Standards.* 3rd Ed. Tolley LexisNexis, 2002.

Cairns, David, and Christopher Nobes. *The Convergence Handbook.* Institute of Chartered Accountants in England and Wales, 2000.

Davidson, Ronald A., Alexander M. G. Gelardi, and Fangue Li. "Analysis of the Conceptual Framework of China's New Accounting System." *Accounting Horizons*, no. 10(1), (March, 1996): 58–74.

Epstein, Barry J., and Abbas Ali Mirza, IAS 2004—Interpretation and Application of International Accounting and Financial Reporting Standards. John Wiley & Sons, 2004.

Financial Accounting Standards Board. *International Accounting Standard Setting: A Vision for the Future.* FASB, 1999.

Gagné, Claire. "Revenge of the Nerds." *Canadian Business* (September 27–October 10, 2004): 47–50.

Gorelik, George. "The Setting of Accounting Standards: Canada, the United

Kingdom, and the United States." *International Journal of Accounting* no. 95 (1994): 95–122.

Gray, Sidney J. "Towards a Theory of Cultural Influence on the Development of Accounting Systems Internationally." *Abacus* no. 3 (1988): 1–15.

Hermsen, Michael L., Philip J Niehoff, and Mark R. Uhrynuk. "An Extraordinary Expansion." *Accountancy U.K.* (October 2002): 110–112.

International Accounting Standards Committee. *IASC Constitution.* IASC, May 2000.

International Accounting Standards Board. *International Financial Reporting Standards (IFRSs)—A Briefing for Chief Executives, Audit Committees, and Boards of Directors.* IASB, 2004.

———. *International Financial Reporting Standards (IFRSs).* IASB, 2004.

International Federation of Accountants. *IES 1-6: International Education Standards for Professional Accountants.* IFAC Education Committee, October 2003.

Lenihan, Donald G., and David Hume. *A Question of Standards: Accounting in the 21st Century.* Centre for Collaborative Government/Certified General Accountants of Canada, 2002.

MacDonald, Linda A. "Right in Principle." *Accountancy U.K.* (January 2003): 89.

Parker, Mushtak. "Islamic Banking Goes Global." *Accounting & Business U.K.* (October 2004): 25–27.

Street, Donna L., and Sidney J. Gray. "How Wide Is the Gap between IASC and U.S. GAAP? Impact of the IASC Comparability Project and Recent International Developments." *Journal of International Accounting, Auditing, and Taxation* no. 8(1) (1999): 133–164.

Street, Donna L., and Kimberley A. Shaughnessy. "The Evolution of the G4+1 and Its Impact on International Harmonization of Accounting Standards." *Journal of International Accounting, Auditing, and Taxation* no. 7(2) (1998): 131–161.

Walton, Peter. "Shattering Complacency: Building Trust." *Accountancy and Business* (October 2002): 20–21.

Zeff, Stephen A. "International Accounting Principles and Auditing Standards." *European Accounting Review* no. 2 (1993): 403–410.

———. "The IASC's Core Standards: What Will the SEC Do?" *Journal of Financial Statement Analysis* no. 4(1) (Fall 1998): 67–78.

# Part Two

# GUIDE TO INTERNATIONAL FINANCIAL REPORTING STANDARDS

*"Accountants have the mentality of children at a circus, they are beguiled by things being balanced."*

—John Harman, *Money for Nothing*.
Headline Book Publishing, 1988, page 72.

# Introduction to the Guide

In April 2001, the International Accounting Standards Board (IASB) announced that future accounting standards would be called "International Financial Reporting Standards" (IFRSs). Standards issued previously by the International Accounting Standards Committee (IASC) were called "International Accounting Standards" (IASs).

The IASB has adopted all of the standards and interpretations issued by the IASC that are still in force. The term IFRS, as now used by the IASB, includes standards and interpretations issued by the IASB, as well as pronouncements from its predecessor, the International Accounting Standards Committee (IASC). For the purposes of this book, the terms *international standard* or *accounting standard* will be used generally unless reference is being made to a specific standard. The term *entity* is also used, as in the standards, to describe a body corporate, partnership, or unincorporated association that is profit-oriented. IAS 1 notes that entities whose share capital is not equity or have not-for-profit activities may need to amend some of the descriptions given in the standards.

Those who are not familiar with the pronouncements issued by the IASB are likely to be surprised by the comprehensiveness and complexity of each standard. For example, IAS 20, one of the less exciting standards for many, since it deals with government grants, is contained within 12 pages. On the other hand, IAS 39 Financial Instruments: Recognition and Measurement covers approximately 80 pages. Of course, it needs to be studied in conjunction with IAS 32 Financial Instruments: Disclosure and Presentation that just manages to fit into less than 50 pages.

We have substantially reduced this great volume of material to provide a succinct review of the main points of the standards that were in force as at 1 January 2005. The background to each standard is explained. The main requirements of the standard and the main disclosures required by organizations are highlighted. Where appropriate, illustrative examples and references to related national standards are given.

The Guide presents an easily accessible summary to the key features but it is not intended to replace the full standard. The official pronouncements of the IASB still remain the only authoritative documents.

## INTERNATIONAL FINANCIAL REPORTING STANDARDS
*(January 1, 2005)*

| *Number* | *Title* | *Issued or last revised* |
|---|---|---|
| | IASB Framework for the Preparation and Presentation of Financial Statements | 1989 |
| IAS 1 | Presentation of Financial Statements | December 2003 |
| IAS 2 | Inventories | December 2003 |
| IAS 3 | Consolidated Financial Statements | Superseded by IASs 27 and 28 |
| IAS 4 | Depreciation Accounting | Replaced by IASs 16, 22, and 38 |
| IAS 5 | Information to be Disclosed in Financial Statements | Superseded by IAS 1 |
| IAS 6 | Accounting Responses to Changing Prices | Superseded by IAS 15 |
| IAS 7 | Cash Flow Statements | December 1992 |
| IAS 8 | Accounting Policies, Changes in Accounting Estimates and Errors | December 2003 |
| IAS 9 | Accounting for Research and Development Activities | Superseded by IAS 38 |
| IAS 10 | Events after the Balance Sheet Date | December 2003 |
| IAS 11 | Construction Contracts | 1993 |
| IAS 12 | Income Taxes | 2000 |
| IAS 13 | Presentation of Current Assets and Current Liabilities | Superseded by IAS 1 |
| IAS 14 | Segment Reporting | 1997 |

| | | |
|---|---|---|
| IAS 15 | Information Reflecting the Effects of Changing Prices | Withdrawn December 2003 |
| IAS 16 | Property, Plant and Equipment | December 2003 |
| IAS 17 | Leases | December 2003 |
| IAS 18 | Revenue | 1993 |
| IAS 19 | Employee Benefits | 1998 and amended December 2004 |
| IAS 20 | Accounting for Government Grants and Disclosure of Government Assistance | April 1983 |
| IAS 21 | The Effects of Changes in Foreign Exchange Rates | December 2003 |
| IAS 22 | Business Combinations | Superseded by IFRS 3 |
| IAS 23 | Borrowing Costs | December 1993 |
| IAS 24 | Related Party Disclosures | December 2003 |
| IAS 25 | Accounting for Investments | Superseded by IAS 39 and IAS 40 |
| IAS 26 | Accounting and Reporting by Retirement Benefit Plans | January 1987 |
| IAS 27 | Consolidated and Separate Financial Statements | December 2003 |
| IAS 28 | Investments in Associates | December 2003 |
| IAS 29 | Financial Reporting in Hyperinflationary Economies | July 1989 |
| IAS 30 | Disclosures in the Financial Statements of Banks and Similar Financial Institutions | 1990 |
| IAS 31 | Interests in Joint Ventures | December 2003 |
| IAS 32 | Financial Instruments: Disclosures and Presentation | December 2003 |
| IAS 33 | Earnings per Share | December 2003 |
| IAS 34 | Interim Financial Reporting | June 1998 |
| IAS 35 | Discontinuing Operations | Superseded by IFRS 5 |
| IAS 36 | Impairment of Assets | March 2004 |
| IAS 37 | Provisions, Contingent Liabilities and Contingent Assets | July 1998 |
| IAS 38 | Intangible Assets | March 2004 |
| IAS 39 | Financial Instruments: Recognition and Measurement | December 2004 |

| | | |
|---|---|---|
| IAS 40 | Investment Property | December 2003 |
| IAS 41 | Agriculture | December 2000 |
| | Preface to International Financial Reporting Standards | May 2002 |
| IFRS 1 | First-time Adoption of International Financial Reporting Standards | June 2003 |
| IFRS 2 | Share-based Payment | February 2004 |
| IFRS 3 | Business Combinations | March 2004 |
| IFRS 4 | Insurance Contracts | March 2004 |
| IFRS 5 | Non-current Assets Held for Sale and Discontinued Operations | March 2004 |
| IFRS 6 | Exploration for and Evaluation of Mineral Resources | December 2004 |

## INTERPRETATIONS OF INTERNATIONAL FINANCIAL REPORTING STANDARDS

| | |
|---|---|
| SIC 1 | Consistency—Different Cost Formulas for Inventory |
| SIC 2 | Consistency—Capitalization of Borrowing Costs |
| SIC 3 | Elimination of Unrealized Profits and Losses on Transactions with Associates |
| SIC 4 | Not Issued |
| SIC 5 | Classification of Financial Instruments—Contingent Settlement Provisions |
| SIC 6 | Costs of Modifying Existing Software |
| SIC 7 | Introduction of the Euro |
| SIC 8 | First-time Application of IASs as the Primary Basis of Accounting |
| SIC 9 | Business Combinations—Classification either as Acquisitions or Uniting of Interests |
| SIC 10 | Government Assistance—No Specific Relation to Operating Activities |
| SIC 11 | Foreign Exchange—Capitalization of Losses Resulting from Severe Currency Devaluation |
| SIC 12 | Consolidation—Special Purpose Entities |
| SIC 13 | Jointly Controlled Entities—Non-Monetary Contributions by Venturers |

| | |
|---|---|
| SIC 14 | Property, Plant and Equipment—Compensation for the Impairment or Loss of Items |
| SIC 15 | Operating Leases—Incentives |
| SIC 16 | Share Capital—Reacquired Own Equity Instruments (Treasury Shares) |
| SIC 17 | Equity—Costs of an Equity Transaction |
| SIC 18 | Consistency—Alternative Methods |
| SIC 19 | Reporting Currency—Measurement and Presentation of Financial Statements under IAS 21 and IAS 29 |
| SIC 20 | Equity Accounting Method—Recognition of Losses |
| SIC 21 | Income Taxes—Recovery of Revalued Non-Depreciable Assets |
| SIC 22 | Business Combinations—Subsequent Adjustment of Fair Values and Goodwill Initially Reported |
| SIC 23 | Property, Plant and Equipment—Major Inspection or Overhaul Costs |
| SIC 24 | Earnings per Share—Financial Instruments and Other Contracts that May be Settled in Shares |
| SIC 25 | Income Taxes—Changes in the Tax Status of an Enterprise or its Shareholders |
| SIC 26 | Not Issued |
| SIC 27 | Evaluating the Substance of Transactions in the Legal Form of a Lease |
| SIC 28 | Business Combinations—"Date of Exchange" and Fair Value of Equity Instruments |
| SIC 29 | Disclosure—Service Concession Arrangements |
| SIC 30 | Reporting Currency—Translation from Measurement Currency to Presentation Currency |
| SIC 31 | Revenue—Barter Transactions Involving Advertising Services |
| SIC 32 | Intangible Assets—Website Costs |
| SIC 33 | Consolidation and Equity Method—Potential Voting Rights and Allocation of Ownership Interests |
| IFRIC 1 | Changes in Existing Decommissioning, Restoration, and Similar Liabilities |
| IFRIC 2 | Members' Shares in Co-operative Entities and Similar Instruments |
| IFRIC 3 | Emission Rights |
| IFRIC 4 | Determining whether an Arrangement Contains a Lease |

## CURRENT ACTIVITIES

| | |
|---|---|
| ED 7 | Financial Instruments: Disclosures |
| Project | Accounting Standards for Small and Medium-Sized Entities |
| Project | Projects Relating to Financial Instruments |
| Project | Issues Relating to IFRS 3 Business Combinations |
| Project | Business Combinations—Phase 2 Application of the Purchase Method |
| Project | Consolidation (including SPEs) |
| Project | Convergence—Convergence Project General Information |
| Project | Convergence—Post-employment Benefits |
| Project | Extractive Activities |
| Project | Insurance Contracts—Phase II |
| Project | Performance Reporting/Reporting Comprehensive Income |
| Project | Liabilities and Revenue Recognition |
| Project | Convergence—Joint Ventures |
| Project | Convergence—IAS 20 Government Grants and Disclosure of Government Assistance |
| Project | Conceptual Framework |
| Research | Leases |
| Research | Extractive Activities |
| Research | Joint Ventures |
| Research | Measurement |

# Framework for the Preparation and Presentation of Financial Statements

**ISSUED**

April 1989

**BACKGROUND**

The "Framework" is not an accounting standard but was issued by the IASC to help develop international standards and to promote harmonization. It was also considered that the "Framework" would assist preparers, auditors, users, and others who are involved with or are interested in accounting and financial reporting issues. The "Framework" was adopted by the IASB in April 2001.

The argument put forward by the IASC was that there are differences in financial statements on a global basis due to national, social, economic, and legal reasons. Different countries have also made various assumptions about the potential users of financial statements and their particular need for certain types of information. The result of this is that different criteria and measurement principles have been adopted, and there are various definitions in use for assets, liabilities, equity, income, and expenses. The purpose of the IASC in issuing the "Framework" was to narrow these differences by seeking to harmonize regulations, accounting standards, and procedures for the preparation and presentation of financial statements.

## ASSUMPTIONS

The "Framework" makes a number of assumptions regarding financial statements, which explain how it arrives at some of its definitions and guidance. Financial statements are regarded as general-purpose documents designed to meet the information needs of a very wide range of users, including investors, employees, customers, the government, and the public. Although the "Framework" emphasizes the economic decision-making needs of users, it also states that financial statements are appropriate for assessing the stewardship of management.

The "Framework" is intended for different accounting models and concepts of capital and capital maintenance. The context, however, is the prevailing model of recoverable historic cost and the nominal financial capital maintenance concept.

The two familiar assumptions that the "Framework" contains are the accruals basis of accounting and the going concern concept.

## STRUCTURE OF THE "FRAMEWORK"

The main headings of the "Framework" are as follows:

- The Objective of Financial Statements
- Underlying Assumptions
- Qualitative Characteristics of Financial Statements
- The Elements of Financial Statements
- Recognition of the Elements of Financial Statements
- Measurement of the Elements of Financial Statements
- Concepts of Capital and Capital Maintenance

We have briefly addressed the first two headings above, and the third, Qualitative Characteristics of Financial Statements, is very similar to Conceptual Frameworks or Statements of Principles issued by various countries. Essentially, the main characteristics are understandability, relevance, reliability, and comparability. These are discussed by reference to a number of supporting characteristics. The section concludes by stating that financial statements that possess such characteristics will normally give a true and fair view or that the information has been presented fairly.

The part of the "Framework" that is possibly the most influential are the sections dealing with the elements of financial statements and their recognition and measurement.

## THE ELEMENTS OF FINANCIAL STATEMENTS

The elements are discussed in two categories: those relating to financial position and those relating to performance. The former covers assets, liabilities, and equity. Performance relates to income and expenditure.

Paragraph 49 offers the following definitions as regards to financial position:

- "An asset is a resource controlled by the enterprise as a result of past events and from which future economic benefits are expected to flow to the enterprise."
- "A liability is a present obligation of the enterprise resulting from past events, the settlement of which is expected to result in an outflow from the enterprise of resources embodying economic benefits."
- "Equity is the residual interest in the assets of the enterprise after deducting all its liabilities."

Paragraph 70 offers the following definitions as regards to performance:

- "Income is increases in economic benefits during the accounting period in the form of inflows or enhancements of assets or decreases in liabilities that result in increases in equity, other than those relating to contributions from equity participants."
- "Expenses are decreases in economic benefits during the accounting period in the form of outflows or depletions of assets or occurrences of liabilities that result in decreases in equity, other than those relating to distributions to equity participants."

The section develops these five definitions by discussions of their various aspects and reference to examples. These definitions have been used as the bedrock of international accounting standards. Although the complications of global business and the sophistication of accounting and financial practices have stretched the boundaries of the definitions, their essence has not been lost.

## RECOGNITION AND MEASUREMENT OF THE ELEMENTS

Elements that meet the criteria for recognition are incorporated in the balance sheet or income statement, as appropriate. There are two hurdles to overcome to achieve recognition. First, it must be probable that any future economic benefit will flow to the enterprise. Secondly, it must be possible to measure the cost or value reliably, and this includes making a reasonable estimate. Measurement is a key criteria underpinning many standards.

The "Framework" explains the following measurement bases:

- Historical cost where assets are recorded at cash, cash equivalents, or fair value at acquisition and liabilities at the amount received in exchange for the obligation
- Current cost where assets are carried at the amount needed to acquire the same asset and liabilities at the undiscounted amount of cash or cash equivalents to settle the obligation currently
- Realizable value where assets are carried at the proceeds expected to be received for their orderly disposal and liabilities at the undiscounted amount of cash or cash equivalent to settle them in the normal course of business
- Present values where assets are carried at the present discounted value of the future net cash flows they are expected to generate and liabilities at the present value of future net cash outflows required to be settled in the normal course of business

The measurement basis most commonly used is historical cost, but in recent years there has been a move at the international level to employ other bases where they seem appropriate. The "Framework" was issued before "fair value" was accepted as a measurement basis, and therefore it does not appear in the document. *Fair value* is defined in several standards issued subsequently.

## CONCEPTS OF CAPITAL AND CAPITAL MAINTENANCE

This section is important, since the choice of concepts will determine the accounting model that will be used. Capital concepts fall into two categories: Financial capital is regarded as the equity or net assets; physical capital is the productive capacity of the enterprise.

In order to maintain financial capital, the amount of net assets at the end of the period must be the same as the net assets at the beginning of the period, excluding transactions with owners. If the net assets at the end of the period are greater, a holding gain or "profit" is made. If the financial capital is defined in terms of nominal monetary units, that "profit" does not reflect increases in the general rise of prices. If financial capital is defined in terms of constant purchasing power units, "profit" represents the increase in invested purchasing power over the period. In this case, only the price increase of assets that is greater than the general level of prices will be regarded as "profit."

To maintain physical capital, the current cost basis of measurement must be adopted. Price changes affecting the assets and liabilities are regarded as changes in the measurement of the physical productive capacity and are referred to as capital maintenance adjustments. It is only the amounts in excess of that required to maintain the physical capital are regarded as "profit."

## CONCLUSIONS

Despite the "Framework" being issued over 15 years ago, there have been no attempts to make amendments. One could argue that this is evidence of its robustness. Critics, however, would claim that it is because the "Framework" is too general in nature, and strengthening it would improve financial statements but could lead to controversy. The conceptual frameworks or statements of principles issued by individual countries do not conflict or depart from the approach of the IASB in any material matters and this has helped its acceptability.

It is important to remember that the "Framework" is not an accounting standard, and, if there is a conflict between the "Framework" and an International Financial Reporting Standard, the requirements of the standard prevails. Where there is not a standard on a particular accounting issue, the framework will help in establishing the appropriate policy and practice.

The "Framework" has been a useful document for both the IASC and the IASB. In particular, under the latter body, the influence of the "Framework" has been apparent in many of the standards. However, many national standard setters have their own conceptual framework. Although these national frameworks have many similarities, there are also differences. In addition, the frameworks were issued prior to the consideration of many complex accounting issues such as derivatives and financial instruments. A major development in convergence would be an agreed and adopted international framework.

Currently, the IASB and the U.S. Financial Accounting Standards Board (FASB) are in early discussions on the convergence of conceptual frameworks. Even at this preliminary stage, it is recognized that convergence cannot take place unless there are significant improvements. It is a lengthy project to devise a new conceptual framework, but it is imperative that this is undertaken in order to achieve international harmonization.

# IAS 1
# Presentation of Financial Statements

## ISSUED OR LAST REVISED

December 2003

## EFFECTIVE DATE

January 1, 2005

## PROBLEM AND PURPOSE

This standard was revised in 2003 as part of the IASB's improvement project. The fundamental approach to the presentation of financial statements has not been altered but user problems in dealing with alternatives and conflicts have largely been resolved. The main issues that the revision has addressed are achieving a fair presentation, classification of liabilities, treatment of extraordinary items, and some additional disclosures.

## SCOPE

All general-purpose financial statements prepared and presented in accordance with IFRSs.

## EXCLUSIONS

- Interim financial reports (IAS 34)
- Special purpose financial reports

## MAIN REQUIREMENTS

The standard states that a complete set of financial statements includes the following:

- A balance sheet
- An income statement
- A statement of changes in equity showing either all changes in equity or those changes arising from transactions with equity holders
- A cash flow statement
- A summary of significant accounting policies and other explanatory notes

Although the standard refers only to these financial statements, they are frequently included with other information in a published document referred to as the Annual Report and Accounts, or similar. The standard includes illustrative examples of the financial statements. The main headings and subheadings of a balance sheet are:

| | |
|---|---|
| ASSETS | |
| Non-current assets | |
| Line by line items | ——— |
| Subtotal | ——— |
| Current assets | |
| Line by line items | ——— |
| Sub-total | ——— |
| Total assets | ═══ |
| EQUITY AND LIABILITIES | |
| Equity attributable to equity holders of the parent | |
| Line by line items | ——— |
| Sub-total | ——— |
| Minority interest | |
| Total equity | ——— |
| Non-current liabilities | |
| Line by line items | ——— |
| Total non-current liabilities | ——— |

| | |
|---|---|
| Current liabilities | |
| Line by line items | ——— |
| Total current liabilities | ——— |
| **Total liabilities** | ——— |
| Total equity and liabilities | ═══ |

Certain information must be disclosed on the balance sheet. The minimum requirements for these line items are as follows:

- Property, plant, and equipment
- Investment property
- Intangible assets
- Held for sale non-current assets and disposal groups
- Financial assets
- Biological assets
- Investments accounted for under the equity method
- Inventories
- Trade and other receivables
- Cash and cash equivalents
- Trade and other payables
- Liabilities included in disposal groups held for sale
- Current tax liabilities and assets
- Deferred tax liabilities and assets
- Provisions
- Financial liabilities
- Minority interest presented as part of equity
- Issued equity capital and reserves

Further details of subclassifications should be disclosed either on the balance sheet or in the notes.

All items of income and expense recognized in the financial period must be included in the profit or loss unless a standard or an interpretation requires otherwise. The income statement can present the analysis of expenses based on either the nature of expenses or their function. With the former, expenses are aggregated in the income statement according to their nature (for example, depreciation, purchases of material, and employee benefits). The second form of analysis is the function of expense, more commonly known as the "cost of sales." This classifies expenses according to their function as part of cost of sales, or the cost of other administrative activities. The most useful difference between the two is that the cost of sales method provides a figure for gross profit. The main headings and subheadings of the income statement are:

THE NATURE OF EXPENSES FORMAT

| | | |
|---|---|---|
| Revenue | | X |
| Other income | | X |
| Changes in inventories of finished goods and work in progress | | X |
| Raw materials and consumables used | X | |
| Employee benefit costs | X | |
| Depreciation and amortization expense | X | |
| Other expenses | X | |
| Total expenses | | (X) |
| Profit | | X |

THE COST OF SALES FORMAT

| | |
|---|---|
| Revenue | X |
| Cost of sales | (X) |
| Gross profit | X |
| Other income | X |
| Distribution costs | (X) |
| Administrative expenses | (X) |
| Other expenses | (X) |
| Profit | X |

The Statement of Changes in Equity is part of the set of financial statements. Changes in equity are attributable to the increase or decrease in net assets during the period, except for those transactions that have taken place directly with the shareholder. The statement should include the following information:

- The profit for the period.
- Each item that has been reported directly in equity rather than the income statement.
- The total income or expense for the period. This is the sum of the first two items with any allocation to minority shareholders clearly separated.

- The effect of any changes in accounting policy, or the correction of an error.

The types of transactions that are taken directly to equity are reversal of impairment losses previously taken to equity (IAS 36), foreign exchange differences arising on consolidation (IAS 21), and revaluation surpluses on non-current assets (IAS 16).

IAS 1 also requires a full reconciliation of each reserve to be presented and the amount of any transaction that has taken place with shareholders to be separately identified.

In preparing the full set of financial statements, the following assumptions and considerations should be applied:

- The business is a going concern and will continue to operate into the foreseeable future.
- The accrual concept is used except for the cash flow statement.
- The presentation and classification of items in the financial statements will be consistent from one financial period to the next.
- Each material class of similar items is presented separately in the financial statements.
- Dissimilar items are presented separately unless they are immaterial.
- No offsetting of assets and liabilities, or income and expenses, is allowed unless this is covered by a standard.
- Comparative information for the previous period should be disclosed for all amounts reported in the financial statements, except where a standard permits or requires.

IAS 1 requires that financial statements present fairly the financial position, financial performance, and cash flows. By complying with IFRSs, and providing any additional information necessary, it is presumed that financial statements give a fair presentation. Where financial statements comply with IFRSs, an explicit and unreserved statement must be made in the notes to that effect.

An important part of the standard addresses the issue of compliance. As discussed in Part One of this book, the United Kingdom has the concept of "true and fair." This means that, in certain limited circumstances, entities are able to depart from a standard where it considers that compliance would result in the financial statements not giving a "true and fair view." This concept is partially weakened but retained in IAS 1. The standard states that where an entity considers that compliance with a particular standard or interpretation would be so misleading, it need not comply with the provisions. This is likely to be a very rare occurrence, and the entity must disclose that it has not complied with a particular standard, the title of the standard and the differences in treatment, and the financial impact of non-compliance.

# IAS 2
# Inventories

## ISSUED OR LAST REVISED

December 2003

## EFFECTIVE DATE

Financial statements covering periods beginning on or after January 1, 2005.

## PROBLEM AND PURPOSE

A major issue in accounting for inventories is determining the amount of cost that will be recognized as an asset and carried forward to the future financial period, when the related revenues are recognized. IAS 2 gives guidance on the methods of determining cost and its subsequent recognition as an expense, including any write-downs to net realizable value. The standard also explains the formulae to be applied in assigning costs to inventories.

In some industries, the value of inventories can be significant. In a manufacturing entity, accounting for inventories will require judgment, particularly in respect of goods in the production process and in identifying costs attributable to specific inventory items. The appropriate determination of the cost of inventories and the proper treatment as an expense is important as it has a direct effect on the profit or loss reported for the financial period.

## SCOPE

- Finished goods that are held for sale in the ordinary course of business
- Work in process in production intended for sale in the ordinary course of business
- Raw materials that comprise materials and supplies to be used in production

## EXCLUSIONS

- Work in progress arising from construction contracts (IAS 11 Construction Contracts)
- Financial instruments (IAS 39 Financial Instruments)
- Biological assets related to agricultural activity and agricultural produce at the point of harvest (IAS 41 Agriculture)

## MAIN REQUIREMENTS

Inventories should be measured at the lower of cost and net realizable value (NRV). Net realizable value is the estimated selling price in the ordinary course of business, less the estimated cost of completion and the estimated costs necessary to make the sale. Inventory losses and any write-downs to net realizable value should be recognized in the financial period in which they occur. If circumstances arise where a reversal of the write-down is justified, then this should be treated as a reduction in expense in the period that the reversal occurs. A reversal of a write-down is unlikely to be a frequent occurrence. The cost of inventories, other than those for which specific identification of costs are appropriate, is to be calculated by using the first-in, first-out (FIFO) or weighted average cost. The last-in, first-out (LIFO) method is not allowed under the standard.

Cost includes the following:

- Costs of purchase (including taxes, transport, and handling) net of trade discounts received
- Costs of conversion (including fixed and variable manufacturing overheads)
- Other costs incurred in bringing the inventories to their present location and condition

Cost excludes the following:

- Abnormal waste
- Storage costs
- Administrative overheads unrelated to production
- Selling costs
- Foreign exchange differences arising directly from the recent acquisition of inventories invoiced in a foreign currency
- Interest cost when inventories are purchased with deferred settlement terms

It is not acceptable to value inventories on a variable cost basis or to exclude a part of the overheads from the value by arguing that prudence has been applied by writing off those overheads in the current period. Fixed overheads should be allocated to each production process on a systematic and consistent basis and should be determined on normal levels of production. Selling or administration overheads should not be included in the valuation, unless there is a firm sales contract, and unless design, marketing, and selling costs were incurred before production started.

Normally, interest cannot be included as part of the valuation of inventories. There is the exception of maturing inventories, such as alcoholic spirits, where it can be reasonably argued that the interest has been incurred in holding the inventory as part of the production process and the product is not ready for sale until that process has been completed. Whisky drinkers will support this argument.

Where an entity may transfer goods internally from one department or division to another at a "transfer" price that does not represent the actual cost, any profits or losses should be eliminated from the inventory valuation.

When inventories are sold, the carrying amount of these inventories should be recognized as an expense in the same period that the revenue is recognized. This expense is usually referred to as the cost of goods sold or cost of sales.

## ILLUSTRATIVE EXAMPLE: THE PRINCIPLE OF THE LOWER OF COST AND NET REALIZABLE VALUE

At the year-end, a manufacturer has 2000 items in inventory and the total production cost per unit is $4. The best estimate of the selling price of the total inventory at that date is $6,500, and it is anticipated that $250 would be incurred in making the sale. At the year-end, the value of the inventory is $6,250; that is, the selling price of $6,500 less the selling costs of $250. The write-down of inventory of $1,750 (cost $8,000 – NRV$6,250) should be recognized as an expense in the period. In subsequent periods, new assessments of the net realizable value will be made until the inventories are sold. If a write-down to realizable value is of such size, incidence or nature that it is deemed exceptional, then it should be separately disclosed.

## MAIN DISCLOSURES

- Accounting policy for measuring inventories including the cost formula used
- Carrying amounts detailing any inventory pledged for securities

- Expensed write-downs and reversals
- Cost of inventories recognized as an expense

## EXAMPLES OF RELATED NATIONAL STANDARDS

Australia: AASB 1019

Canada: CICA Handbook 3030

Malaysia: MASB 2

New Zealand: FRS 4

Taiwan: SFAS 10

United Kingdom: SSAP 9

# IAS 7
# Cash Flow Statements

## ISSUED OR LAST REVISED

December 1992

## EFFECTIVE DATE

Financial statements covering periods beginning on or after January 1, 1994.

## PROBLEM AND PURPOSE

Knowledge of cash flow information is helpful to users of financial statements. The user can assess both the changes in net assets and the financial structure of the entity by evaluating cash flow information in the context of the other financial statements. The potential control that can be effected by an entity over the amounts and timings of cash flows for adapting to changing circumstances and opportunities can also be assessed. IAS 7 requires cash flows to be classified into operating, investing, and financing activities in the cash flow statement. The information enables users to assess the entity's ability to generate cash and cash equivalents, and to use those cash flows. IAS 7 includes an example of a cash flow statement for all entities other than financial institutions. An example of a cash flow statement for a financial institution is also illustrated in the standard.

## SCOPE

All entities producing financial statements that comply with IFRSs.

## MAIN REQUIREMENTS

The purpose of a cash flow statement is to analyze changes in cash and cash equivalents during a financial period. Statements can be drawn up using either the direct method (encouraged by IASB), where each major class of gross cash receipts and gross cash payments are disclosed; or the indirect method (accepted by IASB) that adjusts the net profit or loss for the effects of non-cash transactions. Both methods will give a figure for the cash flow from operation activities. The direct method, however, provides the detail of the cash flows that make up the total of cash flows from operating activities. The indirect method makes adjustments to the net profit or loss for the period (for example adding back depreciation) to arrive at the total cash flow figure.

For the purpose of IAS 7, cash and cash flow equivalents should be incorporated. These include the following:

- Cash on hand and deposits that can be withdrawn immediately in cash without suffering any penalties
- Short-term, highly liquid investments that are readily convertible to a known amount of cash and that are subject to an insignificant risk of changes in value
- Bank overdrafts that are repayable on demand and are an integral part of cash
- Equity investments if they are in substance a cash equivalent (for instance, preferred shares acquired within three months of their specified redemption date)

The cash flow statement must classify the information under three main headings:

*Operating activities:* The main revenue-producing activities of the enterprise, for example, cash received from customers and cash paid to suppliers and employees.

*Investing activities:* The acquisition and disposal of long-term assets and other investments that are not considered to be cash equivalents, for example, acquisition of plant and equipment.

*Financing activities:* Activities that alter the equity capital and borrowing structure of the enterprise, for example, cash from issuing shares.

The standard explains the treatment of certain items, the main ones being:

- Interest and dividends received and paid may be classified as operating, investing or financing cash flows but must be treated consistently.
- Tax cash flows on income are normally classified as operating unless they can be specifically identified under another heading.
- Extraordinary items should be disclosed separately under the most appropriate heading.
- Foreign currency cash flows arising from transactions should be recorded at the rate of exchange applying on the date of the cash flow.
- Cash flows of foreign subsidiaries should be included in the group cash flow statement translated at the exchange rate on the dates of the cash flows.
- Futures, options and swaps held specifically for trading purposes come under the heading of operating activities.

## ILLUSTRATIVE EXAMPLE: EFFECT OF TRANSACTION ON CASH FLOW STATEMENTS, INCOME STATEMENT AND BALANCE SHEET

Machinery with a carrying value of $1.5 million in the balance sheet is sold for $1 million. The cash flow will show the proceeds of $1 million under the heading of investing activities. The loss of $500,000 will be recognized in the income statement. The cost of the asset and the relevant cumulative depreciation will be removed from the balance sheet. In this hypothetical example, it is worthwhile raising the question why an impairment loss was not recognized previously if there was evidence available under IAS 36.

## MAIN DISCLOSURES

- A cash flow statement in the format required by the standard using either the direct or the indirect method
- The components of cash and a reconciliation statement with the corresponding items on the balance sheet
- An explanation of any restrictions on the use of cash balances that are significant

Some cash transactions, such as the issue of shares to acquire assets, and significant lease arrangements, are not shown on the cash flow statement. However, such transactions may have a substantial impact on investing and financing activities and should be stated as a note.

If significant cash or cash equivalent balances are not available for use by the group due to legal or other restrictions in the subsidiary's country of operations, this fact and the amount involved should be stated in the notes.

## EXAMPLES OF RELATED NATIONAL STANDARDS

Australia: AASB 1026

Canada: CICA Handbook 1540

Germany: GAS 2, GAS 2-10, GAS 2-20

Malaysia: MASB 5

New Zealand: FRS 10

Taiwan: SFAS 17

United Kingdom: FRS 1

United States: SFAS 95

# IAS 8

# Accounting Policies, Changes in Accounting Estimates, and Errors

## ISSUED OR LAST REVISED

December 2003

## EFFECTIVE DATE

Financial statements covering periods beginning on or after January 1, 2005.

## SCOPE

Entities producing financial statements that comply with IFRSs.

## PROBLEM AND PURPOSE

The determination of an entity's accounting policies is critical for the appropriate application of accounting standards. The disclosure of accounting policies is essential to assist the user in understanding financial statements. IAS 8 sets out the criteria for selecting and applying accounting policies, and accounting for changes in accounting policies. It also explains the appropriate treatment for changes in accounting estimates and corrections of prior period errors.

## MAIN REQUIREMENTS

The standard deals with three separate matters:

- Accounting policies
- Changes in accounting estimates
- The treatment of material prior period errors

Accounting policies are specific principles, bases, conventions, rules, and practices. They are critical to the understanding of the financial statement and need not be applied only when the effect of applying them is immaterial. Where an existing IFRS or SIC deals specifically with the appropriate accounting treatment of an issue, the entity must comply with that requirement. Where an IFRS or SIC does not address the specific issues, management must use its own judgment by reference to the following criteria in the actual order set out as follows:

- Any other IASB Standard or Interpretation dealing with relevant matters
- Definitions, recognition criteria, and measurement concepts for assets, liabilities; income and expenses contained in the IASB's Framework for the Preparation and Presentation of Financial Statements
- Recent pronouncements by other standard setting bodies that do not conflict with IFRSs and Framework

An entity must apply its accounting policies consistently unless an IFRS specifically requires or permits otherwise. It can only change its policies where required by a standard or interpretation or where the change improves the reliability and relevancy of information in the financial statements. A change in accounting policy, resulting from the initial application of an IFRS, is accounted for in accordance with any specific transitional provisions that are included in the IFRS. If the change is not due to an IFRS, then it is applied retrospectively to all periods presented in the financial statements as if the new accounting policy has always been applied. In other words, the financial statements of the current period and each prior period presented are adjusted, so that it appears as if the new accounting policy had always been applied. The disclosures to be made on changes due to a new standard or interpretation are prescribed by these pronouncements.

Changes in accounting estimates will lead to adjustments in the carrying amounts of assets, liabilities, or related expenses. The change is due to a reassessment of the expected future benefits and obligations. If there is a change in assets, liabilities, or equity, the carrying amount must be adjusted in the period of the change and future periods if they are affected. Financial statements of the prior period when the estimate was originally made do not need to be adjusted because it is assumed that the best estimate was made on the evidence that was available at that time. It is important to note that a change in an accounting estimate is different from a change in accounting policies. This difference is explained in the illustrative example.

Prior period errors, if material, should be adjusted in the financial statement of the prior period where the error occurred. The financial statements for the current period shall not be adjusted for prior period errors, since this would distort the results of the period when the error was identified rather than when it actually occurred. The comparative amounts of the prior period in which the error occurred should be restated. If the error occurred before the earliest prior period presented, the opening balances of assets, liabilities, and equity for the earliest prior period presented should be restated.

IAS 8 sets out the appropriate treatment if it is not practicable to make retrospective adjustments. Prior period errors are fundamental in nature and should only be recognized if it is clear that the original financial statements should not have been issued because of these errors. If the error arises due to a fault in an accounting estimate, but it was the best estimate that could be made at that time with the information available, it is a change in accounting estimates. No prior period adjustments are required.

## MAIN DISCLOSURES

Accounting policies:

- Nature of the change in accounting policies
- Description of transitional provisions
- Details of the amount of adjustments

Accounting estimates:

- Nature of the change
- The financial effect expected in current period or future periods

Prior period errors

- Nature of error
- Details of the amount of correction
- Explanation of error correction if there is no restatement

## ILLUSTRATIVE EXAMPLE: ACCOUNTING POLICIES AND ACCOUNTING ESTIMATES

The ability of management to change accounting policies is severely restricted and should not be confused with accounting estimates. For example, if an entity determines that it should increase its provision for irrecoverable accounts receivable from 3% to 5% because of a poor economy, this is not a change in accounting policy. It is a change in the accounting estimate of the amount that it expects to recover from account receivables.

The application of the standard results in prior periods being adjusted for changes in accounting policies and correction of errors. Prior periods are therefore comparable with the current period. Where there is a change in an accounting estimate, the financial statements of prior periods are not adjusted but the new basis for making estimates will be used in the current and future periods.

## EXAMPLES OF RELATED NATIONAL STANDARDS

Australia: AASB 1001

Canada: CICA Handbook 1505, 1506

Germany: GAS 13

Malaysia: MASB 4

New Zealand: FRS 1

United Kingdom: FRS 18

United States: SFAS 16

# IAS 10
# Events after the Balance Sheet Date

## ISSUED OR LAST REVISED

December 2003

## EFFECTIVE DATE

Annual financial statements covering periods beginning on or after January 1, 2005.

## PROBLEM AND PURPOSE

A situation can arise in which significant events occur between the date of the balance sheet and the date the financial statements are authorized for issue. These events provide information without which the user of the financial statements may not obtain a full understanding of the position and performance of the entity. The standard identifies those events that require adjustments to the financial statements before they are issued, as well as those events in which disclosures are required in financial statements but not adjustments. The standard also requires that an entity should not prepare financial statements on a going concern basis if events occur between the balance sheet date and the date of authorization that indicate that the entity is not a going concern. Entities should disclose the authorization date for financial statements, which is normally the date they are approved for publication. It is essential that users know this date since the financial statements and disclosures will not report any events occurring after the authorization date.

## SCOPE

Accounting for and disclosure of events after the balance sheet date.

## MAIN REQUIREMENTS

Events may occur between the balance sheet date and the date that the financial statements are authorized for issue. Such events may be favorable or unfavorable and can be classed as either adjusting events or non-adjusting events.

Adjusting events give new evidence on conditions at the date of the balance sheet. For example, a factory may be shown at a carrying value of $10 million on the balance sheet. Shortly afterward an independent valuator informs them that this valuation is incorrect and the factory is only to be valued at $8 million at the balance sheet date. Evidence has therefore become available that shows the original valuation to be incorrect, and the financial statements must be restated before they can be authorized.

Non-adjusting events do not provide new evidence on the conditions at the balance sheet date but of events that occurred after that date. These events have no impact on the balance sheet at the date it was drawn up but are of such significance that the users should be informed. For instance, a factory that has been correctly valued at the year-end but is later destroyed by fire, but before the authorization date, is an example of a non-adjusting event. The financial statements are correct as at the year-end and do not have to be restated. However, a non-adjusting event has occurred that is of significant importance and disclosure should be made.

In determining the appropriate classification of the event, it is essential to take all the surrounding circumstances into account. For example, the impairment of a property after the balance sheet date but before the authorization date would normally be considered a non-adjusting event. However, information received after the balance sheet date that demonstrated that the property was, in fact, impaired at the balance sheet date is an adjusting event.

An entity is not required to provide information on the adjusting events, because the redrafted financial statements will incorporate their effect. Entities may consider it appropriate to voluntarily disclose the nature of the event.

If there is evidence before the authorization date that the entity would not be considered a going concern in the foreseeable future, financial statements should not be prepared on a going concern basis, although this evidence was not apparent at the date of the balance sheet .

Dividends are regarded normally as a distribution of earnings for a particular period. However, if dividends are proposed or declared after the balance sheet date, and this is a frequent practice, they do not meet the definition of a liability at the balance sheet date. The dividends only become a present obligation at the date they are proposed or declared. If this date is after the balance sheet date, the dividends should be disclosed as a note to the financial statements and not a liability.

## ILLUSTRATIVE EXAMPLE: AN ADJUSTING EVENT

An entity's financial statements for the year ended 31 December 2004 were completed on 31 March 2005 and were authorized for issue on 12 May 2005. In April 2005, it transpired that fraud had been committed at one of the divisions and that the figure for revenues was overstated by 20%. This event is treated as an adjusting event because evidence has become available on what the correct revenue figure should be at 31 December 2004. Thus, the financial statements should be restated before being authorized.

## MAIN DISCLOSURES

- Date the financial statements were authorized for issue
- Name of person authorizing financial statements
- Nature and financial effect of important non-adjusting events

## EXAMPLES OF RELATED NATIONAL STANDARDS

Australia: AASB 1002

Canada: CICA Handbook 3820

New Zealand: FRS 5

United Kingdom: FRS 21

# IAS 11
# Construction Contracts

## ISSUED OR LAST REVISED

1993

## EFFECTIVE DATE

Financial statements covering periods beginning on or after January 1, 1995.

## SCOPE

The accounting treatment of revenues and costs associated with construction contracts. Such a contract may be for the construction or demolition of an asset.

There must be a firm sales contract. Speculative building work does not come under IAS 11 and is considered as work in progress, which should be valued at the lower of cost and net realizable value.

## PROBLEM AND PURPOSE

Normally with construction contracts, the date that construction activity commences and the date when it is completed fall into different accounting periods. The problem arises on determining the allocation of revenue and costs to the accounting periods when the construction activity is carried out. The standard uses the recognition criteria as set out in the Framework for the Preparation and Presentation of Financial Statements and gives guidance on the application of these criteria. The appendices to IAS 11 contain examples of the calculations required.

## MAIN REQUIREMENTS

A construction contract is specifically negotiated for the construction of an asset or a group of interrelated assets. Contracts may be negotiated on a fixed price basis or on a cost-plus basis. This does not affect the accounting treatment. The contract should be accounted for in its entirety. Only where there are two or more contracts evidenced by submission of separate proposals and negotiations and the costs and revenues of each can be separately identified should they be accounted for separately.

A contract may contain an agreement to construct an additional asset, or the contract may be amended subsequently to permit this. The construction of the additional asset should be treated as a separate contract if the price is negotiated separately or the addition is distinct from the original asset.

There are two methods of accounting permitted. The first is the stage of completion method, also known as the percentage of completion method, where the outcome of the contract can be estimated reliably. In this case, revenues and costs are recognized by reference to the stage of the completion of the contract activity and the illustrative example below shows the calculation. The second method is used when the outcome of a construction contract cannot be estimated reliably. In this case, revenue is only recognized in relation to those costs that are incurred and considered to be recoverable. Contract costs are expensed when incurred and no profit is recognized until the contract is completed or the outcome can be estimated reliably. Any probable loss on a contract must be expensed immediately.

Contract revenue is the amount agreed in the contract. This will include any variations, claims and incentives that will probably result in revenue and can be measured reliably. Contract costs include costs that are directly attributable, for example, site labor costs, construction materials, and rent of plant and equipment used on the contract. Costs such as insurance, design, and technical assistance that can be allocated to the specific contract can be included in the costs.

## ILLUSTRATIVE EXAMPLE: THE PERCENTAGE OF COMPLETION METHOD

The aim of this method is to match contract costs to contract revenues for the stage of completion. This will allow the profit that can be attributed to the stage of completion at the end of a financial period to be reported. The standard does not specify whether the percentage of completion should be calculated on revenues or costs so it is assumed that either method is acceptable.

| | | *Total Contract* |
|---|---|---|
| | $ | $ |
| Revenue | | 10,000 |
| Costs incurred to date | 5,000 | |
| Future expected costs | 3,000 | 8,000 |
| Expected profit | | 2,000 |

The amount of work certified as being complete at the end of the financial period is valued at $5,800. An independent architect, valuer, or surveyor will carry out this certification.

***Percentage Completion:***

| *Sales Basis* | *Cost Basis* |
|---|---|
| $5,800 / $10,000 | $5,000/$8,000 |
| = 58% | = 62.5% |

***Profit for the Financial Period:***

| | | *Sales Basis* | | *Cost Basis* |
|---|---|---|---|---|
| | | $ | | $ |
| Revenue | $10,000 × 58% = | 5,800 | $10,000 × 62.5% = | 6,250 |
| Costs | $ 8,000 × 58% = | 4,640 | $ 8,000 × 62.5% = | 5,000 |
| Profit | | 1,160 | | 1,250 |

## MAIN DISCLOSURES

- Amount of contract revenue recognized
- Methods to determine revenue and stages of completion
- Details of contracts in progress at the balance sheet dates

## EXAMPLES OF RELATED NATIONAL STANDARDS

Australia: AASB 1009

Canada: CICA Handbook 3400

Malaysia: MASB 7

New Zealand: FRS 14

Taiwan: SFAS 11

United Kingdom: SSAP 9

# IAS 12
# Income Taxes

## ISSUED OR LAST REVISED

1996

## EFFECTIVE DATE

Annual financial statements covering periods beginning on or after January 1, 1998.

## SCOPE

Income taxes, including all domestic and foreign taxes, based on taxable profits.

## PROBLEM AND PURPOSE

The liability for current taxes is based on accounting regulations and the requirements of national tax legislation. The tax charge to be paid cannot always be deduced from the entity's reported accounting profit, since this is prepared using GAAP and not tax laws. To ensure that financial statements provide a comprehensive picture, adjustments are made to the current tax expense so that the reported tax charge is consistent with the reported profit for the period. The difference between the current tax expense and the adjusted figure is known as deferred tax. IAS 12 explains the requirement for the recognition and measurement of deferred tax.

It also deals with transactions and other events of the current period that are recognized in the financial statements; recognition of deferred tax assets arising from unused tax losses or unused tax credits; the presentation of income taxes in the financial statements; and the disclosure of information relating to income taxes. IAS 12 also contains a number of worked examples.

## EXCLUSIONS

- Government grants (IAS 20)
- Investment tax credits

## MAIN REQUIREMENTS

Entities should recognize current taxes that are payable with respect to profits or current taxes that are recoverable with respect to losses. The amounts should be calculated using the rates available in the relevant regulations at the balance sheet date.

Deferred tax assets and liabilities arise where there is a difference between the carrying amount of assets and liabilities in the balance sheet, and the tax base of assets and liabilities. A deferred tax asset should only be recognized to the extent that it is probable that a future tax benefit will arise. A deferred tax liability should usually be recognized in full for all tax differences unless it arises from the following:

- Goodwill for which amortization is not deductible for tax purposes
- The initial recognition of an asset/liability that is not part of a business combination and affects neither the accounting nor the taxable profit at the time of the transaction
- Investments where the enterprise is able to control the timing of reversal of the tax difference and it is probable that the reversal will not occur in the foreseeable future

Deferred tax is measured at tax rates expected to apply when the deferred tax asset is realized or a deferred tax liability is settled. The tax rates used must have been enacted or substantially enacted by the balance sheet date. A deferred tax asset or liability is not discounted.

## ILLUSTRATIVE EXAMPLE: THE USE OF TERMS IN THE STANDARD

An entity acquires a non-current asset at the beginning of the year for $20,000. The asset has a useful life of 10 years and zero scrap value. Depreciation will be charged at $2,000 per year. The government permits a tax write-off at 25%. At the end of the year, the entity will have charged only $2,000 for depreciation in calculating net profit whereas the government will have allowed $5,000 to calculate the taxable profits. In the entity's balance sheet, the asset has a carrying value of $18,000 ($20,000 – $2,000) but the amount attributed to the asset for tax purposes will be $15,000 ($20,000 – $5,000).

## MAIN DISCLOSURES

- Current and deferred tax assets and liabilities
- Details of tax income and expense
- Changes in tax rates relating to discontinued operations
- Tax consequences of post-balance-sheet dividends
- Details of deferred tax assets

## EXAMPLES OF RELATED NATIONAL STANDARDS

Australia: AASB 20

Canada: CICA Handbook 3465

Malaysia: MASB 25

New Zealand: SSAP 12

United Kingdom: FRS 16, FRS 19

United States: SFAS 109

# IAS 14
# Segment Reporting

## ISSUED OR LAST REVISED

1997

## EFFECTIVE DATE

Financial statements covering periods beginning on or after July 1, 1998.

## PROBLEM AND PURPOSE

Entities may provide products and services in geographic areas that experience differing rates of profitability, opportunities for growth, future prospects, and risks to other areas where they operate. Aggregate data does not allow the user to assess the importance of these differences, and the standard addresses this issue by setting out the principles for reporting financial information by segments. IAS 14 aims to help users of financial statements to better assess the entity's risks and returns, and to understand the entity's past performance so that users can make more informed judgments about the entity as a whole. The standard contains a decision tree to define segments, illustrative segment disclosures, and a summary of the required disclosures in the appendices.

## SCOPE

Entities whose equity or debt securities are already or are intended to be publicly traded. It is not acceptable to avoid disclosure by arguing that the information can impair an entity's competitive position.

## EXCLUSIONS

- Any other entities that wish to disclose segmental information must comply with all the requirements of the standard.
- Segment information need not be presented in the separate financial statements of a parent, subsidiary, equity method associate, or equity method joint venture when they are presented in the same report as the consolidated statements.

## MAIN REQUIREMENTS

Management is responsible for identifying segments for reporting purposes by examining organizational structure and internal reporting. Segments can be identified as distinguishable components of an entity according to products and services (business segment), or geographic areas of operation. Management must determine which of these two segmentation bases is the more important and that will become the primary segment. An entity must make extensive disclosures about the primary segment with less onerous disclosures required for the secondary segment.

A primary segment for reporting purposes must exceed what is termed the 10% rule. This means that it must exceed 10% with respect to either:

- Its revenue as a percentage of total revenue or
- Its results as a percentage of segment profits or losses or
- Its assets as a percentage of total assets

A primary segment may be either:

- A business where a single product or service or a group of related products and services can be identified and the segment has risks and returns that are different from those of other business segments.
- Geographic where it is within a particular economic environment and has risks and returns that are different from segments in other economic environments.

If total external revenue for the reportable segments identified as meeting the 10% rule is less than 75% of total revenue, additional segments must be identified until the 75% criterion is achieved. The standard requires an accounting policy that entities must prepare segment information in conformity with the accounting policies adopted for preparing and presenting the consolidated financial statements. This approach is not followed in some accounting regimes, but IAS 14 allows additional segment information using different accounting policies. For this to apply, the information should be reported internally for decision-making purposes, and the basis of measurement for the additional information must be clearly described.

## MAIN DISCLOSURE REQUIREMENTS FOR PRIMARY SEGMENTS

- External and intersegmental sales separately
- Assets, liabilities, and depreciation
- The basis of intersegmental pricing
- Capital additions
- Non-cash expenses other than depreciation or cash flows from operating, investing, and financing activities in accordance with IAS 7
- Separate results (before interest and taxes) from continuing operations and discontinued operations
- Profit or loss of investments accounted for under the equity method

## MAIN DISCLOSURE REQUIREMENTS FOR SECONDARY SEGMENTS

- Revenue
- Assets
- Capital additions

## EXAMPLES OF RELATED NATIONAL STANDARDS

Australia: AASB 1005
Canada: CICA Handbook 1701
Germany: GAS 3
New Zealand: SSAP 23
Taiwan: SFAS 20
United Kingdom: SSAP 25
United States: SFAS 14

# IAS 16
# Property, Plant, and Equipment

## ISSUED OR LAST REVISED

December 2003

## EFFECTIVE DATE

Annual financial statements covering periods beginning on or after January 1, 2005.

## PROBLEM AND PURPOSE

For most entities, expenditure on property, plant, and equipment is substantial and raises issues on the timing of the recognition, the determination of their carrying amounts, and the depreciation charge. The proper and consistent treatment of these issues is critical to ensure that the financial statements are not misleading. The standard sets out guidance on these issues for property, plant, and equipment.

## SCOPE

Accounting treatment for property, plant, and equipment.

## EXCLUSIONS

- Property, plant and equipment classified as held for sale under IFRS 5
- Biological assets under IAS 41

## MAIN REQUIREMENTS

Property, plant, and equipment must be recognized as assets when the future economic benefits associated with the asset flow to the enterprise and the cost of the asset can be measured reliably. Recognition should be originally at cost but subsequently may be carried at either cost or at a revalued amount. In both cases, accumulated depreciation and any accumulated impairment losses should be deducted.

Costs include the following:

- Costs incurred initially to acquire or construct an item of property, plant, and equipment to bring it to working condition for its intended use.
- Costs incurred subsequently due to additions to the original property, plant, and equipment or to replace part of it or to service it. Routine servicing should be expensed, but if the asset is improved so that additional economic benefits will flow, the additional costs can be recognized as part of the asset.

As a general rule, costs that add to the value of the finished asset may be capitalized. In addition, costs that are unavoidably incurred in purchasing, installing, or preparing an asset may be capitalized. When deciding whether to capitalize or expense costs, management should exercise prudence.

Examples of costs that are normally recognized for each class of asset are as follows:

- *Land:* purchase price, legal fees, and preparation of land for intended use
- *Buildings:* purchase price and costs incurred in putting the buildings in a condition for use
- *Plant and machinery:* purchase price, transport, and installation costs

Abnormal costs such as rectifying installation errors, design errors, wastage, and idle capacity should not be capitalized. If the revalued basis is used for the subsequent carrying amount, then:

- Revaluations should be carried out regularly, so that the carrying amount of an asset does not differ materially from its fair value at the balance sheet date.
- The entire class of assets to which that asset belongs should be revalued.
- Depreciation is charged in the same way as under the cost basis.
- Increases in revaluation value should be credited to equity under the heading "revaluation surplus" unless they represent the reversal of a revaluation decrease of the same asset previously recognized as an expense, in which case it should be recognized as income.
- Decreases as a result of a revaluation should be recognized as an expense to the extent that they exceed any amount previously credited to the revaluation surplus relating to the same asset.
- Disposal of revalued assets can lead to a revaluation surplus that may be either transferred directly to retained earnings, or it may be left in equity under the heading "revaluation surplus."

The requirement to review revaluations regularly can be interpreted as meaning annually. Each class of assets must be revalued to prevent what is known as "cherry picking," that is, the revaluation of only those particular assets in a class that have increased in value and excluding those in a class that have not increased in value. This practice would obviously benefit the entity's leverage ratios if it were permitted.

Those entities that decide to move to a revalued basis will find that it has an adverse effect on some key financial ratios. The annual depreciation charge will increase, thus lowering earnings, and the higher value of assets will depress the Return on Assets ratio. The higher asset value will have a beneficial effect on leverage ratios.

Depreciation is applied on a component basis. This means that each part of an item of property, plant, and equipment with a cost that is significant in relation to the total cost of the item is depreciated separately. Depreciation applies to both the cost and revalued bases and must be applied in a systematic manner over the asset's useful life. The depreciation charge commences when the asset is available for use and continues until the asset is derecognized, regardless of periods of idleness. It is possible that if the unit of output method of depreciation is used, the charge for the idle period will be zero. Land that is not subject to depletion and does not have any limitations to the owner as regards its useful life should not be depreciated.

Subsequent expenditure that extends the useful life of an asset or increases its productivity may be capitalized. The gain or loss on derecognition of the asset is the difference between the net disposal proceeds, if any, and the carrying amount of the asset. It is included in the income statement. If an asset becomes impaired, this should be accounted for in accordance with IAS 36.

## ILLUSTRATIVE EXAMPLE: CHANGE IN USEFUL LIFE

A non-current asset with a useful life of 10 years and no residual value is acquired for $150,000. The annual depreciation charge is $15,000, and at the end of Year 4, the carrying value is $90,000. The remaining useful life is revised to three years so the annual depreciation charge to the end of the asset's useful life is $90,000/3 years = $30,000 per annum.

## MAIN DISCLOSURE REQUIREMENTS FOR EACH CLASS OF PROPERTY, PLANT, AND EQUIPMENT

- Basis for measuring the carrying amount
- Depreciation methods and the useful lives or depreciation rate
- Gross carrying amount, accumulated depreciation, impairment losses
- Reconciliation details of carrying amounts at the beginning and end of the period

## EXAMPLES OF RELATED NATIONAL STANDARDS

Australia: AASB 1010, AASB 1021, AASB 1041

Canada: CICA Handbook 3061

Malaysia: MASB 15

New Zealand: FRS 3

United Kingdom: FRS 15

United States: SFAS 121, SFAS 144

# IAS 17
# Leases

## ISSUED OR LAST REVISED

December 2003

## EFFECTIVE DATE

Annual financial statements covering periods beginning on or after January 1, 2005.

## PROBLEM AND PURPOSE

Leasing has become an increasingly popular activity in the business world and represents an important source of funding. The accounting treatment applied to leases has a direct impact on the financial statements. In addition, in some taxation regimes, it has been possible to structure agreements so that either, or both, the lessor and lessee have enjoyed significant taxation benefits. These developments meant that greater clarity was required in defining and accounting for different types of leases.

The issues covered by this standard are the proper classification of finance and operating leases and the proper accounting treatment in the financial statements of lessors and lessees. IAS 17 includes contracts in which the right to use assets is transferred, but substantial services are required from the lessor to maintain or operate the asset; for example, a photocopier. Where the assets and services can be separately identified and can be operated independently of each other, only that part of the contract relating to the asset is regulated by IAS 17. The appropriate treatment for sale and leaseback transactions is also dealt with in the standard. Key ratios likely to be impacted by IFRS 17 are leverage and Return on Assets.

## SCOPE

All leases other than exclusions.

## EXCLUSIONS

- Leases for minerals, oil, natural gas, and similar regenerative resources
- Licensing agreements for films, videos, plays, copyrights, and similar items

## MAIN REQUIREMENTS

A lease is classified as a finance lease or an operating lease at its inception, that is, when the agreement or commitment is made. A finance lease is one that transfers substantially all risks and rewards incidental to ownership. All other leases are regarded as operating leases. This classification is critical since it determines the accounting treatment. The standard provides guidance as to what constitutes the transfer of all risks and rewards. For example, all risks and rewards are regarded as being transferred if the agreement transfers legal title at the end of the term or the lessee can purchase the asset at a price lower than the fair value at the exercise date of that option. The standard does not specify rigid, numerical thresholds to decide whether transfer has taken place. In the past, these thresholds have been used by some entities to structure a lease to classify it in a way that gives tax advantages or flatters their financial statements.

The lessee treats an operating lease as an expense on a straight-line basis over the term of the lease. A finance lease is recognized as an asset and a liability in the lessee's balance sheet at the lower of the fair value of the lease and the present value of the minimum lease payments.

Finance lease payments should be apportioned between the finance charge and the reduction of the outstanding liability. The finance charge represents a constant periodic rate of interest on the outstanding liability. The leased asset is depreciated in accordance with IAS 16. The same depreciation policy for all assets should be applied to the asset held under the finance lease and, if there is uncertainty over final ownership, the shorter of the lease term and the life of the asset should be applied.

With regard to lessors, the operating lease assets should appear in the balance sheet according to the nature of the asset. Operating lease income will be recognized over the lease term on a straight-line basis unless another basis is more appropriate. With finance leases, the lease will be recorded in the balance sheet as a receivable at an amount equal to the net investment in the lease. The finance income should be recognized on the basis of a constant periodic rate of return on the lessor's net investment outstanding.

An entity may enter into a sale and leaseback transaction to improve its liquidity by selling an asset to a third party. The arguments used, including those by governments, are that their role is not to own and maintain property but to concentrate on the main operational activities. The entity, having sold the asset, leases it back from the third party and pays rental for its use. Such transactions can be either finance or operating leases. In the case of the former, the entity must defer and amortize the excess of the sales' proceeds over the carrying amount for the period of the lease. With an operating lease, there are four possible alternative transactions as follows:

If at fair value, the profit or loss is recognized immediately.

If sale price is below fair value, the profit or loss should be recognized immediately, but if the loss is compensated by future rentals at below market price, it should be amortized over the period of use.

If sale price is above fair value, the excess should be deferred and amortized over the period of use.

If the fair value at the time of the transaction is less than the carrying amount, the difference should be recognized immediately as a loss.

## MAIN DISCLOSURE REQUIREMENTS FOR FINANCE LEASES—LESSEE

- Carrying amount of asset
- Total minimum lease payments reconciled to their present value
- Details of minimum lease payments
- Description of significant leasing arrangements

## MAIN DISCLOSURE REQUIREMENTS FOR FINANCE LEASES—LESSOR

- Gross investment of the lease reconciled to the present value of the minimum lease payments
- Details of gross investment and present value of minimum lease payments
- Description of significant leasing arrangements

## MAIN DISCLOSURE REQUIREMENTS FOR OPERATING LEASES—LESSEE

- Details of minimum lease payments at balance sheet date under non-cancelable leases
- Total of the future sublease income under non-cancelable leases

- Lease and sublease payments recognized in income
- General description of significant leasing arrangements

## MAIN DISCLOSURE REQUIREMENTS FOR OPERATING LEASES—LESSOR

- Details of minimum lease payment amounts at balance sheet date under non-cancelable operating leases
- General description of significant leasing arrangements

## EXAMPLES OF RELATED NATIONAL STANDARDS

Australia: AASB 1008

Canada: CICA Handbook 3065

Malaysia: MASB 10

New Zealand: SSAP 18

Taiwan: SFAS 17

United Kingdom: SSAP 21

United States: SFAS 13

# IAS 18
# Revenue

## ISSUED OR LAST REVISED

1993

## EFFECTIVE DATE

Annual financial statements covering periods beginning on or after January 1, 1995.

## PROBLEM AND PURPOSE

In some accounting regimes, revenue is referred to as sales or turnover but the IASB uses the term *revenue*. The main issue in accounting for revenue is ascertaining the financial period when revenue is to be recognized. This is a far more complex task than it would first appear. It is surprising how many entities still find that they have misstated revenue in their financial statements and subsequently have to make adjustments. One assumes that these are honest errors and not attempts to mislead. The appropriate allocation of revenue is essential for calculating the correct profit figure for a financial period. IAS 18 defines revenue and identifies the two criteria for its recognition. First, it is highly likely that future economic benefits will flow to the entity and, second, that these benefits can be measured reliably. It defines the circumstances when these two criteria are satisfied and provides guidance on the practical application of the criteria.

## SCOPE

Revenue arising from the sale of goods, the provision of services, and the use of assets yielding interest, royalties and dividends.

## EXCLUSIONS

Revenue specified in other standards, for example, revenue from lease agreements under IAS 17.

## MAIN REQUIREMENTS

Revenue is the gross inflow of economic benefits, for example, cash, receivables, and other assets arising from the ordinary operating activities of an enterprise. Revenue should be measured at the fair value of the consideration that is received or receivable. There are instances where the inflow of cash or cash equivalents is deferred, for example, when the seller provides interest-free credit. In these cases, the fair value of the consideration that is receivable is less than the nominal amount of cash and cash equivalents to be received, and discounting is appropriate. It is critical to determine that a sale has taken place. There have been many examples where a sale has been, in substance, a financing arrangement and should be treated as such.

Recognition from the sale of goods should only be recognized when:

- The seller has transferred to the buyer the significant risks and rewards of ownership.
- The seller retains neither continuing managerial involvement to the degree usually associated with ownership nor effective control over the goods sold.
- The amount of revenue can be measured reliably.
- It is probable that the economic benefits associated with the transaction will flow to the seller.
- The costs incurred or to be incurred in respect of the transaction can be measured reliably.

Revenue from the provision of services should be recognized and the percentage-of-completion method should be used when:

- The amount of revenue can be measured reliably.
- It is probable that the economic benefits will flow to the seller.
- The stage of completion at the balance sheet date can be measured reliably.
- The costs incurred, or to be incurred, in respect of the transaction can be measured reliably.

If these criteria cannot be met, a cost-recovery basis should be used with revenue being recognized only to the extent that the recoverable expenses are recognized. Revenue from interest, royalties, and dividends, assuming that these are probable economic benefits that will flow to the entity and the amount of revenue can be measured reliably, are recognized as follows:

- *Revenue interest:* on a time proportion basis that takes into account the effective yield
- *Royalties:* on an accruals basis in accordance with the substance of the relevant agreement
- *Dividends:* when the shareholders' rights to receive payment are established

The range of possible revenue transactions is extensive and complex. The legal system in the country where the transaction takes place may set down guidelines on when the revenue is recognized. In the absence of legal guidance and if there is uncertainty on the timing of revenue recognition, it is essential to determine the substance of the transaction. The following examples demonstrate some of the variations:

- Goods are only accepted after inspection or installation. In this case the revenue is normally recognized when the buyer formally accepts the goods.
- Consignment sales where the initial buyer sells the goods on behalf of the original supplier. Revenue is normally recognized when the goods have been sold to a third party.
- Advertising commissions where the agency receives a commission for placing advertisements or commercials. The revenue will only be recognized when the advertisement or commercial is in the public domain.
- Real estate sales where the seller retains some form of involvement may mean that revenue is not recognized but the transaction may be treated as a joint venture or lease.

## MAIN DISCLOSURE REQUIREMENTS

- Accounting policy
- Details of each specific classifications of revenue

## EXAMPLES OF RELATED NATIONAL STANDARDS

Australia: AASB 1004

Canada: CICA Handbook 3400

Malaysia: MASB 9

Taiwan: SFAS 32

# IAS 19
# Employee Benefits

## ISSUED OR LAST REVISED

1998 and amended December 16, 2004

## EFFECTIVE DATE

Annual financial statements covering periods beginning on or after January 1, 1999.

## PROBLEM AND PURPOSE

Accounting for employee benefits raises a number of issues. The standard first sets out recognition and measurement criteria for short-term employee benefits such as compensated absence, profit-sharing, and bonus plans. The major part of the standard is concerned with postemployment benefits and the appropriate accounting treatment for defined contribution plans and defined benefit plans. The appendices contain an illustrative example with disclosures. In December 2004, the standard was amended to allow the additional option of recognizing actuarial gains and losses in full in the period in which they occur in a statement of recognized income and expense instead of in the income statement. The original treatment of actuarial gains and losses being recognized in the income statement in the period in which they occur or spread over the service lives of the employees would remain.

## SCOPE

Employee benefits are all forms of consideration given by an entity in exchange for services provided by employees in a financial period. These include the following:

- Short-term benefits, for example, wages, salaries, and holiday pay
- Postemployment benefits, for example, pensions

- Other long-term benefits such as long-service leave and other benefits not payable within 12 months
- Termination benefits, for example, redundancy pay

## EXCLUSIONS

Employee benefits specified in other standards such as share-based payments under IFRS 2 and employee benefit plans under IAS 26.

## MAIN REQUIREMENTS

The guiding principle is that the cost of providing employee benefits should be recognized in the period when the employee earns the benefit, rather than when it is paid or payable. Short-term employee benefits are regarded as those payable within 12 months after service is provided and should be recognized as an expense in the period that service is provided. In terms of non-accumulating compensated absences, the expected cost of compensated absences is recognized when the absences occur. In terms of accumulating compensated absences, the cost is recognized when the service is provided, thus increasing the employee's entitlement to benefits. Profit-sharing and bonus payments should be recognized when the entity has a legal or constructive obligation as a result of past events and a reliable estimate of the expected cost can be made.

Postemployment plans are either defined contribution plans where the employer pays fixed contributions or defined benefit plans where the final benefit is calculated according to certain criteria such as length of service and amount of final salary. For defined contribution plans, contributions are recognized as an expense in the period that the employee provides services. For defined benefit plans, the amount recognized is the present value of the defined benefit obligation at the balance sheet date. This is based on actuarial assumptions, net of the fair value of any plan assets at the balance sheet date.

Other long-term employee benefits are recognized as a liability equal to the present value of the defined benefit obligation minus the fair value of any plan assets at the balance sheet date.

For termination benefits, the standard specifies that amounts payable should be recognized when the enterprise is demonstrably committed to either:

- Terminating the employment of an employee or group of employees before their normal retirement date or
- Providing termination benefits as a result of an offer made in order to encourage voluntary redundancy

## EXAMPLES OF RELATED NATIONAL STANDARDS

Australia: AASB 1028
Canada: CICA Handbook 3461
Malaysia: MASB 29
United Kingdom: FRS 17
United States: SFAS 87, SFAS 88, SFAS 106, SFAS 132

# IAS 20
# Accounting for Government Grants and Disclosure of Government Assistance

## ISSUED OR LAST REVISED

April 1983

## EFFECTIVE DATE

Annual financial statements covering periods beginning on or after January 1, 1984.

## PROBLEM AND PURPOSE

Government grants and assistance do not have a major impact on most entities, but can have a significant effect on the financial statements where they are present. This short standard sets out the accounting treatment and disclosure requirements for government grants and the disclosure requirements for other forms of government assistance.

## SCOPE

All government grants and forms of government assistance.

## EXCLUSIONS

- Government assistance in the form of benefits that are available in determining taxable income
- Government participation in the ownership of an entity
- Government grants covered by IAS 41

## MAIN REQUIREMENTS

Government assistance consists of several types and has various conditions attached to it. Some forms of assistance may be to induce an entity to take an action it would not otherwise perform, for example, to open a new factory in a specific economic area.

Government grants should not be credited directly to equity. Instead they are recognized as income over the period so that they match with the related costs for which they are intended to compensate. A systematic basis should be used for this process. Grants cannot be recognized by an entity unless there is reasonable assurance that:

- The entity will comply with the conditions attached to the grant.
- The grant will be received from the government.

A grant receivable as compensation for costs already incurred or for immediate financial support, with no future related costs, should be recognized as income in the period in which it is received.

If a grant becomes repayable, it should be treated as a change in accounting estimate under IAS 8. If the original grant relates to income, the repayment should be applied first against any related unamortized deferred credit, and any excess should be dealt with as an expense. If the original grant relates to an asset, the repayment should be treated in the balance sheet either as deferred income or as a deduction in determining the carrying amount of the asset.

## MAIN DISCLOSURE REQUIREMENTS

- Accounting policy
- Nature and extent of grants
- Unfulfilled conditions and contingencies relating to recognized grants

## EXAMPLES OF NATIONAL STANDARDS

Canada: CICA Handbook 3800

United Kingdom: SSAP 4

# IAS 21 The Effects of Changes in Foreign Exchange Rates

## ISSUED OR LAST REVISED

December 2003

## EFFECTIVE DATE

Financial statements covering periods beginning on or after January 1, 2005.

## PROBLEM AND PURPOSE

The development of global business has resulted in many entities being involved in various forms of relationships with other entities in different countries. These may include transactions conducted with foreign buyers or sellers, or participation in foreign operations. In these circumstances, foreign currencies are involved. Rules are required to ensure that these currencies are translated in a consistent manner.

The standard addresses the issue where an entity carries out transactions in foreign currencies and/or has foreign financial operations. The transactions in foreign currencies must be expressed in the entity's reporting currency, and the financial statements of foreign operations must be translated into the entity's reporting currency. The standard sets out guidance for the selection of the exchange rate to be used and the recognition of the financial effects of changes in exchange rates.

## SCOPE

Accounting for foreign currency transactions and foreign operations in the financial statements of an entity.

## EXCLUSIONS

- Foreign currency derivatives (IAS 39)
- Hedge accounting of foreign currency items (IAS 39)

## MAIN REQUIREMENTS

The general principle is that an entity should translate foreign currency items and transactions into its functional currency. To do this translation, the spot exchange rate between the functional currency and the foreign currency at the date of the transactions is used. Average rates can be used, but care must be exercised. If exchange rates fluctuate significantly over time or if there are a small number of irregular transactions, the average can be distorted.

At each balance sheet date the following actions are taken:

- Use the closing rate to report foreign currency monetary items (such as cash held, assets to be received, and liabilities to be paid in either fixed amounts or amounts that can be determined).
- Use the exchange rate at the date of transaction to report non-monetary items carried at historical cost.
- Use the exchange rate at the time when fair values were determined for non-monetary items carried at fair value.

Exchange differences arise from translating the same monetary items at different exchange rates. These differences normally occur due to the settlement amounts payable or receivable in a foreign currency and the retranslation during the preparation of financial statements at the period-end. The monetary items that form part of the reporting entity's net investment in a foreign operation are recognized as a separate component of equity in the financial statements that include the foreign and the reporting equity. Such exchange differences are recognized in the income statement as profit or loss on disposal of the net investment. All other differences are recognized in the income statement for that period.

The results and financial position of a foreign operation are translated in the reporting entity's financial statements (the presentation currency) as follows:

- Assets and liabilities for each balance sheet presented (including comparatives) are translated at the closing rate at the date of that balance sheet.
- Income and expenses for each income statement (including comparatives) are translated at exchange rates at the dates of the transactions.
- All resulting exchange differences are recognized as a separate component of equity.

An entity whose functional currency is the currency of a hyperinflationary economy should restate the financial statements as required by IAS 29.

## MAIN DISCLOSURES

- Amount of exchange differences recognized in profit or loss
- Net exchange differences reconciled at the beginning and end of the period and classified into separate components of equity
- Reasons if functional and presentational currencies are different
- Reasons for any change in functional currency for either the reporting entity or the significant foreign operation

## EXAMPLES OF RELATED NATIONAL STANDARDS

Australia: AASB 1012

Canada: CICA Handbook 1650

Malaysia: MASB 6

New Zealand: FRS 21

Taiwan: SFAS 14

United Kingdom: SSAP 20

United States: SFAS 52

# IAS 23
# Borrowing Costs

## ISSUED OR LAST REVISED

December 1993

## EFFECTIVE DATE

Financial statements covering periods beginning on or after January 1, 1995.

## PROBLEM AND PURPOSE

In general, borrowing costs should be treated as an expense, but there are circumstances where they can be capitalized. The effect of these different treatments on the financial statements can be highly significant. Interest that is expensed reduces the profit in that financial year. If the interest is capitalized, the income statement is not charged with the interest, and the asset increases in value by the amount of the capitalized interest. This improves the profit on the income statement and the leverage ratios. Without regulations giving guidance on these two alternatives, an entity may select injudiciously, and the financial statements could be misleading. The standard has expensing as the benchmark treatment, but the allowed alternative treatment permits capitalization subject to certain conditions. The standard gives guidance on the amount of borrowing costs, directly attributable to the acquisition, construction, and production of a qualifying asset that is eligible for capitalization.

## SCOPE

- Interest on bank overdrafts and borrowings
- Amortization of discounts or premiums on borrowings
- Amortization of ancillary costs incurred in the arrangement of borrowings

- Finance charges on finance leases
- Exchange differences on foreign currency borrowings where they are regarded as an adjustment to interest costs

## EXCLUSIONS

Actual or imputed cost of equity capital, including any preferred capital not classified as a liability.

## MAIN REQUIREMENTS

The benchmark treatment is expensing all borrowing costs in the period in which they are incurred. The allowed alternative treatment permits borrowing costs to be considered as part of the cost of the acquisition, construction, and production of qualifying assets. These assets take up a substantial period of time before they are ready for use. Examples include intangible assets that are being developed and investment properties that are being constructed.

The treatment adopted must be applied consistently. The borrowing costs that can be capitalized are not only loan interest but also other costs such as interest on bank overdrafts, finance charges with respect to finance leases, and amortization of ancillary costs incurred when borrowing is being negotiated and arranged.

If the alternative treatment of capitalization is adopted, the following rules apply:

- Costs eligible for capitalization are the actual costs incurred less any income earned on the temporary investment of funds borrowed specifically.
- Where funds are part of a general pool, the capitalization rate is the weighted average of the borrowing costs for the general pool.
- Capitalization commences when expenditures and borrowing costs are being incurred and activities that are necessary to prepare the asset for its intended use or sale are in progress.
- Capitalization ceases when substantially all of the activities are complete.
- Capitalization must be suspended during periods where active development is interrupted.
- Where construction is completed in stages, capitalization should cease when substantially all of the necessary preparatory activities are complete.

## ILLUSTRATIVE EXAMPLE: BORROWINGS CAPITALIZED BY THE WEIGHTED AVERAGE COST OF THE CAPITAL METHOD

An entity has the following general loans:

$2 million @ 5%

$1 million @ 6%

$500,000 @ 8%

It intends to extend its production line at a cost of $600,000. The project will take 3 months from start to completion.

Weighted average calculation is:

($2 million @ 5% + $1 million @ 6% + $500,000 @ 8%)/$3.5 million
= $100,000 + $60,000 + $40,000 / $3.5 million
= 5.714%

Borrowing costs to be capitalized
= $600,000 (cost of asset) × 5.714% × 0.25 year
= $8,571

## MAIN DISCLOSURES

- Accounting policy applied to material borrowing costs incurred
- Accounting policy and the amount of borrowing costs capitalized and the capitalization rate

## EXAMPLES OF RELATED NATIONAL STANDARDS

Australia: AASB 1036

Canada: CICA Handbook 3850

Malaysia: MASB 27

Taiwan: SFAS 3

United States: SFAS 34

# IAS 24
# Related Party Disclosures

## ISSUED OR LAST REVISED

December 2003

## EFFECTIVE DATE

Financial statements covering periods beginning on or after January 1, 2005.

## PROBLEM AND PURPOSE

Normal features of business transactions involve interrelationships and trading connections among different entities. These often have no effect on normal day-to-day operations, but some transactions are conducted between related parties. This is regarded as the situation where one party has the ability to control the other party or exercise significant influence over the other when making financial and operating decisions. Such control and influence may not be applied to all or any transactions. Where such control or influence is exercised, it may have an effect on the financial position and operating results of the reporting entity. The user of the financial statements needs to be aware of this possibility to properly understand the financial statements. This short standard describes examples of relationships where disclosures may be required and the nature of the disclosures.

## SCOPE

- Where one party has the ability to control the other party, exercise significant influence, or exercise joint control over the other party when making financial and operating decisions.
- Where a transfer of resources, services, or obligations between related parties (regardless of whether a price is charged) takes place.

## EXCLUSIONS

- Two enterprises where they simply have a director or key manager in common
- Two venturers who share joint control over a joint venture
- Providers of finance, trade unions, public utilities, government departments, and agencies in the course of their normal dealings with an enterprise
- Economic dependency through a single customer, supplier, franchiser, distributor, or general agent with whom an enterprise transacts a significant volume of business

## MAIN REQUIREMENTS

The standard specifies several circumstances where one party is related to another if:

- Directly or indirectly, through one or more intermediaries, the party controls or is controlled by, or is under common control with, the entity (this includes parents, subsidiaries and fellow subsidiaries).
- One party has an interest in the entity that gives it significant influence.
- One party has joint control over the entity.
- It is an associate of the entity.
- It is a joint venture whereby the entity is a venturer.
- It is a close member of key management personnel of the entity or its parent. The presence of close family members in circumstances where control or significant voting power occurs is deemed to give rise to a related party relationship.
- It is a postemployment benefit plan for the benefit of employees of the entity, or of any of its related parties.

## MAIN DISCLOSURES

- The name of its parent and, if different, the ultimate controlling party, irrespective of whether transactions have taken place. If neither the entity's parent nor the ultimate controlling party produces financial statements available for public use, the name of the next most senior parent that does so must also be disclosed.
- Compensation of key management personnel who have authority and responsibility for planning, directing, and controlling the activities of the

entity, directly or indirectly, including all directors (whether executive or otherwise).
- Details of transactions among related parties and a statement that the related party transactions were made on terms equivalent to those that prevail in arm's length transactions. This statement should be made only if it can be substantiated.

## EXAMPLES OF RELATED NATIONAL STANDARDS

Australia: AASB 1017
Canada: CICA Handbook 3840
Germany: GAS 11
Malaysia: MASB 8
New Zealand: SSAP 22
Taiwan: SFAS 6
United Kingdom: FRS 8
United States: SFAS 57

# IAS 26
# Accounting and Reporting by Retirement Benefit Plans

## ISSUED OR LAST REVISED

January 1987

## EFFECTIVE DATE

Financial statements covering periods beginning on or after January 1, 1988.

## PROBLEM AND PURPOSE

Retirement benefit plans are a common feature of business. They are arrangements by which an entity provides benefits for employees on or after termination of service when such benefits, or the contributions toward them, can be determined or estimated in advance of retirement from the provisions of a document or from the entity's practices. Retirement benefit plans may be required, by regulation or some form of agreement, to make a report to all participants in the plan. The standard applies when such reports are required and it should be read in conjunction with IAS 19.

## SCOPE

Applies to the financial statements of retirement benefit plans.

## MAIN REQUIREMENTS

The standard distinguishes between defined contribution plans and defined benefit plans. Defined contribution plans are those in which payments or contributions into the plan are fixed. The benefits paid to retired members will depend on the value of the investments made from the contributions and the investment returns that are reinvested. Defined benefit plans are those in which the benefits received by a retired member are fixed. Contributions paid into the plan are based on an estimate of the future payments from the plan.

The objective of a defined contribution plan disclosure is to provide information about the conduct of the plan and the performance of the investment. The financial statements of a defined contribution plan contain a statement of net assets available for benefits and a description of the funding policy. The objective of a defined benefit plan disclosure is to provide information about the balance between the future obligations under the plan and the resources it has available to meet these obligations. The financial statements contain one of the following:

- A statement that shows the net assets available for benefits, the actuarial present value of promised retirement benefits distinguishing between vested and non-vested benefits, and the resulting excess or deficit or
- A statement of net assets available for benefits with a note disclosing the actuarial present value of promised retirement benefits, distinguishing between vested and non-vested benefits, or a reference to this information in an accompanying actuarial report.

## MAIN DISCLOSURES

- Accounting policies
- Details of net assets available for benefit
- Details of changes in net assets available for benefit
- Description of funding policy of the plan

## EXAMPLES OF RELATED NATIONAL STANDARDS

Canada: CICA Handbook 3461

Malaysia: MASB 30

New Zealand: FRS 32

United Kingdom: SSAP 24

United States: SFAS 81

# IAS 27
# Consolidated and Separate Financial Statements

## ISSUED OR LAST REVISED

December 2003

## EFFECTIVE DATE

Financial statements covering periods beginning on or after January 1, 2005.

## PROBLEM AND PURPOSE

Investors need to be informed of the combined financial position and performance of all the individual companies in a group in order to make an informed assessment. A parent company, with some exceptions, should present consolidated financial statements. The standard gives guidance on the consolidation procedures, accounting for investment subsidiaries, and the disclosures required.

## SCOPE

- The preparation and presentation of consolidated financial statement for a group of entities under the control of a parent.
- Accounting for investments in subsidiaries, jointly controlled entities, and associates in the separate financial statements of a parent.

## EXCLUSIONS

A parent need not present consolidated financial statements if the following four conditions are met:

> The parent is itself a wholly-owned subsidiary, or is a partially owned subsidiary of another entity and its other owners, including those not otherwise entitled to vote, have been informed about, and do not object to, the parent not presenting consolidated financial statements.
>
> The parent's debt or equity instruments are not traded in a public market.
>
> The parent did not file, nor is it in the process of filing, its financial statements with a securities commission or other regulatory organization for the purpose of issuing any class of instruments in a public market.
>
> The ultimate parent or any intermediate parent of the ultimate parent that produces consolidated financial statements available for public use that comply with International Financial Reporting Standards.

## MAIN REQUIREMENTS

Consolidated accounts should include all of the parent's subsidiaries, both domestic and foreign, except where control is intended to be temporary because the subsidiary is acquired and held exclusively with a view to its subsequent disposal in the near future. A subsidiary is one enterprise controlled by another. The standard concentrates on the substance of the relationship between two entities to determine whether consolidated financial statements are required. There is the presumption that one entity is controlled by another if the investor has more than 50% of the voting rights. However, it is necessary to examine the substance and not rely solely on the numerical threshold. Control can be evidenced by the presence of power, for example, where the parent entity has the ability to appoint or remove the majority of the members of the board of the controlled entity.

Special purpose entities (SPEs) should be consolidated where the substance of the relationship indicates that the SPE is controlled by the reporting enterprise. This may arise even where the activities of the SPE are predetermined or where the majority of voting or equity is not held by the reporting enterprise. For example, an SPE may be created where there are explicit limits restricting the decision-making powers of the governing body. The SPE may have been created to achieve a well-defined aim, and as such the operations are predetermined with little need for changes in operational decisions. In this case, the sponsor will have a significant beneficial interest in the SPE's activities, and the financial statements should be consolidated.

Subsidiaries are not required to be consolidated where they have been acquired and held with the sole intention of subsequent disposal in the near future. In these cases, the subsidiaries will be accounted for under the provisions of IAS 39.

The financial statements of the parent and its subsidiaries must be prepared using uniform accounting policies for like transactions and other events in similar circumstances with the reporting dates being no more than three months apart.

In the parent's/investor's individual financial statements, investments in subsidiaries, associates, and jointly controlled entities should be accounted for, either at cost or conforming to IAS 39. These investments should not be accounted for by the equity method in the parent's/investor's separate statements.

## MAIN DISCLOSURES

- The fact that subsidiaries are not consolidated, and, thus, summarized financial information of such subsidiaries should be disclosed either individually or in groups.
- The nature of the relationship between the parent and a subsidiary when the parent does not own, directly or indirectly through subsidiaries, more than half of the voting power.
- The reasons why the ownership, directly or indirectly through subsidiaries, of more than half of the voting or potential voting power of an investee does not constitute control.

## EXAMPLES OF RELATED NATIONAL STANDARDS

Australia: AASB 1024
Canada: CICA Handbook 1600
Germany: GAS 4
Malaysia: MASB 11
New Zealand: FRS 36
Taiwan: SFAS 7
United Kingdom: FRS 6
United States: SFAS 141

# IAS 28
# Investment in Associates

## ISSUED OR LAST REVISED

December 2003

## EFFECTIVE DATE

Financial statements covering periods beginning on or after January 1, 2005.

## PROBLEM AND PURPOSE

An investor may have a significant influence in an entity that is neither a subsidiary nor a joint venture, so that it does not appear in the consolidated financial statements under the provisions of IAS 27. It is important that the user be made aware of the nature and implications of this investment. The standard sets out the criteria to establish significant influence and provides guidance on accounting for associates in the consolidated financial statements under the equity method and the disclosures required. Generally, significant influence is considered as one entity having the power to participate in the financial and operating policies of another entity but without having control or joint control over these policies.

## SCOPE

All investments where investors have significant influence but do not have control or joint control.

## EXCLUSIONS

Investments held by venture capital organizations or mutual funds, unit trusts, and similar organizations and are:

- Designated at fair value on recognition through the income statement; or
- Held for trading and accounted for under IAS 39.

## MAIN REQUIREMENTS

The presence of significant influence in an entity normally arises where the investor has 20% or more of the voting power. There are exceptions to this rule. For example, an investor may hold more than 20% of the voting rights, but is unable to exercise significant influence because another investor holds the remaining voting rights. The reverse situation can occur where the investor has less than 20% of the voting rights, but circumstances permit significant influence to be applied.

Where there is significant influence, the equity method of accounting for investments in associates should be used in the consolidated financial statements. Under the equity method, an equity investment is initially recorded at cost and is subsequently adjusted to reflect the investor's share of the net profit or loss of the associate. Examples of the key exceptions to the equity method include the following:

- When an investment is held for sale and, therefore, falls under IFRS 5.
- When an investor is itself a subsidiary and its other owners have been informed that the equity method is not being used and they do not object.

The investor should use the financial statements of the associate with the same financial date as the financial statements of the investor unless it is impracticable to do so. In these circumstances, the most recent financial statements should be used as long as the difference is no greater than three months. Adjustments must be made for any significant transactions or events occurring between the different accounting period-ends of the associate and the investor.

Once the significant influence ceases, the equity method is discontinued from that date. The investment should be accounted for in accordance with IAS 39, provided the associate does not become a subsidiary or a joint venture as defined in IAS 31.

## MAIN DISCLOSURES

- Fair value of investments in associates where there are no published price quotations
- Summarized financial information of associates
- Explanations of the reasons for using the equity method where less than 20% of the voting power is held
- Explanation of the reasons for not using the equity method where more than 20% of the voting power is held
- Share of the profit or loss and the carrying amount of equity investments

## EXAMPLES OF RELATED NATIONAL STANDARDS

Australia: AASB 1016

Malaysia: MASB 12

Germany: GAS 8

New Zealand: FRS 38

Taiwan: SFAS 5

United Kingdom: FRS 9

# IAS 29 Financial Reporting in Hyperinflationary Economies

## ISSUED OR LAST REVISED

July 1989

## EFFECTIVE DATE

Periods beginning on or after January 1, 1990.

## PROBLEM AND PURPOSE

The financial statements prepared in a hyperinflationary economy are misleading, since the loss in purchasing power of money makes comparisons of transactions and events at different periods unreliable. The standard does not specify the criteria to identify a hyperinflationary economy but describes some possible characteristics. Where such characteristics are present, the standard specifies the accounting treatment and disclosures required.

## SCOPE

Financial statements of every entity whose functional currency is that of a hyperinflationary economy.

## MAIN REQUIREMENTS

Financial statements of an entity that reports in the currency of a hyperinflationary economy should be stated in terms of the measuring unit current at the balance sheet date. The standard does not specify a hyperinflationary economy but gives examples of the characteristics of such an economy, and the application is a matter of judgment. Hyperinflation is indicated by characteristics of the economic environment of a country that include monetary amounts being expressed in a stable currency rather than in the local currency and the holding of wealth in non-monetary assets such as land and works of art. The only quantitative guidance in the standard is a cumulative inflation rate of approximately 100% or more over a three-year period.

Comparative figures for prior period(s) should be restated into the same current measuring unit. Restatements are made by applying a general price index. A gain or loss on the net monetary position is included in the income statement.

When an economy ceases to be hyperinflationary and the requirements of IAS 29 no longer apply, the amounts expressed in the measuring unit current at the end of the previous reporting period should be used for the carrying amounts in subsequent financial statements.

## MAIN DISCLOSURES

- An explanation that the financial statements have been adjusted to take account of general inflationary increases
- Gain or loss on monetary items
- Whether financial statements are based on historical cost or current cost
- The rate and changes in the price index

# IAS 30
# Disclosures in the Financial Statements of Banks and Similar Financial Institutions

## ISSUED OR LAST REVISED

First issued in 1990, followed by amendments in 1998 and 1999

## EFFECTIVE DATE

Periods beginning on or after January 1, 1991.

## PROBLEM AND PURPOSE

Banks play a major role in the economy, and they have special characteristics in their operation and financing that are not necessarily well understood by the non-expert. Banks are subject to supervision, and they report to regulatory authorities, but users need specific information to understand the financial performance and position as shown by the financial statements of banks. The standard sets out disclosures that it considers to be useful to users but does not require banks to go beyond what can reasonably be required.

## SCOPE

The financial statements of banks and similar financial institutions.

## MAIN REQUIREMENTS

The purpose of the standard is to supplement requirements specified in other standards in order to assist users in evaluating the financial position and performance of banks and to understand their operations.

A bank's income statement should group income and expenses by nature, and details of specific items should be reported. A bank's balance sheet should group assets and liabilities by nature and list them in liquidity sequence.

The general principle is that the offsetting of assets and liabilities or income and expenditure is not allowed under IFRSs. There are, however, transactions where offsetting is allowed, and IAS 30 permits offsetting to be applied in hedge accounting under IAS 39 and in specific circumstances under IAS 32.

## MAIN DISCLOSURES

- Fair value of each class of financial assets and financial liabilities
- Maturity of assets and liabilities based on the remaining period at the balance sheet date to the contractual maturity date
- Concentration of assets, liabilities, and off-balance-sheet items (by geographical area, customer, or industry groups or other aspects of risk)
- Losses on loans and advances
- General banking risks, including future losses and other unforeseeable risks or contingencies disclosed separately as appropriations of retained earnings
- Assets pledged as security

## EXAMPLES OF RELATED NATIONAL STANDARDS

Australia: AAS 32

Germany: GAS 2-10, GAS 3-10, GAS 3-20, GAS 5-10, GAS 5-20

New Zealand: FRS 33, FRS 34, and FRS 35

Taiwan: SFAS 28

# IAS 31
# Interests in Joint Ventures

## ISSUED OR LAST REVISED

December 2003

## EFFECTIVE DATE

Periods beginning on or after January 1, 2005.

## PROBLEM AND PURPOSE

Two or more parties may enter into an agreement to carry out an economic activity that is subject to joint control. This presents particular problems as to the appropriate accounting treatments and the disclosures that should be made. Joint ventures may take many different forms and structures and IAS 31 describes three main types. It provides guidance for the appropriate accounting treatment for each type of joint venture agreement. In addition, the standard explains the benchmark treatment and the allowed alternative treatment in the consolidated financial statements of a venturer.

## SCOPE

All interests in joint ventures and the reporting of joint venture assets, liabilities, income, and expenses in the financial statements of venturers and investors.

## EXCLUSIONS

Investments held by venture capital organizations, mutual funds, unit trusts, and similar entities complying with IAS 39.

## MAIN REQUIREMENTS

The standard identifies three types of joint ventures as jointly controlled operations, jointly controlled assets, and jointly controlled entities. For each of these types, there is a different accounting treatment. Joint control exists only when the strategic financial and operating decisions relating to the economic activity require the unanimous consent of the parties sharing control.

Jointly controlled operations involve the use of assets and other resources of the venturers rather than the establishment of a separate entity. Each venturer uses its own assets, incurs its own expenses and liabilities, and raises its own financing. In these cases, the venturer must recognize in its financial statements the assets that it controls, the liabilities and expenses that it incurs, and its share of the income from the sale of goods or services.

Jointly controlled assets involve the joint control, and often the joint ownership, of assets dedicated to the joint venture. Each venturer may take a share of the output from the assets, and each bears a share of the expenses incurred. In these cases, the venturer must recognize its interest in the assets on a proportional basis. The venturer also recognizes liabilities or expenses incurred by it or its share of those jointly incurred. The income from the sale or its share of output from the joint venture is also recognized. A common example of this type of joint venture is an oil pipeline controlled and operated by several oil companies.

Jointly controlled entities are corporations, partnerships, or other entities where two or more venturers have an interest, under a contractual arrangement that establishes joint control. In these cases, the venturer uses proportionate consolidation (IAS 27) or the equity method in compliance with IAS 28. Proportionate consolidation is the combination of the entity's share of the individual line items of the joint venturer's financial statements. Equity accounting shows the change in the venturer's share of the joint venture for each period. These methods are not used when the asset is held for sale in compliance with IFRS 5. They are also not used if the venturer is itself a subsidiary and the owners do not object to either method being applied, and the debt and equity securities are not publicly traded.

If the venturer decides it is appropriate to use proportionate consolidation, this means that its balance sheet includes its share of the assets it controls jointly and its share of the liabilities for which it is jointly responsible. The income statement includes its share of the income and expenses of the jointly controlled entity.

If a venturer ceases to have joint control, it should cease using whichever of the two methods it has adopted. If it obtains complete control, it should account for it in accordance with IAS 27.

## MAIN DISCLOSURES

- Details about joint venture contingent liabilities
- Details about joint venture commitments
- Details of interests in significant joint ventures

## EXAMPLES OF RELATED NATIONAL STANDARDS

Australia: AASB 1006

Canada: CICA Handbook 3055

Germany: GAS 9

New Zealand: SSAP 25

Taiwan: SFAS 31

# IAS 32

# Financial Instruments: Disclosure and Presentation

## ISSUED OR LAST REVISED

December 2003

## EFFECTIVE DATE

Periods beginning on or after January 1, 2005.

## PROBLEM AND PURPOSE

The use and diversity of financial instruments, from bonds to derivatives, has been increasing in recent years and presents several accounting problems. In order to understand the significance of on-balance sheet and off-balance sheet financial instruments to an entity's financial position, performance, and cash flows, users require more information. This lengthy standard gives guidance on the presentation of on-balance sheet financial instruments and disclosures for off-balance sheet financial instruments. It also incorporates useful examples of the application of the standard. The principles in IAS 32 complement the principles for recognizing and measuring financial assets and financial liabilities in IAS 39.

## SCOPE

Disclosure and presentation of financial instruments, that is, financial assets, financial liabilities, and equity instruments.

## EXCLUSIONS

- Interests in subsidiaries, associates, and joint ventures that are accounted for under IAS 27, IAS 28, or IAS 31
- Insurance contracts and financial instruments within the scope of IFRS 4
- Employee benefit plans within the scope of IAS 19
- Contracts for contingent consideration in a business combination under IFRS 3
- Share-based transactions IFRS 2

## MAIN REQUIREMENTS

The purpose of the standard is to enhance users' understanding of the significance of financial instruments with respect to an entity's financial position, performance, and cash flows. A financial instrument gives rise to a financial asset to one entity and a financial liability or equity instrument to another. Examples of financial assets are cash, account receivables, and equity investments. Examples of financial liabilities are account payables, loans, and leases. The definition of financial instruments includes both primary instruments (for example cash, receivables, creditors, and equities) as well as derivatives (for example options and swaps).

The standard requires the classification of financial instruments as financial assets, financial liabilities, and equity instruments, with compound financial instruments containing both equity and a liability component. This classification must concentrate on the substance of the contract and not the legal form. The classification should be made at the initial recognition, and no subsequent changes are permitted.

Financial instruments can be classified into two types. The first type is classified as financial assets or financial liabilities where the contractual right is to receive cash or pay cash respectively in the future. Examples are trade accounts receivable and payable, notes receivable and payable, and loans receivable and payable.

The second type of financial instrument is classified according to whether the economic benefit to be received or given is a financial asset other than cash. For example, the holder of a note payable in government bonds has the contractual right to receive bonds, and the issuer has the obligation to deliver bonds. Cash is not part of the transaction.

Compound instruments must be treated according to their substance, and the component parts of equity and liability must be accounted for and treated separately. The separation must take place at the date of issue and not revised in later periods. The components are separated for accounting purpose by deducting from the fair value of the instrument the amount separately calculated for the liability. The residual will represent the amount attributable to equity.

Interest, dividends, losses, and gains relating to financial liabilities are recognized as income or expense in the income statement. Distributions to holders of equity instruments are debited directly to equity, net of any related income tax benefit.

Treasury shares (i.e., an entity's own equity instruments that it has reacquired) must be deducted from equity. The offsetting of financial assets and liabilities are only permitted in specific circumstances. The enterprise must have a legally enforceable right to offset the amount and must intend to either settle on a net basis or to realize the asset and settle the liability immediately. In no other circumstances is an entity permitted to offset a financial asset and a financial liability and then report the net amount.

## MAIN DISCLOSURES

Disclosures are extensive and include the following topics:

- Risk management and hedges
- Terms, conditions, nature, and extent of the use of financial instruments and the business purposes they serve

- Interest rate, credit risk, and management's policies for controlling risks
- Fair value of financial instruments
- Derecognition
- Compound financial instruments
- Impairment

## EXAMPLES OF RELATED NATIONAL STANDARDS

Australia: AASB 1033

Canada: CICA Handbook 3860

Malaysia: MASB 24

New Zealand: FRS 31

Taiwan: SFAS 27

United Kingdom: FRS 13

United States: SFAS 107, SFAS 109

# IAS 33
# Earnings per Share

## ISSUED OR LAST REVISED

December 2003

## EFFECTIVE DATE

Periods beginning on or after January 1, 2005.

## PROBLEM AND PURPOSE

Earnings per share (EPS) is information widely used by investors and analysts for the comparison of performance among different entities in the same period and for one organization over several periods. It is one of the fundamental ratios for assessing the financial performance of an entity, but its apparent simplicity in calculation can be misleading. The definition of the terms used is critical in arriving at the correct ratio. The standard concentrates on the calculation of the denominator (the number of shares) to provide consistency and rigor in reporting but accepts that earnings can be affected by different accounting policies applied by entities. The standard requires the calculation and disclosure of diluted EPS as shareholders should be made aware of this and the information should assist them in their decision-making. IAS 33 includes useful examples for calculating the basic EPS and the diluted EPS.

## SCOPE

- Entities whose securities are publicly traded or that are in the process of issuing securities to the public
- Other entities that choose to present EPS information and therefore must comply with IAS 33

## EXCLUSIONS

If both parent and consolidated statements are presented in a single report, EPS is required only for the consolidated statements.

## MAIN REQUIREMENTS

The objective of IAS 33 is to prescribe principles for the determination and presentation of EPS amounts in order to improve performance comparisons between different entities in the same period and between different accounting periods for the same entity.

Basic EPS is calculated by dividing profit or loss attributable to ordinary equity holders of the parent entity (the numerator) by the weighted average number of ordinary shares outstanding (the denominator) during the period. The profit or loss from continuing operations is calculated after deducting all expenses including taxes, minority interests, and preference dividends. The weighted average number of ordinary shares is calculated by adjusting the shares in issue at the beginning of the period by the number of shares bought back or issued during the period, multiplied by a time-weighting factor. IAS 33 includes guidance on appropriate recognition dates for shares issued in various circumstances.

Diluted EPS is calculated by adjusting the profit or loss and the weighted average number of ordinary shares outstanding for the effects of dilutive options and other dilutive potential ordinary shares. Examples of potential ordinary shares are convertible debt, share warrants, convertible instruments, share rights, and employee stock purchase plans. The number of ordinary shares is the weighted average number of ordinary shares outstanding, as calculated for basic earnings per share, plus the weighted average number of ordinary shares that would be issued on the conversion of all dilutive potential ordinary shares into ordinary shares.

The profit or loss attributable to ordinary equity holders of the parent equity, as calculated for basic EPS, is adjusted for the after-tax effects of:

- Any dividends or other items related to dilutive potential ordinary shares deducted in arriving at the profit or loss attributable to ordinary equity holders.
- Any interest recognized in the period related to dilutive potential ordinary shares.
- Any other changes in income or expense that would result from the conversion of the dilutive potential ordinary shares.

## ILLUSTRATIVE EXAMPLE

*Dilutive EPS and Options:*

| | |
|---|---|
| Number of ordinary shares in issues on January 1 | 2,000,000 |
| Average fair value of shares | $10 each |
| Income for the year ended December 31 | $200,000 |

There are options in issue to purchase 100,000 ordinary shares at an exercise price of $7 each.

*Dilutive EPS Calculation:*

| | |
|---|---|
| Proceeds of options exercised (100,000 @ $7) | $700,000 |
| Number of ordinary shares at fair value ($700,000/$10) | 70,000 |
| Number of ordinary shares actually issued | 100,000 |
| Number of shares issued with no "fair value" proceeds | 30,000 |

Diluted EPS = $200,000/2030,000 = $0.985

Options are dilutive because, if exercised, the entity is issuing ordinary shares at less than fair value.

## MAIN DISCLOSURES

- Details of basic and diluted EPS on the face of the income statement
- The amounts used as the profit or loss for ordinary shareholders in calculating basic and diluted EPS
- The weighted average number of ordinary shares used in calculating basic and diluted EPS
- A description of those ordinary share transactions or potential ordinary share transactions that occur after the balance sheet date and would have had a significant effect on the EPS

An entity may decide to disclose an EPS figure using a component of earnings other than the one attributable to ordinary shareholders for the period. In these circumstances, the disclosure must be in addition to the figures required by IAS 33, the entity must use the weighted average number of ordinary shares calculated in accordance with IAS 33, and must provide a reconciliation between the earnings figure used and the reported figure in the financial statements.

## EXAMPLES OF RELATED NATIONAL STANDARDS

Australia: AASB 1027

Canada: CICA Handbook 3500

Malaysia: MASB 13

Taiwan: SFAS 24

United Kingdom: FRS 14

United States: SFAS 128

# IAS 34
# Interim Financial Reporting

## ISSUED OR LAST REVISED

June 1998

## EFFECTIVE DATE

Financial statements covering periods beginning on or after January 1, 1999.

## PROBLEM AND PURPOSE

Investors, creditors, and others relying on annual financial statements do not receive a sufficiently frequent flow of information for decision-making. By the time the annual financial statements are published, the economic environment may have changed dramatically from the time that several of the reported events took place. Interim financial reports can provide timely and reliable information to remedy this situation. One dilemma concerning the preparation of interim statements is whether they should be discrete, that is, a stand-alone statement for the shortened financial period, or whether they should be integral and constitute a part of the 12-month period. The standard addresses this issue and prescribes the minimum content of an interim financial report and the recognition and measurement principles.

## SCOPE

Entities that choose or are required to publish interim financial reports in accordance with IAS 34.

## EXCLUSIONS

Frequency, reportable entities, and publishing date are left to national law or regulations to specify.

## MAIN REQUIREMENTS

IAS 34 defines the minimum content of an interim financial report as a condensed balance sheet, condensed income statement, condensed statement showing changes in equity, condensed cash flow statement, and selected explanatory notes. The standard also prescribes the principles for recognition and measurement in financial statements presented for an interim period.

The periods and items to be covered by the interim financial statements are as follows:

- Balance sheet as of the end of the current interim period and a comparative balance sheet as of the end of the immediately preceding financial year
- Income statements for the current interim period and cumulatively for the current financial year to date, with comparative income statements for the comparable interim periods (current and year-to-date) of the immediately preceding financial year
- Statement showing changes in equity cumulatively for the current financial year to date, with a comparative statement for the comparable year-to-date period of the immediately preceding financial year
- Cash flow statement cumulatively for the current financial year to date, with a comparative statement for the comparable year-to-date period of the immediate, preceding financial year

The interim financial reports should present each of the headings and the subtotals as illustrated in the most recent annual financial statements and the explanatory notes as required by IAS 34. Additional line items should be included if their omission would make the interim financial information misleading. If the annual financial statements were consolidated (group) statements, the interim statements should be group statements as well.

An enterprise should use the same accounting policy throughout the financial year, with the same policies for interim reporting and annual financial statements. The exceptions are accounting policy changes made after the date of the most recent annual financial statements and which would be incorporated in the next annual financial statements. If a decision is made to change a policy mid-year, the change is implemented retrospectively, and previously reported interim data is restated.

The notes to the interim financial statements are essentially an update. They include disclosures about changes in accounting policies, seasonal or cyclical nature of the entity's operations, changes in estimates, changes in outstanding debt or equity, dividends, segment revenue and result, events occurring after balance sheet date, acquisition or disposal of subsidiaries and long-term investments, restructurings, discontinuing operations, and changes in contingent liabilities or contingent assets.

The standard provides guidance for applying the basic recognition and measurement principles at interim and the main points are as follows:

- Revenues received seasonally, cyclically or occasionally within a financial year should not be anticipated or deferred at the interim date if this practice is not used at the financial year-end.
- If this practice is used, costs that are incurred unevenly during a financial year should be anticipated or deferred at the end of the financial year.
- Income tax expenses should be recognized based on the best estimate of the weighted average annual income tax rate expected for the full financial year.

## MAIN DISCLOSURES

- A condensed balance sheet
- A condensed income statement
- A condensed statement of changes in equity
- A condensed cash flow statement
- Selected explanatory notes

## EXAMPLES OF RELATED NATIONAL STANDARDS

Australia: AASB 1029

Canada: CICA Handbook 1751

Germany: GAS 6

Malaysia: MASB 26

New Zealand: FRS 24

Taiwan: SFAS 23

# IAS 36
# Impairment of Assets

## ISSUED OR LAST REVISED

March 2004

## EFFECTIVE DATE

Applied to goodwill and intangible assets acquired in business combinations after March 31, 2004, and to all other assets from annual periods beginning on or after March 31, 2004.

## PROBLEM AND PURPOSE

There is the risk that an entity may be showing an asset at a carrying value that is greater than its recoverable amount in the balance sheet. The recoverable amount is the greater of the asset's net selling price and its value in use. Without this information, users can be misled about the financial strength of the entity and its financial performance. IAS 36 describes the procedures to be followed to ensure that an asset is not carried at greater than its recoverable amount. The standard also explains the accounting treatment for impairment loss. Entities may find that the requirement to write off impairment losses in the financial period they occur has a significant negative effect on earnings and associated performance ratios.

## SCOPE

All assets such as land, buildings, machinery, intangible assets, and goodwill except exclusions below.

## EXCLUSIONS

- Inventories (IAS 2)
- Assets arising from construction contracts (IAS 11)
- Deferred tax assets (IAS 12)

- Assets arising from employee benefits (IAS 19)
- Financial assets (IAS 39)
- Investment property carried at fair value (IAS 40)
- Certain agricultural assets carried at fair value (IAS 41)
- Insurance contract assets (IFRS 4)

## ASSETS HELD FOR SALE (IFRS 5) MAIN REQUIREMENTS

At each balance sheet date, assets should be reviewed for indications of possible impairment; that is, its carrying amount may be in excess of the greater of its net selling price and its value in use. Indications include factors such as market value decline, obsolescence, and physical damage. If there is an indication that an asset may be impaired, then the asset's recoverable amount must be calculated. Annually, irrespective of any indication of impairment, an entity must review intangible assets that have an indefinite useful life, those not yet available for use, and goodwill acquired in a business combination. Those impairment tests may be carried out at any time during the annual period, but the test must be carried out at the same time each year.

If the asset is revalued in accordance with another standard, for example, IAS 16, the impairment loss is then treated as a revaluation decrease in accordance with that other standard.

Where there are indications that an asset may be impaired, the recoverable amount of an asset must be measured. This is the higher of the asset's net selling price (fair value less its selling costs) and its value in use. The calculation of value in use involves an estimate of future cash flows that the entity expects to derive from the asset, which are then discounted to present values. Any impairment loss should be recognized where the recoverable amount is below the carrying amount. The loss is treated as an expense in the income statement.

The discount rate to be applied for measuring value in use should be the pre-tax rate based on the current market assessments of the time value of money and the risk that is specific to the asset. If future cash flows have already been adjusted for asset risk, these should not be included in the discount rate.

If it is not possible to use a market-determined rate, the entity may use either its own weighted average cost of capital, or its incremental borrowing rate, or other market borrowing rates that are appropriate.

Wherever possible, recoverable amounts should be determined for individual assets. Where it is impossible to determine the recoverable amount for an individual asset, the recoverable amount for the asset's cash-generating unit (CGU) should be identified and used. The CGU is the smallest identifiable group of assets that generate cash inflows from continuing use, and that are largely independent of the cash inflows from other assets or groups of assets.

Acquired goodwill requires specific accounting treatment and should be allocated to each of the CGUs or groups of CGUs that are expected to derive benefit. If the recoverable amount of the unit exceeds the carrying amount of the unit, the unit and the goodwill allocated to that unit is not impaired. But where the carrying amount exceeds the recoverable amount, the entity must recognize an impairment loss. An impairment loss for a cash-generating unit is allocated to reduce the carrying amount of the assets of the unit in the following order:

The loss is first charged against the goodwill allocated to the CGU;

If the goodwill is insufficient to absorb the loss, then the loss will be allocated over other assets in proportion to the carrying amount of each asset.

An impairment loss recognized in prior periods is reversed if there is a change in the estimates used to determine the asset's recoverable amount since the last impairment loss was recognized. In this case, the carrying amount of the asset is increased to its recoverable amount, but not exceeding the carrying amount of the asset that would have been determined had no impairment loss been recognized in prior years. Goodwill impairment must not be reversed.

## ILLUSTRATIVE EXAMPLE: IMPAIRMENT OF A CGU

A cash generation-unit to which goodwill has been allocated contains three machines with carrying values as follows:

| | $ |
|---|---|
| Machine 1 | 6,000 |
| Machine 2 | 12,000 |
| Machine 3 | 12,000 |
| Allocated goodwill | 8,000 |
| | 38,000 |

An annual impairment review assesses the recoverable amount of the CGU at $25,000. The impairment loss of $13,000 is to be charged to the income statement. First, the amount of the allocated goodwill is written off. The remainder of the impairment loss of $5,000 will be allocated proportionally to the three machines, reducing their carrying values to the following:

| | $ |
|---|---|
| Machine 1 | 5,000 |
| Machine 2 | 10,000 |
| Machine 3 | 10,000 |
| | 25,000 |

## MAIN DISCLOSURES

- Impairment losses by the class of asset and primary segments
- Allocation of goodwill to CGUs

## EXAMPLES OF RELATED NATIONAL STANDARDS

Canada: CICA Handbook 3063

Malaysia: MASB 23

Taiwan: SFAS 35

United Kingdom: FRS 11

United States: SFAS 121, SFAS 144

# IAS 37
# Provisions, Contingent Liabilities, and Contingent Assets

## ISSUED OR LAST REVISED

July 1998

## EFFECTIVE DATE

Financial statements covering periods beginning on or after July 1, 1999.

## PROBLEM AND PURPOSE

There have been examples where provisions have been used by entities to manipulate the trend of their earnings figure, thus misleading investors. Similarly, the non-reporting of the presence of contingent liabilities and assets means that users do not have a full understanding of the financial performance and position of the entity and of circumstances that could affect its future. The standard establishes recognition and measurement principles for all provisions, contingent liabilities, and contingent assets, and it requires disclosures to assist users to understand their nature, timing, and amount. The appendices to IAS 37 include a decision tree and examples to assist recognition.

## SCOPE

IAS 37 prescribes the recognition criteria, measurement bases, and disclosures that are applied to provisions, contingent liabilities and contingent assets. The standard also applies to financial instruments carried at amortized cost and to non-policy-related liabilities of an insurance company.

## EXCLUSIONS

- Financial instruments carried at fair value
- Non-onerous executory contracts

- Policy liabilities of insurance companies
- Contingent liabilities assumed in a business combination under IFRS 3
- Construction contracts under IAS 11
- Income taxes under IAS 12
- Leases under IAS 17
- Employee benefits under IAS 19
- Insurance contracts under IFRS 4

## MAIN REQUIREMENTS

A provision is a liability of uncertain timing or amount and should only be recognized where:

- A present obligation (legal or constructive) has arisen as a result of a past event.
- Payment is probable in order to settle the obligation.
- The amount can be estimated reliably.

Entities should not make provisions for future operating losses. The amount recognized as a provision should be the best estimate of the expenditure required to settle the present obligation at the balance sheet date. An entity should assess the risks and uncertainties that may operate in reaching a best estimate, and any material future cash flows should be discounted to present values. Examples of provisions include warranty obligations, a retailer's policy on refunds to customers, and obligations to clean up contaminated land.

An annual review of provisions should be conducted, and if the provisions are no longer required, they should be reversed to income. A provision can be applied only to the expenditure for which the provision was originally recognized.

Where there is no realistic alternative for an entity other than to settle an obligation, the standard refers to this as a constructive obligation, and a provision must be made. This would include those circumstances where past practice leads third parties to reasonably assume that the entity will settle the obligation (for instance, a sale or return policy).

A constructive obligation to restructuring can be made only for the sale or termination of a line of business, closure of business locations, changes in management structure, or fundamental reorganizations of the entity. There must be evidence of the planned restructuring and expectations by third parties that this will be implemented. Restructuring provisions should include only the direct expenditures caused by the restructuring, not costs for ongoing activities.

There is an important distinction between provisions and contingent liabilities. The latter must not be recognized in the financial statements as liabilities, but should be disclosed unless the possibility of an outflow of resources is remote. A contingent liability can take two forms. It can be a possible obligation (not a present obligation) that arises from past events, but confirmation is required to determine whether it is a present obligation. Alternatively, it may be a present obligation, but it is uncertain whether the obligation will be settled, or it cannot be measured reliably.

A contingent asset is a possible asset where confirmation is required to establish whether it is an asset. An example is a legal claim that an entity is pursuing, but it is uncertain whether the claim will be successful. Contingent assets should not be recognized, but are disclosed when an inflow of economic benefits is probable.

## ILLUSTRATIVE EXAMPLE: THE BEST ESTIMATE OF A PROVISION

An entity manufactures products carrying a 12-month warranty. It is estimated that 95% of the products will have no defects within the 12 months. It is expected that 4% will require minor repairs and 1% major repairs. If all normal production in the year required minor repairs, the cost is estimated at $50,000. If all normal production in the year required major repairs, the cost is estimated at $200,000.

The provision for repairs is estimated at:

| | *$* |
|---|---|
| $50,000 @ 4% | 2,000 |
| $200,000 @ 1% | 2,000 |
| Estimate of total provision | 4,000 |

## MAIN DISCLOSURES

- The nature, timing, uncertainties, assumptions, and reimbursements for each class of provision.
- Reconciliations for each class of provision.
- Possible obligations (contingent liabilities) are disclosed but not recognized.
- Contingent assets are not recognized but are disclosed when inflows of economic benefits are probable.

## EXAMPLES OF RELATED NATIONAL STANDARDS

Australia: AASB 1044
Canada: CICA Handbook 3290
New Zealand: FRS 15
United Kingdom: FRS 12

# IAS 38 Intangible Assets

## ISSUED OR LAST REVISED

March 2004

## EFFECTIVE DATE

Applied to intangible assets acquired in business combinations after March 31, 2004 and to all other intangible assets for periods beginning on or after March 31, 2004.

## PROBLEM AND PURPOSE

The increasing importance of intangible assets has led to a variety of practices, with some countries ignoring them completely, while entities in other accounting regimes have included brands, publishing titles, and other similar intangible assets on the balance sheet. There have also been a variety of approaches to the question of amortization, with some accounting regimes specifying different periods of time for amortization and others requiring none. IAS 38 requires an entity to recognize an intangible asset only if it meets certain specified criteria. It also specifies how to measure the carrying amount of intangible assets. IAS 38 should be read in conjunction with IAS 36 Impairment of Assets.

## SCOPE

All intangible assets except for exclusions.

## EXCLUSIONS

- Financial assets
- Mineral rights and exploration, and development costs incurred by mining and oil and gas companies
- Intangible assets arising from insurance contracts issued by insurance companies
- Intangible assets covered by another standard (for example, IAS 2 applies to intangible assets held for sale in the ordinary course of business)

## MAIN REQUIREMENTS

Initially, an intangible asset should be recognized at cost if all the following criteria are met:

- It is identifiable and controlled by the entity.
- It is probable that there will be future economic benefits.
- The cost can be measured reliably.

Examples of possible intangible assets include computer software, copyrights, customer lists, import quotas, and franchises. Goodwill arising from an acquisition does not fall within the scope of IAS 38 but is subject to the provisions of IFRS 3.

IAS 38 sets out specific criteria for the recognition of certain internally generated assets. Those assets that should not be recognized as intangible assets include internally generated goodwill, brands, and publishing titles. Although these particular intangibles should not be recognized if internally generated, they may meet the general recognition criteria if purchased by a third party. A similar asset may, therefore, be recognized if purchased, but must be expensed if internally generated. Although some may regard this differing treatment as illogical, the reason for the provision is the uncertainty of measurement with internally generated intangible assets. Users need to be aware that some very famous brands and publishing titles will only appear on a balance sheet if they have been acquired externally. This difference in treatment has a significant effect on accounting ratios, and most analysts will make adjustments in their calculations to allow for this.

Research cost is considered as an expense, but development cost that meets specified criteria may be recognized as an intangible asset.

After initial recognition, an intangible asset may be carried in the balance sheet at:

- Cost less any accumulated amortization and impairment losses.
- A revalued amount (based on fair value) less any subsequent amortization and any accumulated impairment losses, only if fair value can be determined by reference to an active market at the date of the revaluation. The standard considers that active markets are expected to be uncommon for intangible assets.

If an intangible asset does not meet the criteria for recognition as an asset, it should be expensed in the financial period. Expenditure that was initially recognized as an expense cannot be included subsequently as part of the cost of an intangible asset.

Where revaluations are used, increases must be credited directly to the revaluation surplus within equity except to the extent that it reverses a revaluation decrease previously recognized in the income statement. Any revaluation decrease is recognized in the income statement. However, the decrease is debited directly to the revaluation surplus in equity, to the extent of any credit balance previously recognized in the revaluation surplus with respect to that asset.

Intangible assets have either an indefinite life with no foreseeable limit to the period in which benefits will be generated or a finite life with a limited period of benefits accruing. With the former, the intangible asset must be tested for impairment annually. With the latter, the depreciable amount will be amortized on a systematic basis over its useful life. Note that it is an indefinite life and not an infinite life. The IASB has the realistic view that in this mortal world all things come to an end, even if we are unable to predict when that will be.

If an intangible asset is disposed of, the gain or loss is the difference between the carrying amount and the net disposal proceeds. The gain or loss is recognized in the income statement.

## MAIN DISCLOSURES

- Useful life or amortization rate and amortization method
- Gross carrying amount and accumulated amortization and impairment losses
- Reconciliation of carrying amounts at the beginning and end of the period

- Basis for an intangible asset having an indefinite life
- Description and carrying amount of individual intangible assets, if they are material

## EXAMPLES OF RELATED NATIONAL STANDARDS

Canada: CICA Handbook 3062, 3450

United Kingdom: FRS 10

United States: SFAS 142

# IAS 39 Financial Instruments: Recognition and Measurement

## ISSUED OR LAST REVISED

December 2003

## EFFECTIVE DATE

Periods beginning on or after January 1, 2005.

## PROBLEM AND PURPOSE

In 1988, the IASC and the Canadian Institute of Chartered Accountants (CICA) attempted to develop a standard that embraced the recognition, measurement, and disclosure of financial instruments. After some controversy with the proposals put forward, the project was split into two. IAS 32 Financial Instruments, Disclosure, and Presentation, was approved in 1995. The problems of recognition, derecognition, measurement, and hedge accounting were put to one side but were later addressed in IAS 39. The standard sets out the principles for recognizing, measuring, and disclosing information about financial instruments. IAS 39 requires all financial assets and financial liabilities, including derivatives, to be recognized on the balance sheet. The standard also requires derivatives that are embedded in non-derivative contracts to be accounted for separately at fair value through the income statement.

## SCOPE

All financial instruments apart from specified exclusions.

## EXCLUSIONS

- Interests in subsidiaries, associates, and joint ventures under IAS 27, IAS 28, and IAS 31
- Rights and obligations of leases under IAS 17 but with qualifications
- Employers' rights and obligations of employee benefit plans under IAS 19
- Financial instruments that meet the definition of an equity instrument under IAS 32
- Rights and obligations of insurance contracts under IFRS 4 but with qualifications
- Contracts for contingent consideration in a business combination under IFRS 3
- Loan commitments that cannot be settled net in cash or another financial instrument (with qualifications)
- Contracts between a vendor and an acquirer in a business combination to sell an acquiree at a future date
- Financial instruments, contracts and obligations of share-based payment transactions under IAS 2 but with qualifications
- Contracts to buy or sell non-financial items entered into and that continue to be held for the purpose of the receipt or delivery of a non-financial item with respect to the entity's expected purchase, sell, or usage requirements

## MAIN REQUIREMENTS

Financial assets or liabilities are recognized initially at fair value when the entity becomes a party to the instrument contract. Examples of financial instruments are cash, leases, accounts receivable and payable, commercial paper, and repurchase agreements. Derecognition for a liability occurs when the liability is extinguished. Derecognition for an asset occurs when the contractual rights to the cash flows expire, or substantially all the risks and rewards of ownership are transferred, or control is transferred but some of the risks and rewards are retained. IAS 39 defines four categories of financial instruments:

A financial asset (or liability) at fair value through profit and loss

Held-to-maturity investments

Loans and receivables

Available-for-sale financial assets

Financial assets or liabilities at fair value should be remeasured at fair value at each balance sheet date. Changes in fair value are recognized directly in the income statements as part of the profit or loss for the period.

Held-to-maturity financial instruments are non-derivative financial assets and have fixed, or determinable, payments and a fixed maturity date. Financial assets that are held-to-maturity should be recognized initially at fair value, and subsequently measured at amortized cost using the effective interest method. The effective interest rate is the rate that discounts estimated future cash payments or receipts over the expected life of the financial instrument to its net carrying amount.

Loans and receivables are non-derivative financial instruments that have fixed, or determinable, payments, no maturity date, and are not quoted on active markets. Loans and receivables should be measured on the same basis as held-to-maturity financial instruments.

Available-for-sale financial instruments are either specifically designated as such or because they do not fall under one of the other three classifications. They should be measured at fair value at each balance sheet date. Any period gains or losses arising from measuring at fair value should be recognized in equity. On disposal of the financial instrument, cumulative gains and losses will be reported in the income statement.

An embedded derivative is a component of a combined financial instrument that also incorporates a non-derivative host contract. An embedded derivative should not be separated from the host contract and accounted for as a derivative unless its economic character and risks are dissimilar to the host contract, its terms meet the definition of a derivative, and it is measured at fair value with changes recognized in the income statement as part of profit or loss.

An entity must assess the financial asset or group of assets at each balance sheet date to see whether there is any objective evidence of impairment. If there is evidence, a detailed impairment calculation must be carried out to determine whether an impairment loss should be recognized.

Hedge accounting is where the related changes in the fair value of a financial asset and a financial liability are offset against each other. There must be a hedged item and a hedging instrument. Hedge accounting is allowed by IAS 39 under certain circumstances and is classified into two general types of hedging. The standard lays down strict conditions and classifies hedge accounting into cash flow hedging where there is the possibility of changes in cash flows and fair value hedging where there is a possibility of changes in fair value hedge. There is also the hedge of a net investment in a foreign operation under IAS 21.

The conditions that must be met under IAS 39 before hedge accounting is applied are as follows:

- There is formal designation and documentation of a hedge at inception.
- The hedge is expected to be highly effective. For instance, the hedging instrument is expected to almost fully offset changes in fair value or cash flows of the hedged item that are attributable to the hedged risk.
- Any forecast transaction being hedged is highly probable.
- Hedge effectiveness is reliably measurable. For instance, the fair value or cash flows of the hedged item and the fair value of the hedging instrument can be reliably measured.
- The hedge must be assessed on an ongoing basis and be highly effective.

With cash flow hedging, the fair value movements on the part of the hedge that is effective are recognized in equity until such time as the hedged item affects profit or loss in the income statement. Any ineffective part of the fair value movement is recognized in the income statement. With fair value hedging, the fair value movements on the hedging instrument and the corresponding fair value movements on the hedged item are recognized in the income statement.

All derivative contracts with an external counterparty may be designated as hedging instruments except for some written options. External non-derivative financial asset or liability may not be designated as a hedging instrument except as a hedge of foreign currency risk.

## MAIN DISCLOSURES

All disclosure requirements as stated in IAS 32.

# IAS 40
# Investment Property

## ISSUED OR LAST REVISED

December 2003

## EFFECTIVE DATE

Financial statements covering periods beginning on or after January 1, 2005.

## PROBLEM AND PURPOSE

There is a clear distinction between a property that is acquired for use by an entity in its own operation and one that is acquired for investment purposes. Appropriate accounting treatment and disclosures are required, so that the user can gain a better understanding of the financial statements. IAS 40 addresses these issues.

## SCOPE

Investment property (land, building or part of a building, or both) held to earn rentals or for capital appreciation or both.

## EXCLUSIONS

- Property held for use in the production or supply of goods or services or for administrative purposes
- Properties held for sale in the ordinary course of business or in the process of construction or development for such sale (IAS 2)
- Property that is being constructed or developed on behalf of third parties (IAS 11)
- Property that is being constructed or developed for use as an investment (IAS 16)

- Owner-occupied property (IAS 16)
- Property leased to another entity under a finance lease

## MAIN REQUIREMENTS

Investment property should be recognized as an asset when it is probable that the future economic benefits that are associated with the property will flow to the enterprise and that the cost of the property can be reliably measured. The initial measurement should be at cost, including transactions costs but excluding start-up costs, abnormal waste, or initial operating losses incurred before the planned level of occupancy.

Subsequently, investment property may be carried either at:

- Fair value: This is the amount where the property could be exchanged between knowledgeable and willing parties in an arm's length transaction. Gains or losses arising from changes in the fair value of the investment property must be included in net profit or loss for the period in which it arises.
- Cost less accumulated depreciation and any accumulated impairment losses as prescribed by IAS 16.

The selected measurement method must be adopted for all the entity's investment property. The decision on which model to be used must be taken carefully as there can be a substantial impact on the income statement. Transfers to, or from, the investment property classification can take place only when there is a change in use supported by evidence. An investment property sold without development should not be reclassified.

On disposal or permanent withdrawal from use, a property should be derecognized. The gain or loss on derecognition should be calculated as the difference between the net disposal proceeds and the carrying amount of the asset. The gain or losses should be recognized in the income statement.

## MAIN DISCLOSURES

- Whether fair value or cost method used
- Methods and assumptions in determining fair value
- Useful life or depreciation rate, and the depreciation method for the cost method
- Gross carrying amounts and accumulated depreciation

- Whether property interests under operating leases are deemed investment property, if fair value model is used
- Whether a qualified independent valuer has been used
- Details of revenue and direct operating expense

## EXAMPLES OF RELATED NATIONAL STANDARDS

United Kingdom: SSAP 19

# IAS 41
# Agriculture

## ISSUED OR LAST REVISED

December 2000

## EFFECTIVE DATE

Periods beginning on or after January 1, 2003.

## PROBLEM AND PURPOSE

Agricultural activity, particularly in some countries and regions, is a significant part of the economy. This standard sets out the accounting treatment, financial statement presentation, and disclosures for agricultural activity. The standard contains the presumption that a biological asset can be measured reliably by using fair value.

## SCOPE

Activities concerned with the transformation of biological assets (that is, living plants and animals) into agricultural produce.

## EXCLUSIONS

- Land (IAS 16)
- Intangible assets (IAS 38)
- Processing of agricultural produce after harvest (IAS 2)

## MAIN REQUIREMENTS

Biological assets should be recognized only where there is control of the asset as a result of past events, it is probable that future economic benefits will flow to the entity, and the fair value or cost of the asset can be measured reliably. On initial recognition and subsequently, biological assets should be recognized at fair value less estimated point-of-sale costs, unless fair value cannot be reliably measured. Agricultural produce should be measured at fair value less estimated point-of-sales costs at the point of harvest. Point-of-sales costs include commissions, levies, and transfer duties and taxes.

The gain on initial recognition of biological assets at fair value, and changes in fair value of biological assets during a period, are reported in the income statement for that period. A gain on initial recognition of agricultural produce at fair value should be included in the income statement for the period in which it arises.

An unconditional government grant related to a biological asset is recognized as income when the grant becomes receivable, a conditional government grant is recognized when the conditions attached to the grant are met.

IAS 41 presumes that fair value can be measured reliably for most biological assets. If the determination of fair value of a biological asset is not possible at the time when it is initially recognized, then it is measured at cost less accumulated depreciation and impairment losses. All other biological assets should be measured at fair value. If circumstances change and fair value can be measured reliably, the adoption to fair value less point-of-sale costs should be made.

## MAIN DISCLOSURES

- Descriptions and carrying amounts with reconciliation of changes in carrying amounts
- Methods and assumptions for determining fair value
- Changes in fair value during the period
- Fair value of agricultural produce harvested during the period
- Financial risk management strategies
- Additional disclosures if fair value cannot be measured reliably

# IFRS 1
# First-Time Adoption of International Financial Reporting Standards

## ISSUED OR LAST REVISED

June 2003

## EFFECTIVE DATE

- Entities preparing their first IFRS Financial Statements for a period beginning on or after January 1, 2004.
- Interim reports under IAS 34 for any period covered by the first financial statements.

## PROBLEM AND PURPOSE

There is a substantial amount of planning and implementation to be undertaken for those entities adopting IFRSs for the first time. IFRS 1 sets out the regulations and procedures to be followed by an entity whose first IFRS financial statements are for a period beginning on or after 1 January 2004. The standard also applies to interim reports presented under IAS 34 for the part of the period covered by its first IFRS financial statements. The entity must make an explicit and unreserved statement of compliance with IFRSs when it adopts them for the first time.

## SCOPE

Entities that explicitly and unreservedly state compliance with IFRSs for the first time.

## EXCLUSIONS

Specific exceptions where the cost of complying would likely exceed the benefit to users of financial statements.

## MAIN REQUIREMENTS

An entity should comply with each IFRS effective at the reporting date for its first financial statements and on the first balance sheet. In doing so, it should take the following actions:

- Eliminate previous GAAP assets and liabilities if they do not qualify for recognition under IFRS, for example research, advertising, and promotion; provisions that do not meet IAS 37 requirements; reimbursements and contingent assets that are not certain.
- Recognize all assets and liabilities that are required to be recognized by IFRS, even if they were never recognized under previous GAAP, for example derivative financial assets and liabilities, including embedded derivatives (IAS 39) and liabilities under defined benefit plans (IAS 19).
- Reclassify previous-GAAP opening balance sheet items into appropriate IFRS classification.
- Apply IFRSs in measuring all recognized assets and liabilities, unless the standards note exceptions.

The effect of the transition from previous GAAP to IFRS on the financial position, financial performance, and cash flows should be explained. It is essential that the same accounting policies be used throughout the first financial statements. Those policies should comply with each IFRS effective at the reporting date for the first IFRS financial statements, with some limited exceptions.

IFRS 1 does permit some exceptions to the requirement that the opening balance sheet must comply with each IFRS. These allow entities to be exempt from the requirements of some IFRSs and prohibit retrospective application of some parts of other IFRSs. Briefly, the provisions are as follows:

- The requirements in Appendix B of IFRS 1 should be applied to business combinations recognized before the date of transition to IFRSs.
- Property, plant, and equipment may be measured at fair value or revaluation as the deemed cost. This also applies to investment property and intangible assets subject to certain conditions.
- All cumulative actuarial gains and losses at the date of transition for employee benefits even if a corridor approach under IAS 19 is used subsequently.

- Compliance with IAS 21 for cumulative translation differences with certain conditions.
- The retrospective application of IAS 32 requiring the separation of equity from compound financial instruments into two portions is not required if the liability component is no longer outstanding.
- The measurement of assets and liabilities of subsidiaries, associates, and joint ventures depends on the timing of adoption of IFRSs by the subsidiary.
- The designation of financial instruments can be made at the date of transition.
- Encouragement is given to the adoption of IFRS 2 with conditions on dates and disclosures.
- The transitional provisions of IFRS 4 Insurance Contracts can be applied.
- The derecognition of financial assets and financial liabilities in IAS 39 should be applied prospectively for transactions occurring on or after 1 January 2004.
- At the date of transition, all derivatives should be measured at fair value and all deferred losses and gains reported as assets or liabilities eliminated.
- Estimates made at the time of the transition should be consistent with estimates made for the same date under previous GAAP unless there was an error in the estimates.
- If transition to IFRSs is made before 1 January 2005 the transitional provisions of IFRS 5 apply, but, if made after that date, IFRS 5 applies retrospectively.

IFRS 1 does not exempt the requirement to comply with the presentation and disclosure provisions of all other IFRSs. IFRS 1 does require that the first IFRS financial statements include at least one year of comparative information under IFRSs. In other words, an entity intending to prepare its first financial statements under IFRS for the year ended 31 December 2007 must restate its opening balance sheet as at 1 January 2006 in accordance with IFRSs current as at 31 December 2007. There are some exemptions from this requirement for IAS 39 and IAS 4.

## MAIN DISCLOSURES

- Reconciliations of equity reported under previous GAAP and equity under IFRS
- Reconciliation of profit or loss reported in the last period under previous GAAP to IFRS for the same period

- Explanations of material adjustments to the balance sheet, income statement, and cash flow statement
- Separate disclosure of errors in the financial statements revealed during the transition
- Recognition or reversal of impairment losses
- Use of any specific recognition and measurement exemptions

# IFRS 2
# Share-Based Payment

## ISSUED OR LAST REVISED

February 2004

## EFFECTIVE DATE

Periods beginning on or after January 1, 2005.

## PROBLEM AND PURPOSE

Entities may decide to grant share options to employees and to others. Share options and share option plans are a common feature of remuneration for directors, senior executives, and some other employees. There are also circumstances in which entities pay suppliers, particularly for professional services, with the issue of shares or share options. Although such transactions have been increasing, there have been no regulations at the international level. This standard addresses the issue by specifying the financial reporting required when an entity undertakes a share-based transaction. The standard also covers the accounting treatment of expenses for transactions with share options granted to employees.

IFRS 2 prescribes the financial reporting by an entity when it undertakes a share-based payment transaction. It applies to grants of shares, share options, or other equity instruments made after 7 November 2002 that had not yet vested at the effective date of the standard. IFRS 2 applies retrospectively to liabilities arising from share-based payment transactions existing at the effective date.

In those countries that have yet to adopt IFRSs, employee share options are often not recognized in financial statements or are not recognized at fair value. Expenses associated with granting share options, therefore, are omitted from or understated in the income statement. The requirement to apply the provisions of IFRS 2 can have a substantial impact on the financial statements of some entities.

## SCOPE

IFRS 2 applies to all entities.

## MAIN REQUIREMENTS

A share-based payment is where the entity receives or acquires goods or services either as consideration for its equity instruments or by incurring liabilities for amounts based on the price of its shares or other equity instruments, or where equity issue, cash, or equity or cash may settle the transaction. Examples of items falling under the standard are employee share purchase plans, employee share ownership plans, share option plans, and plans where the issuance of shares (or rights to shares) may depend on market- or non-market-related conditions.

Recognition of the transaction takes place when the goods or services are acquired or received. The goods and services are recognized as either an asset or an expense, as appropriate. Employees and others providing similar services that are settled using the share-based payment scheme would have the transaction amount valued at the fair value of the equity instruments at the grant date. The specific terms and conditions of the granting of shares affect the valuation. IFRS 2 explains the variations.

The general measurement principle is that share-based payment transactions are accounted for to show the value of goods or services received. The method used to determine value depends on the type of transactions and with whom they were made. Goods and services are measured at fair value. Fair value is determined in an equity-settled transaction, either directly at the fair value of the goods or services or indirectly by reference to the fair value of the equity instruments granted.

The assumption with equity-based payment to employees is that additional remuneration is being paid by the entity to obtain additional benefits.

It is likely to be extremely difficult to estimate the fair value of the additional benefits and, thus, the fair value of the equity instruments granted may be used.

With cash-settled transactions, the fair value of the liability is used to measure the goods/services received. At each reporting date and the settlement date, any changes in fair value are recognized in the income statement.

## MAIN DISCLOSURES

- Nature and extent of arrangements
- Determination of fair value of goods or services received or equity instruments granted
- Effect of transactions on the profit or loss for the period and on the financial position of the entity

## EXAMPLES OF RELATED NATIONAL STANDARDS

Canada: CICA Handbook 3870

United Kingdom: FRS 20

United States: SFAS 123, SFAS 148

# IFRS 3 Business Combination

## ISSUED OR LAST REVISED

March 2004

## EFFECTIVE DATE

Business combinations where the agreement date is on or after March 31, 2004.

## PROBLEM AND PURPOSE

Entities may seek growth through acquisitions or organic means. Users should be able to conclude from financial statements which strategy has been followed and the way that acquisitions have contributed toward growth. The comparison of financial statements is adversely affected where entities are able to use either the pooling of interest methods or the purchase method to account for business combinations. There is also the danger that each method can give different results and that, therefore, entities may structure a business combination to achieve a particular accounting result. IFRS 3 aims both to improve the accounting treatment for business combinations and to contribute toward international convergence on the issue. The prohibition of the pooling method in Australia, Canada, and the United States was an impetus for the issue of IFRS 3.

## EXCLUSIONS

- Joint venture
- Mutual entities such as mutual insurance companies
- The reorganization of a number of entities that are already under common control
- The combination of separated entities by agreement to form a reporting entity by contract but without obtaining ownership interest

## MAIN REQUIREMENTS

A business combination is the bringing together of separate entities or businesses into one reporting entity and must be accounted for using the purchase method. The pooling of interests method is prohibited. The standard views the business combination from the perspective of the acquirer, and an acquirer must be identified.

One entity is deemed to have control if it acquires more than 50% of the voting rights, but this may be rebutted. Even without 50% of the voting rights, control may be regarded as being achieved by gaining power as follows:

- Obtaining over 50% of the voting rights by means of an agreement with another investor
- To govern the controlled entity's financial and operating policies by means of statute or agreement

- To appoint or remove the majority of the board of directors
- To cast the majority of votes

From the acquirer's perspective, the costs of the business combination are the sum of:

- The fair values, at the date of exchange, of assets given, liabilities incurred or assumed, and equity instruments issued by the acquirer in exchange for control of the acquiree; plus
- Any costs directly attributable to the combination.

If equity instruments are issued as consideration for the acquisition, the market price of those equity instruments at the date of exchange is the best evidence of fair value. If a market price does not exist, or is not considered reliable, other valuation techniques are used to measure fair value.

The acquirer recognizes separately the acquiree's identifiable assets, liabilities, and contingent liabilities at their fair value at the date of acquisition, except for non-current assets that are classified as held for sale in accordance with IFRS 5. Such assets held for sale are recognized at fair value less costs to sell. The acquirer has to satisfy the following recognition criteria at that date, irrespective of whether they had been previously recognized in the acquiree's financial statements:

- Intangible assets of the acquiree at the acquisition date can only be recognized if they meet the definition requirements and can be measured reliably.
- Goodwill is the residual acquisition cost. It is recognized by the acquirer as an asset from the acquisition date and is initially measured as the excess of the cost of the business combination over the acquirer's share of the net fair values of the acquiree's identifiable assets, liabilities, and contingent liabilities. Goodwill must not be amortized but must be tested for impairment at least annually.
- "Negative" goodwill arises where the cost of an acquisition is less than the share of identifiable net assets acquired. The standard considers such an amount as a result of an error either in the measurement of the acquiree's net assets or in the cost of the combination. The cost of these two elements should be reassessed by the acquirer. If "negative" goodwill still exists it should be regarded as a discount arising from a bargain purchase and the amount of discount should be recognized in the income statement.

IFRS 3 specifies the accounting treatment:

- For business combinations that are achieved in stages
- Where fair values can only be determined provisionally in the period of acquisition
- Where deferred tax assets are recognized after the accounting for the acquisition is complete
- For previously recognized goodwill, negative goodwill and intangible assets

## MAIN DISCLOSURES

- Names and descriptions of combining entities
- Acquisition date
- Percentage of voting instruments acquired
- Cost of the combination
- Amounts recognized for assets, liabilities, and contingent liabilities
- Amount of negative goodwill recognized
- Profit or loss of acquiree since acquisition date that is included in the acquirer's profit or loss
- The revenue and profit or loss for the combined entity should be shown as if the acquisition date for all business combinations had been the beginning of the period, where possible

## EXAMPLES OF RELATED NATIONAL STANDARDS

Canada: CICA Handbook 1581

Malaysia: MASB 21

New Zealand: FRS 36

# IFRS 4
# Insurance Contracts

## ISSUED OR LAST REVISED

March 2004

## EFFECTIVE DATE

Periods beginning on or after January 1, 2005.

## PROBLEM AND PURPOSE

There are considerable diverse practices in relation to insurance contracts. The IASB has initiated a two-stage project to address the issues. This standard is the first stage (Phase 1) of the project and aims to establish limited improvements in accounting for insurance contracts and to require certain disclosures. The IASB is currently working on the second stage (Phase II) of the project.

## SCOPE

- Insurance contracts issued
- Reinsurance contracts held
- Financial instruments issued with a discretionary participation feature

## EXCLUSIONS

- Product warranties issued directly by a manufacturer, dealer, or retailer (IAS 18 and IAS 37)
- Employer's assets and liabilities under employee benefit plans (IAS 19) and retirement benefit obligations reported by defined benefit retirement plans (IAS 26)

- Contractual rights or obligations that are contingent on the future use of, or right to use, a non-financial item, as well as the lessee's residual value guarantees on finance leases (IAS 17, IAS 18, IAS 38)
- Financial guarantees entered into or retained on the transfer of financial assets or liabilities under IAS 39
- Contingent consideration payable or receivable in a business combination (IFRS 3)
- Direct insurance contracts that an entity holds as a policyholder

## MAIN REQUIREMENTS

IFRS 4 is concerned with Phase 1 of the IASB's project on insurance contracts. An insurance contract is a "contract under which one party (the insurer) accepts significant insurance risk from another party (the policyholder) by agreeing to compensate the policyholder if a specified uncertain future event (the insured event) adversely affects the policyholder."

Insurers are temporarily exempted from some requirements of other IFRSs until completion of Phase II. This includes the requirement to consider the IASB's Framework in selecting accounting policies for insurance contracts. However, the IFRS:

- Prohibits provisions for possible future claims under contracts that are not in existence at the reporting date (such as catastrophe and equalization provisions).
- Requires assessment of the adequacy of recognized insurance liabilities and an impairment test for reinsurance assets.
- Requires an insurer to keep insurance liabilities in its balance sheet until they are discharged or canceled, or until they have expired, and prohibits offsetting insurance liabilities against related reinsurance assets.

An insurer is allowed to change its accounting policies for insurance contracts only to present information in the financial statements that is more relevant and no less reliable, or more reliable and no less relevant. IFRS 4 identifies several accounting policies that an insurer can continue to use if they represent its existing practices. However, such practices cannot be adopted as new accounting policies. These include the following:

- Measuring insurance liabilities on an undiscounted basis
- Using non-uniform accounting polices for the insurance liabilities of a subsidiary

- Measuring insurance liabilities with excessive prudence
- Measuring contractual rights to future investment management fees at an amount that exceeds their fair value as implied by a comparison with current fees charged by other market participants for similar services

The standard allows the introduction of an accounting policy that involves remeasuring designated insurance liabilities consistently in each period to reflect current market interest rates (and, if the insurer so elects, other current estimates and assumptions). There is a rebuttable presumption that an insurer's financial statements will become less relevant and reliable if it introduces an accounting policy that reflects future investment margins in the measurement of insurance contracts.

When an insurer changes its accounting policies for insurance liabilities, it may reclassify some or all financial assets as "at fair value through the income statement." IFRS specifies the following:

- Embedded derivatives are not required to be accounted for separately at fair value if they meet the definition of an insurance contract.
- Deposit components of some insurance contracts should be accounted for separately ("unbundled").
- "Shadow accounting" may be used (that is, account for both realized and unrealized gains or losses on assets in the same way relative to measurement of insurance liabilities).
- Discretionary participation features contained in the insurance contracts or financial instruments may be recognized separately from the guaranteed element and classified as a liability or as a separate component of equity.

## MAIN DISCLOSURES

- Details of the amounts that arise from insurance contracts
- Details of the amounts, timing, and uncertainty of future cash flows
- Concentrations of insurance risk
- Actual claims compared with previous estimates

# IFRS 5
# Non-Current Assets Held for Sale and Discontinued Operations

## ISSUED OR LAST REVISED

March 2004

## EFFECTIVE DATE

Periods beginning on or after January 1, 2005.

## PROBLEM AND PURPOSE

This standard is the result of a joint project between the IASB and FASB. The United States already has a standard, SFAS 144 Accounting for the Impairment or Disposal of Long-Lived Assets. The IASC had previously issued IAS 35 Discontinuing Operations, which addressed similar accounting issues. The present standard achieves substantial convergence with SFAS 144 as far as the issues of assets held for sale, the timing of the classification of operations as discontinued, and the presentation of such operations. There are still substantial differences between the approaches of IASB and FASB with respect to the impairment of long-lived assets to be held and used. Thus, a complete solution does not appear to be achievable in the short term.

## SCOPE

All non-current assets and disposal groups.

## EXCLUSIONS

- Deferred tax assets (IAS 12)
- Assets from employee benefits (IAS 19)

- Financial assets under IAS 39
- Non-current assets under the fair value model in IAS 40
- Non-current assets measured at fair value less estimated point-of-sales costs under IAS 41
- Contractual rights under insurance contracts in IFRS 4

## MAIN REQUIREMENTS

The standard addresses separately the issues of assets held for sale and discontinued operations separately. A non-current asset or disposal group is classified as held for sale if it is available for immediate sale and its sale is highly probable. It is measured at the lower of fair value less costs to sell, and its carrying amount is not depreciated. In general, the following conditions must be met for an asset (or "disposal group") to be classified as held for sale:

- Management is committed to a plan to sell.
- The asset is available for immediate sale.
- An active plan to locate a buyer is initiated.
- The sale is highly probable, within 12 months of classification as held for sale (with qualifications).
- The asset is being actively marketed for sale at a sale price that is reasonable in relation to its fair value.
- Actions required to complete the plan indicate that it is unlikely that plan will be significantly changed or withdrawn.

A "disposal group" is a group of assets, possibly with some associated liabilities, which an entity intends to dispose of in a single transaction. The measurement basis required for non-current assets classified as held for sale is applied to the group as a whole, and any resulting impairment loss reduces the carrying amount of the non-current assets in the disposal group in the order of allocation required by IAS 36.

A discontinued operation is a component of an entity that has been either disposed of or is classified as held for sale. The discontinued operation may represent the following:

- A separate major line of business or geographical area of operations
- Is part of a single, coordinated plan to dispose of a separate major line of business or geographical area of operations or
- Is a subsidiary acquired exclusively with a view to resale

Businesses frequently change product lines, cease projects, and change the size of their workforces as a response to the demands of the market. These changes are not usually "discontinued operations" as defined by the standard and do not need to be treated as such. These changes can occur in relation to a discontinued operation.

## MAIN DISCLOSURES

- Detailed disclosures of revenue, expenses, pre-tax profit or loss, and related income taxes for the discontinued operations is required either in the notes or on the face of the income statement in a section distinct from continuing operations. Such detailed disclosures must cover both the current and all prior periods presented in the financial statements.
- The gains or loss recognized on measurement to fair value less selling costs or on disposal, and the related income tax expense should also be disclosed.
- The net cash flows attributable to the operating, investing, and financing activities of a discontinued operation shall be separately presented on the face of the cash flow statement or disclosed in the notes.
- Non-current assets held for sale should be shown separately on the balance sheet.
- Assets and liabilities of a disposal group should be shown separately on the balance sheet.
- Details of the nature of assets and the sale.

## EXAMPLES OF RELATED NATIONAL STANDARDS

Australia: AASB 1042

Canada: CICA Handbook 3475

Malaysia: MASB 28

United States: SFAS 144

# IFRS 6
# Exploration for and Evaluation of Mineral Resources

## ISSUED OR LAST REVISED

December 2004

## EFFECTIVE DATE

Financial statements covering periods beginning on or after January 1, 2006.

## PROBLEM AND PURPOSE

Until the publication of this standard, there had been no international guidance on accounting for exploration and evaluation expenditures, including the recognition of exploration and evaluation assets. The practices of accounting for mineral rights and mineral resources, such as oil and natural gas, have varied throughout the world. IFRS 6 seeks to improve transparency by requiring improved disclosures. This is only the first stage of the project since global consensus could not be achieved for a rigorous and comprehensive approach by the deadline of 2005. This is the date set by many countries for the adoption of international standards and it is anticipated that several entities incurring exploration and evaluation expenditures will be presenting their financial statements in accordance with IFRSs from 2005. The second phase of the project was started in 2004 and national standard setters in Australia, Canada, Norway, and South Africa are deliberating on a research project that will address accounting for extractive industries generally.

## SCOPE

Entities should apply the IFRS to exploration and evaluation expenditure that it incurs.

## EXCLUSIONS

- Expenditure incurred before the exploration and evaluation of mineral resources
- Expenditures incurred after the technical feasibility and commercial viability of extracting a mineral resource are demonstrable
- Certain temporary exemptions from IAS 8 paragraphs 11 and 12 relating to accounting policies in the absence of an IFRS applying specifically to that item

## MAIN REQUIREMENTS

Entities must establish and apply consistently an accounting policy specifying which expenditures are recognized as exploration and evaluation assets. Development expenditures cannot be recognized as exploration and evaluation assets. Any obligations for removal and restoration that are incurred as a consequence of having undertaken exploration for and evaluation of mineral resources must be treated in accordance with IAS 37.

After recognition, either the cost model or the revaluation model can be applied to the assets. When there is evidence that the carrying value of the asset may exceed its recoverable amount, an assessment for impairment losses should be conducted. Any impairment loss is recognized as an expense in accordance with IAS 36.

Where expenditures are incurred before the technical feasibility and commercial viability of extracting a mineral resource are determined, such expenditures cannot be treated as assets.

## MAIN DISCLOSURES

- Accounting policies for exploration and evaluation expenditures
- The amounts of assets, liabilities, income and expense, and operating and investing cash flows arising from the exploration for and evaluation of mineral resources
- Exploration and evaluation assets should be disclosed as a separate class of assets and may be intangible assets or tangible assets depending on the nature of the assets

## Part Three

# DICTIONARY

*"Then you should say what you mean," the March Hare went on. "I do," Alice hastily replied. "At least—at least I mean what I say—that's the same thing, you know."*
*"Not the same thing a bit!" said the Hatter.*
*"Why, you might as well say that 'I see what I eat'" is the same thing as 'I eat what I see'!"*

—Lewis Carroll, *Alice's Adventures in Wonderland.* Whitman Publishing Company, 1955, page 70.

# How to Use the Dictionary

The Dictionary includes international accounting and reporting, financial accounting, managerial accounting, and finance terms that are widely used in the international business world. Definitions are given in an easily accessible way with cross-referencing to a particular standard where appropriate.

Many terms that are defined are used in international financial reporting standards (IFRSs) but also have a common theme. In these instances, we have given the general meaning as well as how it is used in the standard. Cross-referencing of a definition to a particular standard is given so that readers can refer to the specific wording within its context. If the term originates from the Framework for the Preparation and Presentation of Financial Statements, we have used the prefix F before the paragraph number.

Terms that are different but have similarities in the meanings they convey are cross-referenced by using the word *See*. In addition, terms are also similarly cross-referenced where this helps the reader's understanding.

# A

**abbreviated accounts** These are sets of summarized accounts drawn from the full financial statements of an organization. They normally contain a summarized income statement, balance sheet, and cash flow forecast. In some countries, abbreviated accounts may be accepted for certain types of organizations, particularly small or medium-sized ones, for the purpose of meeting regulatory requirements.

**abnormal spoilage** An unacceptable number of defective production units that should not arise under efficient operating conditions.

**above-the-line** The entries above the imaginary line on an organization's income statement that establish the profit (or loss) from the entries below the line showing how the profit is distributed. When an expense is denoted as above the line, it is known that it will have an adverse effect on profit and there is an understandable temptation to seek out ways where some expenses may fall below the line.

**abridged accounts** Partial financial statements that have been extracted from the full financial statements but are not normally accepted for regulatory purposes. The purpose of abridged accounts is usually an attempt to make the financial statements more comprehensible for particular users, for example, employees, customers, and the public where there is no legal obligation to do so. Such accounts are used mainly for promotional and marketing purposes and are likely to be only a part of a much larger document.

**absorption costing** A method of accounting for products and services where the total costs of the organization are charged to the operational process to arrive at a total cost per unit. Indirect costs that cannot be directly identified with a unit of production or service are either allocated to a cost or profit center or apportioned using an absorption rate. This method can be criticized because of the arbitrary apportionment of overheads to cost and profit centers.

**absorption rate** A rate used in absorption costing for charging the total overheads to the units of output for a financial period. Absorption rates are normally based on budgets and calculated before the commencement of production. Commonly used absorption rates are rate per unit, rate per direct labor hour, and rate per machine hour.

**accelerated depreciation** The calculation and application of a depreciation charge over a shorter period than the useful-life basis normally used to calculate depreciation. The argument for the higher charge is the uncertainty associated with predicting the useful life of assets, particularly where high technology is involved. The useful life, for example, could be five years when an asset is purchased. As a result of new product innovation, it is replaced after three years. If the useful-life basis had been used, the full cost would not have been charged to the accounts until the end of the fifth year; by accelerating the depreciation, the full charge would be made earlier. The method is not acceptable in most accounting regimes. *Refer to* IAS 16.

**acceptances credit** A mechanism used in international trade for financing the sale of goods. It involves a commercial bank or merchant bank extending credit to a foreign importer whom it regards as an appropriate credit risk. An acceptance credit is opened against which the exporter can draw a bill of exchange. Once accepted by the bank, the bill can be discounted on the money market or allowed to run to maturity. The exporter must pay the bank a fee known as the acceptance commission.

**accord and satisfaction** A subsequent agreement where one party to a prior contract can avoid a contractual obligation, provided that the other party agrees. The accord is the agreement by which the contractual obligation is discharged, and the satisfaction is the consideration making the agreement legally operative. The agreement only discharges the contractual obligation if it is accompanied by consideration. For example, under a contract of sale the seller of goods may deliver goods of different quality from that specified in the contract. If there is an agreement with the buyer (the accord) and a reduction in the contract price (the satisfaction), the contract is valid.

**accountability** A critical concept that refers to the obligation to give an account. The main issues are who is accountable to whom, for what, and by what means. It is usually assumed that the directors and executive officers of an organization are accountable to the owners. This accountability may in part be satisfied by the disclosure of financial information. The accountability aspect of this relationship and how it operates is the basis of Agency Theory.

**account analysis** A method of estimating cost behavior that requires professional judgment to classify costs as either fixed or variable. The total of the costs classified as variable are divided by a measure of activity to calculate the variable cost per unit. The costs that are classified as fixed provide the estimate of fixed cost.

**accountancy** For purists, this term refers only to the professional accountancy bodies, although it is frequently used as a synonym for accounting.

**accountancy bodies** These represent formal organizations of accountants whose members are normally entitled to use the term chartered, certified, certified public, or management accountant. Membership is normally through examination, and the members should comply with the regulations of their body. There are many accountancy bodies throughout the world, but usually recognition by the national government is needed to conduct certain types of work, particularly public audit.

**Accountancy Investigation and Disciplinary Board (AIDB)** The AIDB is an independent, investigative and disciplinary body for accountants in the United Kingdom. It has up to eight members. The AIDB is administered and operated on an independent disciplinary scheme. The Board covers members of the Association of Chartered Certified Accountants (ACCA), the Chartered Institute of Management Accountants (CIMA), the Chartered Institute of Public Finance and Accountancy (CIPFA), and the Institute of Chartered Accountants in England and Wales (ICAEW). The focus of the AIDB is on cases of public interest or those that need to be investigated to determine whether there has been any misconduct by an accountant or accounting firm.

**accountant** It is possible for anyone to hold oneself out as an accountant in most countries but formally it is regarded as a person who has passed the examinations of one of the recognized accountancy bodies, completed the required work experience, and been accepted into membership. The terms *professional accountant* and *qualified accountant* are used to denote somebody who satisfies these criteria.

**account classification method** *See* account analysis.

**accounting** The process of identifying, measuring, recording, and communicating economic transactions and events. Measurement is normally made in monetary terms, and records are maintained so that the activities of an organization can be communicated through financial statements such as the income statement and the balance sheet. Accounting incorporates many activities such as conducting audits, forensic accounting, and taxation as well as preparing financial and statistical information to assist managers in decision-making.

**Accounting and Auditing Organization for Islamic Financial Institutions (AAOIFI)** AAOIFI was registered in 1991 in Bahrain. It is an Islamic International autonomous non-profit corporate body that prepares accounting, auditing, governance, ethics, and Shari'a standards for Islamic Financial institutions. There is an Accounting and Auditing Standards Board with 15 members.

**Accounting and Finance Association of Australia and New Zealand (AFAANZ)** AFAANZ is the premier body representing the interests of accounting and finance academics and other persons interested in accounting and finance education and research in Australia and New Zealand. The current name of the association was adopted in 2002, replacing the name Accounting Association of Australia and New Zealand (AAANZ) and the Australian Association of University Teachers in Accounting (AAUTA).

**accounting assumptions** *See* accounting concepts.

**accounting basis** The method selected by an organization in its accounting policies to apply an accounting concept in the preparation and presentation of financial statements. *Refer to* IAS 1.

**accounting concepts** These are fundamental concepts applied to financial statements. The main ones are going concern, accrual accounting, consistency of presentation, materiality and aggregation, and off setting; but others are also used in practice. Accounting concepts are also referred to as conventions, assumptions, principles, propositions, and axioms. The IASB identifies two underlying accounting assumptions: accrual basis and going concern. *Refer to* F.22-26.

**accounting cushion** The practice of making over-large provisions for expenses in one year thus reducing the actual charge in the income statement in the following year. Earnings are thus understated in the current year and overstated in the subsequent year. These practices are now very difficult to execute without breaching accounting regulations. *Refer to* IAS 37.

**accounting cycle** The sequence of procedural stages in accounting for a financial transaction, from the initial event to the financial statements. The initial transaction, such as a sale or purchase, is recorded in the books of accounts of the organization, summarized in a trial balance at the period end, and incorporated in the financial statements.

**accounting entity** The organization, unit, or group of activities for which accounts are prepared. The entity may be a legal reality or a sole trader or a partnership. The accounts are prepared only for the accounting entity and exclude the private transactions of the owners.

**accounting equation** The formula that is reflected in the balance sheet and can be expressed as:

$$\text{Assets} = \text{Liabilities} + \text{Capital}$$

An increase or decrease in total assets must be accompanied by an equal increase or decrease in liabilities and capital. A balance sheet will, therefore, always balance. The above formula expresses an entity view of the business whereas the proprietary view would deduct liabilities from assets to calculate the owners' stake in the business, i.e.:

$$\text{Assets} - \text{Liabilities} = \text{Capital}$$

**accounting estimates** The assessment of the present basis and expected future benefits and obligations arising from assets and liabilities. One example is the provision for bad debts. Under the standard, accounting estimates are not correction of errors but adjustments are made prospectively by including them in the present and future financial statements. *Refer to* IAS 8.

**accounting manual** A comprehensive document that gives details of an organization's accounting policies and procedures. It normally includes a list of account codes and details of computer procedures and controls.

**accounting period** The period for which an organization prepares its financial statements or other documents. Management accounts, such as budget reports, and internal reports used for control purposes may be produced weekly, monthly or quarterly. Financial reports intended for external purposes are normally produced for a maximum period of 12 months, although in an increasing number of countries companies are producing financial reports, known as interim reports or statements, every three months. *Refer to* IAS 34.

**accounting plan** A detailed, regulatory guide used in some countries with definitions of accounting terms, valuation and measurement rules, model financial statements, and a chart of accounts. This represents a legalistic approach to the preparation of financial statements and is often closely related to the calculation of profit for tax purposes. This approach is not considered useful for general purpose financial statements.

**accounting policies** The specific bases, principles, conventions, rules, and practices adopted and consistently followed by an organization in the preparation of its financial statements. They are the methods determined by the organization to be the most appropriate for presenting fairly its financial results and operations, and will concentrate on specific topics such as pensions, goodwill, research and development, and foreign exchange. *Refer to* IAS 1, IAS 8.

**accounting principles** *See* accounting concepts.

**Accounting Principles Board (APB)** Established by the American Institute of Certified Accountants (AICPA), the APB issued a series of Accounting Opinions during 1959–1973. The Opinions were influential in the formation of Generally Accepted Accounting Principles (GAAP).

**accounting profit** The amount of profit calculated by using the Generally Accepted Accounting Principles (GAAP) of accounting. Profit is calculated by deducting from the revenue for an accounting period all the expenses incurred. There are several theoretical and practical problems in arriving at the amount for revenue and expenses. Accounting standards have attempted to remedy these problems.

**Accounting Rate of Return (ARR)** A ratio that measures the financial performance of an organization for an accounting period by expressing profits as a percentage of the capital employed. Variants of the measure include profit after or before interest and taxation, equity capital employed, and the average of opening and closing capital employed.

**accounting records** The manual or computerized ledgers, journals, and supporting documentation used to record the transactions undertaken by an organization. For a one-person business, minimum accounting records may be maintained mainly for taxation purposes and to meet the requirements of a main lender, for example, a bank. For large organizations, there is normally a legal requirement to maintain proper accounting records.

**Accounting Regulatory Committee (ARC)** The ARC is set up by the European Union (EU) Commission with responsibility for providing an opinion on Commission proposals to endorse international accounting standards. The ARC consists of representatives from the EU Member States and chaired by the Commission.

**accounting standards** Rules and regulations containing both legislative and non-legislative pronouncements governing financial accounting and reporting. A standard-setting body normally issues the pronouncements, and there is some form of legal mandate to ensure compliance by organizations. International Accounting Standards (IASs) were issued by the predecessor body of the International Accounting Standards Board (IASB). The IASB now uses the term International Financial Reporting Standards (IFRSs).

**Accounting Standards Board (AcSB)** The AcSB has the authority to develop and establish standards and guidance covering financial accounting and reporting in Canada. The Board presents its priorities and agenda to an oversight council, the Accounting Standards Oversight Council (AcSoc), and works in conjunction with an Emerging Issues Committee (EIC). The Canadian Institute of Chartered Accountants (CICA) supports the AcSB and pronouncements issued by the Board are encapsulated in the CICA Handbook.

**Accounting Standards Board (ASB)** The national standard-setting body in the United Kingdom that issues Financial Reporting Exposure Drafts (FREDs), Financial Reporting Standards (FRSs), and, through its offshoot the Urgent Issues Task Force, reports known as Abstracts. The ASB is a subsidiary of the Financial Reporting Council. It was established in 1990 as the successor body of the Accounting Standards Committee (ASC).

**Accounting Standards Board of Japan (ASBJ)** The Board is an independent, private-sector body established to develop accounting standards in Japan. It is organized into nine separate committees and a number of working groups.

**accounts** Generally, the account of an organization in which economic transactions and events are recorded. The term is also used to refer to the financial statements of an organization, normally regarded as the income statement, cash statement, balance sheet, statement of changes to equity, and explanatory notes.

**accounts payable** The amounts owed by an organization to suppliers for goods and services to be used in business operations (such as for raw materials). Accounts payable are classed as current liabilities on the balance sheet, but are distinguished from accruals and the other non-trade creditors. The International Accounting Standards Board (IASB) uses the term *trade and other payables*, and some countries use the term *trade creditors*. *See* creditor days ratio.

**accounts receivable** The amounts owing to a business from customers for goods and services provided. Accounts receivable are classified as current assets on the balance sheet. The International Accounting Standards Board (IASB) uses the term *trade and other receivables*, and some countries use the term *trade debtors*. A provision for bad debts is often made against accounts receivable in line with the prudence concept. This provision is based on an organization's past experience of bad debts and its current expectations. *See* days' sales in receivables.

**accounts receivable analysis** A listing of the amounts outstanding from customers, ordered in a chronological sequence. The longest overdue account is normally placed at the top of the list. The analysis enables an organization to expend its efforts on credit control on the longest outstanding debts before they become irrecoverable.
Example:

| *Age of Debts* | *No. of accounts* | *Total outstanding* |
|---|---|---|
| 121+ days | 28 | \$120,500 |
| 80–120 days | 52 | \$154,000 |
| 40–80 days | 75 | \$188,000 |
| Under 40 days | 96 | \$210,500 |
| TOTAL | 251 | \$673,000 |

**accounts receivable collection period** The period, on average, that an organization takes to collect the money owed to it by its trade debtors. If an organization allows one month's credit from the end of the month, then, on average, it should collect the debts within 45 days. The accounts receivable collection period ratio is calculated by dividing the amount owed by trade debtors by the annual sales on credit and multiplying by 365. For example, if accounts receivable are \$25,000 and revenue for the period is \$200,000, the accounts receivable collection period ratio will be:

$$(\$25{,}000 \times 365)/\$200{,}000 = 46 \text{ days approximately}$$

If preferred, the average accounts receivable figure may be used by adding the end-of-the-period balance with the beginning-of-the-period balance and dividing by two.

**accounts receivable turnover** A ratio used to reveal how many times the accounts receivable are collected in one year on average. It is calculated by dividing the net sales by the amount of the accounts receivable. Either the amount of accounts receivable on the closing balance sheet for the period or the amounts on the opening and closing balance sheet can be added and divided by two to give an average figure for the period.

**accretion** An increase in the recorded value of an asset due to physical change (such as a growing crop), as opposed to an increase in value due to a change in its market price. The former represents a holding gain until it is recognized. The latter usually reflects a reduction in the purchasing power of money.

**accrual** An amount in the accounts of an organization showing a liability that is not supported by an invoice or a request for payment at the time the accounts are prepared. An accrual is a current liability on the balance sheet and will be charged under expenses in the income statement. An example of an accrual would be telephone expenses that have not been invoiced at the date the final accounts are prepared.

**accrual accounting** A method of accounting in which revenue is recognized when earned and matched against the expenses incurred. Accrual accounting is a basic accounting concept used in the preparation of the income statement and balance sheet. It differs from cash-based accounting, which recognizes transactions when cash has been received or paid. In preparing financial statements for an accounting period using accrual accounting, there will always be some estimation and uncertainty with respect of transactions, and the reader of the financial statements cannot have the same high level of confidence as in cash-based accounting. *Refer to* F.22.

**accrual basis** *See* accrual accounting.

**accruals concept** *See* accrual accounting.

**accrued revenue** Revenue that has been earned during an accounting period but not received by the end of it. For example, interest may have been earned but not received. The amount owing should be included in the profit or earnings figure and classified as a current asset on the balance sheet. Caution should be exercised that the amount is accrued income and not a contingent asset. *Refer to* IAS 37, IAS 18.

**accumulated depreciation** The total amount of depreciation written off the cost price or valuation of a non-current asset from the date it was brought into the balance sheet of the organization. *Refer to* IAS 16.

**accumulated dividend** A dividend that has not been paid to a holder of cumulative preference shares and is carried forward (that is, accumulated) to the next accounting period. It represents a liability to the company, if proposed or declared prior to the balance sheet date.

**accumulated earnings** The amount of earnings or profits that can be carried forward to the next year's accounts, that is, after paying dividends and taxes.

**acid-test ratio** A ratio calculated to assess the liquidity of a business. Also known as the quick ratio or liquid ratio, it is regarded as a more stringent ratio than the current ratio. It is calculated by excluding inventories from current assets and comparing the balance to liabilities. Assuming current assets are $5,000, inventories are $1,500, and current liabilities are $3,000, the acid test ratio is:

$$\text{Acid test} = \frac{\text{Quick assets}}{\text{Current liabilities}} = \frac{\$3,500}{\$3,000} = 1.17{:}1$$

**acquisition accounting** The accounting procedures that are followed when one organization gains control of another. The fair value of the purchase considerations should, for the purpose of consolidated financial statements, be allocated between the underlying net tangible and intangible assets, other than goodwill, on the basis of the fair value to the acquiring organization. Any difference between the fair value of the consideration and the aggregate of the fair values of the separable net assets (including identifiable intangibles, such as patents, licenses, and trademarks) will represent goodwill. The results of the acquired company should be brought into the consolidated income statement or income statement from the date of acquisition only. Acquisition accounting differs from merger accounting in that shares issued as purchase consideration are valued at their market price, a goodwill figure may arise on consolidation, and pre-acquisition profits are not distributable. *Refer to* IFRS 3.

**acting in concert** Persons or organizations acting together, either through a formal agreement or an informal understanding, for their own benefit but without revealing that they are acting collectively.

**active market** A market of homogeneous items and where there are willing buyers and sellers with prices being publicly available. *Refer to* IAS 36.6, IAS 38.8.

**active stocks** Securities that are frequently traded on a particular stock exchange or in a particular period.

**activity analysis** The development of a detailed identification and description of the specific activities performed in an organization.

**activity-based budgeting (ABB)** A budgeting process that focuses on costs of activities or cost drivers and draws upon the activity-based costing approach.

**activity-based costing (ABC)** An overhead allocation process that employs a variety of cost drivers. In the first stage, costs associated with specific business activities are allocated or assigned to activity cost pools. The second stage involves allocating these pooled costs to designated cost objects through the use of cost drivers. The cost drivers chosen for each cost pool are cost drivers that measure the consumption of activities (such as number of setups, kilograms of material delivered, number of pages typed). The cost drivers are used as allocation bases to improve the accuracy of overhead allocations. For example, if an administrative function spends 60%

of its time dealing with issues raised from the production department, then the production department should bear 60% of the administrative department's costs.

Advocates of activity-based costing argue that this method of allocation is far more logical and accurate than other methods. Critics, however, stress that the costs involved in collecting the information under this method may not provide information that is sufficiently superior to make it worthwhile for some organizations.

**activity-based flexible budget** A flexible budget based on a number of cost drivers rather than on a single, volume-based cost driver.

**activity-based management** A system-wide, integrated management approach that involves analyzing and costing activities with the objective of improving operational efficiency, effectiveness, and customer value. The approach includes driver analysis, activity analysis, and performance evaluation, and draws upon the activity-based costing approach.

**actuals** Commodities that can be purchased and used, rather than goods traded on a futures contract, which are represented by documents. The documents may give a right to physical possession of the goods, but futures contracts are often cancelled out by offsetting a purchase against a sale.

**actuarial assumption** The assumptions made about demographic and financial trends, and that underpin the calculation of the ultimate cost of providing postemployment benefits. *Refer to* IAS 19.

**actuarial valuation method** Entities are required to use the projected unit credit method to determine the present value of its defined benefit obligations, the related service cost and past service costs. *Refer to* IAS 19.

**actuarial gains and losses** Gains and losses arising from the differences between the previous actuarial assumptions and what actually occurs, and changes in actuarial assumptions. *Refer to* IAS 19.

**actuarial method** A method used in lease accounting to apportion rentals on the basis of compound interest and in accounting for pensions to determine the charge to the income statement. *Refer to* IAS 17.

**actuary** A practitioner concerned, among other matters, with the calculation and analysis of insurance probability estimates. The work of the actuary is different from that of the accountant, although there are certain areas where they are required to collaborate.

**adaptive expectation hypothesis** A theory employed in the prediction of interest rates based on the assumption that future movements in variables can be determined by an analysis of past patterns.

**added value statement** Also known as a *value-added statement*, it discloses how much value (wealth created) has been added to the operations of an enterprise and how that value has been allocated among various parties, normally taken to be the government, employees, providers of capital, and reinvestment in the business. Added value is calculated by deducting bought-in goods and services from sales. No major country has a requirement for organizations to publish an added value statement.

**additional paid in capital** The excess received from shareholders over the par value of the shares issued. *See* premium on capital stock.

**adjustable rate mortgage** A mortgage loan in which the interest charged is adjusted at predetermined intervals to be consistent with market rates.

**adjustable rate preferred stock** A type of preference share in which the dividends are determined by the interest rate on treasury bills. There is normally a collar that establishes the minimum and maximum rates that will be paid. Adjustable rate preferred stock may have the right to be converted into ordinary shares at a specified date.

**adjusted trial balance** A trial balance drawn up from the books of account with separate columns added for adjustments, such as prepayments and accruals. Once the trial balance has been adjusted in this way, and the total columns calculated, an income statement and balance sheet can be prepared.

**adjusting entries** Entries made at a balance sheet date under accrual accounting to ensure that all the revenue and expenditure of the business concerned are included in the correct period.

**adjusting events** Events that occur between a balance-sheet date and the date on which financial statements are authorized, providing additional evidence of conditions existing at the balance-sheet date. For example, a subsequent valuation of a property held at the balance-sheet date that provides evidence of a permanent diminution in value at the date of the balance sheet would need to be adjusted in the financial statements. *Refer to* IAS 10.3.

**adjusting journal entry** An entry made in a journal to record a transaction, such as a prepayment at year-end, which has to be entered into a ledger account.

**advance payment bond** A guarantee that any advance payments made by a customer will be reimbursed if the organization cannot fulfill its obligations under the relevant contract. The company's bankers, who are indemnified by the company, normally give such guarantees.

**adverse opinion** An opinion expressed by an auditor in an audit report to the effect that the financial statements do not give a true and fair view of the organization's activities (United Kingdom) or that they have not been presented fairly in accordance with generally accepted accounting principles (United States). This situation can arise if there is a disagreement between the auditor and the directors, and the auditor considers the effect of the disagreement to be so material or persuasive that the financial statements are seriously misleading.

**after-tax cash flow** The net cash generated from operations or investment activities after deducting income taxes.

**agency relationship** A relationship where a principal engages an agent to perform certain services. Since the agent may not always act in the best interests of the principal, the latter incurs costs in monitoring and controlling the behavior of the agent. In turn, the agent will incur bonding costs in convincing the principal that the interests of the principal will not be harmed. The agent may also take decisions that do not always maximize the welfare of the principal; these decisions can result in what is called a residual loss. The sum of the monitoring and bonding costs together with the residual loss form the agency costs. Agents may voluntarily provide or may be legally required to issue financial statements and other information to the principals in order to reduce agency costs. By supplying informative financial statements to external parties on the basis of information held by them, managers may avoid costly disputes and more expensive mechanisms for controlling their actions.

**aging the receivables** *See* accounts receivable analysis.

**agreed bid** A takeover bid that is supported by a majority of the shareholders of the target company.

**all-inclusive income concept** The preparation of an income statement in which all economic transactions in a financial period, whatever their nature, are included in the statement to arrive at the earnings figure. Although it is claimed that this gives the fullest picture of the operation of the enterprise, it results in volatility in the earnings figure, because one-off costs such as redundancies and sale of assets are included. To assist prediction of future profits, users are often more interested in the sustainable profits that are shown under reserve accounting.

**allocation** The assignment of indirect costs to cost pools and cost objects.

**allocation base** The measure of activity (such as labor hours, machine hours, or some other measure of activity or base) used to calculate an overhead rate. It is also referred to as the cost driver.

**allowance method** The generally accepted method used to account for doubtful debts. The amount of doubtful debts is matched against the related revenue recognized, and accounts receivable are valued at the net amount expected to be collected. *Refer to* IAS 8.

**allowed alternative treatment** The alternative to the benchmark treatment permitted in IFRSs. Financial statements comply with the standard whether they use the benchmark treatment or the allowed alternative treatment.

**alpha risk and beta risk** In sampling, an auditor may reject a population that should have been accepted (alpha risk) or accepted it when it should have been rejected (beta risk).

**all-purpose financial statements** *See* general purpose financial statements.

**amalgamation** The combination of two or more organizations. This can be achieved by one organization acquiring others, by the merging of two or more organizations, or by existing organizations being dissolved and a new organization formed to take over the combined business.

**American Accounting Association (AAA)** Established in 1916 as the American Association of University Instructors in Accounting, its present name was adopted in 1936. The AAA's mandate is to foster worldwide excellence in the creation, dissemination, and application of accounting skills and knowledge in accounting education, research and practice. Based in Florida, the AAA is a voluntary organization of persons interested in accounting education and research.

**American Depository Receipt (ADR)** A receipt issued by a U.S. bank to a member of the U.S. public who has bought shares in a foreign country. The certificates are denominated in U.S. dollars and can be traded as a security in U.S. markets. The advantages of ADRs are the reduction in administration costs and the avoidance of stamp duty on each transaction.

**American Institute of Certified Public Accountants (AICPA)** The professional organization of practicing Certified Public Accountants founded in 1887. The Institute provides technical advice and guidance to its members and to such government bodies as the SEC. It issues many influential publications in the areas of accounting, audit, and tax.

**American option** An option that can be exercised on any business day between two dates (the option period). *See* European option.

**American Society of Corporate Secretaries (ASCS)** The American Society of Corporate Secretaries, Inc. was founded in 1946 and has over 4,000 members representing approximately 2,800 companies. Its members deal with public disclosure under the securities laws and matters affecting corporate governance, including the structure and meetings of the board of directors and its committees, the proxy process and the annual meeting of shareholders and shareholder relations, particularly with large institutional owners. *See* corporate secretary, company secretary, chartered secretary.

**American Stock Exchange (AMEX)** This is the primary market for U.S. equities, bonds, options, and derivatives, and was formed in 1921 from the former Curb Exchange. The two main indices used for the market are the AMEX Composite Index and the AMEX Major Market Index. In 1998, it merged with the National Association of Securities Dealers (NASD).

**amortization** *See* depreciation.

**amortization schedule** A schedule that summarizes the dates on which specified amounts must be paid in the repayment of a loan.

**amortized cost** That part of the value of an asset that has been written off; it represents the accumulated amortization to date.

**amortizing loan** A loan in which the repayment is made in installments throughout the life of the loan instead of one full repayment at the end of the term.

**analytical auditing** The comparison of financial data and non-financial data, either with internal or external data, to decide whether a stated financial view is supportable. Analytical auditing can be used at the initial planning stage of an audit, during the audit, or in its final stages, when the tests of details have been completed. Procedures range from simple comparisons (such as comparing current amounts with those of earlier years) to more sophisticated methods using computer audit software and advanced statistical techniques (such as multiple regression analysis).

**annual accounts** The financial statements of an organization at the end of a 12-month financial period. Non-incorporated bodies, such as partnerships, are not legally obliged to produce accounts but may do so for their own information, for potential lenders to access finance, and for taxation purposes.

**Annual General Meeting (AGM)** An annual meeting of the shareholders of an organization. The usual business transacted at an AGM is the presentation of the audited accounts, the appointment of directors and auditors, the determination of their remuneration, and recommendations for the payment of dividends. Other business may be transacted if notice of the agenda has been given to the shareholders.

**annualized net present value** The net present value of a project converted into the equivalent series of annual cash flows over the life of the project to assess the possible margin of risk.

**Annualized Percentage Rate (APR)** A calculation that measures the interest charges on a loan or credit as a percentage of the loan amount outstanding. The application of this method and the publication of the rate is an attempt to ensure that borrowers can compare the true cost of credit from different lenders. APR contrasts with the flat rate method of interest calculation that can be very misleading, since it shows an interest charge that is lower than the effective rate.

**annuity** A contract in which a person pays a premium to an insurance company or other financial institution, usually in one lump sum, and in return receives periodic payments for an agreed period or for the rest of one's life.

**annuity method** A method of calculating the amortization on a non-current asset. The purpose is to achieve an approximately constant annual charge for total amortization and cost of capital for the asset. The method results in a low amortization charge in the earlier years when interest costs are high, and a higher charge in later years when interest costs are lower.

***a priori* theories of accounting** Theories developed from assumptions, rather than experience, that apply deductive reasoning in measurement and valuation systems of accounting. The assumptions may be based on a mixture of empirical observations of accounting practice and the postulates of economic theory.

**application controls** Controls relating to the transactions and standing data for each computer-based accounting system. They are, therefore, specific to each such application. Application controls, which may be manual or programmed, are designed to ensure the completeness and accuracy of the accounting records and the validity of the entries made. An example of an application control designed to check completeness would be a manual or programmed agreement of control totals, i.e. the total of the source documents and the total of the amounts input would be compared.

**application for listing** The procedure for applying to a stock exchange for an organization's securities to be traded. The organization will be required to abide by the rules of the exchange. The advantage in obtaining a listing is that it is easier to raise finance by issuing shares on the stock exchange, and the marketability of the shares will attract investors.

**appreciation** An increase in the value of an asset, usually as a result of inflation. This normally occurs with land and buildings.

**appropriation account** For a partnership, an appropriation account is that section that follows the calculation of partnership profit. It shows the various appropriations, such as interest on capital, salaries, and profit shares to the partners. The term is infrequently used by corporations in respect to the income statement and the section that shows how earnings have been applied. A portion of the earnings may be paid to ordinary shareholders as dividends, another portion may go to preference shareholders, and the remainder will be retained within the organization.

**Arab Society of Certified Accountants (ASCA)** The ASCA has the right to develop and promote accounting standards in Arab countries. The ASCA publishes the Arabic language version of International Accounting Standards (IASs) and International Standards on Auditing (ISAs).

**arbitrage** The non-speculative transfer of funds from one market to another to take advantage of differences in interest rates, exchange rates, or commodity prices between the two markets. It is non-speculative because an arbitrageur will only switch from one market to another if the rates or prices in both markets are known and if the gains outweigh the costs of the operation. For example, a large stock of a commodity in a user country may force its price below that in a producing country. If the difference is greater than the cost of shipping the goods back to the producing country, this could provide a profitable opportunity for arbitrage. *See* Modigliani and Miller (MM) theory.

**arbitrage pricing theory** A model postulating that the return on a security is based on several independent factors, with a particular risk premium attached to each factor. *See* Capital Asset Pricing Model (CAPM).

**arm's length transaction** A transaction entered into by unrelated parties, each acting in their own best interests in paying or charging prices based on fair market values. In the preparation of financial statements it is normally assumed that all transactions are conducted at arm's length, although it is appreciated that this may not be the case with companies belonging to the same group, who make special arrangements between themselves for taxation or other reasons. *Refer to* IAS 24.

**arrears** A liability that has not been settled by the due date.

**articles of association** The document in the United Kingdom that must be prepared and filed on the incorporation of a corporate body. It sets down the rules of the company regarding issues such as the issue of shares, appointment of directors, and the conduct of meetings. The accompanying document that must also be prepared is the memorandum of association.

**articles of incorporation** The document filed by the founders of a corporation in the United States. A certificate of incorporation is issued, and the two documents establish the charter that gives the corporation its legal existence.

**articulated accounts** Accounts prepared under the double-entry bookkeeping system, in which the retained earnings on the income statement equal the increase in net worth of the business on the balance sheet, subject to any other adjustments, such as an injection of new capital or reductions in capital.

**artificial person** An entity whose identity the law recognizes but that is not an individual. For example, a corporate body is a person in the sense that it can sue and be sued, and hold property in its own name.

**Asia-Pacific Economic Co-operation (APEC)** Established in 1989, APEC's role is to promote economic growth in the region. It has 21 members that account for more than one-third of the world's population and approximately 60% of the world's GDP and 47% of world trade.

**Asian Corporate Governance Association (ACGA)** ACGA is an independent, not-for-profit membership organization dedicated to working with investors, corporations and regulators in the implementation of effective corporate governance practices throughout Asia. Established in 1999 and incorporated under the laws of Hong Kong, ACGA's work covers advocacy, education, and research.

**asset** In common terms, any tangible or intangible object that is of value to its possessor. In most cases, it is either cash or another asset that can be turned into cash. Most accounting bodies throughout the world would now define an asset as a source of future economic benefits obtained or controlled as a result of past transactions or events. Tangible assets include land and buildings, plant and machinery, fixtures and fittings, inventories, investments, accounts receivables, and cash. Intangible assets include goodwill, patents, copyrights, and trademarks. *Refer to* IAS 38.8.

**asset classification** The grouping of assets into separate classes on the balance sheet. Assets are usually shown in the order of most fixed to most fluid. Items such as property, plant, and equipment would be shown under non-current assets, while items such as inventories, receivables, and cash would be shown under current assets. *Refer to* IAS 1.

**asset cover** A ratio that provides a measure of the solvency of a company. It is calculated by dividing the net assets by its debt. Those companies with high asset cover are considered more solvent.

**asset deficiency** The position in which the value of an organization's assets, as shown on the balance sheet, are exceeded by its liabilities. An asset deficiency is normally regarded as an indicator that an organization is no longer financially viable, but other factors such as access to finance must be taken into account.

**asset stripping** The acquisition or takeover of a company whose shares are valued on the market below their underlying asset value. The intention is not to maintain the operations of the company but to dispose of its assets to make an immediate profit.

**asset turnover** A measurement of a firm's ability to generate sales from its asset base, calculated by dividing the net sales by the total assets. The principle is that an organization must produce income from its assets; otherwise they represent a drain on its resources or efficiency.

**asset valuation** An assessment of the value at which the assets of an organization, usually the non-current assets, should be entered into its balance sheet. The valuation may be arrived at in a number of ways. The requirements for using the revaluation model are set out in the standards. *Refer to* IAS 16.

**associate** An organization that does not set its operating and financial policies independently but is subject to significant influence by another party. An associate is neither a subsidiary of another nor a party to a joint venture. *Refer to* IAS 28.2.

**Association of British Insurers (ABI)** The Association of British Insurers is the trade association for the insurance industry in the United Kingdom. The ABI represents around 400 companies and deals in approximately 94% of the businesses conducted in the U.K. insurance sector.

**Association of Certified Fraud Examiners (ACFE)** Based in the United States, the Association of Certified Fraud Examiners is a global, 30,000-member professional association whose members are dedicated to fraud prevention, detection, and investigation. Membership consists of accountants, internal auditors, fraud investigators, law enforcement personnel, lawyers, business leaders, educators, and students representing 102 countries around the world. Members must complete an examination prior to getting the Certified Fraud Examiner (CFE) certification.

**Association of Chartered Certified Accountants (ACCA)** One of the largest professional accountancy bodies in the world with 320,000 members and students. Based in the United Kingdom, the ACCA is a major advocate of international accounting and its examinations have covered the topic for several years.

**Association of Corporate Treasurers (ACT)** A U.K. organization established to encourage and promote the study and practice of treasury management. A small organization in relation to the professional accounting bodies, it has become influential in the field of corporate treasurership.

**Association of Chief Executives of Voluntary Organizations (ACEVO)** Established in 1987, ACEVO is the professional body for chief executives in the charitable and voluntary organizations. It has over 1650 members and is based in the United Kingdom.

**Association of International Accountants (AIA)** Based in the United Kingdom, the AIA is one of five Recognized Qualifying Bodies (RQBs) in the United Kingdom for company auditors under the Companies Act 1989. The AIA was founded in 1928 and incorporated in London, England, in 1932. The AIA promotes and supports the advancement of the accountancy profession both in the United Kingdom and internationally.

**Association of International Bond Dealers (AIBD)** Founded in 1969 in Zurich, Switzerland, the Association has more than 350 member institutions.

**at-the-money option** A call or put option in which the exercise price is approximately the same as the current market price of the underlying security. *See* in-the-money option.

**attest** To bear witness to an act or event. In most countries, legislation requires that signatures to a document are required to be witnessed by a third party for that document to be legal and binding.

**attest function** The provision of an audit opinion as to the truth and fairness of the financial statements of an organization.

**attributable profit** The part of the total final profit on a long-term contract attributable to a particular financial period, after allowing for estimated remedial and maintenance costs and any other non-recoverable costs. *Refer to* IAS 11.

**audit** Generally, this involves a formal examination of accounting records or documents and a statement of opinion on their accuracy. An independent auditor performs the audit so that an opinion may be expressed on the financial statements. There are different national rules concerning the status of organizations that require an external audit. In the United States, only those companies registered with the Securities and Exchange Commission have to be audited. The scope tends to be wider in other countries, but the requirements are often relaxed, based on the size of the organization. Auditors within an organization, such as an internal-audit department, will perform internal audit. Internal auditors examine various areas, including financial and non-financial systems, with particular attention to the quality of internal controls.

**audit committee** A committee of knowledgeable and informed individuals with a degree of independence from the organization. There are different forms of audit committees in various countries. Essentially, the Committee has the authority to question executive directors, with particular reference to issues relating to financial reporting, auditing, and corporate governance.

**audit completion checklist** A list of items to be checked by audit staff that includes all statutory disclosures and accounting standard requirements. The checklist may be used throughout the audit but is more specifically designed to be used as a final check before the files are handed to the reporting partner of the audit firm for signature.

**audit evidence** The evidence required by an auditor on which to base an audit opinion about the financial statements of the company whose accounts are being audited. Sources of information include the accounting systems and the underlying documentation of the enterprise, its tangible assets, management, and employees, its customers, suppliers, and any other third parties who have dealings with, or knowledge of, the enterprise or its business. The evidence will be obtained by means of compliance tests and substantive tests.

**audit expectations gap** The difference between the role of an auditor, as perceived by the auditor, and the expectations of the users of financial statements. One aspect of the gap is attributed to poor communications because public expectations are higher than the actual performance required of auditors (for instance, users of accounts may expect all fraud to be discovered by a statutory audit). Ensuring that the users of accounts understand what an audit is and what its limitations are could close the communications gap. The other aspect is where public expectations are reasonable but the auditor's performance does not fulfill them. This gap normally reaches the public domain in the form of high-profile financial scandals.

**Audit Inspection Unit (AIU)** The Professional Oversight Board for Accountancy (POBA) includes an Audit Inspection Unit (AIU) as a separate division. The AIU has taken responsibility from the professional bodies for monitoring the quality of audit of all listed companies and other major audits of public interest. It is committed to improving the quality of audit of major entities that are in the public interest. POBA is responsible for monitoring the activities of the AIU.

**Auditing and Assurance Oversight Council (AASOC)** Established in Canada in 2002, the AASOC oversees the Assurance Standards Board by providing strategic direction, guidance, and the perspective of users into the setting of auditing and assurance standards.

**Auditing Practices Board (APB)** The Auditing Practices Board (APB) was established in April 2002, and replaces a previous APB that had been set up since 1991. APB is one of the five subsidiary boards of the Financial Reporting Council (FRC). The APB is committed to leading the development of the highest standards for auditing practice in the United Kingdom and the Republic of Ireland.

**Auditing Standards Board (ASB)** The authoritative body in the United States responsible for the formulation, revision, and interpretation of generally accepted auditing standards. It issues auditing pronouncements entitled Statements on Auditing Standards.

**audit manual** A written document that explains the auditing policies and procedures of a firm.

**audit opinion** This is the report issued by the independent auditors at the end of their examination. It expresses a view as to whether or not the financial statements audited have been prepared consistently using appropriate accounting policies, in accordance with relevant legislation, regulations, or applicable accounting standards.

**auditor** A person or firm appointed to carry out an audit of an organization. It is normal in most countries to have strict rules on the qualification and experience of a person who is approved as an external auditor.

**auditors' report** A report by the auditors appointed to audit the accounts of a company or other organization. Auditors' reports may take many forms depending on who has appointed the auditors and for what purposes. There is normally specific wording regarding the role, responsibilities, and opinions of the auditor required for an audit conducted under legislation.

**audit program** A document listing the individual audit tests to be performed in compliance with the audit strategy for a particular organization. The audit program gives guidance to the audit staff involved and provides a record of work done and the conclusions drawn. It provides a basis for effective quality control and meeting audit evidence requirements.

**audit report** *See* auditors' report.

**audit risk** The risk that an auditor may not uncover irregularities in the financial records with the result that the financial statements may be materially misleading. The audit risk consists of three components: the inherent risk, the control risk, and the detection risk. A quantification of each of these elements, when multiplied together, gives a measure of the audit risk.

**audit rotation** The practice of appointing an audit firm for a specified number of years after which they will be replaced by another audit firm. The advantage claimed is that it assists the auditors in remaining independent of the directors' influence.

**audit strategy** The overall plan for an audit, which gives the framework for detailed decisions regarding the nature, timing, and extent of the substantive tests to be employed.

**audit trail** The recorded flow of a transaction as evidenced by documents and records examined during an audit. The trail reveals how a transaction has been dealt with from start to finish. Documents will require cross-referencing so that the trail is not broken.

**audit working papers** Files built up during an audit that contain detailed evidence and information of the work performed. Typical contents include information of continuing importance, planning information, assessment of the client's accounting and internal control systems, details of work carried out and by whom, financial information and summaries, evidence of work having been appropriately reviewed, and the conclusions reached. These files provide the reporting partner of the audit firm with the evidence necessary to form an opinion. They are also useful for future reference.

**Australian Accounting Standards Board (AASB)** This organization is responsible for setting accounting standards that apply to public and private organizations. The Board comprises a full-time chairman and nine part-time members and is a technical standard setter. There is an oversight body, the Financial Reporting Council, which comprises key stakeholders from the business community, the professional accounting bodies, government, and regulatory agencies. An Urgent Issues Group reports to the Board.

**authorization date** The date on which the financial statements are signed by the officers (usually CEO and CFO) of an organization responsible for meeting financial reporting requirements.

**authorized capital** The maximum amount of capital that may be issued under an organization's regulations. The actual amount issued is usually lower than the authorized amount.

**average collection period** *See* accounts receivable collection period.

**Average Rate of Return (ARR)** Expressed as the average annual profit as a percentage of the sum invested on a particular project. The ARR can be computed as follows:

$$\frac{\text{total profit over project life / number of years}}{\text{capital outlay on project}} \times 100\%$$

This calculation allows the percentage to be compared with the percentage rates of return on other uses of capital. It can also be judged against the current market rate of interest to assess the amount of percentage return for the risk undertaken.

# B

**b2b** A form of e-commerce between business and business, for example, suppliers to other businesses.

**b2c** A form of e-commerce between business and consumer, for example, on-line provision of goods and services to the end-user.

**backlog depreciation** A depreciation charge that is generated when an asset is revalued upwards. The increase in value not only affects the current depreciation charge but also has an impact on the accumulated depreciation. An additional charge must be made to the current income statement for the backlog.

**back office** The part or department of a stockbroker or trader that is responsible for the operational administration, such as settlements and the maintenance of accounts.

**bad debt** An amount owed to an organization that will not be paid.

***bai-bitahman-ajil*** The Islamic term for deferred payment.

**balanced scorecard** A strategic performance measurement model that incorporates a balanced mix of financial and non-financial critical success factors in four areas: learning and growth, customer satisfaction, internal processes, and financial performance.

**balance sheet** A statement of financial position that shows the total assets, liabilities, and shareholders' equity at a particular date, usually the last day of the financial period. *Refer to* IAS 1.

**balance-sheet asset value** The book value of assets as shown on the balance sheet. Normally, organizations use the historic cost convention so that non-current assets are shown at cost less accumulated depreciation and impairment losses, if any. The value on the balance sheet is unlikely to be closely aligned to the current market value.

**balance-sheet audit** An audit limited to verification of the existence, ownership, valuation, and presentation of the assets and liabilities listed on a balance sheet.

**balloon payment** A substantial payment at the end of a term of a loan that represents repayment of the outstanding amount of the principal. It is designed to defer the burden of debt repayments.

**barometer stock** A security whose financial performance and price is regarded as an indication of the overall financial health of a stock market.

**barter** Trading in which goods or services are exchanged directly without using money as a medium of exchange. The necessity to find matched partners restricts the scope of trading, but where liquidity is poor it may be the only way of conducting transactions. Means of exchange, such as money, enable organizations to trade with each other at much greater distance and through whole chains of intermediaries, which is impossible in a barter system.

**base currency** The currency used as the basis for expressing an exchange rate. A foreign currency rate of exchange is quoted per single unit of the base of currency, frequently in U.S. dollars.

**base inventory** A certain volume of inventory that is established as the norm. Levels are not permitted to fall below that norm. When the total inventory is valued, this proportion of the inventory is valued at its original cost.

**Basel Committee on Banking Supervision** An international organization of banking regulators that announced its support of international accounting standards in 2000.

**base rate** The rate of interest used as the threshold by banks for the rates they charge their customers. Most customers will pay a premium over the base rate to take account of the bank's risk involved in lending.

**basic earnings per share** The earnings per share calculated by dividing the amount of net profit attributable to ordinary shareholders for a financial period by the weighted average number of ordinary shares outstanding during the period. *Refer to* IAS 33.10.

**basis point** One hundredth of 1%. This unit is often used in finance when prices involve fine margins.

**bean counters** A derogatory name for accountants.

**bear** A dealer on a stock exchange, currency market, or commodity market who expects prices to fall. Bears may sell securities at a specific price but without having ownership. They anticipate that they will be able to close this short position by acquiring the securities at a lower price as the market falls and before they have to make their delivery. If they are successful, they will enjoy the profit between the selling price that has been agreed upon and the lower price at which the securities have been acquired.

**bearer** A person who presents for payment a check (cheque) or bill of exchange marked "pay bearer." Since a bearer check or bill does not require endorsement, it is considered a high-risk form of transfer.

**bearer security** A security where proof of ownership is evidenced solely by possessing the security certificate. Since the issuing company does not maintain a register of owners, bonds can be transferred to other owners without registration. Coupons are normally attached to the bond so that interest can be claimed by presenting the coupon.

**behavioral accounting** The study of accounting that encompasses the psychological and social aspects of the discipline in addition to the technical aspects.

**bellwether security** A security that is considered to be a good guide to the direction in which the market is moving.

**below-the-line** The entries below the imaginary line on an organization's income statement that establish the profit (or loss) from the entries above the line that show how the profit is distributed.

**benchmarking** The establishing of competitive performance targets based on the achievements of the most efficient producers within a marketplace. The targets ensure that managers concentrate upon the competitive environment in which the organization operates, instead of only comparing this year's achievements with the previous year.

**benchmark treatment** The accounting treatment that is designated as a reference point by the IASB whenever companies are making choices between allowed alternative treatments.

**benefit-cost ratio** The evaluation of a proposed activity or project by comparing the value of the potential benefits to the costs that will be incurred. If the benefits exceed the costs, the activity is financially attractive, although there may be many non-financial factors to take into account before making a final decision. The benefits, some of which may be of a qualitative nature, may be enjoyed by some groups and the costs borne by others, and this makes the analysis more complex.

**beta coefficient** A measure of the volatility of a share and its systematic risk. When a share has a high beta coefficient, it is likely to respond to market movements by rising or falling in value by more than the market average. In portfolio theory, the beta coefficient is used to compute the appropriate discount rates in the Capital Asset Pricing Model (CAPM).

**beta factor** *See* beta coefficient.

**betterment** A term used to refer to the replacement of a major item of plant and machinery by one that will provide better performance. Betterments thus represent capital expenditure.

**bill broker (discount broker)** A broker who buys bills of exchange from traders and sells them to banks and discount houses or holds them to maturity. Many now deal exclusively in Treasury bills.

**bill of exchange** A formal document signed by the drawer and addressed to another person (the drawee) instructing the drawee to pay to a named person or to the bearer on demand or at a specified future date a sum of money. Bills of exchange are usually used for payments in foreign currency and are drawn for three months after their date. Before a bill has any value, it has to be accepted by the drawee, usually a financial institution. Once the bill has been accepted, the creditor can hold it until it is due for payment, immediately obtain payment at a bank for a fee, or endorse it and pass it onto a second creditor.

**bill of sale** A document transferring the ownership of goods from one person to another.

**bill rate** The discount rate on the market for bills of exchange. It is the difference between the purchase price and the value of the bill when it matures. The rate will depend on the quality of the bill and the risk the purchasers take. First-class bills that are supported by banks or well-respected finance institutions will be discounted at a lower rate then bills involving greater risk.

**biological asset** A living animal or plant. *Refer to* IAS 41.5.

**black knight** A person, group, or organization that makes an unwelcome takeover bid for a company.

**black market** An illegal market for a particular good or service.

**Black-Scholes Model** An option pricing model that assesses whether option contracts are fairly valued. The model states that the value of an option is a function of the short-term interest rate, of the time to expiration, and to the variance of the rate of return on the shares, but is not a function of the expected return on the shares.

**blue chip** The term commonly used for the ordinary shares in the most highly regarded companies traded on a stock market. The name comes from the color of the highest value chip used in poker. Blue-chip companies have a well-known name, a good growth record, and valuable assets. They represent a secure investment, but will not necessarily give the same high returns as other investments that have a higher risk element.

**body corporate** A corporation consisting of a body of persons legally authorized to act as one person, while being distinct from that person. For example, the shareholders of a company are separate from the company.

**boilerplate** The standard language used in legal documents such as contracts and wills. The information is essential and of a formal nature and, therefore, rarely modified.

**bond** A written promise from a borrower to a lender to pay a certain sum of money at a future date and representing a long-term loan. Bonds usually take the form of fixed interest securities issued by governments and corporations, although there are different types of bonds with various conditions attached to them.

**bond discount** The amount by which the maturity value of a bond exceeds the issue price at the date of issue.

**bond indenture** Bond contract that specifies the stated rate of interest, the face value of the bond, and other contractual provisions.

**bond premium** The amount by which the issue price of a bond at the date of issue exceeds the maturity value.

**bonds with warrants** Fixed-rate bonds with warrants attached that offer long-term options related to ordinary shares. The fixed-rate bonds and the warrants can be separated and marketed to different groups of investors.

**bonus issue** The issue of ordinary shares where no consideration is received by the entity. A bonus issue means that shareholders will receive "free" shares in proportion to their existing holding. Normally, the effect is to reduce EPS because earnings are being spread over a larger number of shares. *Refer to* IAS 33.

**book of prime entry** A book or record in which certain types of transactions are recorded before becoming part of the double-entry bookkeeping system. The most common books of prime entry are the day book, the cash book, and the journal.

**book-to-bill ratio** The relationship between orders booked for future delivery and orders now being shipped and thus can be invoiced (billed).

**book value** The carrying amount of an asset or liability as shown in the financial statements. Generally, this is unlikely to represent current market value.

**borrowing costs** The interest and other costs incurred through borrowing of funds. The benchmark treatment is to recognize them as an expense with capitalization permitted, subject to certain conditions. *Refer to* IAS 23.4.

**bottom line** The profit figure used as the earnings figure in the earnings per share calculation of a company.

**bought deal** The raising of capital by a new issue of bonds, without using a rights issue or placing. The borrower invites banks or groups of banks to bid for new issues of bonds or shares, selling them to the highest bidder, who then sells them to the rest of the market in the expectation of making a profit. The borrower is guaranteed that the new issue is successful.

**bourse** *See* stock exchange.

**branch accounting** A record-keeping system in which each department or branch of a business is established as a separate cost center or accounting center. Branch accounts may be prepared to show the performance of both a main trading center (the head office) and subsidiary trading centers (branches) but with all the accounting records being maintained by head office. Alternatively, separate entity branch accounts are prepared in which branches maintain their own records, which are later combined with head-office records to prepare accounts for the whole business.

**brands** Intangible assets such as a product or company name, sign, symbol, design, or reputation that, if operated in combination, will lead to greater benefits from the manufacture and/or sale of a product or service through brand differentiation. *Refer to* IAS 38.

**breakeven analysis** The technique used in management accounting in which costs are analyzed according to cost behavior characteristics into fixed costs and variable costs and compared to sales revenue in order to determine the level of sales volume, sales value, or production at which the business makes neither a profit nor a loss; that is, breakeven. This technique forms a part of cost-volume-profit (CVP) analysis.

**breakeven chart** A graph on which an organization's total costs, analyzed into fixed costs and variable costs, are drawn over a given range of activity, together with the sales revenue for the same range of activity. The point at which the sales-revenue curve crosses the total-cost curve is known as the breakeven point (expressed either as sales revenue or production/sales volume). The breakeven chart is sometimes shown as a profit-volume chart.

**breakeven point** The level of production, sales volume, percentage of capacity, or sales revenue at which the organization makes neither a profit nor a loss. The breakeven point may either be determined by the construction of a breakeven chart or by calculation. The formulae are:

Breakeven point (units) = total fixed costs/unit contribution margin

Breakeven point (sales) = (total fixed costs)/contribution margin ratio

**break-up value** The value placed on an asset where it is assumed that an organization is not a going concern. In these circumstances, it is probable that there will be few willing buyers and that they will make their offer after taking into account the financial condition of the organization.

**British Accounting Association (BAA)** Established in 1947, the BAA is a registered charity organization based in the United Kingdom. It is an academic research-based organization and brings together those interested in teaching and research in accounting and finance. The BAA currently has approximately 800 members, many of whom are employed in higher educational institutions in the United Kingdom.

**British Association of Hospitality Accountants (BAHA)** Established in 1969, BAHA was formed with the aim of bringing together professionals who were involved in accounting, financial management, taxation, valuation, and control areas within the hotel industry. Membership has expanded to include systems specialists, hospitality consultants and accountants, bankers, investment analysts, property professionals, academics, and others who retain an interest in the hotel, catering and leisure sectors.

**bucket shop** A derogatory name for a firm of brokers, dealers, and agents of dubious status and questionable business practices.

**budget** A financial or quantitative statement prepared prior to a specified financial period, containing the plans, policies, and strategies to be pursued during that period. A functional budget is drawn up for each functional area within an organization and it is also usual to produce a capital budget, a cash flow budget, inventory budgets, and a master budget, which includes a budgeted income statement and balance sheet.

**budgetary control** The application of financial control in an organization through the use of budgets that detail income and expenditure for each function of the organization in advance of a financial period. Budgets are compared with actual performance to establish any variances. Individual managers are made responsible for the controllable activities within their budgets and are expected to take remedial action if the adverse variances are regarded as excessive.

**budgetary slack** The process of padding or setting a less rigorous budget by overestimating costs and underestimating revenues. This gives the manager responsible for the budget some slack in the performance levels that should be achieved.

**budget center** A section or area of an organization under the responsibility of a manager for which budgets are prepared. A budget center may be a function, department, section, individual, cost center, or any combination of these that the management wishes to treat as a budget center. It is usual to produce regular financial statements on the basis of each budget center so that each budget-center manager is aware of its budgeted and actual performance and any variances.

**budget committee** A specially established committee in an organization responsible for the budgetary control system. The membership may vary among organizations, but a typical committee may consist of a chief executive as chairman, the functional managers as members, and a financial manager as budget director. The committee must ensure the formulation of the budgets in accordance with the directives and policies communicated by the board of directors. It reviews the budgets set by individual managers for coordination and acceptability, and submits the final budgets to the board of directors for approval. The committee may also have the responsibility for reviewing actual performance against budgeted performance as the financial period progresses.

**budgeted capacity** The productive capacity available in an organization for a budgeted period as stated in the budget for that period. It may be set in terms of direct labor hours, machine hours, standard hours, or output.

**budget period** A period for which a budget is prepared and during which it is intended to apply. The budget period usually coincides with the period used for financial reporting purposes. A budget is normally set for one year in total, but for planning and control purposes monthly or quarterly budget figures will be calculated.

**bull** A dealer on a stock exchange, currency market, or commodity market who expects prices to rise. A bull will buy securities at a specific price anticipating that these can be sold at a higher price once the market price has increased.

**bulldog bond** An unsecured or secured bond issued in the U.K. domestic market by a non-U.K. borrower.

**bullet loan** A loan that is repaid fully in one final amount at maturity, although interest may be paid in interim payments.

**bunny bond** A bond that gives the holder the option of receiving interest or additional bonds.

**burden** The term normally means overheads in the United States.

**burn-out turnaround** The financial restructuring of an organization that is facing liquidation. New financing is secured but at the cost of diluting the interests of existing investors.

**business combination** The bringing together of separate economic entities as a result of one entity uniting with, or obtaining control over, the net assets and operations of another. *Refer to* IFRS 3.A.

**business entity concept** The concept that financial accounting and reporting relate to the activities of a specific business entity and not to the activities of the owners of that entity.

**business segment** A component of an organization that can be separately identified and that provides a product or service that has different risks and returns from other segments of the organization. *Refer to* IAS 14.9.

**buy-in** The purchase of a holding of more than 50% in a company by (or on behalf of) a group of executives from outside the company who wish to run the company.

**buy-in management buyout** A management buyout in which management invests in the venture together with outsider venture capitalists, who have more managerial control than is usual with management buyout.

**buy-out** The purchase of a substantial holding in a company by its existing managers.

**by products** Products from a process that have secondary financial significance to the main product but also possess a value.

# C

**Cadbury Report** The Cadbury Committee was formed in the United Kingdom in 1991 because of increasing public concern over the management of large companies and investors' low trust in financial reporting and auditing. The Committee issued its report in 1992, and the main thrust of their recommendation was a Code of Best Practice to be adopted by the directors of all U.K. public companies. The guidance had no legal backing but the report was influential in establishing the present framework. *See* corporate governance.

**cafeteria plan** An agreement allowing employees to choose a fringe benefit from a range of benefits including cash.

**cage** *See* back office.

**callable bonds** Fixed-rate bonds, usually convertibles, in which the issuer has the right, but not the obligation, to redeem (call) the bond at par during the life of the bond. The call exercise price may be at par, although it is usually set at a premium. A grace period, a period when the borrower is unable to call the bond, will usually be included in the terms of the agreement. Conversion after the grace period will only be possible if certain conditions are met, usually related to the price of the underlying share.

**called-up share capital** The amount of issued share capital for which the organization has requested settlement from shareholders. Sometimes, shares are paid in installments with subsequent calls for additional payment.

**call option** This is an option to buy an asset or a financial instrument. These will be purchased when it is considered that the price of an asset will rise. The call option buyer will only exercise the option if the market price of the asset moves above the exercise price, since the financial benefit will be the excess of the market price over the exercise price. If the share price falls below the exercise price the option will not be exercised as the shares can be bought at a lower price on the open market.

**call provision** A provision, made by an organization issuing bonds or preferred shares, that allows them to be redeemed in part or in total at a date to be determined by the issuer.

**Canadian Academic Accounting Association (CAAA)** The CAAA is an organization of accounting educators, professional accountants, and others who are involved in, or concerned about, research and education in accounting and related areas in Canada.

**Canadian Institute of Chartered Accountants (CICA)** The professional body of practicing accountants in Canada; it was originally founded in 1902 as the Dominion Association of Chartered Accountants. It is a professional self-regulating accounting body whose *CICA Handbook Recommendations* have legal status as the authoritative pronouncements with respect to generally accepted accounting principles in Canada.

**cap** A ceiling on a loan or other financial activity. For example, an interest-rate cap would set a maximum interest rate to be charged on a loan, regardless of prevailing general interest-rate levels. Caps may also limit annual increases to a certain level. The borrower has to pay a fee for the advantage of having a cap. *See* floor.

**capacity utilization** A formula to indicate the extent to which resources are being used at their maximum capacity. It is calculated by expressing the actual output for a period as a percentage of the theoretical maximum output. An organization's capacity utilization is of financial importance, because of the impact of fixed overheads per unit on profit margins. High capacity utilization keeps fixed costs per unit down, by spreading the overheads over many units of output. Low utilization can result in total costs per unit being lower than the selling price. The concept is widely used in a number of industries, for instance, the percentage of rooms occupied in the hotel industry.

**capital** Generally, the investment in an organization that permits it to acquire resources for operations. The owner's interest in an organization is calculated by deducting total liabilities from total assets. Loan capital is the amount provided by financial institutions and others. *Refer to* F.102. *See* capital maintenance concepts.

**Capital Asset Pricing Model (CAPM)** A model used by organizations to establish an investment and financing policy to maximize the price or value of its equity by calculating the equilibrium relationship between return and risk. The model may also be used to determine the discount rate or cost of capital to be used in the organization's investment decisions. It is used in portfolio theory, in which the expected rate of return (E) on an investment is expressed in terms of the expected rate of return ($r_m$) on the market portfolio and the beta coefficient ($\beta$), that is,

$$E = R + \beta(r_m - R),$$

where R is the risk-free rate of return.

**capital assets** *See* non-current assets.

**capital budget** A plan of the future resources required by an organization for expenditure on projects or assets, for example, the acquisition of new machinery or the building of a new factory.

**capital employed** The total of shareholder's equity in an organization plus its long-term debts. This amount equals the non-current assets of a company plus its net current assets. The term is not legally defined, and variations of the formula are used. It is regarded as an important ratio that gives an overview of the organization's entire performance. *See* Return on Capital Employed.

**capital expenditure** The significant expenditure by an organization for the acquisition or improvement of a non-current asset. The expenditure would justify the item being depreciated over an estimated useful life of an extended period. Capital expenditure is not charged against the profits of the organization when it takes place, but is regarded as an investment to be capitalized in the balance sheet as a non-current asset and subsequently charged against profits through depreciation. *Refer to* IAS 16.

**capital instruments** The agreements and documentation used by organizations to raise finance. The term includes shares, debentures, loans, options, and warrants.

**capital intensive** The characteristic of a company with significant funds invested in non-current assets, such as plant and machinery. These companies are regarded as high-risk investments, particularly in times of recession, because a small reduction in sales would cause a sharp reduction in profits. The reason for this is because a substantial part of the company's costs are fixed in the short term.

**capitalization** The recognition of an expense that would normally be regarded as an operating expense, as part of the cost of the acquisition, construction, or production of an asset. *Refer to* IAS 16.

**capitalization of borrowing costs** The capitalization of the costs of borrowing specifically to fund the purchase of a non-current asset or the development of investment property. It may be included in the capitalized cost of the non-current asset. *Refer to* IAS 23.

**capital lease** *See* finance lease.

**capital maintenance concepts** There are two capital maintenance concepts: financial and physical. The financial concept means that the capital of a company is only maintained if the financial or monetary amount of its net assets at the end of a financial period is equal to or exceeds the financial or monetary amount of net assets at the beginning of the period, excluding any distributions to or contributions from, the owners. In maintaining the level of financial capital, it has to be decided whether adjustments should be made for changes in the purchasing power of money. The physical concept means that physical productive or operating capacity, or the funds or resources required to achieve that capacity, is equal to or exceeds the physical productive capacity at the beginning of the period, after excluding any distributions to, or contributions from, owners during the financial period. *Refer to* F.102.

**capital market** A market in which long-term capital is raised by industry and commerce, the government, and local authorities. The money comes from private investors, insurance companies, pension funds, and banks, and is usually arranged by issuing houses and merchant banks. Stock exchanges are part of the capital market in that they provide a market for the shares and loan stocks that represent the capital once it has been raised. Money markets deal in short-term funds.

**capital reserve** A reserve that cannot be distributed to shareholders in the form of a dividend.

**capital stock** The equity shares in a corporation. The two basic types of capital stock are common stock and preferred stock. *See* ordinary shares and preference shares.

**capital structure** The balance between the assets and liabilities of a company, the nature of its assets, and the composition of its borrowings. The assets may be non-current (tangible or intangible) or current inventories or accounts receivables. Borrowings may be long or short-term, fixed or floating, secured or unsecured.

**capital surplus** The difference between the par value of a share and its issue price. It is the equivalent of a share premium in the United Kingdom.

**capital turnover** The ratio of the revenue of an organization to its capital employed. It is calculated by dividing the revenue for a period by the capital employed. Normally, the higher the ratio, the better the use that is being made of the assets in generating revenue.

**captive finance company** A finance company controlled by an industrial or commercial company.

**captive insurance company** An insurance company set up by one or more commercial or industrial companies with the object of insuring their own risks.

**carrying amount** The value of an asset or liability as shown on the balance sheet. For example, a non-current asset, such as a building, will be shown at the historical cost or other allowable basis less the accumulated depreciation to date and accumulated impairment losses, if any.

**carrying cost** The cost of holding inventories from the date of receipt to the date of disposal, or for any other specified period. These costs include warehousing, insurance, and security. These can represent substantial costs for some organizations. These costs can be minimized if an organization adopts the "just-in-time" inventory approach.

**cartel** A group of nations or businesses that agree to work together to influence either the supply and/or the market prices of products by regulating production and marketing.

**cash** A medium of exchange that includes coins, currency, undeposited checks, money orders, and bank drafts and bank deposits in a bank available on demand. *Refer to* IAS 7.6.

**cash basis of accounting** Accounting based on actual movements of cash rather than the accrual concept. Transactions are recorded on the date that cash is received or paid out, and are included in the income statement in which these payments and receipts occur. There is no accounting for outstanding accounts receivable, prepayments, accounts payable, accruals, inventories, and non-current assets.

**cash conversion cycle** The time taken, usually calculated in days, to sell inventory and collect accounts receivable less the number of days taken to settle accounts payable.

**cash cow** A business, or part of an organization, that regularly generates sales and profits without the need for large capital expenditure. Growth prospects, however, are usually expected to be unexciting.

**cash equivalents** Short-term, highly liquid investments that are readily convertible to known amounts of cash and for which there is an insignificant risk of changes in value. *Refer to* IAS 7.6.

**cash flow adequacy** A ratio that measures the number of times that the total of capital expenditure, debt repayments, and dividends paid are covered by the cash flow from operating activities. It is normally expressed as a times basis. For example, an organization may find its cash flows from operating activities covers the payments 1.2 times.

**cash flow hedges** The use of a derivative or other financial instrument to hedge the exposure to variability in cash flows. *Refer to* IAS 39.86.

**cash flow liquidity** *See* cash to current liabilities ratio.

**cash flow margin** A ratio that indicates the ability of an organization to generate cash from net sales. The cash flow from operating activities is expressed as a percentage of the net sales figure for a financial period.

**cash flow multiple** A performance ratio based on an analysis of the cash flow statement and calculated by dividing the total value of the organization by the free cash flow.

**cash flow risk (cash flow interest rate risk)** The risk of changes in future cash flows related to a monetary financial instrument in which interest rates fluctuate but fair values may remain constant. *Refer to* IAS 32.52.

**cash flow statement** A statement showing the inflows and outflows of cash and cash equivalents for a business over a financial period. The cash flows for the period are classified into operating, investing, and financing activities. *Refer to* IAS 7.

**cash flow to capital expenditure ratio** A ratio calculated by dividing an organization's cash flows from operations less dividends by the expenditures for plant and equipment. The ratio evaluates an organization's ability to maintain its plant and equipment from its resources, rather than from borrowing.

**cash flow to total debt ratio** A ratio for assessing the solvency of an organization. It is calculated by dividing the cash flow from operations by total liabilities. The ratio evaluates an organization's ability to satisfy its debts.

**Cash-Generating Unit (CGU)** The smallest identifiable group of assets in an organization that generates cash flows. These cash flows are mostly independent of the cash inflows from other assets or groups of assets. *Refer to* IAS 36.6.

**cash ratio** The ratio of the cash reserve maintained by a bank compared to the amount deposited in current accounts and deposit accounts. Banks attempt to maintain the minimum cash reserves since they earn no interest. However, they must keep sufficient cash to meet customers' demands.

**cash return on assets** A ratio that indicates the return on assets on a cash basis. It is calculated by expressing the cash flow from operating activities as a percentage of the total assets.

**cash to current liabilities ratio** A ratio similar to the liquidity ratio but calculated by using cash figures. The total of cash, marketable securities, and cash flow from operating activities is divided by current liabilities. The ratio evaluates an organization's ability to satisfy short-term financial obligations.

**caveat emptor** The meaning of this term is "let the buyer beware" and is used to caution purchasers to their responsibilities to carry out due diligence in transactions.

**cedant** The policyholder under a reinsurance contract. *Refer to* IFRS 4.A.

**ceiling** The lower of cost or net realizable value with the latter being the selling price minus both the costs to put the item in a marketable condition and any related selling costs.

**certainty-equivalent approach** A method of risk analysis in which the expected cash flows of a project are converted to equivalent riskless amounts. The higher the risk of an expected cash flow, the lower the certainty-equivalent value for receipts and the higher the certainty-equivalent value for payments.

**certificate of deposit (CD)** A negotiable certificate issued by a bank in return for a term deposit of up to five years. They were originally intended to enable merchant banks to attract funds away from the clearing banks with the offer of competitive interest rates. The clearing banks, however, also began issuing CDs since their negotiability and higher average yield made them increasingly popular with investors. The advantage to depositors is that their deposit is in a fixed-term or long maturity arrangement, thus obtaining a higher rate of interest, and the CDs can be sold in a secondary market if there is an urgent need for cash.

**Certified General Accountants Association of Canada (CGA)** Founded in 1908, the Certified General Accountants Association of Canada is a self-regulating, professional association of 62,000 members and students. CGAs work in industry, commerce, finance, government, public practice, and other areas where accounting and financial management is required.

**Certified Internal Auditor (CIA)** A member of the Institute of Internal Auditors (IIA) in the United States. Internal auditors conduct financial and operational audits of the organizations that employ them. *See* Institute of Internal Auditors.

**Certified Management Accountants (CMA) (Canada)** A self-regulatory professional organization of approximately 45,000 members across Canada of whom 19,000 work in Ontario, Canada. CMAs are mainly strategic and financial managers who work in industry, commerce and not-for-profit organizations.

**Certified Public Accountant (CPA)** A member of the American Institute of Certified Public Accountants. State authorities confer the title on those who pass the Uniform CPA examinations and have acquired sufficient practical experience. A certified public accountant is licensed to give an audit opinion on a company's financial statements.

**cessation** The ceasing of trading and the closure of a business.

**chain linked index** An index where movements are calculated on the basis of the number in the preceding period and not against a fixed base.

**chairman's statement** A statement by the chairman of an organization in the Annual Report and Accounts addressed to the members of the organization, giving an overview of the organization's activities during the financial period. These statements are not required by regulation and may present a more favorable view of the activities and future prospects of the organization than would be obtained from an objective interpretation of the financial statements.

**changes in equity** A financial statement that reflects the change in the net assets in the period under the specific measurement model adopted by the entity. The change arises from transactions with shareholders and the total gains and losses generated in the financial period. The changes in equity statement must be presented with the same prominence as the other financial statements. *Refer to* IAS 1.

**chapter 7** The statute of the U.S. Bankruptcy Reform Act (1978) that refers to liquidation proceedings and the appointment of a trustee to make a management charge, secure additional financing, and operate the business in order to prevent further loss. The spirit of the statute is based on fairness and public policy. It assumes that honest debtors may not always be able to discharge their debts fully and should be given an opportunity to make a fresh start both in their business and personal lives.

**chapter 11** The statute of the U.S. Bankruptcy Reform Act (1978) that applies to reorganization of partnerships, corporations, municipalities, and sole traders, who are in financial difficulties. Unless the court rules otherwise, the current owner and management remains in control of the business and its operations. It is intended that by allowing the business to continue, debtors and creditors can enter into arrangements, such as the restructuring of debt, rescheduling of payments, and the granting of loans.

**charge** *See* floating charge, fixed charge.

**charge and discharge accounting** A form of accounting used in the manorial system of Middle Ages in England in which individuals charge themselves with sums or estate they should receive and credit themselves with sums paid out.

**Chartered Institute of Management Accountants** (**CIMA**) A professional accountancy body in the United Kingdom representing 140,000 members and students working mainly as financial managers in industry, commerce, not-for-profit, and public organizations.

**Chartered Institute of Public Finance and Accountancy** (**CIPFA**) A professional accountancy body specializing in the public sector. It has approximately 15,000 members mainly in the United Kingdom.

**Chartered Institute of Taxation** (**CIT**) A professional qualification in the United Kingdom achieved by passing the Institute's examination. Most members with the qualification are partners or senior employees of accountancy or solicitors' firms, working mainly in the tax field. Some members work in banks, the Inland Revenue, insurance, industry, or commerce.

**chartered secretary** A chartered secretary is qualified in company law, accounting, corporate governance, administration, company secretarial practice, and management. They are trained to chart a course through regulation, legislation, and best practice, and to deliver effective operations. Chartered secretaries work as company secretaries and in other senior positions in companies, charities, local government, educational institutions, and trade bodies. The Institute of Chartered Secretaries and Administrators (ICSA) is the professional body for chartered secretaries. *See* company secretary, corporate secretary.

**chartist** An investor who records past movements of the share prices, P/E ratios, turnover, and other financial statistics of individual organizations and constructs charts to predict future share movements. Chartists claim that history repeats itself and that the movements of share prices conform to a small number of repetitive patterns.

**chart of accounts** A detailed listing of all the accounts used by an organization, showing classifications and subclassifications. For example, each letter or number in an account code will indicate a feature, such as transaction type and the department responsible.

**Chief Executive Officer** (**CEO**) The term used in the United States to denote the person who has the responsibility for the operation of an organization. The term used more frequently in the United Kingdom is Managing Director.

**check** (**U.S.**), **cheque** (**U.K.**) A pre-printed form on which instructions are given to an account holder (a bank or building society) to pay a stated sum to a named recipient. It is the most common form of payment of debts of all kinds.

**Chinese Institute of Certified Public Accountants (CICPA)** Founded in 1995, the CICPA regulates the public accountancy profession under the supervision of the Ministry of Finance and the National Audit Office.

**chinese wall** A fictitious barrier between the separate divisions, departments, teams of financial institutions, or intermediaries to prevent price-sensitive, unpublished information passing among them.

**churning** The dubious practice employed by some brokers of encouraging clients to trade actively in their accounts. This improves the commission of brokers but may not improve the returns to clients.

**circularization of accounts receivable** A practice employed during an audit where all accounts receivable or a sample of them are asked to confirm the amounts outstanding (positive circularization) or to reply if the amount stated is incorrect or in dispute (negative circularization). The purpose is to establish that the debts exist and are correctly valued in the financial statements of an organization.

**circulating assets** Assets that consistently change their nature and circulate from cash to goods and back to cash again. Cash is used to purchase raw materials, which become work in progress when issued to a production department. The work in progress becomes finished goods and, once they are sold, becomes accounts receivable or cash.

**class action** A legal action in which a person sues as a representative of a class of persons who share a common claim.

**class of assets** The grouping of assets of a similar nature and use, for example, machinery. *Refer to* IAS 16.37.

**closing rate** The spot exchange rate of two currencies at the balance sheet date. *Refer to* IAS 21.8.

**collar** An option fixing the maximum (cap) and minimum (floor) rate of interest payable on a loan. The purchaser will be required to pay a premium to benefit from the risk of fluctuations in interest rates.

**collateral** Generally, a form of security, especially an impersonal form of security, such as life-insurance policies or shares, used to secure a bank loan. In some senses, such impersonal securities are referred to as secondary collateral, rather than a primary security, such as guarantees where the collateral is in the form of marketable securities.

**collateralize** To pledge assets to secure a debt where the assets will be forfeited if the borrower defaults on the terms and conditions of the agreement.

**collection period** The time, expressed in days, weeks, or months, that it takes an organization to obtain payment of a debt. *See* accounts receivable collection period.

**columnar accounts** Accounts set out in several columns. The extended trial balance is normally constructed in this way so that by adding across the columns adjustments are automatically fed into the financial statements.

**combined financial statement** The aggregation of the financial statements of a related group of entities in order to present the financial information as if the group were a single entity. Intercompany transactions are eliminated from combined financial statements. *Refer to* IAS 27.

**comfort letter** *See* letter of comfort.

**commercial paper** Unsecured promissory notes that are regarded as a relatively low-risk, short-term form of borrowing. Commercial paper is often regarded as a reasonable substitute for Treasury bills and certificates of deposit. The main issuers are large creditworthy institutions, such as insurance companies, bank trust departments, and pension funds.

**commitment fee** A fee charged by a bank for arranging a line of credit or for continuing the availability of unused loan facilities. Usually, the annual charge is made by the lender on the daily drawn balance of the facility and is often expressed in basis points.

**committed costs** Costs, usually fixed, that the management of an organization have a long-term responsibility to pay. Examples include a long-term lease and depreciation on a non-current asset. These costs can restrict the abilities of management to restructure its operations to improve financial performance.

**committed facility** An agreement between a bank and a customer to provide funds up to a specified maximum at a specified interest rate for a certain period. The agreement will include conditions that must be adhered to by the borrower for the facility to remain in place.

**commodity** A raw material traded on a commodity market, such as grain, coffee, cocoa, wool, cotton, jute, rubber, pork bellies, or orange juice (sometimes known as soft commodities or softs) or metals and other solid raw materials (known as hard commodities). The desirability of commodities and thus the demand for them is determined by their physical properties. Their price is directly influenced by the time and place of their availability.

**common-size financial statements** Financial statements of several organizations that are made comparable by expressing the individual elements as percentages of the total. For example, with income statements all the costs would be expressed as a percentage of the revenue. The percentages are compared with those of another organization or the industry average for interpretation. These comparisons enable conclusions to be drawn on the performance of the company.

**common stock** Units of ownership in a publicly traded corporation in the United States. The common stock holders are normally entitled to receive dividends and vote on matters such as the selection of directions. If a corporation is liquidated, the common stock holders' claims come after those of creditors and holders of bonds and preferred stock. *Ordinary share* is the term used by the International Accounting Standards Board (IASB). *See* ordinary shares.

**company** A corporate enterprise that has a legal identity separate from that of its members, it operates as one single unit, in the success of which all the members participate. An incorporated company is a legal person in its own right, able to own property and to sue and be sued in its own name.

**company doctor** A person with wide commercial experience, who specializes in analyzing and rectifying the problems of ailing organizations. The company doctor may either act as a consultant or may recommend policies and be given executive powers to implement them.

**company limited by shares** An incorporated organization in which the liability of members is limited by the constitution and regulations of the organization to the amounts paid, or due to be paid, for shares.

**company secretary** The term refers to an officer of an organization and is widely used in the United Kingdom. In the United States, company secretaries are referred to as corporate secretaries. Company secretaries have a varied range of responsibilities, some of which are defined by company law. These include maintaining company records, sending annual returns to the Company Register or the Stock Exchange, keeping records of the company's property, ensuring that the company and its directors operate within the law, acting as a link between shareholders and directors, organizing board and general meetings. An increasingly important role attached to company secretaries is the added role of being corporate governance officers. Apart from legal responsibilities, company secretaries also have administrative duties. Company secretaries work in many types of organizations, such as business corporations, charities, trade and professional associations, universities, and the not-for-profit sectors. The recognized professional qualification for company secretaries is via membership of the Institute of Chartered Secretaries and Administrators (ICSA). Membership is gained by passing a series of examinations and meeting the required professional experience. *See* chartered secretary, corporate secretary.

**comparability** A qualitative characteristic of financial information. In order to make informed decisions, users must be able to compare financial statements of one organization over several periods and with the financial statements of other organizations. To ensure comparability, there must be consistency in accounting treatments and the disclosure of accounting policies. *Refer to* F.39-42.

**comparable price method** A method for establishing an arm's length price by using the sales prices of similar products made by unrelated organizations.

**comparative information** To assist users' understanding, comparative financial information from the previous period should be disclosed unless an IFRS allows non-disclosure in particular circumstances. *Refer to* IAS 1.

**compensated absences** Periods when employers are obligated to pay employees for time taken off work due to statutory holidays, vacations, and illness. These absences are accrued during the periods when the employee provides services to the employer. *Refer to* IAS 19.

**compensating balance** A sum of money deposited at a bank by a customer as a condition for the bank to lend money to the customer.

**completeness** A qualitative characteristic of financial statements that ensures that information is reliable. Limitations of materiality and cost will detract from the completeness of information. *Refer to* F.38.

**compliance tests** Tests applied by an auditor to assess the effectiveness of an organization's internal control procedures. The extent of compliance testing will depend upon the extent to which specific controls are relied upon. Compliance testing should establish the required level of substantive testing necessary in order to carry out an audit.

**compound discount** The differences between the value of an amount in the future and its present discounted value. For example, if $100 in five years' time is worth $65 now, the compound discount will be $35. The compound discount will depend upon the rate of discount applied.

**compound financial instruments** Financial instruments that contain elements of both equity and liability. For example, convertible bonds are financial liabilities of the issuer but they grant the holder the option to convert them into equity at a future date. *Refer to* IAS 32.28 and IAS 39.

**comprehensive income** Generally, this refers to the total of the operating profits and holding gains of an organization for a financial period. The operating profit is the difference between the operating income and expenditure. The holding gains result from any increases in the value of assets between their dates of purchase and their dates of sale. Using historical cost accounting, no distinction is made between operating profits and holding gains. One criticism of historical accounting is that, by not recognizing holding gains, profits can be overstated and distributed. Decisions will be made by managers and investors on information that is misleading. The IASB regards comprehensive income as the change in equity over a financial period due to transactions and events separate from those transactions with the owners.

**comptroller** The title of the financial director in some organizations or chief financial officer of a group of companies. The title is more widely used in the United States than in the United Kingdom.

**concepts of capital** It is possible to regard capital using either the financial concept or physical concept. In the former, capital is the financial investment and equals the net assets of the entity. The physical or operating capability concept regards capital as the productive capacity of the entity. The particular concept applied will determine the approach to capital maintenance.

**conceptual framework** A statement of theoretical principles that provides guidance for financial accounting and reporting. Many countries have developed conceptual frameworks under different titles. In the United Kingdom, the conceptual framework is called the Statement of Principles and has been issued by the Accounting Standards Board (ASB). In the United States, the Financial Accounting Standards Board (FASB) issued Statements of Financial Accounting Concepts under its conceptual framework project. The International Accounting Standards Board's (IASB) conceptual framework is entitled "Framework for the Preparation and Presentation of Financial Statements." Despite the proclaimed value of conceptual frameworks, in most accounting regimes if there is a conflict between an accounting standard and a conceptual framework, the requirements of the standard prevail.

**condensed financial statements** This is the term used for the abbreviated financial statements prepared for an interim period. *Refer to* IAS 34.

**Confederation of Asian and Pacific Accountants (CAPA)** Established in 1976, CAPA represents over 31 accountancy organizations in 21 countries, with the objective of developing and coordinating the accounting profession in the Asia-Pacific region.

**confiscation risk** The risk that assets in a foreign country may be confiscated, expropriated, or nationalized. Circumstances may arise, particularly in times of war or political unrest, in which the owner's control of the assets may be severely curtailed.

**conglomerate** Several diverse organizations operating in totally different fields that merge into one group. The argument put forward for conglomerates is that risks are being diversified since operations are not confined to one particular industry or geographic location.

**conservatism** *See* prudence.

**consideration** A promise by one party to a contract of the economic benefits they will exchange for securing a promise from the other party to the contract. A consideration must have value and is essential if a contract, other than a deed, is to be valid. It usually consists of a promise to do or not to do something or to pay a sum of money.

**consignee** Any person or organization to whom goods are sent, usually to sell the goods on behalf of a principal (the consignor).

**consignment note** An official note that accompanies a consignment of goods in transit. It is signed by the consignee on delivery and acts as evidence that the goods have been received. The consignment note normally states the names and addresses of both consignor and consignee, details of goods, and gross weight, and states who has responsibility for insuring them while in transit.

**consignment stock** Goods held by one party (the dealer) but legally owned by another. The right to sell the goods or to return them unsold to the legal owner is held by the dealer. It can be difficult to distinguish between the commercial realities of the transaction and the legal agreement. This is because the right to return the goods is held by the dealer although this right is rarely exercised. It is a primary example of a situation in which the substance of the transaction must be accounted for and not the legal form. *Refer to* F.35.

**consignor** Any person or organization that sends goods to a consignee.

**consistency concept** A concept that ensures consistency of treatment of like items within each accounting period and from one period to the next. It also ensures that accounting policies are consistently applied. *Refer to* IAS 1.27.

**consolidated balance sheet** The balance sheet of a group of organizations providing the financial information contained in the individual financial statements of the parent of the group and its subsidiary undertakings, combined subject to any necessary consolidation adjustments. *Refer to* IAS 27 and IFRS 3.

**consolidated cash flow statement** The information contained in the individual cash flow statements of a group of organizations combined by consolidation, subject to any consolidation adjustments.

**consolidated financial statements** The financial statements of a group of organizations obtained by consolidation and presented as those of a single entity. *Refer to* IAS 27.4 and IAS 28.2.

**consolidated goodwill** The difference between the fair value of the consideration given by an acquiring organization when buying a business and the aggregate of the fair values of the separable net assets acquired. Goodwill is generally a positive amount and is treated as an intangible asset subject to an impairment review, at least annually. *Refer to* IAS 38.

**consolidated income and expenditure account** The information contained in the individual income and expenditure accounts of a group of organizations combined by consolidation into a single document for the group. This is subject to any necessary consolidation adjustments. *Refer to* IAS 27 and IFRS 3.

**consolidated income statement** A combination of the individual income statements of the members of a group of organizations, subject to any consolidation adjustments.

**consolidated profit** The combined profit of a group of organizations presented in the consolidated income statement. Any intragroup items should be eliminated by consolidation.

**consolidation** The process of adjusting and combining financial information from the individual financial statements of a parent undertaking and its subsidiaries to prepare consolidated financial statements. These statements should present financial information for the group as a single economic entity. For example, if one subsidiary has sold a non-current asset to another subsidiary in the group for a profit, this transaction should be eliminated in both the consolidated income statement and the consolidated balance sheet. *Refer to* IAS 27.

**consolidation adjustments** Adjustments that need to be made in the process of the consolidation of the accounts of a group of organizations. If there have been intragroup transactions, such as sales from one subsidiary to another, any profits or losses resulting from these transactions should be eliminated from the consolidated financial statements.

**constraint** A shortage in production resources that prevents an organization from achieving higher levels of performance. A constraint results from the impact of a limiting factor (or principal budget factor) that must be eliminated or reduced before the constraint is removed. For example, at various times, a shortage of skilled labor, materials, production capacity, or market demand may constitute a limiting factor.

**construction contracts** Those contracts that are specifically negotiated for the construction of an asset or a combination of assets that are closely interrelated or interdependent in terms of their design, technology, or function or in terms of their ultimate purpose or use. *Refer to* IAS 11.3.

**constructive obligation** An obligation arising from the actions of an organization that leads others to expect that it will accept and discharge certain responsibilities. Past practice, published policies, or current announcements can give rise to third party expectations. *Refer to* IAS 37.10.

**Consultative Committee of Accountancy Bodies (CCAB)** The major accountancy professional bodies in the United Kingdom and Ireland first joined together in 1974 to form the CCAB. The Committee is a limited company with six members: The Institute of Chartered Accountants in England and Wales (ICAEW), The Institute of Chartered Accountants of Scotland (ICAS), The Institute of Chartered Accountants in Ireland (ICAI), The Association of Chartered Certified Accountants (ACCA), The Chartered Institute of Management Accountants (CIMA), The Chartered Institute of Public Finance and Accountancy (CIPFA). The President of ICAEW is the Chairman of CCAB. The Board of CCAB consists of six directors who are senior members of the six member bodies. CCAB provides a platform where matters affecting the profession as a whole can be coordinated to enable the profession to speak with a unified voice to the government.

**Consumer Price Index (CPI)** The measure of U.S. price levels calculated monthly by the Bureau of Labor Statistics. It is commonly known as the cost-of-living index and gives the cost of specific consumer items compared to the base year of 1967.

**contingencies** Potential gains and losses known to exist at the balance sheet date although the actual outcomes will only be known after one or more events have occurred or not occurred. *Refer to* IAS 37.

**contingency theory of management accounting** The theory holds that no single management accounting system can be implemented in all organizations or any one system is appropriate in different conditions in a single organization. It is claimed that management accounting systems are contingent upon the conditions that prevail at any time and in a particular organization. Management accounting systems, therefore, must be flexible to ensure that they can incorporate future changes. These include changes in the environment, competition, organizational structures, and technology.

**contingent asset** A possible asset whose existence will be confirmed by the occurrence or non-occurrence of uncertain events in the future. Such events are not wholly in the control of the organization. *Refer to* IAS 37.10.

**contingent consideration** A payment that is contingent on a particular event or events occurring. The concept is often used in relation to earn-out agreements.

**contingent contract** *See* earn-out agreement.

**contingent gain** A gain that depends upon the outcome of some contingency. For example, if an organization makes a substantial legal claim against another organization and the probability of success is very high, the former will have a contingent gain.

**contingent liability** A possible obligation that arises from past events, whose existence will be confirmed only by the occurrence of one or more uncertain future events not wholly within the organization's control. A present obligation that arises from past events whereby either the amount of the obligation cannot be measured reliably or it is not probable that a transfer of economic benefits will be required to settle the obligation. *Refer to* IAS 37.10.

**contingent rent** A part of a lease payment that is not fixed in amount or subject to change due to the passage of time. The rent is calculated on changes in other factors, for example, movements in future sales. *Refer to* IAS 17.4.

**contingent settlement provisions** Rights and obligations attached to a financial instrument where settlement in cash or equity is dependent on the outcome of uncertain future events that are beyond the control of the parties to the instrument. For example, a bond may have the provision that settlement will be in equity if the market price of the entity's shares exceed a specific price. *Refer to* IAS 32 and IAS 39.

**contingent share agreement** An agreement to issue shares that is dependent on the satisfaction of specified conditions. *Refer to* IAS 33.5.

**continuous improvement** *See* kaizen.

**continuous inventory** A system implemented to ensure that all inventory items are physically counted and reconciled with the accounting records shown on the bin cards and the inventory ledger within a specified period. Continuous inventory identifies the availability of each item of inventory and establishes when inventory levels reach reorder levels. If conducted properly, the system prevents the possibilities of deterioration, waste, and theft. It also avoids the substantial amount of work that is required to conduct one stock-take at the year-end.

**continuously contemporary accounting (cocoa)** A method of accounting that incorporates the recognition of general price level changes in the financial statements.

**contra accounts** An account that can be offset against another. For example, if Corporation A owes money to Corporation B and the latter also owes money to Corporation A, the accounts can be offset against each other, enabling both debts to be settled by one payment of any difference in the two amounts.

**contract** A legally binding agreement arising as a result of an offer by one party and acceptance by another. Several requirements must be met for the agreement to be binding. For example, there must be consideration, the parties have intention to create legal relations, the parties must be competent and be capable of making a contract, the agreement must be legal and not be rendered void by other legislation or regulation.

**contract for service** A contract undertaken by a self-employed individual. The distinction between a contract for service (self-employed) and a service contract (employee) is normally important in establishing various rights and responsibilities appertaining to the contract.

**contribution income statement** The presentation of an income statement using the variable (marginal) costing layout. Fixed costs are not charged to the individual products produced as in absorption costing but are treated as a deduction from the total contribution of all the products. The statement is useful for short-term decision-making. A simplified contribution income statement would appear as follows:

| | *Product A* | *Product B* | *Total* |
|---|---|---|---|
| Sales revenue | 12,000 | 9,000 | 21,000 |
| Variable costs | 6,500 | 4,500 | 11,000 |
| Contribution | 5,500 | 4,500 | 10,000 |
| Total fixed costs | | | 6,000 |
| Total profit | | | 4,000 |

**contribution margin** The contribution margin is the amount remaining to cover fixed costs and to provide a profit. It is calculated by deducting variable costs from revenue. The unit contribution margin is used in cost-volume-profit (CVP) analysis to determine the amount of break-even sales volume.

**contribution margin ratio** The contribution ratio is calculated by expressing the unit contribution margin as a percentage of the unit selling price. It measures the proportion of each sales dollar that contributes towards covering fixed costs and provide for profit. The unit contribution margin can be used in cost-volume-profit (CVP) analysis to identify the amount of break-even sales dollars.

**contributory pension plan** A plan in which employees must either contribute to receive pension or contribute additional amounts to the employers' contribution in order to enhance the benefits that they will receive.

**control** The ability to direct the financial and operating policies of another undertaking with the intention of gaining economic benefits from its activities. *Refer to* IAS 31.3.

**control accounts** Accounts designed to ensure the accuracy of record keeping. The balances on the control accounts should equal the sum of the balances on the individual subsidiary accounts. For example, the balance on the sales ledger control account equals the sum of all individual accounts receivable accounts. The purposes of control accounts are to obtain total figures of the individual accounts at any time without adding up all the balances on the individual records and to have a cross-check on the accuracy of the subsidiary records.

**controller** The chief accounting executive of an organization. The controller will normally be concerned with financial reporting, taxation, and auditing, but will leave the planning and control of finances to the treasurer.

**controlling interest** An interest in an organization that gives the power to govern the financial and operating policies so as to obtain benefits from its activities. In general, in order to gain a controlling interest in an organization, ownership or control of more than half the voting shares is required. In practice, an investor might control the organization with considerably less than half the shares if the ownership of the remainder shares is fragmented. *Refer to* IAS 27.

**control risk** This is part of the audit risk and arises from the possibility that errors in the financial statements will not be prevented or detected on a timely basis by the internal control system of an organization. An assessment of the control risk must be made for each audit objective. In assessing the control risk, an auditor will need to be familiar with the accounting and internal control systems and will test the effectiveness of them by means of compliance tests.

**convergence of accounting standards** The process pursued by the International Accounting Standards Board (IASB) of eliminating the present differences between national accounting standards and the avoidance of future differences to achieve international accounting harmonization.

**conversion cost** Direct labor and overheads costs that are incurred in converting materials into finished goods. Overheads should be charged on a systematic and rational basis with fixed overheads being based on normal production levels. *Refer to* IAS 2.12.

**convertible** A bond issue by an organization that can be converted into shares at the holder's option during the life of the convertible. The holder has the right, but not the obligation, to exchange it for shares or to hold the convertible until maturity. The exchange ratio of shares to bonds (called the conversion premium) is fixed in advance. The dates on which the option to convert (called the conversion intervals) are also set in advance.

**convertible unsecured loan stock (CULS)** Unsecured loan stock that entitles the holder to exchange the loan stock for another security, usually ordinary shares in the company, at some future date.

**cook the books** A derogatory term denoting the falsification of financial records and statements to mislead others regarding the financial performance and position of an organization or in order to commit embezzlement.

**co-operative entities** *Refer to* IFRIC 2.

**copyright** Protection by statute or law, especially for artists and authors, the exclusive right to publish their works or to determine who has the right to publish. It is an intangible asset and should be amortized over the period for which the copyright is granted. *Refer to* IAS 38.

**corporate failure prediction** The application of statistical techniques to predict whether an organization is likely to go into liquidation. One model, devised by Altman, uses financial statements of an organization and applies multivariate analysis to arrive at a Z-score. An Altman's Z-score of 1.8 or less is taken as an indication that the organization may fail. Another technique with a broader approach is Argenti's failure model. It calculates scores for an organization based on defects of the organization, management mistakes, and the symptoms of failure.

**corporate governance** Corporate governance is defined by the Organization for Economic Cooperation and Development (OECD) as the framework by which business corporation are directed and controlled. The framework specifies the distribution of rights and responsibilities among different participants in the corporation, whose interests the Board of Directors and senior managers serve, and how they should discharge their accountability to the shareholders and other stakeholders. Corporate governance provides the structure through which company objectives are set, and the means of attaining those objectives and monitoring performance.

A series of financial scandals in North America and Europe in the late 1980s and early 1990s led to the development of national guidelines on corporate governance. In the United States, the Treadway Report on

Fraudulent Financial Reporting was followed by the Cadbury Committee Report on the Financial Aspects of Corporate Governance in the United Kingdom. Other guidelines were also issued by the Greenbury Committee, Hampel Committee and Turnbull Committee. This is followed by the legislation of the Sarbanes-Oxley Act in the United States in 2002.

**corporate modeling** The use of simulation models to assist the management of an organization in carrying out planning and decision making. A budget is an example of a corporate model.

**corporate report** A comprehensive package of information that describes the economic activities of an organization. Financial statements will be one component of a corporate report, but it will also include qualitative information.

**corporate secretary** The corporate secretary is a senior corporate officer with wide-ranging responsibilities. The officer serves as a focal point for communication with the Board of Directors, senior management, and the company's shareholders. Corporate secretaries occupy a key role in the administration of critical corporate matters. The corporate secretary is often a confidante and counselor to the Chief Executive Officer and other members of senior management, especially on corporate governance affairs. In some companies, the role of the corporate secretary as corporate governance adviser is formalized with a title such as Chief Governance Officer and this is added to the officer's existing title. The professional body for the corporate secretary is the American Society of Corporate Secretaries (ASCS). *See* chartered secretary, company secretary.

**corporate social reporting** The voluntary reporting to various groups of stakeholders on issues that may be considered of interest. From time to time, corporations disclose such information in their annual financial statements, although this remains largely a voluntary activity. Examples include employee reports, ethical reports, and green reports.

**corporation** A number of persons authorized by law to act as one person and having rights and liabilities distinct from the individuals forming the corporation. Royal charter, statute, or common law may create the artificial personality.

**corridor** Specifically, the range of an organization's best estimate of postemployment benefit obligations. In general, it is used to describe the range between a minimum and maximum amount. *Refer to* IAS 19.95.

**cost accounting** A subsection of management accounting that uses specific techniques and methods to collect, process, and present financial and quantitative data within an organization. It is used to determine the cost of cost centers, cost units, and various operations.

**cost behavior** The changes that occur to total costs as a result of changes in activity levels within an organization. This arises because certain costs respond differently at various levels of activity. The total of fixed costs tends to remain unaffected by changes in activity levels in the short term. The total of variable costs tends to increase or decrease in proportion to activity. There are also some costs that demonstrate semivariable cost behavior and, thus, have both fixed and variable elements. The study of cost behavior is important in cost-volume-profit (CVP) analysis and also when applying decision-making techniques.

**cost-benefit analysis** A technique that takes into account the estimated costs to be incurred by a proposed investment or activity and the estimated benefits likely to arise from it. In a financial appraisal, the benefits may arise from an increase in the revenue from a product or service, from saved costs, or from other cash inflows. In a socioeconomic appraisal, however, the benefits due to time saved or fewer accidents resulting from road improvements are often required to be valued.

**cost center** A responsibility center in which the manager is accountable for costs. The area may be a function, department, individual, machine, or activity, and it is a separately identifiable area of the organization.

**cost convention** The measurement basis for entering economic transactions into the accounting records. The cost convention used may be based on historical cost, current cost, realizable value, or present value.

**cost driver** A measure of activity that causes cost to be incurred and is also known as activity base or allocation base. Examples are labor hours, machine hours, or some other measure of activity whose change may cause a corresponding change in the cost object. *See* activity-based costing.

**cost life cycle** The sequence of activities in an organization that begins with research and development, followed by design, manufacturing, marketing, distribution, and customer service.

**cost estimation** The process of developing a well-defined relationship between a cost object and its cost drivers in order to determine a cost equation that will predict cost variables.

**cost object** Any product, department, project, activity, or responsibility center to which costs are measured and assigned.

**cost of capital** The cost, expressed in terms of an interest rate, that an organization pays for the capital used in financing its activities. Since the capital of an organization can be a mix of equity share capital, loan capital, and debt, there is considerable debate as to whether or not the cost of capital increases as leveraging increases. Another approach to establishing the cost of capital is to compute a unique Weighted Average Cost of Capital (WACC) for each organization, based on its particular mix of capital sources. The cost of capital is often used as a hurdle rate in Discounted Cash Flow (DCF) calculations.

**cost of goods sold** The costs to the seller of the products sold to customers in a financial period with adjustments made for opening and closing inventories. This figure will appear on the "Cost of Sales" format for the income statement. *Refer to* IAS 1.

**cost of goods sold percentage** *See* gross margin.

**cost of inventories** Purchase costs, conversion costs, and other costs incurred in bringing inventories to their present location and condition. *Refer to* IAS 2.10.

**cost of quality report** A report that highlights the costs of prevention, appraisal, and internal and external failures. The quality matrix in a cost of quality report illustrates the different categories of quality costs for each operating and support function.

**cost-plus contract** A contract entered into by a supplier in which the goods or services provided to the customer are charged at cost plus an agreed percentage mark-up or at cost plus a fixed fee. This method of pricing is very common if the cost of production of the commodity is unknown, and is frequently used in the construction industry. *Refer to* IAS 11.3.

**cost pools** Costs that are collected into meaningful groups and are assigned to cost objects.

**costs per equivalent unit** The unit cost of product calculated by dividing the total production costs by the number of equivalent whole units. It is used in process costing to allocate product costs between processing departments.

**cost-to-retail ratio** A ratio expressing the cost of goods as a percentage of the retail price of goods. *See* retail method.

**cost-volume-profit (CVP) analysis** A decision-making technique used in costing and management accounting to analyze the interrelationships among sales price, volume, the impact on profitability due to changes in the fixed or variable costs, and the levels of activity required to generate a break-even volume or a targeted profit level.

**coupon** One of several dated slips attached to a bearer bond, which must be presented to the agents of the issuer to obtain an interest payment or dividend. Eurobonds are issued in this form. The coupon rate is the stated rate of interest based on a bond's par value as opposed to the yield in which the interest is calculated as a percentage of the market price.

**coupon stripping** A financial process in which the coupons are detached from a bearer bond and then sold separately as a source of cash, with no capital repayment. The bond, without its coupons, becomes a zero coupon bond and is also sold separately. The process represents a type of synergy, in which the sum of the values of the parts is expected to be worth more than the whole.

**covenant** Generally, a promise made in a deed that may or may not be under seal. A covenant is frequently used as a means of providing funds to a body of persons or a trust established for charitable purposes. In such a deed of covenant, the payer covenants to pay an agreed sum to the charity. Covenants may be concerning the use of land, frequently to restrict the activities of a new owner or tenant (for instance, a covenant not to sell alcohol or build a casino). Specifically, in financial terms it refers to a loan agreement that includes a series of undertakings or agreements, the breaching of which will make the loan repayable immediately. For example, a company obtaining a loan from a bank may agree that the undertakings are split between ratio covenants and non-ratio covenants.

**covered call** This is an investment strategy involving the purchase of shares with the simultaneous selling of a call option on those shares. The principle is that if the share prices fall, the investor will suffer this loss but it will in part be offset by the premium on the option.

**covered put** This is an investment strategy involving the purchase of shares with the simultaneous purchase of a put option. The principle is that if the price of the shares falls, the investor exercises the put and thus limits the loss to the amount of the premium paid for the option.

**creative accounting** Accounting practices that result in the financial statements presenting a more optimistic picture of the financial performance of an organization than is warranted. With some economic transactions, there are ambiguities or omissions in the regulations that permit the unscrupulous to mislead the unwary. Examples of transactions that have been subject to creative accounting in the past include consignment stocks, sale and purchase agreements, and off-balance sheet finance. Much creative accounting is fraudulent, and it attempts to present the apparent legal form of a transaction rather than the actual economic substance. *Refer to* F.35.

**credit note** A document expressing the indebtedness of the organization issuing it, usually to a customer. When goods are supplied to a customer, an invoice is issued. If the customer returns all or part of the goods, the invoice is wholly or partially canceled by a credit note or a refund of any payments made.

**creditor days ratio** A ratio that gives an estimate of the average number of days credit taken by an organization before the creditors are paid. It is calculated by the formula:

$$(\text{Accounts payable} \times 365)/\text{annual purchase on credit}$$

**creditors** Businesses or individuals to whom an organization owes money, for example, unpaid suppliers of raw materials.

**creditors' buffer** The fixed capital of an organization that cannot be reduced or distributed except with special permission. The fixed capital base gives creditors some reassurance that they may be able to obtain settlement if the organization encounters financial difficulties.

**credit rating** An evaluation of the level of credit, and the risk attached, that can be given to an individual or an organization. Banks have provided confidential trade references, but credit rating agencies also gather information from a wide range of sources such as the courts, bankruptcy proceedings, and professional debt collectors.

**credit risk** The risk that one party to a contract will not perform as required and, consequently, the other party will suffer a financial loss (for instance, when a borrower is not able to repay the principal or the interest).

**cross-border listing** The listing by an organization of its shares and other securities on official stock exchanges in more than one country. This allows its shares or securities to be actively traded in more than one country, but the organization must meet the listing requirements of each stock exchange. If international accounting standards are not recognized by the individual exchanges, the organization must either draw up financial statements meeting the requirements of each country or publish a reconciliation statement showing the impact of the differing accounting requirements.

**cross-default clause** The most onerous clause in a loan agreement, stating that if the borrower defaults on one loan, any other loans may become repayable. The cross-default clause is activated when another lender is in a position to call a default on its loan or an event occurs which, with the passage of time, is capable of giving any lender the right to call a default.

**cross-sectional analysis** The comparison of accounting ratios of one organization with those of others in order to assess the profitability, liquidity, and capital structure of the company.

**crown jewel option** A tactic used by an organization to defend itself against a hostile takeover bid. An option is written that allows a sympathetic third party to acquire one or more parts of the business at a favorable price if control of the defending company is lost to the unwelcome predator. The granting of such an option may not always be in the best interest of the shareholders of the defending company.

**cum** A prefix used to include specified benefits when a security is quoted or being sold. Cum all, cum div, cum coupon, cum rights mean that the benefits of the security belongs to the buyer. It has the opposite meaning to ex.

**cumulative preference shares** A preference share that entitles the owner to receive dividends not paid in previous years. Unless otherwise agreed, organizations are not obliged to pay dividends on preference shares if there are insufficient earnings. Cumulative preference shares promise the eventual payment of these dividends in arrears, before the payment of dividends on ordinary shares, if the organization commences to make profits in the future.

**cumulative preferred stock** *See* cumulative preference shares.

**currency exposure** The effect on the worth of an organization due to changes in exchange rates in relation to its financial currency.

**currency risk** The risk that the value of a financial instrument will vary in relation to currency exchange rate changes. *Refer to* IAS 32.52.

**current asset** An asset that is part of operating activities and expected to be realized within 12 months or one operating cycle if longer. Examples of current assets are accounts receivable and inventories. *Refer to* IAS 1.57.

**current-asset investment** An investment intended to be held for less than one year.

**current cost** The cost of assets at the amount of cash or cash equivalents that would have to be paid if the same or an equivalent asset was acquired currently. With liabilities, it is the cost at the undiscounted amount of cash or cash equivalents that would be required to settle the obligation currently. *Refer to* F.100(b).

**current cost accounting (CCA)** A method of accounting in which the concept of capital maintenance is based on maintaining the operating capability of a business. Assets are valued at their worth to the business. This is known as their deprival value and is the loss that a business would suffer if it were to be deprived of the use of the asset. This may be the replacement cost of the asset, its net realizable value, or its economic value to the business. Current cost accounting ensures that a business maintains its operating capacity by separating holding gains from operating profits to prevent them from being distributed to investors. The current cost accounting profit figure is derived by making a number of adjustments to the historical cost accounting income statement. The method was experimented with in the United Kingdom but did not establish itself as an acceptable alternative to historical cost accounting.

**current liabilities** Amounts owed and due to be paid within one year from the balance-sheet date or within the normal course of the organization's operating cycle. These generally consist of accounts payable, amounts owed to group and related companies, taxation, social-security creditors, accruals, deferred income, payments received on account, bank overdrafts, and short-term loans. Current liabilities are distinguished from long-term liabilities on the balance sheet. *Refer to* IAS 1.60.

**current purchasing power (CPP) accounting** A method of accounting in which profit for distribution is calculated after allowing for the maintenance of the purchasing power of the investors' capital. The Retail Price Index (RPI) is used to adjust for general price changes to ensure that the investors' capital maintains the same monetary purchasing power.

**current ratio** The ratio of the current assets of a business to the current liabilities, expressed as x:1. It is used as a test of liquidity and to give an overview performance measure of working capital management. For example, if the current assets are $40,000 and current liabilities are $20,000, the current ratio is 2:1. Care must be taken when making comparisons between companies to ensure that any industry differences are recognized. The acid test ratio is regarded as a more rigorous test of liquidity.

**current replacement cost** The estimated cost of replacing an asset, or the services provided by the asset, at the balance-sheet date. Current replacement costs may be difficult to establish if, for example, the asset cannot be replaced as a result of obsolescence or if it is unique. Normally, current replacement cost is higher than historic cost.

**current tax** The amount of income tax payable in respect of a tax profit and recoverable in respect of a tax loss.

**current value accounting** A method of accounting in which changes in specific prices should be recognized on the financial statements rather than recognizing the changes in the general price level. Assets can be valued at their net realizable value, current replacement cost, or net present value, or a combination of these.

**cycle billing** The method of sending invoices to customers at different time intervals. For example, using the alphabet as a basis, customers starting with the letter A may be invoiced on the first day, B on the second day, and so on. Large organizations with many customers paying relatively small amounts find this an effective practice. This method has the advantage of spreading the workload in the organization and ensuring a steady inflow of cash, providing that there are many customers with comparable accounts.

**cycle time** The amount of time between receipt of a customer order and shipment of the order.

# D

**daisy chain** The creation of a false level of activity by selling and repurchasing the same items continuously in a short period. The practice may be used to attempt to persuade the markets that there is a substantial interest in specific securities, and consequently the price will increase as the market responds favorably.

**damages** Compensation, in monetary form, for a loss or injury, breach of contract, tort, or infringement of a right. The damages awarded by the court may be intended to restore the injured party to the original position. In addition, damages may be set so high as to be considered punitive.

**dangling debit** The deduction of an expense directly from the total shareholders' fund. This was a frequently used method for writing off goodwill in the United Kingdom before regulations were changed.

**dawn raid** An attempt by an investor to acquire a significant holding in the equity of a target organization by acquiring all shares available as soon as the stock exchange opens for the day. This is normally carried out without the knowledge of the target organization and is the prelude to a takeover bid.

**days' sales in inventory** A ratio that is used to assess the effectiveness of an organization in managing its inventory. It is calculated by expressing the amount of inventory in number of days' sales. For example, if 10 items per day are sold and 300 items are held in inventory, this represents 30 days' (300/10) sales in inventory.

**days' sales in receivables** A ratio that is used to assess the effectiveness of an organization's credit control. It is calculated by expressing the amount of receivables in number of days' sales. For example, if $2,000 worth of sales are made each day and the outstanding balance of the total accounts receivable is $100,000, this represents 50 ($100,000/$2,000) days' sales.

**debenture** A long-term loan usually taken by an organization and repayable at a fixed date. Some debentures are irredeemable securities and are referred to as perpetual debentures. Most debentures pay a fixed rate of interest, and this interest must be paid before a dividend is paid to shareholders. In the United Kingdom, debentures are normally secured on the borrower's assets, although some, known as naked debentures or unsecured debentures, are not. In the United States, debentures are usually unsecured, relying only on the reputation of the borrower. Some debentures are convertible and can be converted into ordinary shares on a specified date and at a predetermined rate.

**debenture redemption reserve** A capital reserve into which amounts are transferred from the income statement for debentures that are redeemable at a future date. The aim is to limit the profits available for distribution, although the reserve does not provide the actual funds for redeeming the debentures.

**debit and credit rules** The rules stipulated in the method of double-entry bookkeeping. The fundamental principles are: a debit entry increases asset and expense accounts, but decreases liability and revenue accounts; a credit entry increases liability, capital, and revenue accounts, but decreases asset and expense accounts.

**debt covenant** *See* covenant.

**debt discount** *See* zero coupon bonds.

**debt-equity ratio** Also known as the leverage or gearing ratio, it analyzes the financial structure of a business. The long-term debt is expressed as a percentage of its equity. A highly leveraged (geared) organization is one whereby the debt is higher than the equity, compared to organizations in a similar industry. A highly leveraged organization offers higher returns to investors when it is performing well but enters into a loss very quickly in an economic downturn. The debt-equity ratio may also be computed as the ratio of debt to the sum of debt plus equity.

**debt instrument** A formal document setting out the terms and conditions attached to a short-term loan.

**debtor collection period** *See* accounts receivable collection period.

**debtors** Those who owe money for the sales of goods or provision of services. *See* accounts receivable.

**debt restructuring** The adjustment of a debt, either through legal action or by agreement between the interested parties, to assist the debtor in meeting financial obligations.

**decentralization** The delegation by the central authority of decision-making responsibilities to the subunits and divisions of an organization. It is normal for boundaries to be set on the extent of the decisions that can be made and the activities that can be pursued. As part of decentralization process, it is imperative that divisional managers be provided with information relevant to their needs and responsibilities. The advantages claimed for decentralization are that local managers are more knowledgeable about local situations and circumstances, are more motivated, and thus, have greater control over problems and the ability to take action directly. The disadvantages of decentralization are the possibility of wasteful competition among divisions, lack of central coordination, loss of synergies, and the potential for leaks in confidential information.

**decision-making objective** One of the objectives of financial statements is to meet the needs of users in making economic decisions, for example, to hold or sell investments. Since financial statements mainly present the effects of past events and do not include non-financial information, there are limitations on their value to users. *Refer to* F.14.

**decision model** A model that identifies the various elements in a business decision and their relationships to each other. The model is designed to provide a solution to meet the objectives of the organization and to recognize any constraints that may exist. Decision models include decision trees, discounted cash flow, and cost-volume-profit analysis.

**declaration of dividend** The announcement by directors of an organization that a dividend of a certain amount is recommended to be paid to the shareholders. *See* dividend.

**declining balance method** *See* diminishing-balance method.

**decommissioning costs** The costs incurred in ceasing an operation or activity either entirely or at a particular location. The costs include the costs of removing all non-current assets and rectifying any environmental damage such as closing down a nuclear power station.

**deemed cost** A surrogate for the actual cost or depreciated cost at a given date. *Refer to* IFRS 1.A.

**deep market** A market in which a substantial number of transactions can take place in a short period of time without moving the price of the underlying commodity, currency, or financial instrument.

**deep pocket** A description of a person or organization assumed to have substantial wealth and who would, therefore, be worth suing.

**defalcation** Embezzlement of property belonging to another party.

**default** A failure to fulfill a contractual or other legal obligation. Defaults include failure to settle a debt and failure to defend legal proceedings.

**defective accounts** Accounts that do not comply with legislation or accounting standards. In some accounting regimes, corrected accounts must be issued to replace defective accounts.

**defended takeover bid** A takeover bid for an organization in which the directors of the target organization oppose the bid.

**defensive interval ratio** A ratio that evaluates the ability of a business to satisfy its current debts. It is calculated by deducting inventory from current assets and then dividing by the projected daily operational expenditure. The ratio establishes the number of days an organization can operate without requiring an injection of funds.

**deferral** This refers to a delay in recognizing a cash payment as an expense or a cash receipt as revenue.

**deferred consideration agreement** An agreement in which payment of the consideration is delayed either until a certain date or until a specified and certain event has occurred. *See* earn-out agreement.

**deferred expense** A payment made for goods or services before they are received. The cash expenditure is recorded as an asset initially but will be recognized as an expense in the future as it is used up over time or through the normal course of business. It is also referred to as prepayment or prepaid expense.

**deferred income** A payment that has been received prior to the financial period in which it falls due. It is not shown in the income statement of the period but is shown as a deferred credit balance in the balance sheet. Amounts are transferred from the deferred credit balance to the income statement of future periods until the deferred credit balance in the balance sheet is brought to zero.

**deferred ordinary share** A type of ordinary share where dividends are paid only after all other types of ordinary shares have been paid or where little or no dividend is paid for a fixed number of years. Such shares may entitle their owners to a large share of profit.

**deferred revenue** Cash receipt that is recorded as a liability but will be recognized as revenue in the future when it is earned. It is also referred to as unearned revenue.

**deferred tax assets** Amount of income tax recoverable in future periods with respect to deductible temporary differences. *Refer to* IAS 12.5.

**deferred tax liabilities** Amount of income tax payable in future periods with respect to deductible temporary differences. *Refer to* IAS 12.5.

**defined benefit plans** Postemployment benefit plans that specify the benefits to be received by employees on retirement. The benefits are normally calculated according to a formula incorporating years of service and salary levels. *Refer to* IAS 19.7.

**defined contribution plans** Postemployment benefit plans in which the benefits to be received by the employees are related to the final value of the contributions paid plus investment income. The rate of contribution is normally specified, and the amount of benefits an individual receives will depend on the size of the fund accumulated and the annuity that can be obtained from it at the date of retirement. *Refer to* IAS 19.7.

**deflation** The situation in which there is a general decrease in prices.

**degearing** A reduction in the gearing of an organization carried out through a reduction in the loan capital relative to the total equity.

**delta value** The relationship that is represented by the change in the price of a call option divided by the change in the price of the underlying asset. The relationship is only valid for small price changes. The delta value indicates how much of the asset that the writer of the option should hold in order to hedge the risk of the option position. Delta value is also referred to as the hedge ratio.

**demerger** A business strategy by which a corporation divides its total activities so they are subsequently conducted by two or more independent corporations.

**depletion** The using up of an asset, especially a mineral asset. For example, an oil field is depleted by the extraction of crude oil.

**depletion accounting** The calculation of the annual depreciation charge to the income statement for a wasting asset by calculating the rate the asset is being depleted through use.

**deposit component** A contractual component that falls outside the scope of IAS 39, since it is not a separate instrument. *Refer to* IFRS 4.A.

**depository receipt** A certificate issued by a depository, bank, or other company stating what has been deposited for safekeeping.

**deposits in transit** Cash receipts that have arrived at company's bank too late in the current month to be credited to the depositor's bank statement. An adjustment will therefore be required to the bank reconciliation statement.

**depreciable amount** The cost or value of a non-current asset less its residual value used as the basis for calculating the depreciation charge for the period. When using the diminishing-balance method of depreciation, the depreciable amount is the carrying amount of the asset at the end of the previous financial period. However, when the straight-line method of depreciation is used, the depreciable amount is based on cost or other amount substituted for cost. *Refer to* IAS 16.6.

**depreciation** The measure of the cost or revalued amount of the economic benefits of a non-current asset that have been consumed during a financial period. This includes the wearing out, using up or other reduction in the useful economic life of a non-current asset. A provision for depreciation can be computed by means of different techniques, including the straight-line method, diminishing-balance method, the sum-of-the-digits method, the production-unit method, and the revaluation method. The depreciation reduces the book value of the asset and is charged in the income statement. The term is specifically applied to tangible non-current assets. For intangible assets the term amortization is normally used. *Refer to* IAS 16.41.

**derecognition** The removal from the balance sheet of assets and liabilities that had previously been recognized in the financial statements of an organization. *Refer to* IAS 39.

**deregulation** The removal from market restrictions and controls imposed by a regulatory authority.

**derivative** A financial instrument that derives its value from an underlying asset, interest rate, currency exchange rate, or index. Thus, the value of the derivative has a strong correlation with a related or underlying commodity or financial instrument. The most common derivatives are futures and options. These standard products can be customized with regard to maturity, quantity, or pricing structure for a particular client. A derivative market is a futures or options market derived from a cash market. The standard specifies that derivatives change their value in response to changes in other variables, require a low or no initial net investment, and are settled at a future date. *Refer to* IAS 39.9.

**detection risk** The risk that an auditor will fail to detect any misstatements that have occurred. Unlike the control risk and the inherent risk, the level of the detection risk can be directly controlled by the auditor, who can modify his program of testing.

**devaluation** The action of a government to lower the value of its currency relative to gold or the currency of other countries. The decision is normally made in order to improve a country's economy by encouraging exports through lower prices. The disadvantage is that it increases the price of imports, but this may have the effect of reducing them.

**development costs** The expenditure incurred by an organization in introducing or improving a product, process, system, or service. Such costs can be capitalized if they meet the recognized criteria for intangible assets. *Refer to* IAS 38.45.

**differential cost analysis** *See* incremental analysis.

**differential costs** *See* incremental costs.

**differential pricing** The different pricing of the same product when it is supplied to different customers or different market segments. This approach is based on the principle that to achieve maximum market penetration, the price charged should be what a particular market will bear.

**diluted earnings per share** The amount of net profit for a financial period that is attributable to ordinary shareholders divided by the weighted average numbers of shares outstanding during the period, both adjusted for the effects of all diluted potential ordinary shares. *Refer to* IAS 33.1.

**dilution** A reduction in earnings per share or an increase in loss per share as a consequence of assuming that convertible instruments are converted, that options or warrants are exercised, or that ordinary shares are issued upon the satisfaction of specified conditions. *Refer to* IAS 33.5.

**dilutive potential ordinary shares** Potential ordinary shares that would decrease earnings per share if converted to ordinary shares. *Refer to* IAS 33.41.

**diminishing-balance method** A method of computing the depreciation of a non-current asset in a financial period. The percentage to be charged against income is based on the carrying value at the beginning of the period. This has the effect of reducing the annual depreciation charge against profits each year. The annual percentage to be applied to the annual depreciated value is determined by the formula:

$$\text{Rate of depreciation} = 1 - (s/c)^{1/n}$$

where n = estimated life in years, s = estimated scrap value at the end of its useful life, and c = original cost.

**direct costing** *See* variable costing.

**direct hour** An hour spent working on a product, service, or cost unit of an organization. It is usually expressed as a direct labor hour, machine hour, or standard hour.

**direct labor** The cost of employees working solely on the production of a product, service, or cost unit, such as machine operators, or assembly and finishing operators.

**direct materials** Materials that are directly incorporated in the final product or cost unit of an organization.

**direct method of preparing the cash flow statements** The construction of a cash flow statement by deducting cash payment from cash receipts to identify the net cash relating to operating activities. *Refer to* IAS 7.

**direct method of service department cost allocation** A method of allocating service department costs directly to the production departments.

**director** A person appointed to carry out the day-to-day management of a company. The directors of a company, collectively known as the board of directors, usually act together, although power may be conferred on one or more directors to exercise executive power.

**directors' interests** The interests held by directors in the shares and debentures of the company of which they are a director. The directors' interests can also include options on shares and debentures of the company.

**directors' remuneration** The amounts received by directors from their position or employment, including all salaries, fees, wages, perquisites, and other profit as well as certain expenses and benefits paid or provided by the employer that are considered to form part of the remuneration package.

**direct write-off method** The procedure of writing off bad debts as they occur instead of creating a provision. This approach is acceptable in an organization with a relatively low level of bad debts.

**disbursement** A payment made by a professional person, such as a solicitor or banker, on behalf of a client. This is claimed back when the client receives an account for the professional services.

**disclaimer of opinion** The opinion expressed by an auditor when the audit report is being qualified as a result of the effect of a limitation on the scope of an audit. If the limitation of scope is so material that the auditor has not been able to obtain sufficient evidence to support an opinion on the financial statements, a disclaimer of opinion must be expressed.

**disclosure** Specifically, the publication of financial and non-financial information to those interested in the financial, operational, and economic activities of an organization. The information may be restricted to the financial statements complying with GAAP but may include other financial and non-financial information. Accounting standards set out the information to be disclosed by organizations.

**discontinued operations** These are operations that can be separately identified by an organization. The operations represent a separate major line of business or geographical area, and the organization has plans to dispose of or to sale. *Refer to* IFRS 5.A.

**Discounted Cash Flow (DCF)** The predicted stream of cash flows over the estimated life of a project. The cash flows are discounted by using a cost of capital or hurdle rate to present values or discounted values in order to determine whether the project is likely to be financially feasible. Several appraisal approaches use the DCF principle, namely the Net Present Value (NPV), the Internal Rate of Return (IRR), and the profitability index.

**discounted value** *See* present value.

**discount factor** A factor, when multiplied by a particular year's predicted cash flow, brings the cash flow to a present value. The factor takes into consideration the number of years from the inception of the project and the hurdle rate that the project is expected to earn before it can be regarded as feasible. The factor is computed using the formula:

$$\text{Discount factor} = 1/(1 + r)^t$$

where r = hurdle rate required and t = the number of years from project inception.

**discount rate** The rate of interest applied in a discounted cash flow appraisal calculation. Considerable judgment is required in establishing the appropriate rate for a project. Some organizations apply the cost-of-capital rate adjusted by a risk factor based on the risk characteristics of the proposed investment. Others use the interest rate that the funds could earn if invested in an alternative opportunity. Some organizations establish a policy hurdle rate as the minimum acceptable rate before a project is considered.

**discovery value accounting** The method of accounting used for extractive enterprises, such as oil and gas.

**discrete approach** The measuring of income for an interim period, that is, less than 12 months, by regarding each interim period as separate. *Refer to* IAS 34. *See* integral approach.

**discretionary costs** Costs that are incurred and the amount determined by a specific management decision and are not related directly to levels of activity. Management can, therefore, change these costs since they are avoidable in the short term. A characteristic of such costs is that they are often for a specified amount or subject to a specific formula such as percentage of sales revenue. Examples include advertising, research expenditure, training costs.

**discussion document** A document or memorandum published by some national standard setters prior to issuing a financial accounting standard. The document specifies the topic under consideration, describes the alternative accounting treatments, and explains the perceived advantages and disadvantages of each treatment. Responses to the discussion document will determine whether work will proceed on an accounting standard.

**disinflation** A type of deflation used as part of a government's strategy to reduce inflation by restricting demand.

**disintermediation** The flow of funds between borrowers and lenders, excluding the participation of intermediaries (such as brokers and bankers). Individuals or organizations with excess cash, instead of depositing it with a bank, lend it direct to an end-user. Commercial paper is an example of disintermediation whereby organizations borrow from each other. The improvement in cost has to be offset by the increase in the credit risk.

**disposal group** A group of assets and possibly some directly associated liability that are being held for sale by an entity. The disposal group could be a group of cash generating units, a single cash generating unit or part of a cash generating unit. *Refer to* IFRS 5.

**disposal value** *See* net residual value.

**dissolution** The formal cessation of a business entity. For example, the breaking up of a partnership on the death of one of the partners.

**distributable profits** The profits of a company that are legally available for distribution to shareholders. They normally consist of a company's accumulated realized profits after deducting all realized losses. National regulations or an organization's own constitution may place restrictions on the amount of distributable profits.

**distributable reserves** The retained earnings of an organization that may be legally distributed in the form of dividends.

**diversification** The strategic move by a manufacturer or trader into another range of products, services, or markets. This may be achieved by acquiring organizations already serving the target markets or by extending existing facilities. It is usually undertaken to minimize reliance on one market or to enhance the growth of the organization. It can also mean the lowering of investment risk. This is achieved by spreading an investment portfolio over a wider range of organizations and industries, to benefit from variations in performance levels and to avoid severe losses.

**divestment** The strategic decision of selling or closing down of one or more operating activities of a business.

**dividend** The distribution of all or part of the earnings of an organization, normally by a declaration of the directors, to the holders of equity investments in proportion to their holdings of a particular class of capital. Dividends declared or proposed after the balance sheet date should not appear as a liability. *Refer to* IAS 10.

**dividend cover** A ratio that assesses the potential ability of an organization to pay dividends in the future. It is calculated by dividing the profits available for distribution by the amount of dividend. For example, a net dividend of $400,000 paid by a corporation showing a net profit of $1M will show a dividend cover of 2.5 times. Dividend cover is a measure of the profitability that dividend payments will be sustained. Low cover might make it difficult to pay the same level of dividends if there is poor performance in a future period. High cover implies that the corporation retains its earnings for investment in the business and is likely to meet future dividend payments. The dividend cover can also be expressed as the dividend payout ratio.

**dividend growth model** Shareholders normally expect dividends to increase each year and not to remain constant. The fundamental theory of share values state that the market price of a share is the present value of the discounted future cash flows or revenues from the share. Given an expected constant annual growth in dividends, the market value is illustrated in the formula below. It can also be adapted for uneven growth.

$$P_0 = \frac{d}{r}$$

where $P_0$ is the market price of the share ex div (that is, excluding any current dividend that might be payable), d is the expected annual dividend per share and r is the shareholders' cost of capital, that is, the required rate of return. If the dividend increases annually into the future at a constant rate, g, the following formula may be used:

$$P_0 = \frac{d_0(1+g)}{(r-g)} = \frac{d_1}{(r-g)}$$

where $d_0$ is the dividend in the current year (Year 0) and so $d_0$ (1 + g) is the expected future dividend in Year 1($d_1$). Again, $P_0$ is the market value of the share ex div.

**dividend payout ratio** A ratio expressing the dividends per share as a percentage of earnings per share, thus demonstrating the proportion of earnings paid to shareholders. (for instance, if net earnings are $100,000, cash dividends are $40,000, and common shares outstanding are 10,000, the payout ratio is $4,000/$10,000 = 0.40 or 40%). In general, mature companies tend to have high dividend payout ratios compared to fast-growing companies that reinvest all earnings and pay no dividend.

**dividend policy** An organization's policy on the proportion of profits that should be distributed to shareholders and the proportion of profits that should be retained. The directors will be aware of market expectations when determining the organization's dividend policy.

**dividend valuation model** The assumption that the market value of shares is directly related to the expected future dividends on the shares. This is calculated by the following formula:

$$P_0 + \frac{d}{(1+r)^1} + \frac{d}{(1+r)^2} + \frac{d}{(1+r)^3}. = \frac{d}{r}, \text{ so } r = \frac{d}{P_0}$$

where $P_0$ is the market value of the share ex div, r is the shareholders' cost of capital, and d is the annual dividend per share starting at Year 1 and then continuing annually into perpetuity.

**dividend yield** A ratio that allows comparison of dividends with the return obtained from other forms of investment. It is calculated by expressing the gross dividends paid per share as a percentage of the market price of ordinary shares. The gross dividend yield is used in preference to a net dividend yield so that investors can make a direct comparison with gross interest yields from other forms of investment. (for instance, if a share pays a $1 dividend per year and the market price is $10, the dividend yield is $1/$10 = 10%).

**divisional performance measurement** The measurement of the performance of each individual division in a divisionalized structure to allow control and monitoring by central management. Methods used include the return on capital employed, residual income, and profit-to-sale ratio. The information may be used only by central management or may be made available to local managers.

**documentary credit** A letter from one banker to another authorizing the payment of a specified sum to the person named in the letter on certain specified conditions.

**documentary letter of credit** A financial instrument issued by a bank on behalf of a customer. Payment of a financial obligation to a third party is guaranteed by the bank upon presentation of specified documents. The customer has the obligation to reimburse the bank.

**dollar value LIFO** The calculation of inventory values in monetary terms rather than units. Each homogeneous group of inventory items is converted into base-year prices by using appropriate price indices. Inventory levels are disclosed in monetary terms by the difference between opening and closing levels.

**dominant influence** An influence that can be exercised over a company to achieve the operating and financial policies desired by the holder of the influence, notwithstanding the rights or influence of any other party.

**dormant company** A company that has had no significant accounting transactions for the accounting period in question.

**double-declining balance method** A method of depreciation that accelerates the write-off through the income statements of a non-current asset. The historical cost or revalued amount less the estimated residual value is divided by the number of years of the asset's estimated useful life. The resulting amount is multiplied by two to give the annual depreciation charge. For example, an asset costing $12,000 with an estimated residual value of $2,000 and an estimated useful life of 10 years would have a depreciation charge of $2,000 in the first year. This charge is calculated as: 2 × [($12,000 – $2,000)/10].

**double-entry bookkeeping** A system for recording the financial transactions of an organization. Every transaction has a dual aspect and therefore needs to be recorded in at least two separate accounts. For example, when cash is paid to an organization for goods previously purchased, the cash held is increased, and the amount due from the person is decreased by the same amount. If cash is paid to acquire an asset, the amount of cash held is decreased, and the amount of assets is increased. *See* debit and credit rules.

**double taxation relief** Relief available when income or gains are liable to tax in more than one country. Double taxation relief is given under the provisions of a double taxation agreement between tax country and the country concerned, or it can be given unilaterally.

**doubtful debts** Money owed to an organization for goods and services which may not be settled. A provision of doubtful debts is established based on specific debts or on the assumption that a certain percentage of debtors' amounts are doubtful. If settlement is not made, the debts are written off to the provision for doubtful debts. It is important to note that the so-called provision for doubtful debts is in actual fact an accounting estimate. *Refer to* IAS 8.

**Dow Jones Industrial Average (DJIA)** Dating from 1928, it is an index of security prices based on 30 large corporations used on the New York Stock Exchange (NYSE).

**Dow Jones News/Retrieval** Online information service containing business and investment information from many databases (such as Dow Jones Business Directory, Dow Jones Averages, Down Jones Interactive, DowVision, etc).

**dragon bond** A U.S. dollar bond issued in the Asian bond markets.

**drawdown** The drawing of funds against a bank loan, especially a revolving bank facility.

**drawings** The taking out of cash or goods from an unincorporated business by its owner. This is the normal practice for partnerships with a drawings account recording the various transactions in a financial period.

**drop lock bond** A bond that has both the advantages of a bank loan and the advantages of a bond. The borrower arranges a variable rate bank loan with the agreement that if long-term interest rates fall to a specified level, the bank loan will be automatically refinanced by a placing of fixed-rate long-term bonds with a group of institutions.

**Drum-Buffer-Rope (DBR) system** A system used in the Theory of Constraints (TOC) inventory management system for balancing the flow of production through a constraint. The objective is to reduce the amount of inventory at the constraint and to improve overall productivity.

**drummer** This refers to a major binding constraint in an organization.

**dual aspect** The principle in accounting that every financial transaction has two aspects to record in the books of accounts. This results in a debit entry and a credit entry. *See* double-entry bookkeeping.

**dual cost allocation** An approach to service department cost allocation where variable costs and fixed costs are allocated in proportion to short-term consumption and long-term consumption respectively.

**dual listing** The listing of securities on two stock exchanges by an organization. It is normally carried out by listing on the domestic stock exchange and on one of the international stock exchanges such as the New York Stock Exchange (NYSE) or London Stock Exchange (LSE). Depending on the time zones selected, the number of hours for trading the stock can be extended. The disadvantage is that two financial statements may need to be prepared for the two accounting regimes unless international financial reporting standards are recognized.

**dual pricing** A method of transfer pricing in which goods and services are exchanged between the divisions of an organization. A low price is charged to the buying division and a high price charged to the selling division. The advantage claimed is that this method encourages the divisions to trade with one another internally. This is only likely to be beneficial to the organization as a whole if the selling division has sufficient spare capacity to supply the buying division's needs without sacrificing external sales.

***du Pont* formula** A ratio that assess the Return on Investment (ROI) by examining separately the aspects of margin and turnover. The ROI is defined as:

$$\text{profit margin} \times \text{turnover} = (\text{net income/sales}) \times (\text{sales/ invested capital})$$

# E

**earnings** The net income, profit, or loss of a business calculated by deducting all related costs and expenses, for a specified period from the revenues, using generally accepted accounting principles.

**earnings available for ordinary shareholders** The net profit or loss for a financial period, after deducting preference dividends, that is available for distribution in the form of a dividend to the holders of ordinary shares. *Refer to* IAS 33.

**earnings per share (EPS)** The profit attributable to each ordinary share, based on the consolidated profit for the period after deducting dividends and other appropriations in respect of non-equity shares. This profit figure is divided by the weighted average number of equity shares in issue. *Refer to* IAS 33.11.

**earnings retained** The profit or earning of a company after the distribution of dividends. The earnings retained in the business are used to fund future operations.

**earnings yield** The ratio of the earnings per share of a company to the market price of the share, expressed as a percentage.

**earn-out agreement** An agreement to purchase an organization in which the purchaser pays an agreed sum at the time of the acquisition, with a promise to pay further amounts contingent upon certain criteria. The main criterion is usually that specified earnings levels are achieved for a specified number of years after the acquisition.

**e-business** An abbreviation for electronic business, that is, the use of the Internet for automatic business activities.

**e-commerce** This is the buying and selling of goods and services electronically. It may be in the form of business to consumer (B2C), such as the provision of goods and services from online stores to customers or, business-to-business (B2B), such as suppliers to other businesses.

**economic life** The period over which an asset is expected to be economically usable. This can be measured either on a time basis or an output basis. *Refer to* IAS 17.4.

**Economic Order Quantity (EOQ)** A mathematical model that determines the optimal amount of inventory to be ordered while minimizing the total ordering and holding costs. The EOQ is computed as follows:

$$EOQ = \sqrt{(2AD / H)}$$

where the EOQ is the optimal quantity to be purchased, A is the cost for processing an order, D is the demand required for a particular period, and H is the per unit holding cost of the inventory.

**Economic Value Added (EVA)** The measure is a registered trademark of business consultancy organization Stern Stewart & Co. EVA measures the value created by investing in projects and activities whose returns exceed the organization's cost of capital. One method for calculating this figure is to deduct the cost of capital (equity and long-term debt) from profit after tax. *See* Market Value Added (MVA).

**effective annual rate** The total interest paid or earned in a year expressed as a percentage of the principal amount at the beginning of the year.

**effective interest method** A method for calculating the amortized cost of a financial asset or a financial liability and of allocating the interest income or interest expense over the relevant period. The rate is the one that discounts future cash flows over the expected life of the financial instrument or a shorter period to the net carrying amount of the financial asset or liability. *Refer to* IAS 39.9.

**Efficient Market Hypothesis (EMH)** The hypothesis postulates that stock markets are efficient and share prices move in a rational way by reflecting all new information about future prospects. In order for the hypothesis to be valid, both buyers and sellers should have knowledge of all information relevant to the price of the securities. No individual dominates the market and transactions costs are not too high to discourage trading.

**Electronic Data Gathering, Analysis and Retrieval (EDGAR) system** A database containing submission of financial reports by companies that are required to file forms with the U.S. Securities and Exchange Commission.

**electronic data interchange (EDI)** The transfer of data electronically. This allows organizations to place, process, receive, and pay for goods and services through computers, thus reducing the costs of these activities compared to a paper-based system.

**electronic funds transfer (EFT)** The payment of cash electronically. The transfer of money from one bank account to another by means of computer and communications links.

**electronic funds transfer at point of sale (EFTPOS)** The automatic debiting of a purchase price from the customer's bank or credit-card account by a computer link between the checkout till and the bank or credit-card company.

**elements of financial statements** These are defined in the IASB's "Framework for the Preparation and Presentation of Financial Statements" as assets, liabilities, equity, income, and expenses.

**embedded derivative** A derivative that is part of a hybrid financial instrument that includes both the derivative and a host contract. With such instruments, some of the cash flows vary in a way similar to a stand-alone derivative. *Refer to* IAS 39.10.

**embedded value** The net present value of shareholders' entitlements from existing assets and future cash flows from life insurance policies in force at the reporting date.

**Emerging Issues Task Force (EITF)** The body that is part of the national standard setting structure. The EITF proposes the appropriate treatment of new accounting problems and practices. In the United States, the EITF reports to the Financial Accounting Standards Board (FASB). The comparable body in the United Kingdom is the Urgent Issues Task Force (UITF).

**emission rights** Allowances are issued by certain governments to entities that participate in schemes to emit a specified level of emissions. There are different types of emission rights schemes but the main aim is to encourage a reduction in the level of pollution in a country in conjunction with the Kyoto Agreement. The allowances may be issued free of charge or the entities may have to pay for them. Entities are able to buy and sell allowances and therefore, in many schemes, there is an active market for the allowances. At the end of a specified period, participants are required to deliver allowances equal to their actual emissions. *Refer to* IFRIC 3.

**employee benefits** All forms of consideration given by an entity in exchange for services provided by employees in a financial period. These include wages, salaries, pensions, and redundancy pay. *Refer to* IAS 19.

**employee report** A simplified version of the statutory annual report and accounts of an organization prepared for the employees of the company. Some companies have published employee reports since the beginning of the century. Employee reports were very popular in the 1930s and 1970s.

**Employee Share Ownership Plan (ESOP)** A method in the United Kingdom that provides employees with shares in their organizations. The ESOP buys shares in its sponsoring company, usually with assistance from the company concerned. The shares are ultimately made available to the employees, usually directors, who satisfy certain performance targets. The advantage claimed for ESOPs is that they do not involve dilution of the sponsoring company's share capital by the creation of new shares. In the United States, these are known as employee stock option plans.

**endorsement** Generally, a signature on a document or agreement to make it valid or as acknowledgement of any changes to the original wording. Specifically, a signature on the back of a bill of exchange or check (cheque), making it payable to the person who signs it. A bill can be endorsed any number of times, the presumption being that the endorsement were made in the order in which they appear, the last named being the holder to receive payment.

**engagement letter** A letter sent by a firm of auditors to their client defining clearly the scope of their responsibilities. It provides written confirmation of the auditors' acceptance of the appointment, the scope of the audit, the form of the report, and the details of any non-audit services to be provided. The auditors will agree these terms with the management of the business and the engagement letter is formal confirmation of this agreement.

**engineering method** A cost estimation method in which a detailed study is made of the process that results in cost occurrence.

**Enterprise Resource Planning (ERP)** Systems that computerize inventory and production planning, accounting, human resources, marketing, distribution, customer services, and various e-commerce applications. The systems require substantial funds to implement and maintain. In addition to coordinating the various business processes, reports can be generated that assist managers with planning, controlling, and decision making. Such systems are increasingly popular with large organizations.

**entity** For most accounting purposes, an entity is regarded as a body corporate, partnership, or an incorporated association carrying on a trade or business, with or without a view to profit.

**entity view** The view of an accounting entity as a business or organization completely separate from its owners. It is based on the accounting equation in which the sum of the assets is equal to the claims on these assets by owners and others.

**entry value** The current cost of replacing an existing asset. This value may be used in current-value accounting.

**environmental accounting** A report by an organization on the costs and benefits of its operations in relation to the environment. The increase in concern over the environment has led to a growth in environmental reporting, particularly those operating activities of an organization that may be considered to be environmentally sensitive.

**environment audit (green audit)** An audit of the possible effect of the activities of an organization on the environment. The various stages of the process are to ascertain the organization's environmental policies and that the organization's operations comply with these policies. The policies are regularly reviewed. Environment audits may be conducted internally or externally by environmental consultants.

**equipment trust certificate** A document setting out the details of a loan used to fund the purchase of equipment. The holder of the certificate has a secured interest in the asset in the event of a corporate default.

**equity** In common terms, a beneficial interest in an asset. For example, a person whose house is worth $100,000 with a mortgage of $20,000 may be said to have an equity of $80,000 in the house. For a business, it is the residual interest that remains after deducting both long-term and current liabilities from the total assets. *Refer to* IAS 32.11, IFRS 2.A.

**equity accounting** *See* equity method.

**equity dilution** A reduction in the percentage of the equity owned by shareholders as a result of a new issue of shares that rank equally with the existing voting shares.

**equity dividend cover** *See* dividend cover.

**equity finance** Finance raised from shareholders in the form of ordinary shares, as opposed to non-equity shares and to debt finance.

**equity gearing** *See* leverage.

**equity instruments** Generally, an instrument, including non-equity shares, warrants, and options that provide evidence of an ownership interest in the assets of an enterprise after deduction of all liabilities. Specifically, an equity instrument must satisfy two conditions. First, it must not have a contractual obligation to deliver cash or another financial asset to another entity, or to exchange financial assets or financial liabilities with another entity on potentially unfavorable terms. Secondly, if the instrument will or may be settled in the issuer's own equity instruments, it is a non-derivative, including no contractual obligation for the issuer to deliver a variable number of its own equity instruments, or a derivative that will be settled by the issuer exchanging a fixed amount of cash or another financial asset for a fixed number of its own equity instruments. *Refer to* IAS 32.

**equity method** A method of accounting in which the investor initially discloses in its financial statements the amount of the investment at cost. In subsequent periods, the carrying amount is adjusted by the postacquisition changes in the investor's share of the investee's net assets. The investor's share of the results from operations is included in the income statement. *Refer to* IAS 28, IAS 31.

**equity share capital** The share capital of a corporation that consists of its equity shares as opposed to its non-equity shares.

**equivalent unit** A measure of the amount of production effort applied to a physical unit of production. For example, a physical unit that is 25% completed represents one-quarter of an equivalent unit.

**estimates** *See* accounting estimates.

**ethical investment** *See* socially responsible investment.

**EU Accounting Directives** A policy established in the European Union to bring about accounting harmonization among member countries.

**Euro** The Euro has been a currency in its own right since the Economic and Monetary Union (EMU) was set up on 1 January 1999. Participating member states at that date had their local currencies fixed to the Euro and, thus, the currency differences were eliminated. SIC 7 states that the requirements of IAS 21 should be strictly applied on the adoption of the Euro, at whatever date the country joins the EMU. *Refer to* SIC 7.

**eurobond** A bond issued in a currency other than the currency of the market or country in which it was issued. The eurobond market is popular because secondary market investors can remain anonymous. Issues of new eurobonds normally take place in London, largely through syndicates of U.S. and Japanese investment banks. Eurobonds are bearer securities, unlike the shares registered in most stock exchanges, and interest payments are free of any withholding taxes.

**Euro-Commercial Paper (ECP)** Commercial paper issued in a euro currency. The system makes it much easier and quicker to obtain same-day funds by the issue of unsecured notes, for example, in Europe for use in New York. The market for ECPs is in London.

**eurocurrency** A currency held in a European country other the its country of origin. For example, U.S. dollars deposited in a bank in Switzerland are eurodollars, yen deposited in Germany are euroyen. The eurocurrency market provides a cheap and convenient form of liquidity for the financing of international trade and investment. Eurocurrency is used for lending and borrowing with the main participants being the commercial banks, large corporations, and the central banks.

**eurodollars** Dollars deposited in financial institutions outside the United States. The eurodollar market evolved in London in the late 1950s when the growing demand for dollars to finance international trade and investment coincided with a greater supply of dollars. The prefix "euro" indicates the origin of the practice, but it now refers to all dollar deposits made anywhere outside the United States.

**euromarket** A market that emerged in the 1950s for financing international trade. Its principal participants are commercial banks, large corporations, and the central banks of members of the European Union. Its main business is in eurobonds, euro-commercial paper, euronotes, and euroequities issued in eurocurrencies. The largest euromarket is in London. Smaller ones are in Paris, Brussels, and Frankfurt.

**euronote** A form of euro-commercial paper consisting of short-term, negotiable bearer notes. They may be in any currency but are usually in dollars or euros. The euronote facility is a form of note issuance facility set up by a syndicate of banks that underwrites the notes.

**European Accounting Association (EAA)** Established in 1977, the EAA aims to bring together accounting scholars and researchers in Europe, to provide a platform for a wider dissemination of European accounting research.

**European Corporate Governance Institute (ECGI)** Registered in Belgium, the ECGI is an international scientific non-profit association that provides a forum for debate and dialogue between academics, legislators and practitioners, focusing on major corporate governance issues and thereby promoting best practice. The Institute's role is to undertake, commission and disseminate research on corporate governance.

**European Financial Reporting Advisory Group (EFRAG)** EFRAG was established in 2001 to provide the European Commission with support and advice on the adoption of International Accounting Standards and to provide input to the International Accounting Standards Board.

**European option** An option that can be exercised only on a specific date. *See* American option.

**events accounting** A method of accounting in which data is stored and reported in respect of particular events rather than being transaction-based with financial statements issued at regular intervals.

**events after the balance sheet date** Events that may occur between the date of the balance sheet and the authorization date of the financial statements. Such events may be favorable or unfavorable and the accounting treatment depends on whether they are classified as adjusting or non-adjusting events. *Refer to* IAS 10.

**ex** A prefix used to exclude specified benefits when a security is quoted or being sold. A share is described as ex-dividend to indicate that the share is quoted without a recently declared dividend, the right to which remains with the seller. Similarly, ex-rights, ex-script, ex-coupon, ex-capitalization (ex-cap) and ex-bonus mean that the benefits of the security remain with the seller. *See* cum.

**exceptional items** It is generally believed that the users of the accounts of an organization should be informed of any events or transactions of an exceptional nature. It has been difficult, however, to reach agreement on how to define and report exceptional items. IAS 8 has clarified the position by stating that exceptional items are income or expenses incurred as part of the ordinary activities but are of such size, nature, or incidence that separate disclosure should be made. Included in the examples the standard gives are the write-down of inventories to net realizable value, restructuring, and disposal of items of property, plant, and equipment. *Refer to* IAS 8.16.

**exchange difference** The difference as a result of translating units of one currency into another currency at different exchange rates. *Refer to* IAS 21.8.

**exchange gain or loss** A gain or loss resulting from an exchange-rate fluctuation arising from the conversion of other currencies into the domestic currency.

**exchange rate** The number of units of one currency, usually the home currency, expressed in terms of a unit of another currency.

**executive director** A director of an organization who has management responsibilities for the day-to-day activities of a business.

**executive share option scheme** A share option scheme that entitles a specified class of directors or senior executives to purchase shares in the organization in which they are employed.

**exercise price** In terms of an option contract, the exercise price is the price for which the underlying commodity or financial instrument can be bought in the case of a call option or sold in the case of a put option. The exercise price is also referred to as the strike price.

**existing use value** The price at which a property can be sold on the open market assuming that it can only be used for the existing use and that there is vacant possession.

**exit value** The net realizable value of an asset calculated by deducting the expenses of selling the asset from its market price. Exit values can be regarded as break-up values and are not consistent with the going-concern concept that assumes operations will continue into the foreseeable future.

**expectation gap** The possible difference between what the public perceives as the duties and responsibilities of an auditor and the role of auditors as set by regulations.

**expenditure** The costs or expenses incurred by an organization. They may be capital expenditure or revenue expenditure.

**expenses** The outflow or depletion of assets or the occurrence of liabilities during a financial period resulting in the reduction in equity but excluding distributions to equity participants.

**exploration and evaluation assets** Expenditure on exploration and evaluation that is recognized as assets in accordance to the entity's accounting policy. *Refer to* IFRS 6.

**exploration and evaluation expenditure** Expenditure incurred before the technical feasibility and commercial viability of extracting mineral resources are demonstrable. *Refer to* IFRS 6.

**exposure draft** A draft document issued by some national standard setters for final comment before the issuing of the accounting standard.

**extended trail balance** A trial balance comprising columns for debit and credit balances plus additional columns for adjustments, accruals, and prepayment. There are two final columns that aggregate all the debit and credit balances. These are the figures used to generate the income statement and the balance sheet.

**extendible bond issue** A bond, the maturity of which can be extended at the option of all parties.

**external audit** An audit of an organization carried out by an auditor who is external to, and independent of, the organization. An example would be a statutory audit carried out on behalf of the shareholders of an organization.

**external failure costs** Costs incurred to rectify quality defects after products that fail to conform to requirements are sold to customers. Examples include warranty claims, product recalls, product liability lawsuits, lost sales.

**extraordinary items** Gains or losses that are unusual in nature, occur infrequently, and are not derived from the ordinary activities of the organization. In the past, organizations had been able to exclude extraordinary items (particularly losses) from their earnings figure. IAS 8 makes it clear that nearly all items of income and expenditure are incurred by an organization in the ordinary course of business and extraordinary items must be considered as rare. The two examples it gives are the expropriation of assets and an earthquake or other natural disaster, although these would not be considered extraordinary if the organization had insurance protection. Even with natural disasters, it is questionable whether an organization located in an area that is subject to severe and regular flooding or seasonal hurricanes could claim that these were extraordinary. The standard requires the total of extraordinary items to be shown on the face of the income statement but does not specify where. It is assumed that they would be shown after income tax expense and minority interests. *Refer to* IAS 8. *See* exceptional items, ordinary activities.

# F

**face value** *See* par value.

**facility** An agreement between a bank and an organization whereby the bank offers a line of credit to the organization. The bank will normally charge a facility fee for this service.

**factoring** The acquisition of accounts receivable from an organization and accepting the responsibility for debt collection and bad debts. A factoring organization buys the debts at a discount, but the seller of the debts has the advantage of obtaining cash immediately.

**fair value** The amount of consideration that would be agreed upon for which an asset or liability could be exchanged or settled in an arm's length transaction between informed and willing parties.

**fair value hedges** The use of derivatives or other financial instruments to hedge potential changes in the fair value of the whole or part of a recognized asset or liability. *Refer to* IAS 39.86.

**fair value interest rate risk** A part of market risk that is the specific risk that the value of a financial instrument will fluctuate because of changes in market interest rates. These fluctuations have the potential for gain and loss. *Refer to* IAS 32.52.

**faithful representation** A qualitative characteristic of financial statements that ensures that information is reliable. Financial information should faithfully represent transactions and other events, but may or may not always do so because of difficulties in recognition, measurement, and presentation. *Refer to* F.33-34.

**feasibility study** An investigation to determine the range of decisions that are likely to give a satisfactory return in a financial or economic appraisal of the alternatives.

**Fédération des Experts Comptables Européens (FEE)** FEE represents the European Federation of Accountants. Established in 1987, FEE is the representative organization for the accountancy profession in Europe. FEE's membership consists of 41 professional institutes of accountants from 29 countries. The member bodies represent more than 500,000 accountants in Europe. Roughly 45% of these accountants work in public practice, providing a wide range of services to clients. The other 55% work in various capacities in industry, commerce, government and education. The organization is based in Brussels and is created under Belgian law. FEE is recognized by a Royal Decree and is registered as a not-for-profit organization.

**Fédération Internationale des Experts Comptables Francophones (FIDEF)** Based in Paris, France, FIDEF represents the International Federation of French-speaking auditors. Member bodies include professional institutes of accountants from the African continent, Europe, the Middle East, the Caribbean islands and Canada.

**fidelity bond** An insurance policy that provides cover against specified losses occurring from dishonest acts or defalcations by an employee.

**final dividend** A dividend recommended by the directors of a company to be paid, subject to the shareholders giving approval at the annual general meeting.

**finance lease** A lease that transfers substantially all the risks and rewards related to ownership of an asset, although title need not be transferred. The risks include those of technological obsolescence and the rewards of profitable operation through the use of the asset. The standard does not specify when all the risks and rewards are deemed to have been transferred, but describes a number of situations that could indicate that transfer has taken place. *Refer to* IAS 17.

**financial accounting** The subdiscipline of accounting concerned with identifying, measuring, and recording economic transactions of an organization and reporting the results to those who have a right to receive them. At the end of a financial period, an income statement, balance sheet, cash flow statement, statement of changes in equity, and accompanying notes are prepared in order to show the performance and position of the organization. Financial accounting is conducted in the context of accounting concepts, regulation, and accounting standards. Financial accounting can be classified into a number of specific activities, such as auditing, taxation, bookkeeping, and insolvency. *See* managerial accounting.

**Financial Accounting Foundation (FAF)** The funding body of the Financial Accounting Standards Board (FASB). It appoints its members and reviews the process of setting standards and accounting principles.

**Financial Accounting Standards Board (FASB)** A non-government body founded in 1973 with the responsibility of promulgating generally accepted accounting principles (GAAP). This is achieved by the issue of statements of financial accounting standards (SFASs), which practicing Certified Public Accountants (CPAs) are expected to follow. The American Institute of Certified Public Accountants (AICPA) and the Securities and Exchange Commission (SEC) officially recognize the SFASs.

**financial adaptability** The ability of an entity to take effective action to alter the amounts and timing of cash flows so that it can respond to unexpected needs or opportunities.

**financial analysis** The use of financial statements and the calculation of ratios to monitor and evaluate the financial performance and position of a business. Interpretations are conducted by comparing the ratios of one organization over a period of time, comparing the ratios of one organization with others, and comparing with the industry average or other indices.

**financial asset** An asset that is either cash, or an equity instrument of another entity, or a contractual right to receive cash, or the right to exchange a financial instrument with another entity under potentially favorable terms. It may also be a contract that will or may be settled in the entity's own equity instruments and can be a derivative or a non-derivative. *Refer to* IAS 32.11.

**financial capital maintenance** *See* capital maintenance concept.

**financial control** The monitoring, review, and control of the costs incurred and revenue generated by an organization to ensure that these costs and revenue are at acceptable levels. Financial control is assisted by the provision of financial information to management on a frequent basis. Extensive use is made of techniques such as budgetary control, activity-based costing, standard costing, comparative statements, and variance analysis to assist in decision making.

**financial engineering** The combination or splitting of financial instruments so as to create new financial instruments.

**financial flexibility** The ability of an organization to control the timing and amount of future cash flows, including the ability to access additional finance.

**financial futures** A futures contract in currencies or interest rates. Unlike simple forward contracts, future contracts themselves can be bought and sold on specialized markets.

**financial gearing** *See* leverage.

**financial highlights** A voluntary disclosure made by organizations in their annual reports and accounts. Key financial data such as revenues, profits, and dividends are summarized, and often presented in graphic form.

**financial instrument** Any contract that gives rise to both a financial asset of one entity and a financial liability or equity instrument of another entity. *Refer to* IAS 32.11.

**financial intermediary** An individual or an institution, such as a commercial bank or credit union, that facilitates the flow of funds between savers and lenders.

**financial liability** A contractual obligation to deliver either cash or another financial asset to another entity, or to exchange financial instruments with another entity on potentially unfavorable terms. It may also be a contract that will or may be settled in the entity's own equity instruments and is either a non-derivative for which the entity is or may be obliged to deliver a variable number of the entity's own equity instruments or a derivative that will or may be settled other than by the exchange of a fixed amount of cash or another financial asset for a fixed number of the entity's own equity instruments. *Refer to* IAS 32.11.

**financial modeling** A process of simulation by the generation and application of planning and decision models based on financial data. This can assist in the prediction of the potential implication of various decisions and activities. The financial models include discounted cash flow, economic order quantity, decision trees, learning curves, and budgetary control.

**financial performance** The most common measure of financial performance is profit calculated by deducting expenses from income for a financial period. Distinguishing between items of income and expenses, and combining them in different ways can provide different measures of profit. It is usual to assess performance by using financial ratios. *Refer to* F.469.

**financial period** The period falling between one balance sheet date and the next balance sheet date for which financial statements are prepared. For statutory accounts, the period is normally 12 months. In some accounting regimes, organizations may be required or encouraged to publish condensed financial statements more frequently. *See* interim accounts.

**financial position** The assets, liabilities, and equities of an organization as shown on the balance sheet at the end of a financial period. *Refer to* F.47.

**financial ratio** The calculation of a ratio from two or more related figures that is used to analyze and interpret the financial performance and position of an organization. Ratios may be expressed as a percentage (such as return on investment), in days (such as accounts receivable collection period) or as a multiple (such as inventory turnover).

**Financial Reporting Council (FRC)** A body initially set up in 1990 in the United Kingdom to promote good financial reporting. The FRC's original mandate has now been enlarged to include a more active role with respect to corporate governance, compliance with company law and accounting standards. The Council assumes new responsibilities in relation to audit, auditing standards and the oversight of the self-regulatory professional bodies. The FRC aims to increase investor confidence in financial reporting and governance, and the underpinning regulatory processes. The FRC is the parent to five subsidiary boards: the Accounting Standards Board (ASB), the Financial Reporting Review Panel (FRRP), the Auditing Practices Board (APB), the Accountancy Investigation and Discipline Board (AIDB) and the Professional Oversight Board For Accountancy for Accountancy (POBA). The latter encompasses the Audit Inspection Unit (AIU). Although the organizational structure has been expanded, the fundamental operational framework remains the same. The FRC is the parent of all the subsidiary boards, but each board is independent in exercising its functions. The FRC and its subsidiaries are all companies limited by guarantee. Several measures are in place to provide for accountability and transparency of process.

**Financial Reporting Exposure Draft (FRED)** A document issued by the Accounting Standards Board (ASB) in the United Kingdom for discussion and debate prior to the issue of a Financial Reporting Standard (FRS).

**Financial Reporting Release (FRR)** Policy pronouncements made by the Securities and Exchange Commission (SEC) in the United States.

**Financial Reporting Review Panel (FRRP)** The Financial Reporting Review Panel (FRRP) was established in 1990 as a subsidiary of the Financial Reporting Council. The panel forms part of the financial reporting process in the United Kingdom. It has statutory authority to examine the financial statements of organizations to ensure that there is compliance with the requirements of company legislation or accounting standards. If the panel considers that the accounts are defective, it can seek the organization's agreement to revise them or it can apply to the courts to compel the organization to revise them.

**Financial Reporting Standard (FRS)** The term used in a number of countries to refer to accounting standards and pronouncements issued by an accounting standard setting body.

**Financial Reporting Standard for Smaller Entities (FRSSE)** An accounting standard issued by the Accounting Standards Board (ASB) in the United Kingdom that is intended to be applied to smaller entities. It is consistent with the full accounting standards issued, and summarizes and simplifies the relevant requirements into one volume of guidance. The argument in favor of the FRSSE is that many accounting standards are too complex and not relevant for smaller organizations, but guidance is required. The International Accounting Standards Board shares the same philosophy and is seeking to adopt a similar approach.

**financial risk** A term defined in reference to insurance contracts under IFRS 4. The risk of a possible future change in one or more of a specified interest rate, financial instrument price, commodity price, foreign exchange rate, index of prices or rates, credit rating or credit index, or other variables. When the variable is non-financial, then it must not be specific to a party to the contracts. *Refer to* IFRS 4.A.

**financial stability measures** Ratios used to assess whether an organization can meet its financial obligations including interest, dividends, and capital repayments. The measures include the leverage ratio and interest cover.

**financial statement analysis** The analysis and interpretation of the financial statements of an organization in order to draw conclusions on its financial performance, position, and stability. Ratios are normally calculated to assess the profitability, solvency, working capital management, liquidity, and financial structure. Ratios are calculated for a series of financial periods for one organization to identify any trends, or compared for one financial period to the ratios for similar organizations or to industry averages. *See* ratio analysis.

**financial statements** The annual statements summarizing an organization's economic activities over a financial period. They consist of the income statement, balance sheet, statements showing changes in equity, cash-flow statement, supporting notes, and accounting policies. They are normally prepared in accordance with an accounting model that uses recoverable historic cost and the nominal financial maintenance concept. *Refer to* IAS 1.8.

**financial structure** *See* capital structure.

***Financial Times* share indexes** A number of shares indexes published in the U.K.'s *Financial Times* as a guide to the performance of share prices on the London Stock Exchange.

**financial year** Any period of 12 months for which financial information is collected and issued either internally or externally. It is commonly used to refer to the 12 months covered by the published financial statements of an organization, but can refer to internal documents, such as budgets.

**financing activities** A heading to be shown separately on the cash flow statement as required by IAS 7. It includes resources obtained and returned to owners, short-term and long-term borrowings, and their repayment. *Refer to* IAS 7.6.

**finished goods inventory** The products that have passed through the complete production cycle and are being held awaiting sale or transfer to another location.

**first-in-first-out cost (FIFO cost)** A method of valuing units of raw material or finished goods issued from inventory. FIFO is based on using the earliest unit value for pricing the materials issued to production until all inventory at that price has been used up. The next latest price is then used for pricing the issues. The method may also be used in process costing to value the work-in-progress at the end of an accounting period. *Refer to* IAS 2.27.

**fixed asset** *See* non-current asset.

**fixed-asset investment** The acquisition of assets that are intended to be used in the operating activities of the organization and not for subsequent sale.

**fixed-asset to equity-capital ratio** A ratio used to assess an organization's ability to meet the financial obligations of long-term debt. The value of the non-current assets are divided by the equity capital. A ratio greater than 1 means that some of the non-current assets are financed by debt.

**fixed-assets register** A listing of the non-current assets of a company. It records a description of the assets, their location, cost, revaluation, estimated net value, and estimated useful economic life.

**fixed-assets turnover ratio** A ratio used to evaluate an organization's level of activity over a period. The ratio is calculated by dividing revenues by the balance-sheet value of the non-current assets. The non-current asset values may be taken either at the beginning or the end of the period or the average of the two. The higher the turnover ratio, the more active, and efficient the organization is deemed to be. The formula is:

Fixed assets turnover ratio = revenue/non-current assets

**fixed budget** A budget that remains unchanged for a period of time, regardless of changes in the level of actual activity compared to the budgeted level. This approach is appropriate for costs that are fixed in nature, but does not recognize the impact on actual variable costs due to the changes in activity levels.

**fixed charge** A charge in which a creditor has the right to have a specific asset sold and applied to the repayment of a debt if the debtor defaults on any payments. The debtor is not at liberty to deal with the asset without the charge-holder's consent.

**fixed price contract** A contract in which the price is fixed, either in total or by the units of output. The contract may incorporate cost escalation clauses. *Refer to* IAS 11.3.

**fixed production overheads** Those indirect costs of production that remain relatively constant, irrespective of changes in the volume of production. *Refer to* IAS 2.12.

**fixed-rate loan** A loan in which the interest rate is fixed at the inception of the loan and prevails for the life of the loan.

**flash report** A management report that highlights key data and identifies weaknesses in operational performance which requires corrective action.

**floating charge** A charge that "floats" over the assets of an organization and will only be crystallized by some predetermined event. For example, a floating charge may be created over all the assets of an organization including its inventories. The assets may be freely dealt with until a crystallizing event occurs (such as the organization going into liquidation). No further dealing may take place, but the debt may be satisfied from the charged assets. Such a charge ranks in priority after legal charges (such as a mortgage) and after preferred creditors in the event of a winding-up.

**floating-rate loan** A loan that does not have a fixed interest rate throughout its life, but the interest rate is normally linked to a short-term market indicator. Such a loan can represent a risk to a borrower when the economic environment suggests that interest rates generally will be increasing.

**floor** An agreement that sets a minimum rate of interest for a borrower. *See* cap.

**flotation** *See* initial public offering.

**Ffootsie** *See Financial Times* share indexes.

**401(K) plan** A U.S. employee investment plan. It allows employees to take part of their gross salary and invest in securities, bonds, or the money markets. No tax is paid on the investment until funds are withdrawn by the employee. The 401(K) plan is also known as a salary reduction plan.

**foreclosure** The legal right of a lender to dispose of property of the borrower if the loan is not repaid on the due date. The lender must apply to a court to permit the sale of the property that has been held as security for the debt. This procedure can occur when the security is the house that the mortgagor occupies but fails to pay the mortgagee (such as the bank) the installments as they fall due. The bank has the power to foreclose the mortgage, thus dispossessing the mortgagor.

**foreign currency** A currency other than the currency of the primary economic environment in which the entity operates. *Refer to* IAS 21.8.

**foreign currency transactions** Transactions that are conducted in a foreign currency or payment is made in a foreign currency. *Refer to* IAS 21.20.

**foreign currency translations** Converting amounts that were originally in a foreign currency into the domestic currency of the organization. *Refer to* IAS 21.38.

**foreign exchange (FX)** The currencies of foreign countries that are bought and sold on a foreign-exchange market. The foreign-exchange spot market is for transactions in which two currencies are exchanged within a few days. The forward market in foreign exchange is intended for transactions in which the exchange occurs at a specified future date. *Refer to* IAS 27.

**forensic accounting** Accounting that involves investigating the financial aspects of situations when it is suspected that fraud has taken place, irregularities have occurred, or there are differences of opinion on the correct accounting requirements or procedures. Such cases are often subject to litigation, and accountants may be called upon to provide expert opinion.

**form 8-k** A report describing any unscheduled material event that is required to be filed with the Securities and Exchange Commission (SEC) by publicly traded corporations.

**form 10-k** The form that is required to be filed annually with the Securities and Exchange Commission (SEC) by publicly traded corporations. Comprehensive information is required, including audited financial statements. The information on the Form 10-k is more detailed, but otherwise similar, to the Annual Report and Accounts.

**form 10-q** The form that is required to be filed quarterly with the Securities and Exchange Commission (SEC) by publicly traded corporations. The form contains the interim financial statements and may be presented for a single quarter, or it may be cumulative. It may contain unaudited financial information. Comparative figures are provided for the same period in the previous year.

**form 20-f** The form required by the Securities and Exchange Commission (SEC) for the filing of annual results by non-U.S. companies trading in the U.S. stock exchanges.

**formation expenses** The expenses incurred on setting up a corporation.

**forward differential** *See* forward points.

**forward interest rate** The rate of interest that will apply to a loan or deposit beginning on a future date and maturing on a second future date.

**forward margin** *See* forward points.

**forward points** The amount to be added to or deducted from the spot foreign-exchange rate to calculate the forward exchange rate.

**Forward Rate Agreement (FRA)** A form of forward contract that is designed to allow interest rates to be fixed in advance for a specified period commencing at some agreed future date. Usually conducted between banks and clients, the interest rate is fixed on a specified amount of money. The agreement relates only to the interest rate, and there is usually no intention to borrow or lend the specified amount of money.

**founders' shares** The shares issued to the founders of a company. These shares sometimes carry special dividend rights and voting rights.

**fragmentation** A situation that arises when two transactions, especially foreign transactions, offset each other commercially but not in terms of taxation.

**Framework** The "Framework for the Preparation and Presentation of Financial Statements" was issued by the IASC in 1989. It is not an accounting standard but is intended to assist in the development of international standards and to promote harmonization. The document is also helpful to preparers, auditors, users and others who are involved with or are interested in financial accounting and reporting issues. The "Framework" was adopted by the IASB in 2001.

**free cash flow** A measure used to determine the amount of cash available to pay dividends, pay debts, and expand. There is no agreed method for calculating this figure, although one calculation is to deduct new investments from the net cash flow.

**free in and out** Denoting a selling price that includes all costs of loading goods into a container, road vehicle, ship, etc. and unloading them out of the carriers.

**free issue** *See* scrip issue.

**free on board** An agreement in which goods are transported by the seller with no cost to the buyer. The seller is financially responsible for all risks of transportation, and the title to the buyer is not transferred until the goods are delivered to the agreed destination.

**front-end fee** A fee payable to a financial institution from which a corporation has arranged a loan. The fee is paid at approximately the same time as signing the loan agreement. The fee applies even if the loan is only taken in part, subsequently cancelled or repaid before the agreed date. It is usually made up of four components: a lead management fee; general management fee; underwriting fee and the participation fee.

**front-end loading** The initial charge for administrative expenses and commission included in the first payment of a loan installment, unit trust investment, or insurance premium. It increases the first payment in relation to subsequent payments.

**frozen assets** Assets that for one reason or another cannot be used or realized; for example, when a government refuses to allow certain assets to be exported.

**frustration of contract** The termination of a contract as a result of an unforeseen event that makes performance impossible or illegal. A contract to sell an aircraft could be frustrated if it crashes before the contract was due to be implemented. Similarly, an export contract could be frustrated if the importer was in a country that declared war on the country of the exporter.

**full costing** *See* absorption costing.

**fully diluted earnings per share** The earnings per share that are calculated on the number of shares in actual issue as well as those that may be issued as a result of such factors as convertible loans, options, or warranties. *Refer to* IAS 33.

**fully paid capital** *See* paid-up share capital.

**fully paid share** A share where calls for payment of all installments have been made and payment has been made. The total paid will be the par value plus any premium.

**functional analysis** A feature of value engineering in which the performance and cost of each major function of a product are analyzed.

**functional currency** The currency of the primary economic environment where a business operates. It is usually, although not necessarily, the currency in which the business will produce its audited accounts. *Refer to* IAS 21.8.

**fundamental analysis** A detailed analysis of the financial statements as well as other managerial and organizational information to assess future share value and price movements. Fundamental analysis differs from technical analysis, since the latter focuses on market indicators such as price movements and trading volumes in the market.

**fundamental error** A material mistake in, or omission from, the accounts of a business. It is not a recurring adjustment or the correction of an accounting estimate made in a prior period. When a fundamental error is discovered applying to a prior period, a prior-period adjustment should be made.

**funded pension scheme** A pension scheme in which the future liabilities for benefits are provided for by the accumulation of a fund of assets, held externally to the business of the employer.

**funding risk** *See* liquidity risk.

**funds flow statement** A financial statement detailing in a structured format the differences between the balance sheet at the beginning and end of the financial period. Normally, such statements are not drawn up on a cash basis but on an accruals basis.

**fungible issue** A bond issue on the same terms and conditions as a bond previously issued by the same organization. It has the advantage of having paperwork consistent with the previous bond and of increasing the depth of the market for that particular bond. The gross redemption yield on the fungible issue will probably be different from that of the original issue, which is achieved by issuing the bond at a discount or a premium.

**fungibles** Interchangeable goods and securities, that allow one to be replaced by another without loss of value. For example a $10 note could be exchanged for a bearer bond of the same denomination.

**futures contract** These are "exchange traded derivatives," since they can be bought and sold on organized exchanges. In general terms, the contracts take the form of an agreement to buy or sell a fixed quantity of a particular commodity, currency, or security for delivery at a fixed date in the future at a fixed price. Unlike an option, a futures contract involves a definite purchase or sale, and not an option to buy or sell, and therefore may entail a potentially unlimited loss. However, futures provide an opportunity for those who purchase goods regularly to hedge against changes in price. For hedging to be possible, there must be speculators willing to offer these contracts. In fact, trade between speculators usually exceeds the amount of hedging taking place by a considerable amount. Futures contracts can reduce financial risk, but usually do not result in gains from favorable movements in the prices of the underlying instruments.

**future economic benefits** Flows of cash or cash equivalents or reductions in cash outflows. The term is a critical concept in the definition of an asset. *Refer to* F.5.

# G

**gains** These are economic benefits, and the International Accounting Standards Board (IASB) does not distinguish between gains and revenue or between losses and expenses.

**gain-sharing plan** An incentive system that specifies a formula in which cost savings from productivity gains accomplished by an organization are shared with the employees who assisted in achieving the improvements.

**gamma value** The relationship that indicates the change in delta value relative to price changes of the underlying asset.

**gearing** *See* leverage.

**gearing ratios** *See* leverage ratios.

**Generally Accepted Accounting Principles (GAAP)** A term regarded as incorporating the conventions, rules, procedures, and regulations that define accounting practices. It serves as the basis for financial reporting to external parties. Developed through historical usage and pronouncements of authoritative bodies, GAAP is a dynamic concept because regulations and conventions change over time in order to improve existing practices and to respond to emerging practices. In some countries, for example New Zealand and the United States, there is statutory support for the concept whereas in others, for example in the United Kingdom, the term is applied more loosely.

**Generally Accepted Auditing Standards (GAAS)** These are the broad rules and guidelines set down by the Auditing Standards Board of the American Institute of Certified Public Accountants (AICPA). In carrying out work for a client, a certified public accountant would apply the Generally Accepted Auditing Standards. If they fail to do so, they can be held to be in violation of the AICPA'S code of professional ethics.

**general meeting** A meeting that all the members of an association may attend.

**general price level** An index that gives a measure of the purchasing power of money. In the United Kingdom, the best-known measure is the Retail Price Index (RPI). In the United States, it is the Consumer Price Index (CPI).

**general purpose financial statements** The financial statements prepared by organizations that are intended to meet the needs of a range of users and are therefore regarded as general purpose documents. Specific purpose statements are sometimes prepared to meet the needs of a particular group of users. IFRSs are intended to apply to general purpose financial statements.

**geographical segment** An area consisting of an individual country, group of countries, or economic environment in which an organization operates and where the risks and returns are different from other geographic segments. *Refer to* IAS 14.9.

***gharar*** The Islamic term for deception or uncertainty due to a non-disclosure or non-availability of full facts relevant to a transaction.

**gilt-edged security** Commonly known as gilts, these are fixed-interest securities or stock issued by the British government in the form of exchequer stocks or treasury stocks. Gilts are regarded as very low risk investments, since it is highly unlikely that the government will default on interest or principal repayments. Redeemable gilts are classified as long-dated gilts or longs and are normally not redeemable for 15 years or more. Medium-dated gilts or mediums are normally redeemable in 5 to 15 years. Short-dated gilts or shorts are redeemable in less than 5 years.

**global bond** A single bond for the total amount of a new issue of bonds, issued on a temporary basis to the bank (normally the paying agent) that has responsibility for distributing the actual bonds to investors. In due course the global bond, sometimes referred to as a global bearer bond, is exchanged for the actual bond.

**going-concern concept** The assumption used in the preparation of financial statements that an organization will continue in operation for the foreseeable future: that is, the accountants assume no intention or necessity to liquidate or significantly curtail the scale of the organization's operation. There is also the implicit assumption that the organization will be profitable in the long term. The consequences of the going-concern concept is that non-current assets are shown at cost, or at cost less depreciation, and not at their break-up values. It is also assumed that liabilities that would only become applicable on liquidation are not included in the financial statements. The going concern value of a business is normally higher than the value that would be achieved by disposing of its individual assets. *Refer to* F.23.

**going public** The process of a private company offering its shares to the public. It is also known as Initial Public Offering (IPO).

**golden handcuffs** Incentives written into a contract with key employees that make it financially better to remain with the employing organization than to move to another organization.

**golden handshake** A payment for loss of office made by an employer to an employee if the contract of employment is terminated; for example, in the case of a takeover.

**golden hello** Financial inducement made to encourage a prospective employee to join an organization.

**golden key** The key that unlocks the golden handcuffs. It usually consists of a single payment to a key employee who has a golden handcuffs contract but whose services are no longer required.

**golden parachute** A clause in the employment contract of a senior executive that provides for financial and other benefits if the executive is dismissed or leaves voluntarily through changes in organizational ownership.

**golden share** A share that gives at least 51% of the voting rights in an organization.

**goodwill** Generally, the difference between the value of the separable net assets of a business and the total value of the business. Purchased goodwill is the difference between the fair value of the price paid for a business and the aggregate of the fair values of its separable net assets. Specifically, future economic benefits arising from assets that cannot be individually identified and separately recognized. *Refer to* IFRS 3.A.

**goodwill write-off reserve** National accounting standards sometimes have not included requirements for the appropriate accounting treatment of goodwill or have allowed considerable flexibility. In such cases, organizations have written off goodwill to a special reserve, thus avoiding charging any part of it as an expense against profits.

**government grant** Assistance in various forms given by the government to an organization. In return, the organization is normally expected to comply with certain conditions relating to its activities (such as operating in certain industries or regions). *Refer to* IAS 20.3.

**gray knight** A counter-bidder in a take-over who has not made public its ultimate intentions for the future of an organization.

**gray market** Generally, any market for goods that are in short supply. It differs from a black market since a gray market is legal; a black market is usually not. Specifically, a market in shares that have not been issued, although they are due to be issued in a short time. Market makers will often deal with investors or speculators who are willing to trade in anticipation of receiving an allotment of these shares or are willing to cover their deals after flotation. This type of gray market provides an indication of the market price after flotation. An investor who does not receive the anticipated allocation has to buy the shares on the open market, often at a loss.

**Greenbury Report** A report on corporate governance, issued in 1995, that followed from the Cadbury Report in the United Kingdom. It concentrated mainly on directors' pay and recommended a remuneration committee be set up in every company and that there should be certain public disclosures regarding the total remuneration of the directors of a company. The majority of the recommendations of the Greenbury Report have been included in the rules of the London Stock Exchange.

**green mail** The purchase of a significant amount of shares in a corporation by a potential bidder for control. The shares are sold back at a premium over the market price in return for a promise not to launch a bid.

**green reporting** *See* environmental accounting.

**grey knight** *See* gray knight.

**grey market** *See* gray market.

**gross dividend** The amount of a dividend prior to the deduction of tax.

**gross dividend per share** The total of the gross dividends paid by an organization in a year divided by the total number of ordinary shares on which the dividend is paid.

**gross margin** *See* gross profit.

**gross margin ratio** A ratio of financial performance calculated by expressing the gross profit as a percentage of revenue. With retailing organizations in particular, it is regarded as a prime measure of their trading success.

**gross profit** The difference between the revenue of an organization and the cost of goods sold. It does not include finance costs, administration, or the cost of distributing the goods.

**gross redemption yield** The internal rate of return of a bond bought at a specified price and held until maturity. The yield calculation includes all the income and all the capital payments due on the bond but ignores the tax payable on the interest and the capital repayments.

**gross up** To convert a net amount into its equivalent gross amount. For example, an amount payable net of 20% can be grossed up by multiplying the net amount by 1.20.

**group** A parent undertaking and its subsidiary or subsidiaries. *Refer to* IAS 21.8, IAS 27.4.

**group accounts** *See* consolidated financial statements.

**group company** A corporation that is a subsidiary undertaking or a holding company.

**growth rate** The amount of change over a period of time in an organization's financial characteristics, for example, revenue or profits. The rate is calculated as a percentage and can be compared to indices or average rates to evaluate the performance of the organization. A common comparison is with an index of general inflation to determine whether the growth is real or merely a consequence of movements in the value of money.

**guarantee** A promise made by a guarantor to accept liability if one of the parties to a contract fails to fulfill contractual obligations. For example, the bank may make a loan to a person, provided that a guarantor is prepared to repay the loan if the borrower fails to do so.

**guaranteed bond** A bond issued by one party with payment guaranteed by another party. A common example is a bond issued by a subsidiary undertaking that is guaranteed by the holding company.

# H

**Hampel Committee Report** Issued in 1998, the report was a continuation of the work of the Cadbury Report and the Greenbury Report in the United Kingdom. The London Stock Exchange published the Hampel Committee's Principles of Good Governance and the Code of Practice, known as the Combined Code, in 1998. There is a detailed list of disclosures to be made by companies listed on the stock exchange, including explanations in the company's annual report on how the principles in the Code have been applied. *See* corporate governance.

**Hang Seng index** The index of stock prices used on the Hong Kong Stock Exchange (HKSE). It is calculated on the arithmetically weighted index of 33 stocks.

**hard currency** A currency that is acceptable in international business transactions. Traditionally, hard currencies have been those of the western industrialized countries, such as U.S. dollars. Holdings of hard currencies are desired because they offer purchasing power across national borders.

**harmonization** The process of increasing the similarity of national accounting standards by setting restrictions on the number of alternative accounting treatments that are permitted for certain economic transactions. It was the process used to bring about change in the European Union, particularly in the 1970s. It was advocated by the International Accounting Standards Committee. It differs from standardization, since that term implies the imposition of a rigid and narrow set of rules. The term *harmonization* is often used as a synonym for convergence, although the latter implies a gradual process of a number of different national standards moving towards an agreed regulatory pronouncement.

**harvesting strategy** The strategy of making the maximum short-term profit from a particular product or service prior to withdrawing it from the market. This is achieved by eliminating or reducing as many of the costs as possible that would be necessary if there was the intention to continue to sale the product. For example, current marketing costs may be reduced on the assumption that advertising incurred earlier will continue to have an effect until the cessation of the product. Sometimes, there is no public announcement of the intention to cease production because this could lead to an adverse affect on sales.

**head lease** The main or first lease, out of which subleases may be created. For example, if A grants a 99-year lease to B and B then grants a 12-year lease of the same property to C, the 99-year lease is the head lease, and the 12-year lease is a sublease.

**hedge effectiveness** The degree to which changes in the fair value or cash flows of a hedged item that are attributable to a hedged risk are offset by changes in the fair value or cash flows of the hedging instrument. *Refer to* IAS 39.9.

**hedge funds** Funding in which the managers invest in liquid instruments, such as currency and interest rate derivatives, with the aim of making profits from movements in foreign-exchange or bond markets.

**hedge ratio** *See* delta value.

**hedging** An activity undertaken now by an organization to reduce future financial risk. It involves offsetting two transactions against each other, for example, cash flows arising from ordinary transactions by buying or selling a derivative instrument. Hedging is normally carried out with respect to a sale or purchase of a commodity, currency, security, and so forth that is likely to fluctuate in price over a future period. For example, a manufacturer may realize that it will not have sufficient raw material in inventory in six months time. There is the risk that the raw materials will increase in price before they are required. This position can be hedged by buying the raw material required on a forward contract so that the raw materials can be purchased in six months time but at a price fixed now. The organization thus reduces the risk by the payment of a premium on the forwards contract, but loses the chance of a gain if the price falls within the next six months.

**hedging instrument** A designated derivative whose fair value or cash flows are expected to offset changes in the fair value or cash flows of a designated hedged item. When the hedge is for the risk associated with changes in foreign currency exchange rates, the hedging instrument can be a non-derivative financial asset or liability. *Refer to* IAS 39.9.

**held-to-maturity investment** Financial assets that have the characteristics of being non-derivative, with fixed or determinable payments, and fixed maturity. The organization must have the intention and ability to hold such financial assets to maturity. *Refer to* IAS 39.9.

**highlights** Brief summaries of financial information that are often given some prominence in the annual reports and accounts.

**high-low method** An algebraic method of estimating fixed and variable cost components in which a straight line is fitted to two data points representing the highest and lowest levels of activity.

**hire purchase contract** A contract for the hire of an asset in which the hirer has an option to acquire title to the asset upon the fulfillment of agreed conditions. *Refer to* IAS 17.6.

**historical cost** A method of valuing assets based on the original cost incurred by the organization in conducting a transaction. The advantages of historical cost are that it is relatively objective, easy to apply, difficult to falsely manipulate, and suitable for audit verification. It also fulfils the stewardship function. In times of high inflation, however, the results of historical cost accounting can be misleading since profit can be overstated and assets understated in terms of current values. In addition, capital maintenance is only concerned with the nominal amount of the capital invested rather than its purchasing power. *Refer to* F.100.

**historical cost convention** Under this convention, assets are carried in the books of account at their historic cost less any accumulated depreciation and impairment losses, if any.

**historical summary** A voluntary statement appearing in the annual reports and accounts of some organizations where selected financial results are given for previous financial periods for comparative purposes. There are no regulations concerning the publication of such information, but details such as revenue, earnings, and earnings for a 5- or 10-year period are often given.

**holding company** A corporation that owns shares and manages one or more other companies.

**holding gain** A gain that results from the length of time an asset has been held due to increases in prices. A holding gain is realized when the asset is sold. It remains unrealized if the asset is still held in the business. In times of inflation, holding gains can be illusory unless adjustments are made for changes in purchasing power.

**homogeneous cost pools** A collection of overhead costs in which each cost component is consumed in equal proportion by each product line. In addition, the overhead costs are associated with activities that share the same process, and thus the same activity driver can be used to assign costs to the products.

**horizontal analysis** An analysis that focuses on the year-to-year percentage changes in financial statement items.

**horizontal form** The presentation of a financial statement in which the debit balances are given on one side of the statement and the credit balances on the other. In the case of a balance sheet, the assets would be shown on the left-hand side of the statement and the equity and liabilities on the right-hand side. This format has now largely been replaced by the vertical format.

**horizontal integration** The combination of two or more corporations in the same business, carrying out the same process or production. The arguments for horizontal integration are that it reduces competition and gains economies of scale. It does not, however, offer diversification.

**hostile bid** The attempt to take over another company against the wishes of the board of directors. Although the directors are opposed to the bid, shareholders may accept the bid if the price offered by the bidder is sufficiently high.

**hot money** Used to describe speculative flows of currency on foreign exchange markets. For example, the speculative selling of a specific currency increases the supply and thus drives the value down.

**human resource accounting** The recognition of the human resources of an organization. It is suggested that a value can be calculated by using such factors as discounted future earnings or market prices. The "value" placed on members of professional sporting teams is often referred to as an example. It is also claimed that organizations may invest heavily in the recruitment and training of employees, and this expenditure should be capitalized and not expensed. There is occasional academic interest shown in the topic, but there is no general agreement about whether such human assets should be recognized, and there is no sound method of measurement. Industry has not expressed interest in this form of accounting.

**hurdle rate** The minimum return expected from an investment when selecting from a range of alternatives.

**hybrid** A synthetic financial instrument formed by combining two or more individual financial instruments, such as bonds with warrants.

**hybrid product-costing system** A product costing system that incorporates features of two or more alternative systems such as job order and process costing.

**hyperinflation** A very high rate of increase in the general price level to the extent that historical financial statements are meaningless. *Refer to* IAS 29.2.

**hypothecation** In banking, it is the use of property as collateral for a loan. The title is not passed, but the bank does have the right to sell the property if certain terms of the agreement are not met; for instance, through default on interest payments. The term is also used when securities are pledged to brokers as collateral for loans.

# I

**if-converted method** The method used for determining the dilution of convertible securities that are not common stock equivalents in the calculation of fully diluted earnings per share.

***ijarah*** The term refers to leasing under Islamic finance.

**immaterial** Denotes any item or economic transaction that is not significant in relation to the entire activities of which it forms part and thus does not require any specific accounting treatment.

**immediate holding company** A company that has a direct controlling interest in another company, even though it is itself controlled by a third corporation, which is the holding company of both companies.

**impairment** A reduction in the recoverable amount of a non-current asset or goodwill below its carrying amount. The recoverable amount is the higher of an asset's net selling price and the present value of estimated future cash flows arising from the continued use of an asset. *Refer to* IAS 36, and IAS 38.

**impairment losses** The amount by which the carrying amount of an asset exceeds its recoverable amount. *Refer to* IAS 36.

**impersonal account** A ledger account that does not bear the name of a person. These accounts normally comprise the nominal accounts, having such names as heat and light, and inventories.

**imprest account** A system for controlling petty cash expenditure. The person responsible for petty cash is given a certain sum of money. As expenditure is incurred, periodically the receipts and other vouchers are totaled, and the petty cashier is reimbursed for the expenditure, thus restoring the cash held to the original amount. Control is maintained by ensuring that, at any time, the total of the receipts held but not yet reimbursed and the cash held is equal to the original amount of cash.

**Improvements Project** Commenced by the International Accounting Standards Board (IASB) in 2002, the project is designed to implement relatively minor amendments to standards.

**incentive stock option** The right given to employees to purchase a specified number of shares in the organization at a specified price during a specified period.

**income** Inflows or enhancement of assets or decreases of liabilities that result in increases in equity over a financial period other than those relating to owners. Income, in the opinion of the International Accounting Standards Board (IASB), incorporates both revenues and gains. *Refer to* F.70.

**income and expenditure account** An account, similar to an income statement, prepared by a not-for-profit organization. It records the income and expenditure of the organization and results in either a surplus of income over expenditure or of expenditure over income.

**income gearing** *See* interest cover.

**income generating unit** A group of assets, liabilities, and associated goodwill that generates income that is largely independent of the organization's income streams from other activities.

**income smoothing** The manipulation of items in an organization's financial statements to reduce significant movements in profit so that a smooth trend over a number of years can be reported. This practice is followed to maintain investors' confidence since steady increase in profits is being reported annually. One consequence of the implementation of International Financial Reporting Standards is that profits are likely to become more volatile.

**income statement** The term used by the International Accounting Standards Board (IASB) for the statement that shows financial performance for a period of time. Terms used in other countries include the profit and loss account, statement of performance, statement of earnings, and statement of operations.

**incomplete records** Accounting records from which some details are missing thus preventing the construction of a trial balance and the drawing up of financial statements. For example, some transactions may not have been recorded at all, or some may have been partially recorded. To complete the records, the cash book must be examined, and with the other information available missing items are then calculated.

**incorporation** The process of becoming a corporate body by establishing a business as a legal entity.

**incremental analysis** An analysis of the revenues and costs that will change when a decision alternative is chosen. Incremental costs and incremental revenues are relevant for decision-making.

**incremental costs** Costs that differ among alternative decisions or opportunities and are relevant for decision making. These costs are also referred to as differential costs.

**independence of auditors** A fundamental principle is that auditors must be, and must be seen to be, independent of their clients to enable them to behave with integrity and make objective professional and business judgments. They are responsible to the owners of the company and not to the directors. The reality of independence is often questioned, and financial scandals often cast doubt on the independence of auditors.

**index-linked gilt** A gilt-edged security in which there is an obligation to increase both interest and redemption payments pro rata to increases in the Retail Price Index (RPI). Interest payments are normally calculated using the ratio of the RPI for the start date to RPI for the end date of the interest period.

**indirect method** The construction of a cash flow statement by adjusting the net income or loss for the period for transactions of a non-cash nature, deferrals or accruals of past or future operating cash receipts, or payments and income or expenses related to investing or financing activities. It is also acceptable to provide the revenues and expenses as shown in the income statement to arrive at net income. *Refer to* IAS 7.18.

**inflation** A general increase in prices in an economy and consequent fall in the purchasing power of money.

**inflation accounting** A method of accounting that takes account of the fact that a monetary unit does not have a constant value over time and therefore obscures trends in profit. Although the theoretical arguments for using some form of inflation accounting are persuasive, it has not been possible to agree on a method.

**information intermediaries** Individuals and groups who obtain, analyze, and interpret information, and communicate their findings to others. An example is the analyst who uses financial statements and other information to advise clients whether to buy, hold, or sell shares. The information intermediary will make use of not only the annual report and accounts, preliminary announcements of profits and interim financial statements, but also any other financial and non-financial information that is available, including those not on public record, although this could lead to the accusation of insider dealing.

**Information Systems Audit and Control Association (ISACA)** Based in the United States, ISACA was first incorporated as EDP Auditors Association in 1969. The association is a worldwide organization that provides education, training, certification, publications, and standards. The mandate is to expand the knowledge and value of the IT governance and control field. ISACA has more than 35,000 members worldwide. Members live and work in more than 100 countries and cover a variety of professional IT-related positions.

**inherent goodwill** The goodwill presumed to be present in an existing business, although it has not been evidenced by a purchase transaction. Internally generated goodwill should not be recognized as an asset in the financial statements. *Refer to* IAS 38.36.

**initial disclosure event** A binding sale agreement or the approval and announcement by an organization of the discontinuance of an operation.

**Initial Public Offering (IPO)** This is a corporation's offer of shares to the public for the first time.

**initial yield** The gross initial annual income from an asset divided by the initial cost of that asset.

**inside director** An employee of a company who has been appointed to the board of directors.

**insider dealing** Dealing in securities with a view to making a profit or avoiding a loss while in possession of price-sensitive information. The information may be obtained illegally and, if the information were publicly available, it would affect the market price of the securities. In most countries, insider dealing is unlawful.

**insolvency** The inability to pay one's debts when they fall due. In the case of individuals, it may lead to bankruptcy and, in the case of organizations, to liquidation.

**Institute of Chartered Accountants in Australia (ICAA)** Originally established by Royal Charter in 1928, the ICAA now operates under a Supplemental Royal Charter granted in 2000. It is governed by a Board of Directors consisting of 11 members: 10 are elected by members in each respective region and 1 elected by members on the overseas register. Directors and Regional Councilors will be elected for a three-year term, with one-third of the positions on the Board and Regional Councils being up for election each year. The Board elects the President and Deputy President annually.

**Institute of Chartered Accountants in England and Wales (ICAEW)** The Institute was incorporated by Royal Charter in May 1880 following the coming together of six local societies of accountants in London, Liverpool, Manchester, and Sheffield. The Institute is the largest professional accountancy body in Europe, with over 124,000 members working in business and public practice in 142 different countries. Members of the Institute are entitled to the description Chartered Accountant and to the designatory letters ACA or FCA. The Institute undertakes or facilitates a wide range of professional activities, including education and training of students, continuing professional development for members, maintenance of professional and ethical standards, and the provision of advice and services to members.

**Institute of Chartered Accountants in Ireland (ICAI)** The Institute of Chartered Accountants in Ireland is the largest and longest established accountancy body in Ireland. The Institute was established by Royal Charter in 1888. Its activities and those of its members are governed by its Bylaws and by Rules relating to professional and ethical conduct. It has over 13,000 members, and it is the leading body for the accountancy profession in Ireland. The Institute is governed by a Council and it is responsible for determining policy and monitoring its implementation. The Council is led by the Officer Group and supported by the Management Team and staff.

**Institute of Chartered Accountants of New Zealand (ICANZ)** The Institute of Chartered Accountants of New Zealand is the only professional accounting body in New Zealand and represents nearly 27,000 members. There are three "Colleges" or membership groupings within the Institute:

Chartered Accountants; Associate Chartered Accountants; and Accounting Technicians. The Institute has branches throughout New Zealand, and in Sydney, Melbourne, London, and Fiji. Within this framework, volunteer committees and special interest groups work together to share ideas and create opportunities for members to continually develop their skills.

**Institute of Chartered Accountants of Scotland (ICAS)** The Institute of Chartered Accountants of Scotland (ICAS) received its Royal Charter in 1854 and is the oldest professional body of accountants in the world. It was the first to adopt the designation "Chartered Accountant," and the designatory letters "CA" are still an exclusive privilege in the United Kingdom for members of the Scottish Institute.

**Institute of Chartered Secretaries and Administrators (ICSA)** Established in 1891 in London, United Kingdom, the ICSA is the professional body for chartered secretaries. The ICSA's mandate is to promote the interests of company secretaries and administrators. It has 44,000 members and 28,000 students in over 70 countries. Members are qualified in company law, accounting, corporate governance, administration, company secretarial practice, and management. They work as company secretaries and in other senior positions in companies, charities, local government, educational institutions, and trade bodies. The ICSA has international divisions and offices in Australia, Canada, Hong Kong, Malaysia, New Zealand, Singapore, South Africa.

**Institute of Cost and Executive Accountants (ICEA)** The ICEA is a professional and examining body representing cost and executive accountants. It promotes the study and adoption of scientific methods in industrial and commercial enterprises, public sector, and internal audit streams. The Institute was the first accounting body in the world to provide an examination in Management Auditing for its members. The Institute commenced as the Institute of Industrial and Commercial Accountants in 1939. In 1958 it was incorporated as a company limited by guarantee and adopted its present name. Members are entitled to designate themselves as "Incorporated Executive Accountant" using the letters FCEA (for Fellows) and ACEA (for Associates). The Institute has over 3,500 members, 2,000 registered students, 14 branches in the United Kingdom, and 18 overseas branches.

**Institute of Internal Auditors (IIA)** Established in 1941, the IIA has 98,000 members in 160 countries and territories worldwide. Members work in internal auditing, governance and internal control, IT audit, education, and security worldwide. The Institute serves as the profession's watchdog and resource on significant auditing issues around the globe. The IIA provides internal audit practitioners, executive management, boards of directors, and audit committees with standards, guidance, and information on best practices in internal auditing.

**Institute of Management Accountants (IMA)** Originally established in 1919 as the National Association of Cost Accountants in the United States, the IMA has 67,000 members mainly engaged in management accounting and financial management.

**institutional investor** An organization such as a bank, insurance company, or pension fund that trades in substantial volumes of securities on a daily basis. Institutional investors tend to dominate stock markets in many countries.

**instrument** *See* financial instrument.

**insurance risk** Risk, other than financial risk, transferred from a holder of a contract to the issuer. *Refer to* IFRS 4.A.

**intangible assets** Assets of a non-monetary nature that are identifiable, have no physical substance, and are held for use in the production or supply of goods or services. Historically, the accounting treatment for intangible assets has been a controversial topic, and assets, such as brands and publication titles, have appeared on the balance sheets of a number of well-known corporations. The current position is that intangible assets should only be recognized if they meet the criteria set out in the International Financial Reporting Standard and must be measured in accordance with the guidance provided. *Refer to* IAS 38.

**integral approach** A basis for the recognition and measurement of assets, liabilities, income, and expenses for an interim period, that is, less than 12 months. The assumption used is that the interim period is an integral part of the total annual period and not an independent, stand-alone period. *Refer to* IAS 34.28.

**integrated accounts** A system of maintaining both the financial accounts and cost accounts of an organization in one set of books in an integrated form. This avoids the necessity of reconciling separate financial and cost books, and at the same time ensures that both records are based on the same data.

**intellectual property** An asset that arises from the invention, generation, or ownership of patents, trade markets, logos, and similar items that give rise to future economic benefits. If the asset meets the recognition and measurement criteria in the accounting standard, it will appear in the financial accounts. *Refer to* IAS 38.

**inter-company transactions** Transactions conducted between separate companies or parts within a group of companies. The transactions may be the transfer of goods or services from one part to another or may be certain charges. In the preparation of consolidated financial statements, intragroup balances and intragroup transactions should be eliminated in full. *Refer to* IAS 27.

**interest** The charge made for lending a sum of money or received for investing it. The interest rate is normally expressed as a percentage of the total sum loaned, for a stated period of time. In simple interest, the charge is calculated on the sum loaned only, thus i = prt, where i is the interest, p is the principal sum, r is the rate of interest, and t is the period. In compound interest, the charge is calculated on the sum loaned plus any interest that has accrued in previous periods. In this case $i = p[(1+r)^n - 1]$, where n is the number of periods for which interest is separately calculated.

**interest cover** A ratio that evaluates the financial strength of an organization by calculating the number of times interest charges are covered by earnings before interest and tax. For example, an organization with interest charges of $12 million and earnings before interest and tax of $36 million would have its interest covered three times. The ratio is one way of analyzing leverage and reflects the vulnerability of an organization to changes in interest rates or profit fluctuations. A highly leveraged corporation with a low interest cover may find that it has no earnings after interest charges to provide dividends to shareholders if the interest rate increases.

**interest rate** The rate charged for a loan, usually expressed as a percentage of the sum borrowed. Conversely, the amount paid by a bank or a financial institution, to a depositor of funds, expressed as a percentage of the sum deposited.

**interest rate guarantee** An indemnity sold by a bank, or similar financial institution, that protects the purchaser against the effect of future movements in interest rates. It is similar to a forward-rate agreement, but the terms are specified by the customer.

**interest rate options** A contract giving the holder the right, but not the obligation, to fix the interest rate on either a notional or an agreed amount for a fixed term or on a specific future date. These contracts are a device for hedging against fluctuating interest rates.

**interest rate risk** The risk that the value of a financial asset or liability can vary during its life due to fluctuations in market interest rates.

**interest rate swaps** An agreement between two parties in which each party agrees to pay the interest of the other for a specified period. The normal practice is for a fixed rate of interest to be swapped for a floating rate based on a "notional" principal amount. Each party remains responsible for the actual payment of their own interest on the loans they hold and to settle between themselves the net difference arising from any differential rates on interest payments. Properly structured, both parties can benefit financially from the swap.

**interim account** *See* interim financial reporting.

**interim audit** The work performed in stages by auditors during the course of a financial year. This reduces the amount of audit work to be completed at the year-end.

**interim dividend** A dividend paid midway through a financial year. Shareholders normally regard it as a signal of good financial performance.

**interim financial reporting** Financial statements issued for a period of less than a financial year, normally three or six months. The report may be a complete set of financial statements or a condensed version. *Refer to* IAS 34.4.

**interlocking accounts** A record keeping method of maintaining cost accounting and financial accounting information separately. To ensure the reliability of the records, regular reconciliations are normally conducted by the use of control accounts.

**intermediate holding company** A corporation that is both a holding company of one group and a subsidiary undertaking of a larger group.

**intermediation** The involvement of a bank, similar financial institution, or a broker, in a financial arrangement between two parties to a transaction. The intermediary, as well as offering guidance and support, can accept all or part of the credit risk or other commercial risks.

**internal audit** An audit that an organization carries out on its own behalf, normally to ensure that its own internal controls are operating satisfactorily. The internal audit may also be used to conduct investigations to detect any theft or fraud. As well as strengthening internal controls, the operation of an internal audit department may reduce the fees charged by external auditors.

**internal control** The activities, procedures, and systems used by an organization to ensure the effective and orderly conduct of operations. The system will also ensure that opportunities for fraud or misconduct are minimized. Examples of internal control procedures include requiring more than one signature on certain documents, security arrangements for inventory handling, division of tasks, keeping control accounts, use of special passwords, and handling of computer files. The system should ensure that management policies are adhered to, assets are safeguarded, and the records of the company's activities are both complete and accurate. A principal concern in the internal audit is to ensure that internal controls are working properly so that external auditors can have faith in the accounts produced by the organization. Internal controls should also reassure management of the integrity of its operations and contribute to good corporate governance.

**internal control risk** The risk that material errors are not prevented or detected by the internal control system of an organization.

**internal failure cost** Costs incurred to rectify quality defects of products found prior to product sale. These costs include scrap, spoilage, and rework costs.

**Internal Rate of Return (IRR)** A measure of the return, expressed as a percentage that may be anticipated from a long-term project. It is calculated by identifying the interest rate that gives a net present value of zero (where both cash inflows and outflows are equal) when applied to the projected cash flows of a project. The financial decision whether to proceed with the project would depend on the IRR compared with the organization's cost of capital.

**International Accounting Standards (IASs)** Accounting standards issued originally by the International Accounting Standards Committee and adopted by its successor, the International Accounting Standards Board (IASB). A total of 41 International Accounting Standards were issued, and those still in existence have retained the term IASs. However, the IASs have been incorporated under the general heading of International Financial Reporting Standards (IFRSs) by the IASB.

**International Accounting Standards Board (IASB)** In 2000, the International Accounting Standards Committee Foundation was established with the responsibility of appointing the members of the International Accounting Standards Board. The IASB commenced operations in 2001 with Sir David Tweedie as Chair. The IASB has 14 Board members, each with one vote. The IASB Board has full responsibility for all technical matters, including the preparation and issuing of accounting standards and final approval of Interpretations by the Interpretations Committee.

**International Accounting Standards Committee (IASC)** A committee that came into existence in 1973 as a result of an agreement by professional accounting bodies of Australia, Canada, France, Germany, Japan, Mexico, the Netherlands, the United Kingdom and Ireland, and the United States. The objectives of the IASC were the formulation and publication of accounting standards, the promotion of their worldwide acceptance, and the harmonization of regulations, accounting standards, and procedures relating to the presentation of financial statements. In 2000, the IASC approved the recommendations of a strategic working party and the restructuring of the organization. In April 2001, the new International Accounting Standard Board became effective.

**International Association for Accounting Education and Research (IAAER)** Established in 1984, the IAAER promotes the quality of accounting education and research at the international level. It supports the globalization of accounting standards and contributes to their academic development.

**International Association of Bookkeepers (IAB)** The IAB was founded in 1973. The qualification is appropriate for those working at the first level of financial accounting in small to medium-sized organizations.

**International Association of Financial Executives Institutes (IAFEI)** Based in Zurich, Switzerland, IAFEI is a non-profit association with a total membership of over 30,000 Financial Executives. Founded in 1969, IAFEI currently has 21 Member Institutes. The Association is organized under the provisions of Articles 60–79 of the Swiss Civil Code and, accordingly, has its own legal personality. IAFEI is recognized in accounting, financial, and governmental circles around the world. Its aim is to promote international cooperation and integrity among financial executives toward making financial systems and regulations more uniform and harmonious worldwide.

**International Association of Practising Accountants (IAPA)** Based in the United Kingdom, the IAPA was established in 1979. It has membership offices in over 340 cities and business centers around the world. The Association coordinates the activities of its members and administers the affairs of the Association under the strategic guidance of its International Board.

**International Auditing Practices Committee (IAPC)** A standing committee of the International Federation of Accountants (IFAC). It has a specific responsibility to issue exposure drafts and guidelines on auditing and related services. It also issues International Standards on Auditing (ISA). The members of the committee are nominated by the member bodies in the countries selected by the council of the IFAC. Whenever possible, the subcommittees of IAPC would include representatives from countries that are not members of IAPC in order to obtain a broad spectrum of views.

**International Bank for Reconstruction and Development (IBRD)** A specialized agency working in coordination with the United Nations, established in 1945 to help finance postwar reconstruction and to help raise standards of living in developing countries, by making loans to governments, or guaranteeing outside loans. It lends on broadly commercial terms, either for specific projects or for more general social purposes; funds are raised on the international capital markets. The bank and its affiliates, the international development association and the international finance corporation, are often known as the World Bank.

**International Federation of Accountants (IFAC)** A body formed in 1977 with the objective of developing an international accountancy profession with harmonized standards. Based in the United States, it has a membership of accounting bodies representing approximately 80 countries. It works through a number of committees responsible for education, ethics, financial and management accounting, the public sector, and international auditing practices. Although it does not issue standards, the federation supports international accounting standards and makes a significant contribution to the annual running costs of the International Accounting Standards Board (IASB).

**International Financial Reporting Interpretations Committee (IFRIC)** The International Financial Reporting Interpretations Committee is the successor to the Standards Interpretation Committee. IFRIC has the responsibility for interpreting requirements of standards that may be controversial or capable of being applied in a way other than that intended by the IASB. The Committee develops Draft Interpretations (Numbered D1, D2, and so forth) and releases these for public comment. When approved by IFRIC, they are sent to the IASB for review, approval, and release as Final Interpretations. Organizations cannot claim that their financial statements comply with IFRSs unless they comply both with the requirements of the standard and any interpretation that has been issued.

**International Financial Reporting Standards (IFRSs)** The term used by the International Accounting Standards Board to include standards and interpretations it has issued and the International Accounting Standards that it has adapted and were issued by its predecessor the International Accounting Standards Committee (IASC).

**International Forum for Accountancy Development (IFAD)** The IFAD was created as a working group among these organizations: the Basel Committee, the International Federation of Accountants (IFAC), IOSCO, the large Accounting Firms, OECD, UNCTAD, the World Bank, and the regional development banks, which flowed from the East Asian crisis. The IFAD's mission is to improve market security and transparency, and financial stability on a global basis.

**International Monetary Fund (IMF)** The IMF was established after the Second World War to promote international monetary cooperation, expand international trade, stabilize exchange rates, and help countries experiencing short-term balance of payments difficulties to maintain their exchange rates. The fund assists members by supplying the amount of foreign currency it wishes to purchase in exchange for the equivalent amount of its own currency. The member repays the amount by buying back its own currency in a currency acceptable to the fund, usually within three to five years. The fund is financed by subscriptions from its members, the amount determined by an estimate of their means. Voting power is related to the amount of the subscription: the higher the contribution, the higher the voting rights.

**International Organization for Securities Commissions (IOSCO)** A body formed in 1987 with the objective of establishing internationally agreed accounting standards to aid in multinational share offering by companies. IOSCO agreed with the International Accounting Standards Committee to support the development of a core set of standards. The core standards project resulted in 15 new or revised standards and was completed in 1999. IOSCO spent a year reviewing the results of the project and released a report in 2000. They recommended that its members allow multinational issuers to accept IASC standards for cross-border listings. However, it also allowed its members to require reconciliation, disclosure, and interpretation where necessary to address outstanding substantive issues at a national or regional level.

**International Organization of Supreme Audit Institutions (INTOSAI)** Based in Austria, INTOSAI is the professional organization of supreme audit institutions (SAI) in countries that belong to the United Nations or its specialized agencies. SAIs play a major role in auditing government accounts and operations and in promoting sound financial management and accountability in their governments. National governments depend on SAIs to help ensure public accountability. INTOSAI supports its members in this task by providing opportunities to share information and experiences about the auditing and evaluation challenges facing them in today's changing and increasingly interdependent world. Founded in 1953, INTOSAI has grown from the original 34 countries to a membership of over 170 supreme audit institutions.

**International Regional Federation of Accountants and Auditors "Eurasia" (IRFAA-EURASIA)** Established in Kiev in 1999, the body is an international federation of accounting and audit associations in the Eurasian region (New Independent States of the Former Soviet Union). Member countries currently include the Republic of Armenia, Republic of Azerbaijan, Republic of Belarus, Georgia, Republic of Kazakhstan, Kyrgyzstan, Republic of Moldova, Russian Federation, Ukraine and Republic of Uzbekistan. With the assistance of the Organization for Economic Co-operation and Development (OECD) and the United States Agency for International Development (US-AID), the body's overall goal is to improve financial disclosure, accounting and audit practices in the Eurasian region in support of corporate governance, transparency and accountability.

**International Standards on Auditing (ISA)** Standards issued by the International Auditing Practices Committee (IAPC). They do not override the local regulations of countries. If the IASs conform to local regulations on a particular subject, the audit of the financial information in that country will automatically comply with the international regulations.

**International Valuation Standards Committee (IVSC)** Established in 1981 and based in the United Kingdom, the IVSC is comprised of 50 professional valuation associations from around the world. The IVSC works closely with IFAC and the IASB. The Committee has released International Valuation Standards (IVSs) since 1985.

**interpretations** Pronouncements issued by IFRIC with the objective of developing conceptually sound and practicable interpretations. These may concern newly identified financial reporting issues that are not specifically addressed in the IFRSs. Interpretations are also required where unsatisfactory, conflicting, divergent, or other unacceptable practices have developed or are likely to develop without appropriate guidelines.

**in-the-money option** A situation with respect to a call option when the current market price of the share or other underlying asset is higher than the exercise price at a time when the option is exercisable. *See* at-the-money option.

**intrinsic value** The amount by which the market price of the underlying share exceeds the exercise price of an option.

**introduction** A method of issuing shares on a stock exchange in which a broker or issuing house takes small quantities of the corporation's shares and issues them to clients at appropriate stages.

**inventory** The products and supplies of an organization on hand or in transit at any time in the ordinary course of business. For a manufacturing organization, the types of inventory are raw materials, work in progress, and finished goods. *Refer to* IAS 2. *See* days' sales in inventory.

**inventory accounting** The accounting records and systems used for the ordering, receipt, issuing, and valuation of the materials bought by an organization. It includes the recording of the entries on bin cards and in the inventory ledger as well as the procedures adopted to carry out an effective inventory count.

**inventory appreciation** An increase in the value of an organization's inventory, generally due to inflation. As company profits are boosted by increases in inventory values, inventory appreciation gives an artificial boost to profits, causing higher tax and possibly higher dividend payments. The standard accounting procedure for preventing this distortion of real profitability is the adoption of last in, first out (LIFO).

**inventory control** A control system to ensure that adequate but not excessive levels of inventories are maintained by an organization, taking into account the consumption levels, delivery lead times, and reorder levels of each commodity.

**inventory turnover** A ratio that shows the effectiveness of the organization in its inventory control. It is calculated by dividing the number of units of inventory used per annum by the number of units in inventory. The number of units in inventory may be taken at the start or the end of the year, or may be the average of both. Because the information required for this ratio is only likely to be available from management accounts, a different formula using the figures from final accounts is often used as an overall measure of inventory turnover. This is calculated by dividing the cost of sales in the financial period by the value of the inventory.

**inventory valuation** The valuation of inventories of raw materials, work in progress, and finished goods. Inventories are normally valued at lower of cost or net realizable value and the cost incurred up to the stage of production. This means that finished goods and work in progress should include both fixed and variable production costs but exclude the selling and distribution costs. *Refer to* IAS 2.

**investing activities** A heading required by IAS 7 for the cash flow statements. It shows details of acquisition and disposal of long-term assets and other activities not included in cash equivalents. *Refer to* IAS 7.

**investment center** A responsibility center in which the manager is accountable for its profit and for the capital investment decisions. The center is normally a division, subsidiary, department, or area of activity.

**investment properties** Properties owned by an investor for the purpose of rental income or capital appreciation rather than for operating use. The standard permits organizations to choose either the fair value model or the cost model. *Refer to* IAS 40.

**invisible assets** *See* intangible assets.

**issue by tender** A method of issuing shares in which an issuing house asks investors to tender for them. The stocks or shares are then allocated to the highest bidders. It is usual for the tender documents to state the lowest price acceptable.

**issued shares** The number of shares issued by an organization and held by shareholders.

***istisna*** Under Islamic finance, the term refers to construction financing.

# J

**Japanese Institute of Certified Public Accountants (JICPA)** Originally founded as a self-disciplinary association in 1949, the Institute was reorganized under the Certified Public Accountants Law in 1966. It is the sole representative body for the CPA profession in Japan. Those who wish to practice using the designation of CPA in Japan must register and become a member of JICPA.

**job order costing** A product costing system in which costs are collected and assigned to units of production for each individual job. Job costing is used by organizations that produce relatively small numbers of unique or dissimilar products.

**joint and several liability** An agreement is entered into by a group of individuals, in business with a view to profit, that if any individuals become insolvent, liability must be shared by the remainder. A partnership is an example of a joint and several liability relationship.

**joint audit** An audit carried out by two or more accounting firms in which the audit report is prepared jointly.

**joint costs** The costs incurred in a joint production before the joint products become identifiable as separate products at the split-off point.

**jointly controlled assets** Two or more parties agree to control certain assets jointly. The costs of the operation of these assets are shared, and each venturer may take a share from the output from the assets. Examples of such ventures can be found in the oil, gas, and mineral extraction industries. *Refer to* IAS 31.13.

**jointly controlled entities** Two or more parties agree to a share of control in an enterprise, a partnership being an example. A jointly controlled entity operates as a business, and each venturer is usually entitled to a share of the results or of the output. *Refer to* IAS 31.19.

**jointly controlled operations** Two or more parties agree on assigning the use of certain assets or other resources to specified operations. There may not be an entity legally separate from the owners, but, in fact, there may be an accounting entity for reporting purposes. An example of a joint venture is the combinations of certain resources and operations of the individual venturers to produce and sell a particular product. *Refer to* IAS 31.8.

**joint production process** The manufacturing process that results in two or more joint products.

**joint products** The outputs of a manufacturing process that consist of two or more separately identifiable products with similar economic importance.

**joint venture** A contractual arrangement in which two or more parties control an economic activity jointly. Joint ventures can have different forms and structures requiring different accounting treatments. The standard identifies three types: jointly controlled assets; jointly controlled entities; jointly controlled operations. *Refer to* IAS 31.3.

**junk bond** A bond that offers a high rate of interest but a low level of security.

**just-in-time techniques (JIT techniques)** A technique used in manufacturing to match production to demand by only supplying materials to production as needed. This has the effect of reducing inventories, encouraging those production activities that add value to the output, and minimizing the levels of scrap and defective units.

# K

**kaizen** A Japanese term meaning continuous improvement. Instead of special projects to implement improvements to processes and products, kaizen is a continuous process involving all employees. Kaizen involves the constant effort of eliminating waste, reducing response time, minimizing defects, streamlining the design of products and processes, and improving quality and customer service. The technique has gained popularity worldwide, particularly in manufacturing industries.

**kanban** The Japanese system of order cards that forms the basis of the *just-in-time* production system. The system reduces the amount of semicompleted stock within the factory, focusing attention on the critical need to ensure a smooth flow of production to prevent the processes coming to a halt.

**kite** An informal name for an accommodation bill. Kite-flying or kiting is the act of discounting a kite at a bank knowing that the person on whom it is drawn will dishonor it.

**know-how** Industrial information and techniques that assist in manufacturing and processing goods or materials.

# L

**lapping** The fraudulent practice of concealing the theft of cash by delaying the recording of cash receipts. There are several variations of this practice, but frequently cash received from the first customer is stolen, and this action is concealed by recording cash received from the second customer as attributable to the first, and continued with subsequent customers. The cashier hopes to be in a position to replace the cash before the dishonesty is discovered.

**last-in-first-out (LIFO) cost** A method of valuing units of raw material or finished goods by using the latest unit value for pricing the issues until all the quantities received at that price are used up. The next earliest price is then used for pricing the issues. Since the issues are based on a LIFO cost, the valuation of closing inventories is described as being on LIFO basis.

**leading and lagging** Techniques that may be used at the end of a financial year to improve the appearance of the financial statements. For example, outstanding liabilities could be settled to reduce the borrowings figure or delayed to enhance the cash position.

**lease** A contract between the owner of a specific asset, the lessor, and another party, the lessee, allowing the latter to use the asset for a specified period of time in exchange for payments. Leases may be classified as either financial leases or operating leases with different accounting treatments for the lessor and the lessee. *Refer to* IAS 17.3.

**leaseback** An arrangement in which the owner of an asset (such as land or buildings) sells it to another party but immediately enters into a lease agreement with the purchaser to obtain the right to use the asset.

**leasehold** The right acquired under a lease to use land and buildings for a specified period in return for the payment of a specific rental.

**ledger capital** The amount of equity, which cannot be reduced by the payment of dividends.

**legal obligation** An obligation that arises from a contract, legislation, or other operation of law.

**letter of comfort** A letter to a bank from the parent company of a subsidiary that wishes to obtain a loan. The letter gives no guarantee for the repayment of the loan but offers the bank the comfort of knowing that the subsidiary has made the parent company aware of its intentions and, at least, some reassurance that there is the apparent intention that the subsidiary will remain in business.

**letter of credit** *See* documentary credit.

**letter of representation** A letter signed by both management and auditors regarding issues for which the auditor is unable to obtain independent corroborative evidence. These matters might include any future legal claims and adjusting events.

**leverage** The relationship between the funds provided by ordinary shareholders and the long-term funds with a fixed interest charge, such as debentures and preference shares. A company is highly leveraged when its long-term funds are significantly higher than those for other companies. A highly leveraged company is considered to be a speculative investment for the ordinary shareholder. It should have high returns when the company is doing well, but quickly enters into a loss situation if there is a downturn.

**leveraged buyout (LBO)** The acquisition of one organization by another through the use of borrowed funds. Usually, the acquirers use their own assets as security for the funds. The intention is that the loans will be repaid from the cash flow of the acquired organization.

**leverage ratios** Ratios that examine the relationship between equity and debt. There are a number of different ratios that can be extracted from information on either the balance sheet or income statement. Ratios based on the balance sheet usually express debt as a percentage of equity or as a percentage of debt plus equity. Ratios based on the income statement usually examine the relationship of interest charges to earnings.

**liability** A present obligation to transfer economic benefits, for example cash, other assets, or services. Liabilities arise through past transactions or past events. For example, the acquisition of goods that are not paid for immediately will result in trades payable. *Refer to* F.60.

**license** A legal permission or right granted to perform a particular act, to exercise a certain privilege, or to pursue a particular business or occupation, e.g. a taxi license. It is an intangible asset and should be amortized over the period for which the license is granted. *Refer to* IAS 38.

**life cycle costing** A management technique used to identify and monitor the cost of a product throughout its life cycle. It is also known as cradle-to-grave costing. For instance, the life cycle of a nuclear plant would take into account the decommissioning costs.

**limited liability company (LLC)** An organization in which the financial liability of the investors is limited to an agreed amount. The liability may be limited by shares, in which case the liability of the investors on a winding-up is limited to the amount (if any) unpaid on their shares. The liability of the investors may alternatively be limited by guarantee, in this case the liability is limited to a specified amount that the investors undertake to contribute on the event of liquidation.

**linear depreciation** Depreciation charges that, when plotted on a graph against time on the x-axis, result in a straight line, as a constant amount per annum is written off the assets concerned. The straight-line method of depreciation is an example of linear depreciation.

**linear interpolation** A technique used in the Discounted Cash Flow (DCF) method for project appraisal when calculating the approximate Internal Rate of Return (IRR). The cash flows for the project are discounted at two discount rates in order to obtain a small positive and a small negative net present value. A linear relationship is assumed between the two results in order to calculate the discount rate that would give a net present value of zero.

**liquid assets** Cash or other assets that can be readily turned into cash (such as deposits in bank checking (chequing) accounts, short-term deposit savings accounts, accounts receivable, marketable investments). The ratio of these assets to current liabilities provides an assessment of an organization's liquidity or solvency.

**liquidation** The distribution of an organization's assets among its creditors and investors prior to its dissolution.

**liquid ratio** The liquid ratio is regarded as a stringent test of an organization's solvency and is also known as the acid-test ratio or quick ratio. It is calculated by comparing the liquid (quick) assets (that is, the current assets less the inventory) to the current liabilities. The result is expressed either as a percentage or as x:1. For example, a company with current assets of $40,000 including inventory of $15,000 and liabilities of $32,000 will have a liquid ratio of the following:

($40,000 – $15,000)/$32,000 = $25,000/32,000 = 0.78:1

This may be interpreted as the company having 78 cents of liquid or current assets for every $1 of current liabilities. If, for some reason, the company is obliged to repay the current liabilities immediately, there would be insufficient liquid assets to allow it to do so. In such circumstances, it may be difficult to find either sources of finance to remedy the position.

**liquid instruments** A negotiable instrument that the purchaser is able to sell before maturity.

**liquidity** The extent to which an organization's assets are liquid, enabling debts to be paid as they fall due. The concept of liquidity encompasses cash and non-cash position as well as the timing of future cash flows that are part of normal business activity.

**liquidity index** A measure of an organization's liquidity assessed by calculating the number of days it would take for current assets to be converted into cash.

**liquidity risk** This risk is associated with financial instruments. It is the possibility that an organization is unable to sell a financial asset quickly at close to fair value, thus having difficulty in meeting commitments. *Refer to* IAS 32.52.

**listed company** A corporation in the United Kingdom that has a listing agreement with the London Stock Exchange and whose shares therefore have a quotation on the main market. These corporations were formerly called quoted companies, and the term is still frequently used.

**loan capital** Capital used to finance an organization that is subject to payment of interest over the life of the loan, at the end of which the loan is repaid.

**loan creditor** A person or institution that has lent money to a business. For example, when a bank loan is obtained, the bank becomes a loan creditor.

**loans and receivables** These are financial assets that are non-derivative, with fixed or determinable payments, and are not quoted in an active market. There are a number of exceptions, mainly in respect of the intention of the entity to sale the assets. *Refer to* IAS 39.9.

**loan stock** *See* debentures.

**London Stock Exchange (LSE)** Based in London, United Kingdom, the LSE is one of the world's oldest stock exchange. The LSE was originally known as "Jonathan's Coffee House" and dealings in securities began as early as the seventeenth century. The name stock exchange was first used in 1773, although it was not formally instituted until 1801. The development of the industrial revolution encouraged many other share markets to flourish throughout the United Kingdom. These amalgamated in 1973 to form the Stock Exchange of Great Britain and Ireland. It later became the International Stock Exchange of the United Kingdom and the Republic of Ireland, and finally it was called the London Stock Exchange. *See* stock exchange.

**long-form report** A detailed report made by an auditor on a client's financial statements.

**long hedge** A strategy to protect the value of future cash flows. A derivative is purchased now, at a price fixed today, of equivalent value to the future cash flows. The value of the future cash flows is therefore protected from adverse fluctuations.

**long position** A position held by a dealer in securities, commodities, or currencies, where current holdings exceed sales. The dealer expects prices to rise, enabling a profit to be made by selling at the higher levels.

**long-term contract** A contract that commences in one financial period but will not be completed until a subsequent period. Such a contract may be for the design, manufacture, or construction of a single, substantial asset (as in the construction or civil engineering industries). From an accounting point of view, there is a problem in determining how much profit can be reasonably allocated to each accounting period when the contract is only partially completed. *Refer to* IAS 11.

**long-term debtors** Debtors who are not expected to settle in the present financial period the amounts outstanding.

**long-term liability** A sum owed that does not have to be repaid within the next accounting period of a business. In some contexts, a long-term liability may be regarded as one not due for repayment within the next 3, or possibly 10, years.

**loss** The amount by which expenses of a transaction or operation exceed the income generated.

**lowballing** The practice of auditors offering to reduce the fees for statutory audit in order to be appointed by a prospective client. The lower audit fees are compensated by carrying out highly lucrative non-audit work, such as consultancy and tax advice, for the client.

**lower of cost and net realizable value rule** The method of valuing inventories at the lower of cost and net realizable value. *Refer to* IAS 2.6.

# M

**mad dog** A term used to describe an organization with the potential to expand rapidly, but the risks associated with the rapid expansion are likely to be high. The computer industry is an example of a sector that has included several mad dogs.

**make or buy decision** A short-term decision on whether to make a product or component internally or to buy it from an external party. If an organization has spare capacity, only the variable costs of manufacture will be incurred and should be compared to the buy-in cost to make the decision. If there is no spare capacity, the opportunity costs of manufacture may have to be taken into account.

**management accounting** *See* managerial accounting.

**management audit** An independent review of the management of an organization. This is conducted normally by management consultants specializing in this service. The review will cover all aspects of running the organization including the control of production, marketing, sales, finance, and personnel.

**Management by Objectives (MBO)** A management technique in which all levels of management are encouraged to specify and agree upon quantitative and/or qualitative targets with their immediate superiors. The agreed targets should be achieved within a set period, and actual performance achieved is compared against these objectives.

**Management Buy Out (MBO)** The acquisition of an organization or part of it by its managers, usually because the original owners are unable to manage it effectively or it no longer fits in with the corporate strategy. The management usually obtains loans from venture capitalists or other financial institutions, and the expectation is that the company will be listed on a stock exchange when it is sufficiently profitable.

**Management Discussion and Analysis (MD&A)** The section in the annual report to shareholders and in Form 10-k that is required by the Securities and Exchange Commission (SEC). The purpose of the MD&A is to assist investors to understand the impact of changes in accounting and business activities that have affected comparisons with results of previous years. Management should summarize and discuss, among other matters, the reasons for changes in the results of operations, capital resources, and liquidity.

**Management Information System (MIS)** An information system designed to provide financial and quantitative information to all levels of management in an organization for the purposes of planning, control, and decision making. Most modern information systems provide the data from an integrated computer database that is constantly updated from all areas of the organization in a structured way. Access to the data is usually restricted to managers responsible for specific functions with confidential information being confined to senior management.

**management letter** A letter written by an auditor to the management of a client organization at the end of the annual audit to suggest possible improvements that could be made to the organization's accounting and internal control system.

**managerial accounting** The techniques used to collect, process, analyze, and interpret financial and quantitative data within an organization, to enable managers to plan, control organizational operations, and make decisions.

**mandate** Written authority given by one person (the mandator) to another (the mandatory), giving the latter the power to act on behalf of the former. The mandate comes to an end on the death, mental illness, or bankruptcy of the mandatory.

**manufacturing account** An accounting statement forming part of the internal final accounts of a manufacturing organization. It is prepared for a financial period and is structured to provide details on the prime costs of production, manufacturing overhead, total production costs, and manufacturing costs of finished goods. Depending on the policies of the organization, the manufacturing cost may be the basis for calculating the final profit on the sale of the goods, or there may be a transfer price fixed that is higher than the manufactured cost, thus showing a manufacturing profit.

**manufacturing profit** The difference between the value of the goods transferred from a manufacturing account to a trading account at a price other than the manufactured cost of finished goods.

**marginal cost** *See* variable cost.

**marginal revenue** The additional income that accrues to an organization from selling an extra unit of sales.

**margin of safety** The difference between the level of activity at which an organization breaks even and a given level of activity higher than the breakeven point. The margin of safety may be expressed in terms of sales dollars, number of units, or percentage of capacity. The margin of safety shows how much activity can decline before the organization enters into a loss.

**margin of safety ratio** The margin of safety expressed as a percentage of a given level of activity. For example, if the sales level achieved is $800,000 and the sales level breakeven point is $600,000, the margin of safety is $200,000 and the margin of safety ratio will be:

$$(\$200{,}000/\$800{,}000) \times 100\% = 25\%$$

**markdown** A reduction in the price of a good or service below the normal price.

**markup** The amount by which the cost of a service or product has been increased to arrive at the selling price. It is calculated by expressing the profit as a percentage of the cost of goods or services. For example, if a product cost $48 and is sold for $60, the markup would be:

$$\text{Profit} = \$12/\$48 \times 100 = 25\%$$

The markup is widely used in the retailing industry, both for setting prices and as a ratio for control and decision making.

**marker rate** The base interest rate defined in a loan agreement. The spread is added in order to establish the interest rate payable on a variable-rate loan.

**market capitalization** The value of an organization obtained by multiplying the number of ordinary shares in issue by the market price per share.

**market risk** The risk that the value of a financial instrument will fluctuate as a result of changes in market prices. These changes may affect all securities traded in the market or may be specific to the individual security. Market risk offers the opportunity of loss or gain. There are three types: currency risk; fair value interest rate risk; price risk. *Refer to* IAS 32.52.

**market valuation** *See* market capitalization.

**market value** *See* market price.

**Market Value Added (MVA)** The difference between the recorded value (or book value) of an organization's share capitalization and the current market value of the shares. A high MVA measure indicates that the organization has created substantial wealth for its shareholders. MVA is equivalent to the present value of all future Economic Value Added (EVA) measures for the organization. A negative MVA suggests that the value of investments of the organization is less than the value given by the capital markets. In essence, this means that the wealth of the organization has been adversely affected or destroyed.

**matched bargain** A transaction in which a sale of a particular quantity of stock is matched with a purchase of the same quantity of the same stock.

**matching concept** Revenue and expenditure are not allocated to financial periods on the basis of cash received or paid, but matched within one particular period so that the income for the period can be determined. The revenue to be recognized for a period is determined, and the costs incurred in achieving that revenue are matched against it. *Refer to* F.95.

**materiality** The extent to which an item of accounting information is material. Information is considered material if its omission from a financial statement could influence the decision making of its users. Materiality is therefore not an absolute concept but is dependent on the size and nature of the item and the particular circumstances in which the accounting information arises. *Refer to* F.30.

**matrix accounting** The use of a matrix to record accounting transactions and events rather than using a T-account. Entries are made into the cells of the matrix that contains formulae to produce the appropriate results.

**maturity date** The date on which a document, such as a bond, bill of exchange, or insurance policy, becomes due for payment. In some cases, especially for redeemable government stocks, the maturity date is known as the redemption date.

**measurement** Generally, the determination of the monetary amounts of transactions and events that are to be recognized and entered into the books of account. Specifically, determining the monetary amounts of the assets, liabilities, and equity on the balance sheet and the revenue and expenses on the income statement. *Refer to* F.99.

**medium-term notes** Debt instruments with maturities ranging from 9 months to 30 years that are offered on a continuous basis. Offered on a continuous basis means that they are issued and sold as buyers request them rather than on a single-issue date.

**memorandum of association** An official document used to form a corporate body in the United Kingdom. It contains the following information: the corporation's name; a statement that the corporation is a public company; the address of the registered office; the objects of the corporation; a statement of limited liability; the amount of the guarantee; and the amount of authorized share capital and its division. *See* articles of association.

**merger** *See* uniting of interests.

**merger accounting** *See* pooling of interests.

**mezzanine finance** Funds, provided by specialist financial institutions, that are neither pure equity nor pure debt. This type of financing can take many different forms and can be secured or unsecured. This form of financing is usually at a higher rate of interest than pure debt and carries a higher risk. It usually has a lower rate of return than equity but has a lower risk.

**minority interest** Generally, the interest of shareholders (individuals, partnerships, and corporations) in a subsidiary that own less than 50% of a subsidiary's outstanding voting shares. These minority shareholders will receive their full share of profits in the form of dividends. However, they are unable to determine company policy since they are outvoted by the majority interest held by the holding company. *Refer to* IAS 27.4.

**modified historical-cost convention** A modification of the historical-cost convention in which certain assets are included at revalued amounts rather than at their original costs.

**Modigliani and Miller (MM) Theory** A theory in financial management developed by Modigliani and Miller postulating that investors would use arbitrage to keep the weighted average cost of capital (WACC) constant when changes in an organization's leverage occurs. *See* arbitrage.

**monetary assets** Generally, assets such as cash and accounts receivable have fixed monetary exchange value and are not affected by a change in the price level. If no regulations require organizations to account for changing price levels, monetary assets remain in the financial statements at their original amounts. If the principle of accounting for changes in price levels is applied, the monetary assets will be linked to a particular index.

**monetary measurement convention** The accounting convention that states transactions are only recognized in financial statements if these transactions can be measured in monetary terms. Hence, some assets, such as a highly trained work force or a sound customer base, will not be shown.

**money laundering** The practice of converting money from an illegal source, such as drug dealing, into an apparently legitimate source. Although monetary and financial channels are used for money laundering, cash purchases of high-value goods is also a method employed. Increasingly, legislation is being enacted to reduce such activities and the main thrust is to compel accountants and other professionals to report their suspicions concerning clients.

**money market** Where buyers and sellers of financial securities and loans come together at an agreed price, usually a rate of interest called the discount rate. The transactions are conducted in large quantities, and individuals do not participate. There is no single physical market place, since transactions are usually conducted over the phone, through online computer links, or through faxes.

**money market line** An agreement between a bank and an organization that entitles the latter to borrow up to a certain limit each day in the money markets, on a short-term basis.

**monopsony** A single purchaser of goods and services in a situation where there are a number of competing suppliers. The buyer is in a strong position to exploit the supplier of the good or service required. This can be done by forcing suppliers to lower the price or agree to delayed payment terms or by imposing unrealistic quality standards.

**mortgage** An interest in property created as collateral for a loan or a debt. A mortgage is terminated on payment of the loan or debt. The borrower, who offers the security, is the mortgagor; the lender, who provides the money, is the mortgagee.

**mortgage bond** A bond where a debt is secured by a real asset. Senior mortgage bonds have first claim on assets, and junior mortgage bonds are subordinate. A mortgage bond may have a closed-end provision that prevents an organization from issuing further, similar bonds on the same asset or bonds with open-end provision since the latter permits further issues with the same status.

***mudaraba*** This refers to trust financing in Islamic banking.

**multilateral netting** A method of reducing bank charges where the subsidiaries of a group offset their receipts and payments with each other, usually monthly, resulting in a single net intercompany payment or receipt made by each subsidiary to cover the period concerned.

**multinational** An organization with production and/or other facilities outside of the country of origin. Multinational organizations are strong supporters of international accounting standards.

***murabaha*** Under Islamic finance, the term refers to cost-plus financing.

***musharaka*** The Islamic term for equity participation.

**mutual entity** Organizations such as mutual insurance companies that are not investor owned but in which the policyholders or participants in the entity receive lower costs or other economic benefits. *Refer to* IFRS 3.

# N

**naked option** An option contract that is not held for the purpose of hedging.

**National Association of Securities Dealers (NASD)** A not-for-profit U.S. organization whose members are most of the investment banks and firms dealing in the over the counter market. It is supervised by the Securities and Exchange Commission.

**National Association of Securities Dealers Automated Quotation System (NASDAQ)** An electronic system providing quotations for securities traded on the over-the-counter market as well as for many New York Stock Exchange listed companies. It is owned and operated by the National Association of Securities Dealers.

**near final drafts** A document issued by the International Accounting Standards Board (IASB) of forthcoming Exposure Drafts of standards. Near final drafts are for information only and the IASB is not seeking comments on these drafts. Comments will be sought on the Exposure Drafts as subsequently published.

**near money** A term used to describe an asset that is immediately transferable and may be used to settle some but not all debts. It is not as liquid as bank notes and coins. Bills of exchange are examples of near money.

**negative cash flow** Cash paid out by the organization.

**negative goodwill** The goodwill arising on consolidation in which the price paid for an acquisition is less than the fair value of its net tangible asset. *Refer to* IFRS 3.56.

**negative pledge** A covenant in a loan agreement whereby a borrower either promises that no secured borrowings will be made during the life of the loan or ensures that the loan is secured equally with any new borrowings as specified.

**negative yield curve** A graph that shows interest rates for deposits or securities against different maturities when short-term interest rates are higher than longer rates. The result is a graph that starts at a high level and curves downward.

**negotiability** The characteristic of a document that can be transferred so that legal ownership passes by delivery or endorsement of the document. For a document to be negotiable, it must also entitle the holder to bring an action in law if necessary.

**negotiable instruments** A document of title that can be freely negotiated. For example, a check where the stated payee of the instrument can negotiate it by either inserting the name of a different payee or by making the document "open" by endorsing it (signing one's name), usually on the reverse. Holders of negotiable instruments cannot pass on a better title than the one they possess.

**net asset turnover** A ratio that shows the efficiency with which net assets have been used to generate revenue. It is calculated by dividing the revenue for a financial period by the net assets; that is, total assets less current liabilities.

**net asset value (NAV)** The value of an investment in an organization calculated by dividing the value of the net assets of the organization as shown in the balance sheet by the number of shares in issue. Since the balance sheet does not reflect current values, the net asset value of a share is normally below the market price.

**net book value (NBV)** The value at which a non-current asset appears in the books of an organization. It is the cost or revalued amount less accumulated depreciation and impairment losses. The net book value cannot be higher than the market price, since this would suggest there has been an impairment loss that has not been recognized.

**net cash flow** The difference between the cash inflows and cash outflows in a financial period. The difference may be positive, meaning there is a surplus of cash, or negative, in which case there is a deficit.

**net current assets** *See* working capital.

**net dividend** The dividend paid by a corporation to its shareholders after making any appropriate deductions for taxation.

**net earnings** The profit or loss for the financial period after deducting all expenses from the net sales.

**net margin** The gross margin less all other costs of an organization in addition to those included in the cost of goods sold.

**net present value (NPV)** The difference between the present values of cash outflows and the present values of cash inflows for a long-term project. The NPV is the application of a discount rate to cash flows so that the future cash flows are expressed in present values. For example, a cash inflow of $100 expected in one year's time is worth approximately $91 now if a discount rate of 10% is used. The selection of the appropriate discount rate is critical, and an organization will wish to ensure that a project shows a return in excess of the discount rate. If the NPV is positive, the required rate of return is likely to be earned, and the project should be considered. If the NPV is negative, the project should be rejected.

**net profit or loss** The amount of profit or loss earned by an organization after deducting all expenses from revenues for the financial period.

**net profit ratio** A ratio drawn from information on the income statement that assesses the financial performance of an organization. To calculate the ratio, the net profit for a financial period is expressed as a percentage of the revenue.

**net realizable value (NRV)** The estimated selling price of an item in the ordinary course of business less the costs incurred in putting the item in a saleable condition and the costs of making the sale. *Refer to* IAS 26, IAS 27.

**net revenue** Total revenue for the financial period less returns and allowances.

**net worth** The value of an organization calculated by deducting the total liabilities from the value of the total assets on the balance sheet. It is the equivalent of equity. The term can be misleading because the method of asset valuation will affect the net worth figure.

**netting** A method of reducing bank charges where the number of payments and receipts between connected parties is reduced by offsetting transactions between them.

**netting off** The deduction of one amount from another. For example, accounts receivable are usually shown in a balance sheet after netting off (or deducting) a provision for doubtful debts.

**neutrality** A qualitative characteristic of financial information. It contributes to the reliability of financial information by ensuring that it does not contain any bias. *Refer to* F.36.

**New York Stock Exchange (NYSE)** The main U.S. stock exchange, it is also known as the Big Board. It was founded in 1792 under the Buttonwood Agreement (the name of the tree under which 24 merchants agreed to give each other preference in their dealings). It moved to Wall Street in 1793, and the New York Stock & Exchange Board was formally established in 1817. It was then re-named the New York Stock Exchange in 1983. Most of the members of the NYSE will act on behalf of individuals.

**next-in-first-out (NIFO) cost** A method of valuing units of raw material or finished goods issued to production by using the next unit price at which a consignment will be received for pricing the issues. It is effectively using replacement cost as an inventory valuation method.

**Nikkei stock average** The index of share prices used on the Tokyo Stock Exchange. It is a price-weighted index of 225 Japanese corporations.

**nil paid shares** Shares issued without payment, usually as the result of a rights issue.

**nominal price** A minimal price is used as the consideration for a transaction that may have no relationship to the market value of the item or service being exchanged.

**nominal share capital** *See* authorized share capital.

**nominal share value** *See* par value.

**nominee** A person named by another (the nominator) to act on his or her behalf, often in financial matters.

**nominee shareholding** A shareholding held in the name of a bank, stockbroker, corporation, or individual for the beneficial owner of the shares. A shareholding may be in the name of nominees to facilitate dealing or to conceal the identity of the true owner.

**non-adjusting event** Events occurring between the balance sheet date and the date on which the financial statements are issued. If significant, these events require disclosure but not adjustments to the financial statements. *Refer to* IAS 10.3.

**non-contributory pension scheme** A pension scheme in which the contributions to the scheme are made by the employer and no contributions are made by employees.

**non-cumulative preference share** A share that does not have the right to the unpaid dividends of previous years.

**non-current assets** An asset of a business intended for continuing use in the organization, rather than a short-term asset that is consumed during operations, such as inventory. Non-current assets must be classified in the balance sheet as intangible, tangible, or investments. Examples of intangible assets include goodwill, patents, and trademarks. Examples of tangible non-current assets include land, buildings, plant, and machinery. Non-current assets normally should be written off to the income statement over their useful economic life. This is achieved by the amortization of intangible non-current assets and the depreciation of tangible non-current assets. Non-current assets should also be adjusted for any impairment. Although the International Accounting Standards Board (IASB) refers to non-current assets, other terms such as fixed assets may be used as long as their meaning is clear. *Refer to* IFRS 5A.

**non-equity share** A share in an organization that has any of the following characteristics: any rights to receive payments are for a limited amount, any rights to participate in a surplus on liquidation are limited to a specific amount, or the share is redeemable either according to its terms or because the holder, or any other party other than the issuer, can require its redemption.

**non-executive director** A director of a company who is not involved in the day-to-day management of the business but who is appointed to bring independent judgment on issues of strategy, performance, resources, and standards of conduct.

**non-participating preference share** A preference share that does not carry a right to participate in the profits of an organization beyond a fixed rate of dividend. This is the most common type of preference share.

**non-purchased goodwill** Goodwill that has been internally generated by an organization rather than purchased on the acquisition of another business. It should not be recognized as an asset. *Refer to* IAS 38.36.

**non-ratio covenant** A form of covenant in a loan agreement that includes conditions relating to the payment of dividends, the granting of guarantees, disposal of assets, change of ownership, and a negative pledge. Breaching such a covenant will usually empower the lender to request repayment of any of the loan then outstanding, and the loan then becomes null and void.

**non-recourse finance** A bank loan in which the lending bank is only entitled to repayment from the profits of the project the loan is funding and not from other resources of the borrower.

**non-revolving bank facility** A bank loan in which there is flexibility as to the amount and timing of withdrawals. An organization can therefore, with careful planning, reduce its total interest costs, but once drawn an amount takes on the characteristics of a term loan.

**non-statutory accounts** Any balance sheet or income statement dealing with a financial period of the company that does not form part of the statutory accounts.

**no par value capital stock** Shares that have no par value or assigned value. The advantage of this share is that it avoids a contingent liability to shareholders in the event of a share discount.

**normal production capacity** The production capacity expected under normal operating conditions, allowing any losses resulting from planned maintenance.

**normative theories of accounting** Theories of accounting, often based on deductive reasoning, that prescribe the accounting procedures and policies that should be implemented to improve accounting practices.

**Norwalk Agreement** An agreement entered into in 2002 by the Financial Accounting Standards Board (FASB) and the International Accounting Standards Board (IASB), marking a significant step in formalizing the commitment of the United States toward convergence and international accounting standards. The FASB and IASB agreed to undertake a short-term project aimed at removing a variety of individual differences between U.S. GAAP and IFRSs that remained as of 1 January 2004 by working mutually and concurrently on discrete substantial projects.

**notes payable** A current liability on the balance sheet representing promissory notes to suppliers or financial institutions.

**notes to the financial statements** Information supporting that given on the face of financial statements. Many notes are required to be given by regulation; other information may be provided to help users' understanding. *Refer to* IAS 1.

**not-for-profit organization** An organization that provides goods or services with no intention to make profits and normally follows a policy that no individual or group will share in any profits or loss, for example, charitable organizations.

**notional amount** The amount that is considered as principal when interest and other payments are calculated for derivative contracts.

**not negotiable** Words marked on a check indicating that it ceases to be a negotiable instrument.

**novation** A cancellation of the rights and obligations under one loan agreement and their replacement by new ones under another agreement. The principal effect is to change the identity of the lender.

**number of days' inventory held** A ratio that demonstrates an organization's abilities in inventory management by measuring the average number of days inventory is held. The following formula is used:

$$(\text{Number of units of inventory held} \times 365)/\text{usage in units per annum}$$

The number of units held may be taken at the start or the end of the year, or may be the average of both. Because the information required for the above ratio is only likely to be available from internal management accounts, a different formula using figures from the final accounts is often used as an overall measure of inventory levels:

(Value of inventory × 365)/revenue or cost of sales per annum

# O

**objectives of financial statements** The reasons or purposes for producing financial statements for users. It is essential to identify these to determine what information should be provided in financial statements and how economic transactions and events should be measured. The current thinking is that the main objectives include the provision of information useful for economic decision making and the results of the stewardship of management. *Refer to* F.12.4.

**objectivity** An accounting concept aimed at minimizing subjective decisions by the preparer of accounts. The objectivity concept seeks to enable users to compare financial statements for different organizations over a period with some confidence that the statements have been prepared without bias. *See* neutrality.

**obligation** A commitment given to comply with the terms of a contract to act or perform in a certain way, for example, to settle a debt. *Refer to* F.60.

**obsolescence** A fall in the value of an asset for reasons such as changes in production or outdated technology. Obsolescence is an important factor both for depreciation and inventories. In terms of depreciation, changes in technology or markets may mean that a non-current asset becomes obsolete before reaching the end of its predicted useful life. In terms of inventories, obsolescence may mean that the total cost of outdated items must be charged against the income statement immediately.

**occupational pension scheme** A pension scheme run by an employer for its employees.

**off-balance sheet financing (OBSF)** Funding an organization's activities in such a way that some or all of the finance and the corresponding assets are not shown on the balance sheet. This practice can enhance its accounting ratios, such as the leverage ratio, and also avoid breaking any agreements made with banks with respect to the total amount that may be borrowed. The most common method used was the creation of a subsidiary that was so structured that it was not incorporated into the consolidated accounts. This subsidiary may have obtained the loans essential for funding the entire group, but these were not listed on the consolidated accounts. In most accounting regimes, regulations have come into force to prevent, or at least minimize, the practice.

**offer** The price at which a seller is willing to sell a product or service. If there is an acceptance of the offer by another party, a legally binding contract has been entered into.

**offer by prospectus** An offer to the public of a new issue of shares or debentures made directly by means of a prospectus, a document giving a detailed account of the aims, objects, and capital structure of the organization, as well as its past history.

**offer for sale** An invitation to the public to purchase the shares of an organization, normally through a financial intermediary. An offer for sale can be in one of two forms: at a fixed price that requires some form of balloting or rationing if the demand exceeds supply, or in an issue by tender in which individuals offer to purchase a fixed quantity of shares at or above some minimum price and the share allocations are made to the highest bidders.

**offset account** An account that reduces the gross amount of another account by calculating a combined net balance. An example is a non-current asset that remains in the books of accounts at cost as a debit balance and is then offset by a provision for depreciation account. The latter accumulates the annual charge for depreciation as a credit balance.

**offsetting** The practice of setting a financial asset and a financial liability and reporting only the net amount. Under IAS 32, this is only permitted when an organization has a legally enforceable right to set off the amounts and intends either to settle on a net basis, or to realize the asset and settle the liability simultaneously. *Refer to* IAS 32.42.

**offsetting revenues and expenses** Under IAS 1, one item may only be offset by another if it is immaterial or permitted by another standard.

**old lady of Threadneedle Street** Popular term for the Bank of England in London.

**onerous contracts** A contract entered into where the unavoidable costs of fulfilling the contract exceed any expected revenues and compensation has to be paid to the other party if the terms of the contract are not fulfilled. *Refer to* IAS 37.10.

**opening inventory** The inventory held by an organization at the beginning of an accounting period as raw materials, work in progress, or finished goods. The closing inventories of one period become the opening inventories of the succeeding period. *Refer to* IAS 2.

**open position** A trading position in which a dealer either has commodities, securities, or currencies bought but unsold or unhedged, or sales that are neither covered nor hedged. In either case, there is a level of risk, and the dealer is vulnerable to market fluctuations until the position is closed or hedged.

**operating activities** A heading on the cash flow statement required by IAS 7. The cash flows are from the activities of an organization undertaken to earn revenue. Investing or financing activities are excluded from this definition. *Refer to* IAS 7.

**operating and financial review** A statement in the annual accounts and reports of U.K. companies that is not dissimilar to the U.S. management discussion and analysis statement.

**operating cycle** The period of time that elapses between the acquisition of materials in an organization and the subsequent realization into cash or cash equivalents.

**operating lease** A lease that that does not transfer substantially all the risks and rewards related to the ownership of an asset. *Refer to* IAS 17.4.

**operating performance ratios** Various ratios for analyzing and interpreting the financial performance of an organization in terms of the return generated for a financial period. The ratios usually incorporate some form of profit from the income statement, and this is compared to another factor such as revenue or net assets to calculate a ratio. Generally, the higher the ratio, the higher the profitability of the organization.

**operating profit (or loss)** The profit (or loss) made by an organization as a result of its principal trading activity. This is arrived at by deducting the operating expenses from its trading profit or adding its operating expenses to its trading loss.

**operational gearing** A ratio that measures the extent to which an organization's costs are fixed in relation to output.

**opportunity cost** The income or benefit forgone due to the selection of one specific alternative rather than another when resources are limited or when mutually exclusive projects are involved. The opportunity cost of making a particular product is the revenue forgone by ceasing production of another product. Opportunity cost is an important factor in decision making, although it represents costs that are not recorded in the accounts of the organization.

**option** A contract that gives the right, but not the obligation, to buy or sell a fixed quantity of a commodity, currency, or security, at a particular date at a particular price (the exercise or strike price). The purchaser of the option pays a premium for the option to the seller of the contract to compensate the risks of the seller for the risks of payment. The premium is non-refundable.

**ordinary activities** These are defined very broadly under the international accounting standard. It is those activities that are part of the normal business of an organization and any other related activities engaged in incidental to, or arising from the main activities. The inclusive nature of the definition is such that very few items of income or expense are outside the normal activities. If so, they would fall under the definition of extraordinary items and would be treated accordingly. *Refer to* IAS 8. *See* extraordinary items.

**ordinary share** A share (equity instrument) in an organization that carries the right to a share of the profits without limit. Ordinary shares generally carry the right to vote. It is subordinate to all other classes of equity instruments. The U.S. term is common stock. *Refer to* IAS 33.5.

**ordinary share capital** The total share capital of a corporation consisting of ordinary shares.

**ordinary shareholders' equity** The value of the total assets of an organization less its total liabilities and any amounts of capital due to holders of non-ordinary shares (such as preference shares). If the organization were to go into liquidation, this would be the equity available for distribution to the ordinary shareholders.

**Organization for Economic Cooperation and Development (OECD)** Established in 1961, the membership comprises the main industrialized countries. Its objectives are to promote economic growth with stability, to foster international trade, and to contribute to the economic progress of the developing countries and of non-member countries.

**original cost** The cost of an item at the time of purchase or creation. It is also referred to as the historic cost. The composition of the original costs of non-current assets is set out in the standards. *Refer to* IAS 16.

**outside director** A person who is a member of the board of directors but is not an employee of the organization and has no executive responsibilities. Such directors are appointed because they offer wide business experience or specialist knowledge not available from the executive directors. As the responsibilities of outside directors have increased over recent years because of regulations, there are indications that some individuals are relinquishing some of the many well-reimbursed positions they once held.

**over-capitalization** A condition in which an organization has too much capital for the demands of current operations or expected growth. Overcapitalization results in either extremely high interest charges or payment of low dividends to shareholders. The situation can be resolved by settling long-term debt or buying back shares.

**overhang** A large quantity of shares available for sale on the market that results in depressing the market price of the shares.

**override provisions** Under IAS 1, it is permitted to depart from the compliance of a standard when it is necessary to provide a fair presentation. This would be rare, and the organization must disclose the standard from which it has departed, the reason, and the financial impact. *Refer to* IAS 1.13.

**over-the-counter market** A market for two-way trading in securities that are not listed on the established stock exchanges.

**over-the-counter option** An option contract that is specifically created to suit the specific requirements of the company.

**over-the-counter trading** Trading of shares and other financial instruments outside the official supervised and regulated stock exchange.

**overtrading** The position in which an organization has rapid growth in operations but not the necessary long-term financing to support it. This places immense pressure on working capital, and the increased demand creates the need for more cash to finance extra raw material inventories and work in progress. Short-term strategies may be used to delay accounts payable and actively push accounts receivable. Overtrading is a particular problem for small organizations in high growth sectors where there may be difficulties in obtaining long-term funding. It also occurs where the economy is emerging from recession, thus creating increasing demand during the recovery before the financial infrastructure has been developed.

**owner-occupied property** A property used by the owner or lessee for the production or supply of goods or services or for administrative use.

# P

**paid-in-capital** The section of shareholders' equity on a corporation's balance sheet that shows the amount of shares issued, the premium or discount from selling the shares, shares received from donations, and the re-sale of treasury stock.

**paid-up share capital** The total amount of money that shareholders have paid the corporation for their fully paid shares.

**parent** An enterprise that has one or more subsidiaries. *Refer to* IAS 27.4, IFRS 3A.

**pari passu clause** The term means "equally," and it is sometimes a provision in a loan agreement whereby a borrower promises to ensure that the loan will rank equally with its other debts.

**participating preference share** A preference share that is entitled to a fixed rate of dividend and a further share in the profits of the corporation.

**partly paid shares** Shares for which the full nominal or par value has not been paid. Shareholders pay an initial sum for their shares and subsequently pay one or more calls on specified dates. There is the advantage to the organization that funds are only acquired when needed, and the source of the funding is secure. There is the advantage to the shareholders that they are not required to pay the full amount at once, but there is the disadvantage that they are subject to future calls.

**partnership** An association of two or more people who have combined for the purpose of carrying on a business with a view to making profit. There is normally a formal agreement that will include matters such as the treatment of partnership loans, payments of salaries, and share of profits. Partners are personally liable for all the debts incurred by the partnership.

**partnership accounts** The accounts kept by a partnership. They include an appropriation account in which the profit of a partnership is shared between the partners in accordance with the partnership agreement. Each partner also has a capital account and a current account. The former is used to account for the capital contributions, goodwill, and revaluation, and the latter for all other transactions such as appropriations of profit and drawings.

**par value** The nominal price of a share or other security. If the market value of a security exceeds the nominal price, it is said to be above par; if it falls below the nominal price, it is below par.

**patent** An official document that gives a person or organization the legal right to exploit an invention for profit. It is an intangible asset and should be amortized over the period for which the patent is granted. *Refer to* IAS 38.

**pathfinder prospectus** An outline prospectus designed to test the market reaction to the initial public offering (IPO) of a new corporation.

**payable to bearer** Describing a bill of exchange where neither the payee nor endorsee is named. Holders can make the bill payable to order by adding their names.

**payback period** A simple technique used in capital investment appraisal. The payback period is the length of time over which future cash flows from an investment are expected to recover the initial outlay. The project with the shorter payback period is chosen. The technique is low risk, but does not account for the return on the investment. In addition, it is not usual to discount future cash flows to their present value so that no recognition is given to the time value of money.

**payments in advance** *See* prepayments.

**penny shares** Securities with a very low market price traded on a stock market. They can be attractive to small investors since they can acquire a significant holding in a corporation for a very low cost. Although a small increase in the market price of the share can represent a high percentage profit, such shares are usually considered to carry a high risk.

**pension scheme** An arrangement of which the main purpose is to provide a group of employees with pensions. A pension scheme may include benefits other than a pension and may provide a pension for dependents of deceased members.

**p/e ratio** *See* price/earnings ratio.

**percentage of completion method** In construction contracts, a method of matching revenue with costs at different stages of completion so that the reported profit can be attributed to the proportion of work completed within the financial period. *Refer to* IAS 11.25.

**percentage of sales method** The accounts receivable that may not be collectable for a financial period calculated by expressing the historic bad debts figure as a percentage of historic gross credit revenue. This percentage is then applied to current credit revenue.

**performance** *See* financial performance.

**performance bond** A guarantee given to customers in some industries that goods will be delivered to a specific standard. The organization's bankers, who are indemnified by the organization, normally give the bond.

**performance measures** Measures used to evaluate the performance of whole organizations or parts of organizations, for example, profit centers, departments, sections, and the managers responsible for these parts of the business. Performance measures may consist of quantitative, qualitative, or financial measures. These include measures based on profitability or comparison with budgets and standard costs, as well as figures for previous periods.

**period concept** The accounting concept that the financial statements of an organization should be produced for equal periods of time and at regular intervals. It is obviously impractical to prepare financial statements after every transaction or event, but the period concept does raise issues concerning the proper allocation of revenues and expenses to each period.

**period costs** Another term for fixed costs, since they are allocated to a time period rather than to specific output, for example, rent and straight-line depreciation.

**periodic inventory** A method for accounting for the inventory of an organization at the end of an accounting period by a physical count and the calculation of total value by the application of an agreed unit price. A method that is commonly used is FIFO.

**perks** Benefits arising as a result of employment, in addition to regular remuneration. This could be inducements such as company cars and generous expense accounts. The term is an abbreviation of the word perquisites.

**perpetual inventory system** The maintenance of records in a ledger or on a bin card where the balance of the quantity of inventories held is entered after each receipt or issue. In some systems, the value of the balance may also be entered after each transaction.

**petty cash** The amount of cash in notes or coins that an organization keeps on site and that is readily available to settle small items of expenses. This is to be distinguished from cash, which normally refers to amounts held in the banks. Petty cash transactions are normally recorded in a petty cash book under the imprest system.

**physical capital maintenance** *See* capital maintenance concept.

**physical inventory** The process of counting the physical balance of items at a particular time with a view to carrying out a stocktaking under a system of either inventory control or continuous inventory.

**placed deal** The marketing of a new issue of bonds or securities by a bank or a group of banks. Unlike a bought deal, the borrower is not guaranteed that the new issue will be successful. The smaller financial institutions, such as merchant banks, which do not have large marketing departments, favor such transactions.

**placement** The sale of shares by an organization to a selected group of individuals or institutions. Placements can be used either as a means of an initial public offering (IPO) or to raise additional capital for a quoted company. Placements are normally the cheapest way of raising capital on a stock exchange, and they also allow the directors of a corporation to influence the selection of shareholders. The success of a placement usually depends on the placing power of the corporation's broker.

**pledging** An agreement in which an asset is used as collateral for a loan.

**point of sale (POS)** The location where a customer makes a purchase, usually at a retail shop. The purchase may also occur as a doorstep transaction (as in door-to-door selling), at a market stall, or as a mail-order transaction. *Refer to* IAS 41.

**poison pill** A defensive strategy used to discourage an unwanted takeover by ensuring that a successful takeover bid will trigger an event that substantially reduces the value of the corporation, for example, the sale of assets to a friendly organization.

**policyholder** The party to an insurance contract who has a right to compensation on the occurrence of an insured event. *Refer to* IFRS 4.A.

**political credit risk** The credit risk that arises as a result of actions by a foreign government that may affect the management of a foreign business, control of its assets, and its ability to make its payments to its creditors.

**pooling-of-interests** The method of accounting used in a business combination where the acquiring organization has issued voting ordinary shares in exchange for voting ordinary shares of the acquiree. The features of this method are that the acquirer's net assets are brought forward at book value, retained earnings and paid-in-capital are brought forward, the net income is recognized for the full financial year regardless of the date of acquisition, and the expenses of pooling are immediately charged against earnings. This method of accounting for business combinations is now prohibited. *Refer to* IFRS 3.

**portfolio** The list of holdings in securities owned by an individual or an organization. The components of a portfolio will depend on the mix of income and capital growth the investor is seeking and the risk that can be accepted.

**portfolio theory** The theory that rational investors are averse to taking increased risk unless they are compensated by an adequate increase in expected return. The theory also assumes that for any given expected return, most rational investors will prefer a lower level of risk and for any given level of risk they will prefer a higher return than a lower return. There is the assumption that diversifying holdings can reduce risk.

**positive accounting theory** A theory that attempts to explain the nature of accounting, the role and activities of accountants, and the relationships of accounting with the economy. Unlike normative theories of accounting, it does not set out to state what accounting procedures and policies should be, but rather to explain why they are what they are.

**post-date** To insert a date on a document that is later than the date on which it is signed, thus making it effective only from the later date. A post-dated (or forward-dated) check cannot be negotiated before the date written on it irrespective of when it was signed.

**post-employment benefits** Benefits provided by an employer to an employee after the completion of employment. For example, some employers provide health care and other benefits in addition to pensions.

**potential ordinary share** A financial instrument or other contract that may entitle the holder to ownership of ordinary shares in the future. Examples are convertible instruments, share warrants, share options, employee stock purchase plans, and shares that will be issued subject to certain conditions being met. The presence of such financial instruments or contracts have a dilutive effect on the earnings per share figure. *Refer to* IAS 33.5.

**pre-acquisition profits** The profits of an organization that were made prior to a takeover.

**preference dividend** A dividend paid to the holders of preference shares. Dividends of preference shares not paid in previous periods will only be due to holders of cumulative preference shares.

**preference share** A share that is entitled to a fixed percentage dividend rather than a variable dividend; for example, a 5% preference share pays a dividend of 5% per annum on the par value of the share irrespective of the level of earnings. If an organization goes into liquidation, the preference shares are paid out after debt capital, but before ordinary share capital.

**preference share capital** Share capital consisting of preference shares and regarded as non-equity shares.

**preferential creditor** A creditor whose debt will be met in preference to those of other creditors and who has the best chance of being paid in full on the bankruptcy of an individual or the winding-up of an organization.

**preferential debt** A debt that will be repaid in preference to other debts.

**preferred stock** *See* preferred share.

**preliminary announcement** An early public announcement of an organization's profit or loss for a financial period before the full financial statements are released to the financial markets.

**premium on capital stock** *See* premium on share capital.

**premium on share capital** This arises where the price for the share issued by the organization is higher than the par value. The premium account is shown in the balance sheet under the paid-in-capital section of shareholders' equity and should not be regarded as income.

**prepaid expense** *See* deferred expense.

**prepayment** *See* deferred expense.

**presentation currency** This is the currency in which the financial statements are presented and is an amendment to the original term "reporting currency" used in the standard. *Refer to* IAS 21.8.

**present value** The value obtained using a discounted cash flow calculation to future cash flows expected from an investment. The projected annual cash flow figure is multiplied by a discount factor to provide the present value of those cash flows. A project that gives a positive present value is financially worth adopting.

**price-dividend ratio (PDR)** A ratio that shows the return investors are receiving in the form of dividends. The current market price of a share is divided by the dividend per share for the previous year.

**price-earnings (P/E) ratio** A ratio that shows the total return that investors are receiving. To calculate the ratio, the current market price of a share is divided by the earnings per share. The P/E ratio usually refers to the annual earnings per share and is expressed as a number (such as 2 or 18), and is often called the multiple. High multiples, usually associated with low yields, indicate that the organization is growing rapidly, while a low multiple is associated with dull, no-growth shares. *Refer to* IAS 33.

**price-level accounting** A system of accounting that attempts to take into account changes in price levels, thus improving the quality of financial information provided to users and overcoming some of the deficiencies of historical cost accounting.

**price risk** Price risk refers to the potential for loss and for gain due to the value of a financial instrument fluctuating because of changes in market prices. The changes may be related directly to the specific financial instrument or its issuer, or may affect the entire market. *Refer to* IAS 32.52.

**price sensitive information** Information about an organization's financial performance, operating activities, or other matters of substance that are not in the public domain. Once the information is released, it is likely to cause its share prices to move.

**price variance** *See* direct materials price variance.

**pricing** The determination of selling prices for the products and services supplied by an organization. In many cases, selling prices are based on prevailing market prices for similar products or services. There are circumstances in which pricing is based on costs, using information provided by the management accounting system.

**primary earnings per share** A calculation for assessing the performance of organizations with complex capital instruments. The net income available to holders of ordinary shares is divided by the weighted average of the ordinary shares outstanding plus securities that can be converted into ordinary shares.

**primary financial instrument** These are non-derivative financial instruments such as receivables, payables, and equity securities. *Refer to* IAS 32. AG 15.

**primary market** The market where a new issue of bonds or any other form of medium or long-term money-market paper is launched.

**prime cost** The total of direct material costs, direct labor costs, and direct expenses incurred in the manufacture of a product.

**prime documents** The documents used to initiate and record the accounting entries in an accounting and management accounting system. Prime documents include invoices, material requisitions, materials return notes, and direct charge vouchers.

**prime rate** The rate of interest charged by banks to their best borrowers. The prime rate is therefore a lending rate, while the base rate is a benchmark to which a margin will be added.

**prior period errors** Errors in the financial statements of prior periods arising from the failure to properly use reliable information that was available, or could be reasonably obtained, at that time in the preparation of the financial statements. These errors can arise from mathematical mistakes, errors in applying accounting policies, oversights, misinterpretation of facts, and fraud. *Refer to* IAS 8.5.

**privatization** The sale of a publicly owned company to the private sector. Privatization may be pursued for political as well as economic reasons.

**pro-forma financial statements** Financial statements that give projections of future revenues, expenses, financing, and working capital management based on a set of assumptions.

**process costing** A product costing system that produces large numbers of identical items in a continuous production process. The costs are accumulated for the whole production process and averaged over a large number of product units.

**process value analysis** *See* activity analysis.

**product financing arrangements** An arrangement whereby a seller obtains finance for inventory by selling inventoriable items to a financial institution and repurchases at the sales price plus carrying and finance costs over a specified period of time. The substance of the transaction is that of borrowing. *Refer to* F.35.

**product warranties** The guarantee by an organization that will repair or replace any defective products. These represent liabilities that may be incurred by an organization and should be recorded in the financial statements. *Refer to* IAS 37.14.

**Professional Oversight Board for Accountancy (POBA)** POBA is one of the five subsidiary boards of the Financial Reporting Council (FRC) in the United Kingdom. The Board's fundamental aim is to support investor, market, and public confidence in the financial and corporate governance of entities. POBA monitors the quality of the auditing process of economically significant entities and provides independent oversight of the regulation of the auditing profession.

**profit** Generally, the excess of the selling price over the cost of providing the goods or services sold. Gross profit is the excess of selling price over the cost of the goods sold. Net profit is the gross profit less all other costs, such as administration and distribution costs. Specifically, the residual amount after expenses have been deducted from revenue and any adjustments made to maintain capital at the beginning of the period. *Refer to* F.105, F.107.

**Profitability Index (PI)** A method used in discounted cash flow for ranking a range of products under consideration where standard cash flow patterns are projected. It is based on the ratio:

(total net present values of cash inflows)/initial investment

The projects with a PI of less than 1 are not expected to earn the required rate of return and are rejected. The projects with a PI in excess of 1 are ranked according to the magnitude of the PI.

**profit and loss account** An account in the books of an organization showing the profits (or losses) made on its business activities with the deduction of appropriate expenses. The account is also known as an income statement or a statement of financial performance.

**profit and loss account reserve** A reserve that contains the balance of retained earnings to carry forward. It is fully distributable and shown as part of shareholders reserves on the balance sheet.

**profit center** A separable identifiable area of an organization to which revenue and matching costs can be attributed to calculate a profit. The center is normally a division, subsidiary, department, or area of activity.

**profit margin** *See* gross margin; net margin.

**profit-sharing ratio** The ratio in which profits or losses of a business are shared between the owners. For a partnership, the profit-sharing ratio will be set out in the partnership agreement. This will show the amount, usually given as a percentage of the total profits, attributable to each partner.

**profit-volume chart (PV chart)** A graph showing the profits and losses occurring at various levels of activity. The profit/loss line is usually plotted as a linear function, and the graph shows the total fixed cost level as the loss at zero activity, the breakeven point activity level, and the profits or losses at each level of production or sales.

**profit-volume ratio (PV ratio)** *See* contribution margin ratio.

**pro-forma financial statements** Financial statements for a period prepared before the end of the period and, therefore, would contain estimates.

**pro-forma income** A figure of earnings that some organizations emphasize in their financial statements, although it is calculated before negative items such as goodwill amortization and impairment charges. The Sarbanes-Oxley Act requires that pro-forma income must be prominently reconciled with GAAP earnings in the financial statements.

**progress payment** A payment made to a contractor based at different stages of work completed at a specified date, as certified by an agreed authority. It is used in the costing of long-term contracts, such as civil engineering, shipbuilding, or large items of plant and machinery.

**projected unit credit method** An actuarial valuation method that regards each period of employee service as generating additional units of post-employment benefit entitlement. Each unit is separately measured to calculate the entity's final obligation. *Refer to* IAS 19.

**promissory note** A document that is a negotiable instrument and contains a promise to pay a certain sum of money to a named person, to that person's order, or to the bearer at a specified time in the future. It must be unconditional, signed by the drawer, and delivered to the payee or bearer.

**property, plant, and equipment** These are tangible assets that are expected to be used for more than one financial period for the production or supply of goods and services, for rental or for administration. Such assets should be depreciated and can be classified as either non-current assets or fixed assets in the balance sheet. *Refer to* IAS 16.6.

**proportion consolidation** With a jointly controlled entity, the method of incorporating the venture's share of the assets, liabilities, income, and expenses on a line-by-line basis in its own financial statements. *Refer to* IAS 31.3.

**proprietary company (PTY)** The name given to a private limited company in Australia and South Africa.

**proprietary view** The view of an accounting entity in which the enterprise is seen from the shareholder's view rather than stressing the perspective of the enterprise itself. This view can be applied to consolidated accounts where the assumption is that the group accounts are prepared primarily for use of the shareholders of the controlling parent company.

**prospectus** A document containing company information in connection with an issue of shares.

**provision** Generally, an amount set aside out of profits in the accounts of an organization for a known liability, although the timing or the specific amount might not be known. Commonly, the term provisions are for doubtful debts and for depreciation, although these do not fall under the standard that restricts the term to items that are disclosed in the balance sheet under the heading for liabilities and are of uncertain timing or amount. *Refer to* IAS 37.10.

**provision for doubtful debts** A provision calculated to cover the debts during an accounting period that are not expected to be paid. It is important to note that the so-called provision for doubtful debts is in fact an accounting estimate. *Refer to* IAS 8.

**prudence concept** A qualitative characteristic of information that contributes to the reliability of financial statements. It is the acknowledgement of uncertainties and attempts to implement the exercise of caution into the making of judgments by ensuring that assets and income should not be overstated in the financial statements, and liabilities or expenses are not understated. *Refer to* F.37.

**Public Accounting Council (PAC)** Under the Public Accounting Act 2004 in Canada, the Public Accountants Council (PAC) implements new regulatory standards that accounting organizations need to meet in order to grant the licenses, harmonize the process with evolving national and international standards, and improve transparency, accountability, and independence within the field. The legislation allows the three principal accounting bodies in Ontario, Canada—the Institute of Chartered Accountants of Ontario, the Certified General Accountants of Ontario, and the Society of Management Accountants of Ontario—to license and regulate individual public accountants once they meet the standards set by the PAC. To promote accountability and transparency, the accounting bodies would be required to file annual reports with the government and would be subject to rotating audits by the PAC.

**Public Company Accounting Oversight Board (PCAOB)** Established by the Sarbanes-Oxley Act, the Board is a private sector, non-profit corporation. Its role is to oversee the auditors of public companies in the preparation of informative, fair, and independent audit reports. Its rules must be approved by the Securities and Exchange Commission (SEC) before they take effect.

**public issue** A method of making a new issue of shares or loan stock. The public is invited, through advertisements in the national press, to apply for shares at a price fixed by the corporation.

**public limited company (PLC)** A company registered in the United Kingdom that can, if it wishes, issue shares to the public. Its name must end with the initials 'PLC.'

**purchased goodwill** Goodwill acquired when an entity is purchased, as opposed to goodwill that is internally generated. Positive goodwill arises where the purchase cost exceeds the aggregate, fair values of the identifiable assets and liabilities. *Refer to* IFRS 3.

**purchase method** The method of accounting for business combinations required under IFRS 3. The acquirer must measure the cost of a business combination at the date of exchange as the aggregate of fair values of the assets given, liabilities incurred or assumed, and equity instruments issued by the acquirer, in exchange for control of the acquiree. *Refer to* IFRS 3.

**purchasing power** The strength of money to purchase goods and services at a specific price. In times of inflation, the loss of purchasing power occurs when monetary assets are held, and a gain in purchasing power will arise if monetary liabilities are held.

**push down accounting** The incorporation of the fair value adjustments on acquisition made by the acquiring company into the financial statements of the acquired subsidiary.

**put option** This is an option to sell an asset or an instrument. A contract entered into where it is expected that the price of specific shares may fall. The buyer will only sell the shares if the market price falls below the exercise price, and therefore a profit will be made of the difference between the lower market price and the exercise price, less the premium paid for the option. *Refer to* IAS 33.5.

# Q

**qualified acceptance** An acceptance of a bill of exchange in which the drawee changes the terms of the bill from how it was originally drawn.

**qualified audit report** *See* qualified opinion.

**qualified opinion** An audit report in which the auditor makes a qualification of the financial statements. This may be due to some limitation on the scope of the audit examination or because the accounting treatment or disclosures of certain transactions and events do not meet the satisfaction of the auditor or are not in accordance with generally accepted accounting principles (GAAP). *See* unqualified opinion.

**qualified stock option** An agreement giving employees the right to purchase company shares at a later date at a specified option price that is normally lower than the market price.

**qualifying assets** This is a term used to denote those assets where borrowing costs can be capitalized under the alternative treatment in IAS 23. To fall within the definition, such assets must necessarily take a substantial period of time to be put into a condition suitable for their intended use or sale. Examples include manufacturing plants, investment properties, aircraft being built, and wine and spirits being aged. *Refer to* IAS 23.10.

**qualitative characteristics of financial statements** All conceptual frameworks and similar pronouncements issued by national standard setters contain a section on the qualitative characteristics of financial statements. This is also the case at the international level. The Framework for the Preparation and Presentation of Financial Statements refers to the attributes of the information in financial statements that make them useful. It identifies the four main qualitative characteristics as understandability, relevance, reliability, and comparability. These are in turn supported by a number of subcharacteristics. *Refer to* F.24.

**quality of earnings** The degree to which the net profit of an organization reflects accurately its operating performance, and no manipulation or events have occurred that distorts the profit figures.

**quarterly report** A financial report issued every three months. The prescribed contents are a condensed income statement, condensed balance sheet, condensed statement showing changes in equity, condensed cash flow statement, and selected narrative notes. *Refer to* IAS 34.8.

**quick assets** *See* liquid assets.

**quick ratio** *See* liquid ratio.

**quoted company** A company listed on a stock exchange.

# R

**random walk theory** A theory postulating that share price movements have no predictable pattern and that it is impossible to extrapolate from previous movements.

**ratchet effect** A change in an economic variable, usually upwards, that is highly unlikely to be reversed, for example, an increase in wage rates. The consequences are that other variables throughout the economy may also change, thus leading to inflation.

**rate of return** The gain or economic benefit earned from the investment of resources in a project or other activity. The return is evaluated by comparing it to the amount of the investment in some way, usually in percentage terms. The return from investment in a division or subsidiary may be expressed as an accounting rate of return or return on assets. For a capital project, the rate of return may be expressed as the internal rate of return.

**rate of turnover** The frequency with which some activities or assets of an organization are used or "turned over" in a financial period. For example, the revenue for a financial period can be divided by the total assets to arrive at an asset turnover figure. This can be compared with previous periods or other organizations to assess the organization's efficiency in using resources to generate revenue. The more rapid the rate of turnover, the more efficient an organization normally is.

**rating agency** An organization that monitors the credit backing of bond issues and other forms of public borrowings. The two best known are Standard & Poor's and Moody's, both of which have been in existence for over 100 years.

**ratio analysis** The use of ratios to evaluate various aspects of an organization's operating performance, financial solvency, and efficiency. For example, financial performance can be evaluated by calculating profit margins, solvency by calculating the current ratio, and financial structure by calculating leverage ratios. In conducting an analysis, comparisons will be made for one organization over a number of financial periods, with other organizations, and with industry averages or other indices. Users of ratio analysis include managers wanting to measure their own performance compared with previous years and with their rivals, creditors for whom the security of loans or credits would be the prime consideration, shareholders interested in the return on their investment, and employees interested in the financial security of the organization and its profitability. *See* financial statement analysis.

**ratio covenant** A form of covenant in a loan agreement that includes conditions relating to ratios such as the leverage ratio and interest cover. If the borrower breaches one of these conditions (for instance, does not maintain the agreed leverage ratio), the lender normally has the right to request full repayment of the loan. Because of the importance of ratio covenants, organizations that are in danger of breaching them can be tempted to adopt accounting policies and practices that flatter their ratios. There is also the critical necessity for those organizations adopting IFRSs for the first time to assess the impact on their accounting ratios and to discuss the implications with their creditors.

**raw materials inventory** The goods that have been purchased and delivered and are being held before entering the production process.

**real rate of interest** The rate of interest charged on loans or received on investments after adjusting for the effect of inflation within an economy. For example, if the rate charged for borrowed funds is 6% and the inflation rate is 2% per annum, the real rate of interest is 4%. In economies where there is a very high level of inflation, the real rate of interest may be a negative figure.

**realizable value** This is the amount that could be obtained if an asset were sold in a normal and orderly manner as opposed to a liquidation. *Refer to* F.100.

**realization account** An account drawn up on the dissolution of a partnership. The account is debited with the assets of the partnership and any expense on realization. It is credited with the proceeds of any sales made. The balance on the account is either a profit or loss on realization and should be shared between the partners in the profit-sharing ratio.

**realization convention** The general basis used in financial statements prepared under historical cost accounting where increases or decreases in the market values of assets and liabilities are not recognized as gains or losses until the assets are sold or the liabilities paid.

**realized profit** The profit generated from a completed transaction such as the sale of goods or services. It is calculated within the context of generally accepted accounting principles. The introduction or amendment of an accounting standard can have a significant impact on the realized profit declared.

**recapitalization** The process of changing the balance of debt and equity financing of a corporation, usually to reduce the amount of interest that has to be paid on loan capital. Recapitalization is often required as part of restructuring of an organization that would otherwise go into liquidation.

**receipts and payments basis** The preparation of financial statements on a cash basis rather than an accruals basis. The amounts actually paid or received are shown, and this method may be appropriate for a small, informal social organization.

**receivables** These include claims held against customers and others for money, goods or services, notes receivables, trade acceptances, and third party instruments. They appear on the balance sheet of an organization under current assets.

**receivership** A situation in which a lender holds a mortgage or charge, especially a floating charge, over an organization's property. If the organization defaults on the loan, a receiver can be appointed to realize the charged assets in order to repay the debt.

**reciprocal method** A method that considers two-way associations among service centers simultaneously, as well as allocates service costs to all user departments. It gives full consideration to interactions among support departments.

**recognition** The process of incorporating economic transactions and events into the financial statements of an organization. The transaction should generate future economic benefits and have a cost or value that can be reliably measured. Not only is the recognition process essential for revenue and expenditure activities, but it has became increasingly important in the proper disclosure of off-balance-sheet financing. *Refer to* F.82.

**Recognized Qualifying Body (RQB)** There are five statutorily Recognized Qualifying Bodies (RQBs) for company auditors under the Companies Act 1989 in the United Kingdom: the Association of International Accountants (AIA), the Institute of Chartered Accountants in England and Wales (ICAEW), the Institute of Chartered Accountants of Scotland (ICAS), the Institute of Chartered Accountants in Ireland (ICAI), and the Association of Chartered Certified Accountants (ACCA). Statutory audit rules are laid out in the Companies Acts 1985 and 1989 and reflect the EU 8th Company Law Directive. The Department of Trade and Industry (DTI) in the United Kingdom designates professional bodies as RQBs.

**recourse** The right of a lender to demand that a loan be repaid.

**recoverable amount** The recovery amount of an asset is the greater of its net realizable value and its value in use. This amount is compared to an asset's carrying value to determine whether impairment has taken place. *Refer to* IAS 36.6.

**recovery rate** *See* absorption rate.

**redeemable shares** Shares that the issuer has the right to redeem under the terms specified on the share issue. Redemption may be funded from distributable profits or from a fresh issue of shares. Under IAS 7, redeemable preference shares acquired within three months of their predetermined redemption date are regarded as cash equivalents.

**redemption** The repayment of shares, stocks, debentures, or bonds. The amount payable on redemption is usually specified on issue. The redemption date or dates may or may not be specified on issue.

**reduction of capital** A reduction in the issued share capital of an organization.

**registrar of companies** An official charged with the duty of registering all companies in the United Kingdom. There is one registrar for England and Wales, and one for Scotland. The registrar is responsible for carrying out a wide variety of administrative duties connected with registered companies, including maintaining the register of companies and the register of charges, issuing certificate of incorporation, and receiving annual returns.

**registration statement** A lengthy document that has to be lodged with the Securities and Exchange Commission. It contains all the information relevant to a new securities issue that will enable an investor to make an informed decision as to whether or not to purchase the security.

**Regulatory News Service (RNS)** A screen-based service operated by the London Stock Exchange for the rapid dissemination of information on listed companies.

**re-insurance** An agreement in which one insurer indemnifies another insurer in part, or in total, for the risks of a policy issued by the latter.

**re-investment rate** The interest rate that an investor is able to reinvest the income earned on an existing investment.

**related parties** One party is considered to be related to another if it can control or significantly influence the other party in making financial and operating decisions. *Refer to* IAS 24.

**related party transactions** The transfer of assets, liabilities, or the performance of services by, to, or for a related party, regardless of whether a price is charged. *Refer to* IAS 24.9.

**relevance** A qualitative characteristic of financial information. It is considered to be one of the main attributes that make financial statements useful. For information to be relevant, it should assist in the evaluation of past, present, or future events. *Refer to* F.26.

**relevant range** The range of activity for which a cost relationship is likely to be valid for the normal operations of the organization. For instance, fixed costs for activity levels in the relevant range do not change in the short run.

**relevant cost** The cost items that managers need to consider when analyzing decision alternatives, since these costs will differ across decision options.

**reliability** A qualitative characteristic of financial information. To be reliable, financial statements must represent faithfully what they are intended to represent. Reliability assumes that the information is free from error and bias. *Refer to* F.31.

**reload feature** An automatic grant of additional rights to subscribe for shares for a fixed or determinable price for a specified period of time. This arises where an option holder exercises previously granted options, using the entity's shares rather than cash to satisfy the exercise price. *Refer to* IFRS 2A.

**replacement cost** The cost of replacing an asset with the same or a similar asset with equivalent productive or service capabilities. It may be the cost of a new or a used asset.

**reporting accountants** A firm of accountants who report on the financial information of an organization provided in a prospectus. The accountants may be organization's own auditors. It is usual for reporting accountants to have previous experience of new issues and the preparation of prospectuses.

**reporting currency** *See* presentation currency.

**reporting entity** The organization for which financial statements are prepared. The statements are the main source of financial information to those external parties who have an interest in the organization's operations and financial stability.

**reporting period** Financial statements must state precisely the period or point in time to which the information relates, for example, "for the six months ending December 31, 2005."

**reproduction cost** The cost of replacing an asset with one that is exactly the same in all aspects.

**re-purchase agreement** An agreement in which a financial asset is transferred to another party for cash or other consideration with a concurrent obligation to re-acquire the financial asset at a future date for an equal amount of cash or consideration plus interest. There can be an attempt to use this type of agreement as a device for obtaining a loan without showing it on the balance sheet.

**re-purchase of own debt** The action of an organization buying its own debt at an amount different from the amount of the liability shown on the balance sheet.

**resale price method** A transfer pricing method that determines an appropriate markup based on the gross profits of various organizations selling similar products.

**research** An original and planned activity with the aim of gaining new knowledge or understanding. Expenditure on research should be charged as an expense in the period that it is incurred, whereas development may be capitalized subject to certain criteria. *Refer to* IAS 3.8.

**reserve** Part of the capital of an organization, other than the share capital, that arises largely from retained earnings or from the issue of share capital at a premium. They are attributable to equity holders and appear on the balance sheet. *Refer to* IAS 1.68.

**residual income (RI)** A dollar amount equal to the operating income of a business unit less a charge for the investment in the unit. This can be measured as follows:

$$\text{RI} = \text{Net Operating Income} - (\text{Minimum Rate of Return on Investment} \times \text{Operating Assets})$$

RI is used as a performance measure when evaluating the performance of profit and investment centers and is a popular alternative to the Return on Investment (ROI) ratio. RI, unlike ROI, is an absolute amount of income dollars rather than a rate of return. RI is considered to be superior as a performance measure to ROI because the former encourages managers to accept investment opportunities that have greater rates of return than the charge for invested capital.

**residual value** The expected proceeds from the sale of an asset, net of the costs of sale, at the end of its estimated useful life. It is used for computing the straight-line method and diminishing-balance method of depreciation, and also for inclusion in the final year's cash inflow in a discounted cash flow appraisal. *Refer to* IAS 16.6.

**responsibility accounting** A system of accounting that measures the performance of business units, divisions, and individuals with related responsibilities for generating revenues and controlling costs.

**responsibility center** A subunit or division in an organization whose manager is held accountable for specified activities and financial results.

**restrictive covenant** A clause in a contract that restricts the freedom of one of the parties in a specified way. Employment contracts, for example, may include a clause by which a departing employee cannot open a competing business for a specified period or in a specified location.

**restructuring** Material changes introduced by management to an organization's scope of business or the way business is conducted. *Refer to* IAS 37.10.

**Retail Price Index (RPI)** An index in the United Kingdom of the prices of goods and services in retail shops purchased by average households, expressed in percentage terms relative to a base year. The base year is taken as 100. The RPI is one of the standard measures of the rate of inflation and is similar to the Consumer Price Index (CPI) used in the United States and some other countries.

**retained earnings** The net profit retained in the organization after dividends and any other distributions have been made to investors.

**return on assets** An accounting ratio that shows the profitability of an organization and the efficiency with which it uses its assets to generate profit. It is calculated by expressing the amount of profit for a financial period as a percentage of assets. Depending on the focus of interest, total assets or net assets may be used.

**return on capital employed (ROCE)** An accounting ratio assessing the return on the resources employed by the organization. It is calculated by expressing the profit of an organization for a financial period as a percentage of capital employed. There are several different definitions of the terms used. For instance, profit may be regarded as the profit before interest and tax while capital employed refers to non-current assets plus current assets minus current liabilities. Management may consider that profit before interest and tax expressed as a percentage of total assets is a useful measure of performance. Shareholders, however, may be more interested in taking profit after interest and comparing this to total assets less all liabilities. *See* Return on Investment (ROI).

**Return on Equity (ROE)** A ratio that shows the benefits accruing to shareholders. It is calculated by expressing the profit after interest of an organization as a percentage of the equity capital.

**Return on Investment (ROI)** Similar to the Return on Capital Employed (ROCE) ratio. ROI measures the earning power of assets and reveals the organization's profitability on its business operations. The rate of return is commonly used to evaluate divisional performance. The disadvantage of ROI is that divisional managers who are evaluated using ROI may not accept new investments that lower their current ROI, even though the investments may be desirable for the entire organization. *See* Residual Income (RI).

**revaluation** A change in the value of an asset or liability that is incorporated in the financial statements. *Refer to* F.81.

**revaluation method** A method of determining the depreciation charge on a non-current asset against profits for an accounting period. The asset is revalued each year, and the decrease in value is the amount of depreciation to be written off the asset and charged against the income statement for the period. It is often used for depreciating assets such as loose tools or a mine from which materials are extracted.

**revaluation reserve** When an organization revalues non-current assets to fair values, a reserve account is created to record the difference between the historical cost of an asset less depreciation and the revalued amount. *Refer to* IAS 16.

**revaluation surplus** Where the revaluation of an asset under IAS 16 indicates a fair value, which is higher than the carrying value, the difference should be credited to shareholders' equity under the heading of "revaluation surplus." *Refer to* IAS 16.

**revenue** Generally, the receipts and receivables of an organization generated from the sale of goods or services and the amount appearing on the income statement for a financial period. It can include such items as interest and royalties. Other terms used for revenue are turnover and net sales. Specifically, it is the gross inflow of economic benefits resulting in increases in equity other than those due to contributions from equity participants. The economic benefits must arise in the course of ordinary activities and do not include amounts collected on behalf of third parties such as sales tax. Revenue should be measured at the fair value of the amounts received or receivable. *Refer to* IAS 18.7.

**revenue center** A responsibility center where the manager is accountable for sales.

**revenue recognition** The process of recording revenue in the accounts of an organization in the appropriate financial period. Revenue from the sale of goods should only be recognized where the significant risks and rewards have been transferred, the amount of revenue and the costs incurred can be measured reliably, and it is probable that economic benefits will flow to the enterprise. Services may spread over more than one financial period and it is important that the outcome of the transaction can be measured reliably and only the revenue for the stage of completion at the end of the period is recognized. *Refer to* IAS 18.

**reverse acquisition** This can take place where one organization obtains the shares of another but issues a sufficient number of shares as consideration that the control of the combined enterprise passes to the owners of the acquiree rather than the acquirer. *Refer to* IFRS 3.21.

**reverse takeover** The acquisition of a public company by a private company. This can be an inexpensive method for a private company to obtain a listing on a stock exchange, since it avoids the expenses of an initial public offering and the assets of the public company may be purchased at a discount.

***riba*** The Islamic term for interest or usury. The receipt or payment of interest is prohibited under Islamic or *Shariah* laws.

**rights issue** A method by which quoted companies on a stock exchange raise new capital by offering existing shareholders the right to purchase shares in proportion to their current holding. For example, with a one for six rights issue, shareholders would be invited to purchase one new share for every six they currently hold. As rights are usually issued at a discount to the market price of existing shares, those not wishing to take up their rights can sell them in the market. *Refer to* IAS 33.

**risk analysis** The recognition, analysis, and assessment of the risk associated with specific economic activities. Risks are inherent in the unpredictability of future events, but a range of possible outcomes can be identified and an estimate made of their probability. This can lead to an informed decision being taken based on the potential rewards compared against the possible risks.

**risk-based audit** An method of audit that evaluates the degree of risk attached to different areas of an organization's system. The results are used to design the appropriate conduct of the audit by concentrating on areas of highest risk in order to improve the chances of detecting errors.

**risk-free rate of return** The rate of interest that an investment with no perceived element of risk is capable of generating. Government securities in certain countries are often regarded as offering a risk-free rate of return.

**risk premium** The difference between the expected rate of return on an investment and the risk-free return over the same period. If there were any risk element, the rate of return would be higher than if no risk is involved.

**risk:reward ratio** This ratio is rarely calculated but intuitively applied by identifying the possible risks of making an investment compared with the anticipated rewards. The data is rarely available, but the anticipated rewards can be assumed to be of such a substantial magnitude that they overwhelm, at least in the opinion of the optimistic investor, any possible risks.

**royalty** A payment made or a benefit received for the right to use the long-term assets of an organization. This may be an intellectual property, such as an invention or copyright, or an activity such as the grant of mineral rights to someone else with the royalties being based on the amount of minerals extracted. *Refer to* IAS 18.

# S

***salam*** This refers to forward sale in Islamic finance.

**salary reduction plan** *See* 401(K) plan.

**sale and lease back** A transaction in which the owner of an asset sells and immediately purchases back from the buyer the right to use the asset under a lease. The lease may be a finance lease or an operating lease. The capital released through this process can enable the organization to expand or to survive a difficult trading year. *Refer to* IAS 17.49.

**sale and repurchase agreement** *See* repurchase agreement.

**salvageable value** *See* scrap value.

**samurai bond** A bond issue by a foreign issuer, in the Japanese domestic market, denominated in yen. It is the Japanese equivalent of a Yankee bond.

**Sarbanes-Oxley (SOX) Act** Formally titled the Public Accounting Reform and Investor Protection Act, it was passed in the United States in 2002 following high profile financial scandals such as Enron. The Act established a Public Company Accounting Oversight Board (PCAOB) with particular responsibilities in relation to the audit of public companies. Other sections include issues relating to the independence of auditors, corporate responsibility, enhanced financial disclosures, and corporate and criminal fraud accountability. One part of the Act required the Securities and Exchange Commission (SEC) to examine the possibility of the United States adopting a principles-based approach to financial reporting.

**scatter diagram** A set cost observations denoted by X and Y data points at various activity levels plotted on the graph. For cost analysis purposes, X denotes the activity consumption, and Y denotes the associated cost for that activity level.

**scattergraph** *See* scatter diagram.

**scrap value** The net realizable value of an asset at the end of its useful life when it is no longer suitable for its original use. Non-current assets, inventories, or waste arising from a production process can have a scrap value.

**scrip issue** *See* stock split.

**secondary market** A market in which existing securities are traded, as opposed to a primary market where securities are sold for the first time. Stock exchanges largely fulfill the role of a secondary market, with the initial public offering of new issues representing only a small proportion of its total business.

**secret reserve** Funds accumulated by an organization over a period of time but not disclosed in the financial statements. Concealment can take place by deliberately undervaluing an asset or accounting for a transaction with the intention of not showing the effect on the balance sheet. Historically, such reserves were used to smooth profits, but regulations have greatly reduced the opportunities to create these reserves.

**secured creditor** A creditor who holds either a fixed charge or a floating charge over the assets of its debtor.

**secured liability** A debt against which the borrower has provided sufficient assets as security to safeguard the lender in case of non-repayment.

**Securities and Exchange Commission (SEC)** Established in 1934, the SEC is the federal government agency in the United States monitoring and controlling corporate financial reporting, auditing practices, and trading activity. The SEC follows, to a very large extent, the accounting and auditing pronouncements of bodies organized by the public accounting profession such as the Financial Accounting Standards Board (FASB) and the Auditing Standards Board (ASB).

**securitization** An arrangement in which one party (the originator) sells a portfolio of high-quality assets, such as property mortgages, to a special purpose entity (the issuer), which issues loan notes to finance the purchase. In summary, it is the process by which financial assets are transformed into securities.

**segment expenses** Those expenses that result from operating activities and are directly attributable or reasonably allocable to a segment. Interest expense and related security losses are only included if the segment is a financial segment such as a bank. Segment expenses never include extraordinary items, losses on investments accounted for by the equity method, income taxes, and general corporate administrative and head-office expenses. *Refer to* IAS 14.16.

**segment reporting** The disclosure in the financial statements of certain results of major business and geographical segments of a diversified group of companies. A business segment is one that is a distinguishable part of the organization that is subject to risks and returns different from other parts. A geographic segment is a distinguishable part of the organization providing goods and services within a particular economic environment that is subject to risks and returns different from other economic environments. *Refer to* IAS 14.

**segment revenue** Revenue that is directly attributable or reasonably allocable to a segment. This includes intersegment revenue but only includes interest, dividend income, and related security gains if the segment is a financial segment, for example, a bank. *Refer to* IAS 14.16.

**self-sustaining foreign operation** A foreign operation that is financially and operationally independent of the reporting entity such that the exposure to changes in exchange rate is limited to the reporting entity's net investment in the foreign operation.

**separate entity concept** The concept that the financial statements of an organization should describe the business as if it were entirely separate from its owners. With certain organizations, such as corporate bodies, this is legally the case, but the concept should also be applied to partnerships and sole traders.

**serial bonds** Bonds that mature in installments, rather than on one maturity date. *See* term bonds.

**service concession** An arrangement where an enterprise (the concession operator) agrees with another enterprise (the concession provider) to provide services that give the public access to major economic and social facilities.

Examples include motorways, car parks, tunnels, bridges, airports and telecommunication networks. *Refer to* SIC 29.

**set off** An agreement between relevant parties to set off one debt against another or one loss against a gain. A banker can set off a credit balance on one account against a debit balance on another, if the accounts are in the same name and in the same currency.

**shadow director** A person who is not a director of a company but the directors are accustomed to act on that person's instructions.

**shallow discount bond** A bond issued in a primary market at a price where the discount normally does not exceed 10%.

**share** One of several terms used for the document or agreement representing ownership of the whole or part of an organization. A share confers on its owner a legal right to a part of the profits, usually by payment of dividends, and to any voting rights attached to the share. The normal classes of shares are as follows: ordinary shares that have no guaranteed amount of dividends but carry voting rights, and preference shares. The term used in the United States is *stock* but IFRSs use the term *share*.

**share-based payment transaction** Transactions involving the receipt of goods or services as consideration for equity instruments, including shares or share options, and transactions involving the acquisition of goods and services by incurring liabilities based on the price of the entity's shares or other equity instruments. *Refer to* IFRS 2A.

**share capital** The finance an organization receives from its owners (its members or shareholders) in exchange for shares.

**share certificate** A document that provides evidence of ownership of shares in an organization. It states the number and class of shares owned by the shareholder and the serial number of the shares. Shares are not negotiable instruments.

**shareholders** Individuals, businesses, and groups owning shares in a corporation.

**shareholders' equity** The share capital and reserves of a corporation. It represents the ownership interest of shareholders. The amount is the difference between the total assets and total liabilities. Share capital should be classified on the balance sheet as equity shares and non-equity shares. Specific information relating to the share capital must be disclosed in the organization's financial statements. *Refer to* IAS 1.76.

**share issued at a discount** A share issued at a price (the issue price) below its par or nominal value. The discount is the difference between the par value and the issue price.

**share issued at a premium** A share issued at a price (the issue price) above its par or nominal value. The premium is the difference between the issue price and the par value.

**share options** The right to buy a fixed quantity of shares at a particular price within a specified period of time. An option is a right, not an obligation, so the holder does not have to buy the shares. Share options are sometimes given to employees and executives on favorable terms. For example, a manager may be given an option to buy 500 000 shares at a price of $1 at any time between three and five years from the date of the option. If the share price rises to $1.20 the manager can exercise the option by buying at $1. The shares can then be sold at the market price of $1.20 per share giving a profit of 20 cents each. Thus, total profit = 20 cents per share x 500,000 shares = $100,000. *Refer to* IFRS 2A.

**share premium** *See* premium on capital stock.

**share repurchase** The purchase by an organization of its own shares to reduce the number of shares in the market. The organization uses surplus funds to do this and therefore reduces its dividends commitment. The term used in the United States is Treasury stock, and the International Accounting Standard Board (IASB) uses Treasury share. *Refer to* IAS 11.3.5.

**share splitting** The division of share capital of an organization into smaller units. The effect of the share split is the same as a scrip issue, although the technicalities differ. Share splits are usually carried out when the existing shares reach such a high price that trading in them becomes difficult for shareholders.

**share warrant** A certificate giving the holder the right to purchase a security at a particular price at a particular date or dates in the future.

***shariah*** The code of law derived from the Qur'an and the teachings of the Prophet Mohammed. *Shariah* laws underpin the fundamental principles, features, and practice of Islamic markets and financial systems.

**shell company** A non-trading company, with or without a stock-exchange listing, used as vehicle for various organizational maneuvers or kept dormant for future use in some other capacity.

**short call** The position in which the seller is obliged to sell an asset at the exercise price but only has to do so when the option is exercised by the buyer.

**short-form audit report** A standard audit report that conforms to the short-form reporting requirements of the Securities and Exchange Commission (SEC) and the American Institute of Certified Public Accountants (AICPA). The first paragraph of the report indicates the work the auditor has carried out, and the second paragraph gives the findings.

**short position** A position held by a dealer in securities, commodities, currencies, and so forth, where sales exceed holdings because the dealer expects prices to fall, enabling the shorts to be covered at a profit.

**short-termism** Any policy that aims to maximize current profits rather than long-term development and wealth. For example, cutting back on research and development or advertising reduces immediate costs but may lead to products becoming obsolete or unmarketable in the future. The argument is put forward that financing companies through shares increases directors' short-termism approach because they have to satisfy market expectations on a annual, or even more frequent, basis.

**significant influence** The power of an investor to participate in, but not control, the financial and operating policy decisions of an economic activity. Significant influence can be acquired through holding shares, by statute, or by agreement. *Refer to* IAS 28.2. IAS 31.3.

**simplified financial statements** Simplified versions of the full financial statements intended for readers who do not possess sophisticated financial knowledge. The financial statements may use easier financial terminology, contain graphs and diagrams, provide more extensive explanations, and reduce the amount of information. One form of simplified financial statement is the employee report that is intended for employees.

**single-entry book-keeping** A book-keeping system that only records one aspect of each transaction; that is, either a debit or a credit.

**sinking fund** Funds that are set aside for payment periodically so as to reduce a financial obligation or to meet future redemption commitments; for example, a bond with a sinking fund provision. The objective is to accumulate sufficient income to retire the bonds at the maturity date.

**social accounting issues** Issues that are concerned with the impact of an organization's operations on society or particular aspects of it. Social accounting issues may include charitable donations of equipment and time, education initiatives, community involvement, employment of disadvantaged groups, and the provision of sports equipment or sponsorship.

**social audit** An audit of the impact of an organization's activities on society. An environmental audit is one example of a social audit.

**socially responsible investment** An investment made in an organization not engaged in any activity that investors may consider unethical (such as armaments or tobacco) or an investment in an organization that investors approve on ethical grounds (such as social or environmental activities).

**social responsibility reporting** The reporting of the costs and benefits of the operations of an organization that impact on society. This information may be included in a separate report or as part of the annual accounts. For example, costs to the business may include equipment donated, sponsorship given, or monetary support of charities.

**Society of International Accounting Technicians (SIAT)** Based in the United Kingdom, SIAT is a professional body for the Accounting Technicians, sponsored by the London Chamber of Commerce and Industry Examinations Board (LCCIEB) and the Association of International Accountants (AIA). SIAT offers an internationally recognized qualification for Accounting Technicians.

**soft currency** A currency that is not freely convertible and for which there is only a thin market.

**solvency** Generally, the financial ability of a person or an organization to pay all debts as they fall due. Specifically, the availability of cash over the long term to meet commitments as they fall due. *Refer to* F.16.

**source and application of funds statement** A financial statement that identifies the inflow and outflow of funds by calculating changes on the balance sheets at the beginning and end of the financial period and adjusting with information from the income statement.

**source document** The first document to record an economic transaction. This is the authority to enter the transaction into the books of account.

**South Eastern European Partnership on Accountancy Development (SEEPAD)** Established in December 1999, SEEPAD is a regional accountancy reform initiative comprising of principal accounting and auditing associations in South Eastern Europe. The SEEPAD initiative is sponsored by the Organisation for Economic Co-operation and Development (OECD), the U.S. Agency for International Development (USAID) and the EU Stability Pact for South Eastern Europe. The objectives of SEEPAD are also supported by the International Accounting Standards Board (IASB), the International Federation of Accountants (IFAC) and the United Nations Conference on Trade and Development (UNCTAD).

**sovereign risk** The risk inherent in an oversees project that the assets on which the cash flow for repaying loans or generating profits is dependent could be expropriated by the local government. In countries where such a risk is present, either a high level of return is expected, or there are political considerations to be taken into account.

**Special Purpose Entities (SPEs)** These are normally created solely to achieve a narrow and closely defined objective, such as research and development, or securitization of financial assets. There have been examples where SPEs have been created by organizations to conceal the true nature of the transactions that are being entered into, particularly in relation to financing. An SPE should be consolidated when it is evident that the SPE is controlled by another organization.

**special purpose vehicles (SPVs)** *See* Special Purpose Entities (SPEs).

**split-off point** The point in a joint production process at which the joint products become identifiable as separate products.

**spot exchange rate** The price at which a currency can be bought or sold with immediate delivery. *Refer to* IAS 21.8.

**spot market** A market that deals in commodities or foreign exchange for immediate delivery. Immediate delivery in foreign currencies usually means within two business days. For commodities, it usually means within seven days.

**spread** Generally, the difference between two prices (the buying and selling price) or two rates (the interest rate charged by banks for loans and the rate at which they borrow funds). The term is also used for the simultaneous purchase and sale of commodity futures (for example, futures contracts) in the hope that movement in their relative prices will enable a profit to be made. This may include a purchase and sale of the same commodity for the same delivery but on different commodity exchanges, or a purchase and sale of the same commodity for different deliveries.

**stabilization** The activities of a lead manager of a bond issue in the gray market that are intended to reduce fluctuations in the price of the bond before and immediately after issue.

**stag** A person who applies for shares in new issue in the hope that the price when trading begins will be higher than the issue price. Measures are normally taken by the issuers to prevent excessive stagging.

**stage of completion method** *See* percentage of completion method.

**staggered directorships** A measure used in the defense against unwanted takeover bids where the periods of appointment of present directors are staggered and no directors can be removed from office without due cause. In these circumstances, a bidder cannot gain control of the board for some years, even with a controlling interest in the share capital.

**stakeholders** An individual or group with a direct interest in an organization's performance. The main stakeholders are employees, shareholders, customers, suppliers, financiers, government, and the community. Stakeholders may not hold any formal authority over the organization, but may be users of its financial statements. They may also, to some degree, be dependant on the organization's financial position and performance, or affected by the operations it carries out.

**standby letter of credit** A financial instrument issued by a bank on behalf of a customer whereby the issuing bank has guaranteed payment of a financial obligation to a third party should the customer fail to meet its obligation to the third party.

**standard costing** A system of planning and control of production operations that establishes predetermined costs for products and processes, and compares these with the actual costs incurred. The predetermined costs are referred to as standard costs and are the costs that should be incurred in specified working conditions. The differences, known as variances, between standard cost and actual cost are examined and analyzed to ascertain the reasons for the differences. In an organization using a standard costing system, standard costs will be established for direct materials and direct labor costs as a minimum.

**Standards Advisory Council (SAC)** A council appointed by the trustees of the International Accounting Standards Committee Foundation (IASCF).

Its role is to act as a means of participation by organizations and individuals and to give advice to the International Accounting Standards Board (IASB) on priorities and major projects for standard setting.

**Standards Interpretation Committee (SIC)** Appointed by the trustees of the International Accounting Standards Committee Foundation (IASCF), the Committee later become the International Financial Reporting Interpretations Committee (IFRIC). SIC reviews accounting issues that are likely to receive divergent or unacceptable treatment in the absence of authoritative guidance, with a view to reaching consensus as to the appropriate accounting treatment. *See* International Financial Reporting Interpretations Committee (IFRIC).

**start-up costs** The initial expenditure incurred in the setting up of an operation or project. The start-up costs may include capital investment costs plus the initial revenue expenditure prior to the start of operations.

**Statement of Changes in Equity** An additional financial statement required under IAS1. The purpose of the Statement is to report changes in equity between two balance sheet dates and to provide details on the increase or decrease in net assets or wealth during the financial period. *Refer to* IAS 1.36.

**Statement of Financial Accounting Concepts (SFAC)** The pronouncements issued by the Financial Accounting Standards Board (FASB) to identify the fundamental concepts of financial accounting and reporting. They identify the objectives of financial statements, qualitative characteristics of accounting information, elements of financial statements and recognition and measurement issues.

**Statement of Financial Accounting Standards (SFAS)** The pronouncements detailing the financial accounting and reporting requirements of the Financial Accounting Standards Board (FASB). These accounting standards are regarded as forming Generally Accepted Accounting Principles (GAAP) and should be followed by accountants responsible for the preparation of financial statements.

**Statement of Movements in Shareholders' Funds** *See* Statement of Changes in Equity.

**Statement of Principles** The equivalent of a conceptual framework in the United Kingdom. There are seven chapters:

The objectives of financial statements
Qualitative characteristics of financial information
The elements of financial statements
The recognition of items in financial statements
Measurement in financial statements
Presentation of financial information
The reporting entity

**Statement of Total Recognized Gains and Losses** A statement showing the extent to which shareholders' equity has increased or decreased from all the various gains and losses recognized in the period. It includes profits and losses for the period, together with all other movements on reserves, reflecting recognized gains and losses attributable to shareholders.

**statutory accounts** Accounts required by law.

**stewardship** The historical function of accounting in which stewards or agents, such as directors, provide relevant and reliable financial information relating to resources over which they have control but which others own, for example, shareholders. The disclosure of information relating to the stewardship or accountability of management allows shareholders to decide whether to hold or sell their investment or whether to discharge management. *Refer to* F.15.

**stock** *See* share.

**stock appreciation** *See* inventory appreciation.

**stock control** *See* inventory control.

**stock dividends** The issue of additional shares to existing shareholders in proportion to their current holdings.

**stockholders** *See* shareholders.

**stockholders' equity** *See* shareholders' equity.

**stock market** *See* stock exchange.

**stock exchange** A market for the sale and purchase of securities in which the prices are influenced by supply and demand. The first stock exchange was set up in Amsterdam, where in 1602, shares in the United East India Company could be traded. Stock exchanges in the United Kingdom date from 1673, with the first daily official price lists being issued in London in 1698. Their basic function is to allow public corporations, governments, local authorities, and other incorporated bodies to raise capital by selling securities to investors. The greatest activity takes place in its role as a secondary market in which investors can buy and sell securities.

**stock split** The issue of new share certificates to existing shareholders to reflect the retained earnings in the reserves of an organization. The shareholders do not pay for the new shares but benefit from the issue. For example, in a one for three scrip issue, the shareholders receive one new share for every three existing shares they own. This automatically reduces the price of the shares by 25%, meeting the preference of shareholders to hold low-priced shares rather than high-priced ones. Should the shares recover to their former value, the shareholders will have made a capital gain. Although there are technical reasons for doing this, the main motive is to reduce the market share price.

**stock turnover** *See* inventory turnover.

**stock valuation** *See* inventory valuation.

**stock watering** The creation of more new shares in a corporation than is justified by its tangible assets, even though the company may be making considerable profits. This may result in dividends not being maintained at the old rate on the new capital, and if the corporation were to be liquidated, its shareholders may not be paid in full.

**straddle** The purchase of a put option and a call option at the same time.

**straight bond** A bond issued in the primary market that carries no equity or other incentive to attract the investor; its only reward is the bi-annual interest coupon together with a promise to repay the capital at par on the redemption date.

**straight-line depreciation** A method of calculating the amount at which a non-current asset is to be depreciated in a financial period. The depreciation to be charged against income is based on the original cost or valuation less the asset's estimated net residual value, divided by its estimated economic life in years. This has the effect of a constant annual depreciation charge against profits year by year. *Refer to* IAS 16.47.

**strike price** *See* exercise price.

**subjective goodwill** The goodwill of an organization calculated by deducting its net tangible assets from the Net Present Value (NPV) of its estimated future cash flows.

**subordinated debt** A debt that can only be claimed by an unsecured creditor, after the claims of secured creditors have been met in the event of liquidation. Subordinated, unsecured loans are issued by institutions such as banks where the rights of the holders of the stock are subordinate to the interests of the depositors. Debts involving junk bonds are always subordinated to debts to banks, irrespective of whether or not they are secured.

**subsidiary** An organization, including corporations and partnerships, that is controlled by another (the parent). *Refer to* IFRS 3.A.

**substance over form** A qualitative characteristic of information that contributes to the reliability of financial statements and ensures that information faithfully represents transactions and other events. The concept holds that transactions and other events should be accounted for by their commercial reality rather than their legal form. Off-balance sheet finance and creative accounting depend on the legal form, often established in complex agreements. For information to represent transactions and events faithfully, accounting must be based on the substance and not according to the legal form. *Refer to* F.35.

***sukuk*** This refers to Islamic bonds or securities that do not pay interest but make regular payments based on the profits from *shariah*-compliant investments.

***sukuk al-ijara*** This refers to a leasing certificate for a transaction that normally involves the sale and leaseback of an asset under Islamic finance.

**summary financial statement** An abbreviated form of the full financial statements that, providing certain conditions are met in some countries, may be issued to shareholders instead of the full financial statements.

**summary of significant accounting policies** A required disclosure that must accompany financial statements. It describes the accounting policies used in the preparation of financial statements. *Refer to* IAS 8.

**sum-of-the-digits method** The calculation of the depreciation charge for a non-current asset in an accounting period. The estimated life is expressed in years, and the digits for each year of its life are added up. The proportion of the asset's cost or valuation less residual value to be written off as depreciation in a particular year is determined by the number of years remaining before the asset's removal from commission, expressed as a proportion of the sum of the years of the asset's life. For example, for an asset with an estimated life of 5 years, the sum of the digits is 5+4+3+2+1 = 15. Thus 5/15 is written off in the Year 1, 4/15 in Year 2, 3/15 in Year 3 until the full depreciation charge has been made. *Refer to* IAS 16.47.

**sunk costs** Costs that have been incurred or committed in the past and are, thus, irrelevant for decision making, since they cannot be affected by a future decision.

**sunrise industry** An industry in a rapidly growing market, usually based on new technology and innovation.

**sunset industry** An industry considered to be in terminal decline, with obsolete technology and an obsolete product.

**supply risk** The inherent risk in limited recourse financing of a construction project that the raw materials necessary for the operation of the future plant may become unavailable.

**sushi bond** A bond issued in the Euro market by a Japanese-registered corporation in a currency other than yen but targeted primarily at Japanese institutional investors.

**suspense account** A temporary account in the books of an organization to record balances in order to correct mistakes or balances that have yet to be finalized.

**swaps** An arrangement in which a borrower can exchange the type of funds most easily raised for the type of funds required, usually through the intermediary of a bank. For example, a Canadian organization may find it easier to raise a Canadian dollar loan although it requires Deutschmarks. A German corporation may have exactly the opposite problem. A swap will enable them to exchange the currency they possess for the currency they need. The other common type of swap is an interest-rate swap where borrowers exchange fixed interest rates for floating interest rates.

**swaption** An option to enter into a swap contract.

**swingline loan** A facility that enables a borrower to have access to funds at very short notice, usually on a same-day basis, often to cover shortfalls in other credit arrangements. It may form part of a multioption facility.

**syndicated loan** A substantial loan made to one borrower by a group of banks. The syndicate will be headed by one lead bank that may take only a small percentage of the loan but will syndicate the rest to other banks and financial institutions. There is only one loan agreement, and the loans are usually made on a small margin. The borrower can reserve the right to know the names of all the members of the syndicate. If the borrower states which banks are to be included, it is known as a club deal.

**synthetic lease** A financial device that has similar characteristics to a mortgage but neither the asset nor the debt appear on the balance sheet of the organization.

**System for Electronic Document Analysis and Retrieval (SEDAR)** The System for Electronic Document Analysis and Retrieval (SEDAR) was developed for the Canadian Securities Administrators (CSA) to facilitate the electronic filing of securities information as required by the securities regulatory agencies in Canada. SEDAR enables the public dissemination of information collected in the securities filing process and provides electronic communication between electronic filers and the Canadian securities regulatory agencies.

**systematic risk** That part of risk of an investment that cannot be reduced by diversification. *See* beta coefficient, portfolio theory.

# T

**takeover bid** An offer made to shareholders by an individual or organization to buy their shares in a specific entity at a specified price. This takeover bid will allow control to be gained if the offer to existing shareholders is successful. In a welcome takeover bid, the directors will advise shareholders to accept the terms of the bid. If the bid is unwelcome, or the terms are unacceptable, the board will advise against acceptance. In the ensuing takeover battle, the bidder may improve the terms offered and will then usually write to shareholders outlining the advantages that will follow from the successful takeover. In the meantime, bids from other sources may be made, or the original bidder may withdraw as a result of measures taken by the Board of the target company. In an unconditional bid, the bidder will pay the offered price irrespective of the number of shares acquired, while the bidder of a conditional bid will only pay the price offered if sufficient shares are acquired to provide a controlling interest.

**tangible assets** Assets that have physical substance, such as land, buildings, and machinery, as compared to intangible non-current assets, such as goodwill.

**tap stock** A gilt-edged security from an issue that has not been fully subscribed and is released onto the market slowly when its market price reaches pre-determined levels. Short taps are short-dated stocks, and long taps are long-dated stocks.

**target cost** A strategic pricing approach that enables an organization to compete successfully with the organization's competitors. The target cost is equal to the competitive sales price less the desired target profit.

**target costing** An integrated approach to determining the target cost of a product to enable an organization to earn the desired profit at the estimated market-driven price. The estimated price is referred to as the target price, the desired profit margin is called the target profit, and the cost at which the product must be manufactured is known as the target cost. The design of the product and the processes use to manufacture it are planned accordingly, so that the target profit is achieved.

**tax base** The amount attributed to an asset or liability for tax purposes. *Refer to* IAS 12.5.

**tax profit (loss)** The profit or loss for a period calculated according to the regulations established by the tax authorities rather than according to GAAP. *Refer to* IAS 12.5.

**technical analysis** A method of analyzing price trends in the share, commodity, and futures market by evaluating market factors, trading volumes, charts, and computer programs to predict price movements. It differs from fundamental analysis since the latter focuses on the analysis of financial statements to forecast future price movements.

**technological risk** The inherent risk in limited recourse financing of a project that the final technological outcome will not operate as favorably as initially anticipated.

**teeming and lading** *See* lapping.

**temporary differences** The differences between the carrying amount of an asset or liability and its tax base. *Refer to* IAS 12.5.

**tender bonds** A guarantee given by an organization that it will not withdraw from a contract, if it is awarded, after having submitted a tender.

**tenor** The time that must elapse before a bill of exchange or promissory note becomes due for payment, as stated on the bill or note.

**term bonds** Bonds that mature on one maturity date, rather than in installments. *See* serial bonds.

**term loan** A loan from a bank to an organization in which the term of the loan is fixed and the principal must be repaid in full at the end of the term.

**terminal value (TV)** The value of an investment at the end of an investment period, taking into account a specified rate of interest over the period. The formula is the same as that for compound interest, that is:

$$TV = P(1 + r)^t$$

where TV = the final amount at the end of the period, P = the principal amount invested, r = the interest rate, and t = the time in years for which the investment takes place.

**Theory of Constraints (TOC)** A management approach that focuses on managing bottlenecks or constrained resources by identifying and relaxing the constraints. An example of a TOC inventory management system is the Drum-Buffer-Rope (DBR) system.

**thin capitalization** A form of capitalization in which the capital of an organization consists of too few equity shares and too much loan stock from the viewpoint of tax authorities. In this case, the tax authorities may treat the interest from the loan stock as if it were dividends, thus denying the organization the right to a tax deduction on the interest payment.

**thin market** A market with few securities in which the price of the underlying commodity, currency, or financial instrument may change if sizable transactions are carried out.

**throughput costing** A product costing system for short-term decision making in manufacturing that assigns only material costs as direct costs and treats all conversion costs as fixed costs when resource constraints exist.

**throughput margin** A Theory of Constraint (TOC) measure of product profitability. The throughput margin equals selling price less materials cost, including all purchased components and materials handling costs. All conversion costs are treated as fixed costs.

**times interest earned** A ratio that measures the relationship between the amounts of periodic interest expense to earnings before interest and tax. The ratio is used to assess an organizations' ability to sustain its regular interest payments.

**time value of money** The discounted or compounded value of an amount of money over a specified period of time, using a specified discount or compound rate.

**Tokyo Stock Exchange** The Tokyo Stock Exchange was established in 1878 and is one of the three central stock exchanges in Japan. It was closed during the Second World War but resumed trading in 1949.

**tom next** A deal starting from tomorrow and maturing the following day.

**Toronto Stock Exchange** The exchange was established by 24 individuals in 1861 and was formally incorporated by legislation in 1878. It is now Canada's sole exchange for the trading of senior equities. It became a for-profit company in 2000.

**trade and other receivables** The term used in IAS 1 for the item on the balance sheet that is equivalent to accounts receivable.

**trade and other payables** The term used in IAS 1 for the item on the balance sheet that is equivalent to accounts payable.

**trade creditors** *See* accounts payable.

**trade date** The date that an organization commits to purchase a financial asset.

**trade debtors** *See* accounts receivable.

**traded options** Options that can be bought or sold on the market throughout their life.

**trademark** A distinctive symbol that identifies particular products. The symbol may consist of a logo, device, words, or a combination of these. The symbol is normally depicted along with the superscript ™ or ®. The owner of a trademark may assign it or allow others to use it. If anyone uses a registered trademark without the owner's permission or uses a mark that is likely to be confused with a registered trademark, the owner can sue for an injunction and damages or an account of profits. A trademark is an intangible asset and should be accounted for under IAS 38.

**trading account** The part of an income statement in which the cost of goods sold is deducted from the sales revenue to arrive at the gross profit.

**trading investments** Investments that have been obtained mainly to make a profit by disposing of them in a relatively short period of time.

**trading profit** The profit of an organization before deductions for items such as interest, directors' fees, auditors' remuneration, and so forth.

**traditional options** Options that are normally three-month contracts that must be held to the expiration date. At that date, the right to buy or sell the underlying asset or instrument must be exercised or allowed to lapse.

**tranche** One part or installment of a substantial amount of funds. In tranche funding, successive installments become available on a prearranged basis to an organization. This is often linked to the progress of a particular project.

Such an arrangement is helpful to the borrower because interest is only charged on the tranche and not the full amount of the loan.

**transaction** An external event (such as purchase or sale) or internal event (for example, depreciation of an asset) that gives rise to a change affecting the operations or finances of an organization.

**transaction costs** Costs arising from transactions such as buying and selling a financial asset or liability.

**transaction date** The date on which a transaction in the money market took place.

**transaction exposure** The risk that the cost of a transaction will change because of exchange rate movements between the date of the transaction and the date of settlement.

**transferable loan facility (TLF)** A bank loan facility that can be traded between lenders in order to reduce the credit risk of the bank that provided the loan. It is a form of securitization, but can have an adverse effect on relationship banking.

**transfer pricing** The fixing of a price for the transfer of goods and services from one part of an organization to another. For example, goods that are manufactured and sent to other divisions for retailing can be transferred at their production cost or at a higher figure to include an element of internal profit. Large organizations often use transfer pricing for internal purposes to control costs or, in the case of multinationals, to reduce taxation. This is achieved by a business division in a low-tax country charging another division in a high-tax country a higher transfer price. The effect of a higher transfer price would result in higher cost, thus reducing the tax liability for the organization in the high-tax country.

**transitional provisions** Guidance given in international standards, when they are issued, as to the adjustments and disclosures organizations should make if changing their accounting practices and/or policies because of the requirements of that specific standard.

**translation of foreign currencies** This refers to the restating of assets and liabilities initially recognized in more than one currency into a common currency, that is, into the functional currency. *Refer to* IAS 21.

**treasurer** A person who is responsible for looking after the money and other assets of an organization. A treasurer's responsibilities include overseeing the provision of the organization's finances as well as stewardship over the way money is spent.

**treasury bills** Short-term (three months) government securities. They are sold on the stock exchange in order to make up for any shortfall in government spending in excess of tax revenue. Because they are short-term in nature, they provide a very flexible way for governments to borrow.

**treasury shares** The organization's own shares that it has reacquired. The cost is deducted from equity. Gains or losses are not recognized on the purchase, sale, issue, or cancellation of treasury shares. Treasury shares can be acquired and held by the organization and other members of a group. Any consideration paid or received is recognized directly in equity. *Refer to* IAS 32.33.

**treasury stock method** A method of recognizing the use of proceeds that can be obtained upon exercise of options and warrants in calculating the diluted earnings per share. The method assumes that any proceeds would be used to purchase common shares at the average market price during the period.

**trial balance** A listing of the balances on all the accounts of an organization with debit balances in one column and credit balances in the other. If accurate accounting records have been maintained, the totals of each column should agree. If they do not, investigations must be carried out to find the discrepancy. The figures in the trial balance after adjustments (that is, for closing stocks, prepayments, accruals, depreciation, and so forth) are used to prepare the final accounts (income statement and balance sheet).

**true and fair view** This is an important concept in the United Kingdom in the preparation of financial statements, and it may be used as an override to depart from regulatory requirements. Thus, an organization may decline to comply with a particular accounting standard on the grounds that to do so would mean that the financial statements do not present a true and fair view. Despite its importance, there is no legal definition of the expression, and the concept conflicts with the U.S. rules-based approach.

**turnover** A term used in some countries to denote the total revenue of an organization for a stated period. It is also used in ratio analysis to measure the effectiveness or stability of an activity or operation, for example inventory turnover.

**two-tier board** A method of running a large organization where, in addition to a board of management, there is a supervisory board. It is claimed that this provides an effective method of corporate governance.

# U

**unbundle** To account for the components of a contract as if they were separate contracts. *Refer to* IFRS 4.A.

**uncommitted facility** An agreement between a bank and an organization in which the bank agrees to make funding available when required but has no obligation to provide a specified amount of funding. If a loan is made, it is usually only for a short period, and the bank may request repayment of the loan at any time.

**under-capitalization** The financial position of an organization that does not have sufficient capital or reserves for the size of its operations. This may be due to over-rapid growth or poor decisions on financial structuring. Although profits may be generated, there could be problems in converting these quickly into cash to pay debts as they fall due.

**understandability** A qualitative characteristic of financial information. The preparers of financial statements should assume that users have a reasonable knowledge of business, economics, and accounting, and are willing to study the financial statements with reasonable diligence. Preparers cannot omit complex information from financial statements based on the argument that some users would be unable to understand it. *Refer to* F.25.

**under-subscribed** The situation in which investors do not take up all of a new issue, and the underwriters must take up the remainder.

**undertaking** A body corporate, partnership, or an unincorporated association carrying on a trade or business with a view to making a profit.

**underwriter** In the insurance industry, an underwriter is an individual who assesses a risk, decides whether or not it can be insured, and works out the premium to be charged. The premium is usually based on the frequency of past claims for similar risks. In the financial markets, an underwriter is an institution, usually an issuing house or merchant bank, that guarantees to buy a proportion of any unsold shares when a new issue is offered to the public.

**unearned revenue** *See* deferred revenue.

**uniform commercial code** A legal code that standardizes business law. It consists of regulations on commercial paper, warranties, uncertified checks, security agreements, written agency agreements, and bankruptcy.

**United Nations Intergovernmental Work Group of Experts on International Standards of Accounting and Reporting (ISAR)** ISAR was established in 1982 by resolution of the Economic and Social Council of the United

Nations (ECOSOC), with the mandate of promoting the international standardization of the accounting and release policies practices of transnational companies. ISAR is a subsidiary of the Transnational Companies and Investments Division, an entity of the United Nations Conference for Trade and Development (UNCTAD).

**uniting of interests** A business combination in which there is a mutual sharing as opposed to an acquisition where one party gains control over the net assets and operations of another. With a uniting of interests, the combining enterprises share control over all of their combined net assets and operations. The risks and benefits of the combined entity are shared, and neither party can be identified as an acquirer. *Refer to* IFRS 3.

**units-of-production depreciation method** A method that provides depreciation expense based on the productive output of the asset, taking into account the total expected productive capacity of the asset over its useful life.

**unlimited liability** The liability of an individual or a group of individuals to pay all debts incurred by a business. For a sole proprietor or partnership, the liability of the owners is not limited solely to the amount the owner has invested. All debts of the business must not only be paid out of the assets of the business but also, if necessary, out of personal assets.

**unlisted securities** Securities (usually equities) in companies that are not on an official stock-exchange list. They are, therefore, not subject to the regulatory monitoring and controls of a stock exchange. Unlisted securities are usually issued in relatively small corporations, and although they may promise high returns, their shares usually carry a high degree of risk.

**unqualified opinion** Opinion on financial statements audited by a professional accountant indicating that the financial statements overall are fairly presented in accordance with generally accepted accounting principles (GAAP). *See* qualified opinion.

**unrealized profit (or loss)** A profit or loss that results from holding assets rather than using them. It is, therefore, a profit or loss that has not been realized in cash.

**unsystematic risk** That part of risk of an investment that can be reduced by diversification if the investor holds a diversified portfolio of investments. *See* portfolio theory.

**Urgent Issues Task Force (UITF)** A body established in 1991 as part of the Accounting Standards Board (ASB) in the United Kingdom. It is responsible for tackling urgent matters not covered by existing standards in which the timescale of the normal standard setting process would not be practicable.

**useful economic life** The period over which the present owner of an asset derives economic benefits from its use. This can be either a period of time or the anticipated output of the asset measured in suitable units.

# V

**value-added statement** *See* added value statement.

**value analysis** *See* value engineering.

**value chain analysis** A strategic tool used to evaluate an organization's relationships with suppliers, customers, and competitors. The set of interrelated activities required to design, develop, produce, market, and deliver products or services to customers are examined in order to identify where value to customers can be increased or costs reduced.

**value engineering** This is a cost-reduction and process improvement technique that is used in target costing to minimize product cost. Value engineering uses information from product design and production processes and evaluates the trade-offs between the different categories of product functionality and attributes in order to identify areas for further improvement.

**value for money audit** An audit of a government department, charity, or other not-for-profit organizations to assess whether it is operating effectively and efficiently, and giving value for the funds expended in achieving its agreed objectives.

**value in use** The value of an asset calculated by discounting the future cash flows obtainable from the asset's continued use. This would include any costs associated with its disposal. *Refer to* IFRS 5.A.

**value to the business** The value of an asset taken as the lower of the replacement cost and the recoverable amount. The latter is the greater of Net Realizable Value (NRV) and Net Present Value (NPV).

**variable cost** Costs that, in total, vary in direct proportion to changes in the level of activity achieved. For example, direct materials cost will tend to double if output doubles. Direct costs are also known as variable costs.

**variable costing** A costing and decision-making technique that charges only the variable costs to the cost units and treats the fixed costs as a total sum to be deducted from the total contribution, in obtaining the final profit or loss for the period. Finished goods inventory is valued only on the basis of variable manufacturing costs, and fixed costs are ignored. Although excellent as a decision-making technique, variable costing is not acceptable for external financial reporting.

**variable-rate note** A bond, usually with a fixed maturity, in which the interest coupon is adjusted at regular intervals to reflect the prevailing market rate. A variable-rate note differs from a floating rate note in that the margin is not fixed and is adjusted to take into account market conditions at each coupon-setting date.

**variance analysis** An analysis of the difference between actual and standard costs or between actual and budgeted costs. Variances can be classified as either favorable or adverse variances. *See* standard costing, budgetary control.

**velocity** The amount of output or units that can be manufactured in a given period of time.

**vendor placing** A type of placing used to acquire another organization. For example, if an acquirer wishes to buy a business from Company Y, it issues Company X shares to Company Y as payment. There will be a prearranged undertaking that these shares will be placed with investors in exchange for cash. Vendor placing has been popular with some companies as a cheaper alternative to a rights issue.

**venture capital** A source of finance for new businesses or turn-around situations, where high returns are offered but high risks are expected.

**vertical analysis** An analysis that focuses on various account balances of financial items as a percentage of a base. The base is revenue when analyzing the accounts in the income statement and total assets when analyzing balance sheet accounts. Vertical analysis is also known as common-size analysis. *See* common-size financial statements.

**vertical integration** The combination of two or more businesses at different stages in the same industry. For example, a manufacturer could purchase a supplier of raw materials and a wholesaler or distributor.

**vest** The establishment of a right, under share-based payment arrangements, to receive cash, other assets, or equity instruments upon satisfaction of any specified vesting conditions. *Refer to* IFRS 2.

**vesting conditions** Conditions that must be satisfied for a party to a share-based payment agreement to become entitled to receive cash, other assets or equity. *Refer to* IFRS 2.

**virement** The offsetting of overspending in one budget expenditure classification against underspending in another budget classification. If virement is not allowed, each expenditure category must be treated individually and show its respective under- and overspending.

**visual-fit method** *See* scatter diagram.

**volume-based cost driver** A cost driver or activity base that is closely associated with production volume such as direct labor hours or machine hours.

**voting shares** Shares in an organization that entitle their owner to vote at the annual general meeting and any extraordinary meetings of the organization. Shares that carry voting rights are usually ordinary shares rather than preference shares or other classes of shares.

# W

**warrant** A security that offers the owner the right to subscribe for ordinary shares at a fixed date at a fixed price. Warrants are themselves bought and sold on stock exchanges and are equivalent to stock options. Subscription prices usually exceed the market price, since the purchase of a warrant is an anticipation that the organization will flourish. *Refer to* IAS 33.5.

**wasting asset** An asset that has a finite life due to a specified period of time or the nature of production. For example, a lease will lose value throughout its life and become valueless when it terminates, and an oil well will lose value in relation to its output.

**website development costs** A website that has been developed for the purposes of promoting and advertising an entity's products and services does not meet the requirement in IAS 38 to generate probable future benefits. Thus, costs incurred in its development should be expensed as incurred. *Refer to* SIC 32.

**weighted average cost of capital (WACC)** The calculation of an organization's cost of capital by taking each source of funds and assigning a required rate of return to each individual source. The amounts for each source of funds are used as weights to be applied to the required returns, and the total return is divided by the total weights so that the WACC is expressed as a percentage.

**white knight** A person or organization making a welcome takeover bid on improved terms to replace an unacceptable and unwelcome bid from a black knight.

**windfall gains and losses** Gains and losses from actual or prospective receipts that differ from those initially predicted.

**window dressing** The practice of making the financial statements look better than they actually are. For example, to conceal a deteriorating liquidity position, an organization may enter into a sale and leaseback agreement, therefore obtaining an inflow of cash and improving its current ratio. To enhance profits, organizations may attempt to bring forward as many invoices and deliveries as possible to draw next period's revenue into the current one.

**working capital** The amount of funding required for the organization's day-to-day operations. It is the sum of current assets (for example, inventory, accounts receivable, prepayments, cash-in-hand, and cash at bank) less current liabilities (such as accruals and accounts payable).

**working-capital ratio** *See* current ratio.

**work-in-process** The balance of partially finished work remaining in the production operation or a long-term contract at a particular time.

**World Bank** The name by which the International Bank for Reconstruction and Development combined with its affiliates, the International Development Association and the International Finance Corporation, is known.

**write off** Generally, to make a charge to the income statement. For example, bad debts will be written off and impairment losses to non-current assets will be written off.

# Y

**yankee bond** A bond issued in the U.S. domestic market by a borrower that is not a U.S.-resident organization.

**yellow book** The term used in the United Kingdom for the regulations that deal with the admission of securities to listing. It is a book issued by the London Stock Exchange that sets out the regulations for admission to the official list and the obligations of the corporations with listed securities.

**yield** The income from an investment expressed in various ways. The nominal yield of a fixed-interest security is the interest it pays, expressed as a percentage of its par value. For example, a $100 stock quoted as paying 4% interest will yield $4 per annum for every $100 of stock held. The current yield will depend on the market price of the stock. If the $100 stock had a market price of $90, the current yield would be $100/90 \times 4 = 4.45\%$.

**yield curve** A curve on a graph on which the yield of fixed-interest securities is plotted against the length of time they have to run to maturity. The yield curve usually slopes upwards, indicating that investors expect to receive a premium for holding securities that have a long time to run. However, when there are expectations of changes in interest rate, the slope of the yield curve may change.

# Z

**zero-based budgeting** A budgeting approach in which the initial budget for each department has to be justified from scratch (zero) at the start of each budget period.

**zero coupon bond** A bond issued at a discount to mature at its face value. The discount is fixed at a level so that no interest will be paid during the life of the bond and the only gain is from the discount.

**z-score** A score that attempts to assess the probability of a corporate failure. It is a single figure calculated by applying beta coefficients to a number of selected ratios taken from an organization's final accounts using the multiple discriminant analysis technique. *See* corporate failure prediction.

## APPENDIX A

# List of Acronyms

| | |
|---|---|
| **AAA** | American Accounting Association |
| **AAOIFI** | Accounting and Auditing Organization of Islamic Financial Institutions (Bahrain) |
| **AARF** | Australian Accounting Research Foundation |
| **AAS** | Australian Accounting Standards |
| **AASB** | Australian Accounting Standards Board |
| **AASOC** | Auditing and Assurance Oversight Council (Canada) |
| **ABB** | Activity Based Budgeting |
| **ABC** | Activity Based Costing |
| **ABI** | Association of British Insurers (United Kingdom) |
| **ACCA** | Association of Chartered Certified Accountants (United Kingdom) |
| **ACEVO** | Association of Chief Executives of Voluntary Organizations |
| **ACGA** | Asian Corporate Governance Association (ACGA) |
| **AcSB** | Accounting Standards Board in Canada |
| **AcSOC** | Accounting Standards Oversight Council (Canada) |
| **ACT** | Association of Corporate Treasurers (United Kingdom) |
| **ADR** | American Depository Receipts |
| **AFAANZ** | Accounting and Finance Association of Australia and New Zealand |

| | |
|---|---|
| **AGM** | Annual General Meeting |
| **AIA** | Association of International Accountants (United Kingdom) |
| **AIBD** | Association of International Bond Dealers |
| **AICPA** | American Institute of Certified Public Accountants |
| **AIDB** | Accountancy Investigation and Disciplinary Board (United Kingdom) |
| **AIU** | Audit Inspection Unit (United Kingdom) |
| **AMEX** | American Stock Exchange |
| **AMPS** | Auction Market Preferred Stock |
| **APB** | Accounting Principles Board (United States) |
| **APB** | Auditing Practices Board (United Kingdom) |
| **APC** | Auditing Practices Committee (United Kingdom) |
| **APEC** | Asia-Pacific Economic Cooperation |
| **APR** | Annualized Percentage Rate |
| **ARC** | Accounting Regulatory Committee (European Union) |
| **ARDF** | Accounting Research and Development Foundation (Taiwan) |
| **ARR** | Accounting Rate of Return, Average Rate of Return |
| **ASB** | Accounting Standards Board (New Zealand, United Kingdom) |
| **ASB** | Auditing Standards Board (United States) |
| **ASBJ** | Accounting Standards Board of Japan |
| **ASC** | Accounting Standards Committee (United Kingdom) |
| **ASCA** | Arab Society of Certified Accountants |
| **ASCPA** | Australian Society of Certified Public Accountants |
| **ASCS** | American Society of Corporate Secretaries |
| **ASSC** | Accounting Standards Steering Committee (United Kingdom) |
| **BAC** | Business Accounting Council (Japan) |
| **BAHA** | British Association of Hospitality Accountants |
| **CAPA** | Confederation of Asia and Pacific Accountants |
| **CAPM** | Capital Asset Pricing Model |
| **CASC** | China Accounting Standards Committee |
| **CCA** | Current Cost Accounting |
| **CCAB** | Consultative Committee of Accountancy Bodies (United Kingdom) |
| **CD** | Certificate of Deposit |
| **CEO** | Chief Executive Officer |
| **CESR** | Council of European Security Regulators |

| | |
|---|---|
| **CFC** | Conselho Federal de Contabilidade (Brazil) |
| **CGA** | Certified General Accountants Association of Canada |
| **CGU** | Cash Generating Unit |
| **CIA** | Certified Internal Auditor (United States) |
| **CICA** | Canadian Institute of Chartered Accountants |
| **CICPA** | Chinese Institute of Certified Public Accountants |
| **CIMA** | Chartered Institute of Management Accountants (United Kingdom) |
| **CIPFA** | Chartered Institute of Public Finance and Accountancy (United Kingdom) |
| **CIT** | Chartered Institute of Taxation (United Kingdom) |
| **CMA** | Certified Management Accountants (Canada) |
| **CNC** | Conseil National de la Comptabilité (France) |
| **CPA** | Certified Public Accountant |
| **CPI** | Consumer Price Index |
| **CPP** | Current Purchasing Power |
| **CULS** | Converted Unsecured Loan Stock |
| **CVP** | Cost-Volume-Profit Analysis |
| **DASC** | Danish Accounting Standards Committee |
| **DBR** | Drum-Buffer-Rope |
| **DCF** | Discounted Cash Flow |
| **DJIA** | Dow Jones Industrial Average |
| **EAA** | European Accounting Association |
| **ECGI** | European Corporate Governance Institute |
| **ECP** | Euro-Commercial Paper |
| **ECU** | European Currency Unit |
| **EDGAR** | Electronic Data Gathering, Analysis, and Retrieval System |
| **EDI** | Electronic Data Interchange |
| **EFT** | Electronic Funds Transfer |
| **EFRAG** | European Financial Reporting Advisory Group |
| **EFTPOS** | Electronic Funds Transfer at Point of Sale |
| **EIC** | Emerging Issues Committee (Canada) |
| **EITF** | Emerging Issues Task Force |
| **EMH** | Efficient Market Hypothesis |
| **EMU** | Economic and Monetary Union |
| **EOQ** | Economic Order Quantity |

| | |
|---|---|
| **EPS** | Earnings Per Share |
| **ERP** | Enterprise Resource Planning |
| **ESOP** | Employee Share Ownership Plan |
| **EVA** | Economic Value Added |
| **FACPCE** | Federación Argentina de Consejos Profesionales de Ciencias |
| **FAF** | Financial Accounting Foundation (United States) |
| **FARR** | Financial Accounting and Reporting Rules for Entities (China) |
| **FASAC** | Financial Accounting Standards Advisory Council (United States) |
| **FASB** | Financial Accounting Standards Board (United States) |
| **FASC** | Financial Accounting Standards Committee (Taiwan) |
| **FASF** | Financial Accounting Standards Foundation (Japan) |
| **FEE** | Fédération des Experts Comptables Européens (Belgium) |
| **FER** | Fachempfehlungen zur Rechnungslegung—Swiss GAAP (Switzerland) |
| **FIDEF** | Fédération Internationale des Experts Comptables Francophones (France) |
| **FIFO** | First In, First Out |
| **FRA** | Forward Rate Agreement |
| **FRC** | Financial Reporting Council (United Kingdom) |
| **FRED** | Financial Reporting Exposure Draft (United Kingdom) |
| **FRF** | Financial Reporting Foundation (Malaysia) |
| **FRR** | Financial Reporting Release (United States) |
| **FRRP** | Financial Reporting Review Panel (United Kingdom) |
| **FRS** | Financial Reporting Standards (New Zealand, United Kingdom) |
| **FRSB** | Financial Reporting Standards Board (New Zealand) |
| **FRSSE** | Financial Reporting Standard for Smaller Entities (United Kingdom) |
| **FSR** | Foreningen af Statsautoriserede Revisorer (Denmark) |
| **FX** | Foreign Exchange |
| **GAAP** | Generally Accepted Accounting Principles |
| **GAAS** | Generally Accepted Accounting Standards |
| **GASB** | German Accounting Standards Board |
| **GASB** | Government Accounting Standards Board (United States) |
| **GSCCAB** | Gibraltar Society of Chartered & Certified Accountancy Bodies |
| **HKICPA** | Hong Kong Institute of Certified Public Accountants |

| | |
|---|---|
| **HKSE** | Hong Kong Stock Exchange |
| **IAAER** | International Association for Accounting Education and Research |
| **IAASB** | International Auditing and Assurance Standards Board |
| **IAB** | International Association of Bookkeepers |
| **IAFEI** | International Association of Financial Executives Institutes |
| **IAPA** | International Association of Practising Accountants (United Kingdom) |
| **IAPC** | International Auditing Practices Committee |
| **IAS** | International Accounting Standard |
| **IASB** | International Accounting Standards Board |
| **IASC** | International Accounting Standards Committee |
| **IBRD** | International Bank for Reconstruction and Development |
| **ICAA** | Institute of Chartered Accountants in Australia |
| **ICAC** | Instituto de Contabilidad y Auditoría de Cuentas (Spain) |
| **ICAEW** | Institute of Chartered Accountants in England and Wales |
| **ICAI** | Institute of Chartered Accountants in Ireland |
| **ICAN** | Institute of Chartered Accountants of Nepal |
| **ICANZ** | Institute of Chartered Accountants of New Zealand |
| **ICAS** | Institute of Chartered Accountants of Scotland |
| **ICSA** | Institute of Chartered Secretaries and Administrators (United Kingdom) |
| **IFAC** | International Federation of Accountants (United States) |
| **IFAD** | International Forum for Accountancy Development |
| **IFAEC** | International Federation of Accountants Education Committee |
| **IFRIC** | International Financial Reporting Interpretations Committee (IASB) |
| **IFRS** | International Financial Reporting Standard |
| **IGC** | Implementation Guidance Committee |
| **IIA** | Institute of Internal Auditors |
| **IMA** | Institute of Management Accountants (United States) |
| **IMF** | International Monetary Fund |
| **INTOSAI** | International Organization of Supreme Audit Institutions (Austria) |
| **IOSCO** | International Organization for Securities Commissions |
| **IPO** | Initial Public Offering |

| | |
|---|---|
| **IRFAA-EURASIA** | International Regional Federation of Accountants and Auditors "Eurasia" |
| **IRR** | Internal Rate of Return |
| **ISA** | International Standards on Auditing |
| **ISACA** | Information Systems Audit and Control Association (United States) |
| **ISAR** | United Nations Intergovernmental Work Group of Experts on International Standards of Accounting and Reporting |
| **IVSC** | International Valuation Standards Committee (United Kingdom) |
| **JICPA** | Japanese Institute of Certified Public Accountants |
| **JIT** | Just-In-Time |
| **KASB** | Korean Accounting Standards Board |
| **LBO** | Leveraged Buy Out |
| **LIFO** | Last In, First Out |
| **LLC** | Limited Liability Company |
| **LSE** | London Stock Exchange |
| **MAS** | Malaysian Accounting Standards |
| **MASB** | Malaysian Accounting Standards Board |
| **MBO** | Management By Objectives, Management Buy Out |
| **MD&A** | Management Discussion and Analysis (United States) |
| **MIS** | Management Information Systems |
| **MVA** | Market Value Added |
| **NASD** | National Association of Security Dealers |
| **NASDAQ** | National Association of Security Dealers Automated Quotation System |
| **NAV** | Net Asset Value |
| **NBV** | Net Book Value |
| **NRS** | Norsk RegnskapsStiftelse (Norway) |
| **NIFO** | Next-In-First-Out |
| **NPV** | Net Present Value |
| **NRV** | Net Realizable Value |
| **NYSE** | New York Stock Exchange |
| **OBSF** | Off Balance Sheet Financing |
| **OECD** | Organization for Economic Cooperation and Development |
| **PAC** | Public Accounting Council (Canada) |
| **PCAOB** | Public Company Accounting Oversight Board (United States) |

| | |
|---|---|
| **PDR** | Price Dividend Ratio |
| **P/E** | Price/Earnings |
| **PI** | Profitability Index |
| **PLC** | Public Limited Company |
| **POBA** | Professional Oversight Board for Accountancy (United Kingdom) |
| **POS** | Point of Sale |
| **PSAB** | Public Sector Accounting Board (Canada) |
| **PSASB** | Public Sector Accounting Standards Board (Australia) |
| **PSR** | Profit Sharing Ratio |
| **PTY** | Proprietary Company (Australia) |
| **PV** | Profit Volume |
| **RI** | Residual Income |
| **RNS** | Regulatory News Service (United Kingdom) |
| **ROCE** | Return on Capital Employed |
| **ROE** | Return on Equity |
| **ROI** | Return on Investment |
| **RPI** | Retail Price Index |
| **RQB** | Recognized Qualifying Body (United Kingdom) |
| **SAC** | Standards Advisory Council (IASB) |
| **SEC** | Securities and Exchange Commission (United States) |
| **SEDAR** | System for Electronic Document Analysis and Retrieval (Canada) |
| **SEEPAD** | South Eastern European Partnership on Accountancy Development |
| **SFAC** | Standards of Financial Accounting Concepts (United States) |
| **SFAS** | Statement of Financial Accounting Standards (United States) |
| **SFC** | Securities and Futures Commission (Taiwan) |
| **SIAT** | Society of International Accounting Technicians (United Kingdom) |
| **SIC** | Standards Interpretations Committee (IASB) |
| **SOX** | Sarbanes-Oxley Act 2002 |
| **SPE** | Special Purpose Entities |
| **SPV** | Special Purpose Vehicles |
| **SSAP** | Statement of Standards Accounting Practice (United Kingdom) |
| **TFOSS** | Task Force on Standards Setting (Canada) |

| | |
|---|---|
| **TLF** | Transferable Loan Facility |
| **TOC** | Theory of Constraints |
| **TV** | Terminal Value |
| **UITF** | Urgent Issues Task Force (United Kingdom) |
| **UNCTAD** | United Nations Conference on Trade and Development |
| **USAID** | U.S. Agency for International Development |
| **WACC** | Weighted Average Cost of Capital |

APPENDIX B

# Accounting Standard Setting Bodies

International Accounting Standards Board (IASB)
30 Cannon Street
London EC4M 6XH
United Kingdom
Phone: +44 (0) 20 7246 6410
Fax: +44 (0) 20 7246 6411
Email: iasb@iasb.org
Web site: www.iasb.org
Publications telephone: +44 (0) 20 7332 2730
Publications fax: +44 (0) 20 7332 2749
Publications email: publications@iasb.org

**Argentina**

Federación Argentina de Consejos Profesionales de Ciencias (FACPCE)
The Argentine Federation of Professional Councils
Email: facpce@facpce.org.ar
Web site: http://www.facpce.org.ar/
Web site in English not available to date

**Australia**

Australian Accounting Standards Board (AASB)

| Postal Address: | Street Address: |
|---|---|
| PO Box 204 | Level 4 |
| Collins St West | 530 Collins Street |
| VIC 8007 | Melbourne, VIC 3000 |
| Australia | DX 30897, Document Exchange MEL VIC, Australia |

Phone: +61 (03) 9617 7600
Fax: +61 (03) 9617 7608
Email: standard@aasb.com.au
Web site: www.aasb.com.au
Publications email: publications@aasb.com.au

**Bahrain**

Accounting and Auditing Organization for Islamic Financial Institutions (AAOIFI)
P.O. Box 1176
Manama, Bahrain
Phone: +973 244496
Fax: +973 250194
Email: aaoifi@batelco.com.bh
Web site: www.aaoifi.com

**Brazil**

Conselho Federal de Contabilidade (CFC)—Brazil
SAS Quadra 05 Lote 03 Bloco 'J'
Edificio CFC
Cep : 70070-920, Brasilia-DF
Brazil
Phone : +55 (61) 314 9600
Fax : +55 (61) 322 2033
Email : cfc@cfc.org.br
Web site: http://www.cfc.org.br/
Web site in English not available to date

**Canada**

Accounting Standards Board (AcSB)
Canadian Institute of Chartered Accountants
277 Wellington Street West
Toronto ON

M5V 3H2
Canada
Phone: +1 (416) 977 3222
Fax: +1 (416) 977 8585
Web site: http://www.acsbcanada.org

**Chile**

Colegio de Contadores de Chile A.G.
Chilean Accountants Association
Email: informaciones@contach.cl
Web site: http://www.contach.cl/colegio/
Web site in English not available to date

**Denmark**

Foreningen af Statsautoriserede Revisorer (FSR)
The Institute of State Authorized Public
Accountants in Denmark
Danish Accounting Standards Committee (DASC)
Revisorernes Hus
Kronprinsessegade 8
DK-1306 Copenhagen K
Phone: +45 3393 9191
Fax: +45 3311 0913
Email: fsr@fsr.dk
Web site: www.fsr.dk

**France**

Conseil National de la Comptabilité (CNC)
French Accounting Standards Council
(National Accounting Board)
This is the body responsible for issuing the Plan Comptable Général (National Accounting Code) which sets out the prescribed format of accounts in France.
http://www.finances.gouv.fr/CNCompta/
Ministry of Economy, Finance and Industry
Main Web site: http://www.minefi.gouv.fr/minefi/minefi_ang/index.htm

### Germany

German Accounting Standards Committee
Deutsches Rechnungslegungs Standards Committee e.V. (DRSC)
Zimmerstrasse 30
D-10969 Berlin
Germany
Phone: +49 (030) 20 64 12 - 0
Fax: +49 (030) 20 64 12 - 15
Email: info@drsc.de
Web site : http://www.standardsetter.de/drsc/news/news_eng.php?list_id=1&language=English

### Gibraltar

Gibraltar Society of Chartered & Certified Accountancy Bodies (GSCCAB)
Email: http://www.gibraltaraccountants.com/

### Hong Kong

Hong Kong Institute of Certified Public Accountants (HKICPA)
4th Floor, Lippo Centre
Tower Two
89, Queensway
Hong Kong
Phone: +852 2287 7228
Fax: +852 2865 6603, 2865 6776
Email: hkicpa@hkicpa.org.hk
http://www.hkicpa.org.hk/

### India

Accounting Standards Board, India
Web site: http://www.icai.org/resource/o_ac_standard.html

### Israel

Israeli Accounting Standards Board
38 Kalisher St.
Tel Aviv, Israel
Phone: +972 (03) 510 9977
Fax: +972 (03) 510 9988
Web site: www.iasb.org.il

### Japan

Accounting Standards Board of Japan (ASBJ)
Financial Accounting Standards Foundation
No. 9 Kowa Building,
1-8-10 Akasaka, Minato-ku
Tokyo 107-0052
Japan
Fax: +81 (3) 5561 9619
Web site: http://www.asb.or.jp/index_e.html

### Korea

Korean Accounting Standards Board (KASB)
Yonsei Severance B/D 24F
Chung-gu Namdaemunro 5-ga 84-11
Seoul 100-753
South Korea
Phone: +82 (2) 2259 0150, 2259 0152
Fax: +82 (2) 2259 0170
Email: webmaster@kasb.or.kr
suklim@kasb.or.kr
Web site: http://www.kasb.or.kr/enghome.nsf

### Malaysia

Malaysian Accounting Standards Board (MASB)
Suites 5.01-5.03, 5th Floor
338 Jalan Tuanku Abdul Rahman
50100 Kuala Lumpur
Malaysia
Phone: +60 (03) 2715 9199
Fax: + 60 (03) 2715 9212
Email: masb@masb.org.my
Web site: www.masb.org.my

### Nepal

Institute of Chartered Accountants of Nepal (ICAN)
Post Box No: 5289
Babar Mahal
Kathmandu
Nepal
Phone: 4269130, 4258569

Fax: 4258568
Email: ican@ntc.net.np
http:// www. ican.org.np/main.aspx

**Netherlands**

De Raad voor de Jaarverslaggeving
Netherlands Accounting Standards Board
A.J. Ernststraat 55, Postbus 7984
1008 AD Amsterdam
Netherlands
Phone: +31 (020) 3010391
Fax: +31 (020) 3010279
Email: rj@rjnet.nl
Web site: www.rjnet.nl
Only Dutch version of Web site available to date

**New Zealand**

Financial Reporting Standards Board (FRSB)
Level 2, Cigna House
40 Mercer Street
P.O. Box 11342
Wellington 6034
New Zealand
Phone: +64 (4) 474 7840
Registry helpdesk: +64 (4) 460 0606
Fax: + 64 (4) 473 6303
Email: registry@icanz.co.nz
Web site: www.icanz.co.nz

**Norway**

Norsk RegnskapsStiftelse (NRS)
The Norwegian Accounting Standards Board
P.O. Box 5864 Majorstuen, N - 0308 Oslo
Phone: + 47 23 36 52 00
Fax: + 47 22 69 05 55
Email: nrs@revisornett.no
Web site: http://www.regnskapsstiftelsen.no/

**Singapore**

Council on Corporate Disclosure and Governance
The Secretariat, c/o Accounting and Corporate Regulatory Authority
55 Newton Road #11-03, Revenue House
Singapore 307987
Fax: +65 6225 1676
Email: Feedback_CCDG@acra.gov.sg
Web site: www.ccdg.gov.sg

**South Africa**

South African Accounting Standards Board
Menlyn Square
1st Floor, East Block
Cnr Lois and Gobie Ave
Menlyn
Phone: 012 470 9480
Fax: 012 348 4150
Email: ernas@asb.co.za
Web site: http://www.asb.co.za/

**Spain**

Instituto de Contabilidad y Auditoría de Cuentas (ICAC)
Official Institute of Accounting and Audit
C/Huertas, 26
28014 Madrid
Spain
Phone: +34 (91) 389 56 00
Fax: +34 (91) 429 94 86
http://www.icac.mineco.es/icacpr.htm
Web site in English not available to date

**Sweden**

Swedish Accounting Standards Board (Redovisningsrådet)
Box 6417
11382 Stockholm
Sweden
Phone: +46 (08) 506 112 75
Fax: +46 (08) 32 12 50
Email: mail@redovisningsradet.se
Web site: http://www.redovisningsradet.se/forening-english.html

**Switzerland**

Swiss GAAP FER
Fachempfehlungen zur Rechnungslegung (FER)
Neue Briefadresse
Stiftung für Empfehlungen zur Rechnungslegung
Postfach 6140
8023 Zürich
Fax: +41 (0)1 267 75 85
http://www.fer.ch/de/index.htm
Web site in English not available to date

**Taiwan**

Accounting Research and Development
Foundation (ARDF)
9th Floor, 1 Nan-Hai Road
Taipei 100
Taiwan, Republic of China
Phone: +886 (2) 2394 5291
Fax: +886 (2) 2393 6216
+886 (2) 2391 9434
Email: research@ardf.org.tw
Web site: www.ardf.org.tw

**United Kingdom**

Accounting Standards Board (ASB)
David Loweth
Secretary, Accounting Standards Board
5th floor, Aldwych House
71-91 Aldwych
London WC2B 4HN
United Kingdom
Phone: +44 (0) 20 7492 2300
Fax: +44 (0)20 7492 2301
Email: d.loweth@frc-asb.org.uk
http://www.frc.org.uk/asb/

**United States**

Financial Accounting Standards Board (FASB)
401 Merritt 7
P.O. Box 5116
Norwalk, Connecticut
06856-5116, USA
Phone: +1 (203) 847 0700
Fax: +1 (203) 849 9714
Web site: www.fasb.org
Email: techinq@fasb.org

Governmental Accounting Standards Board (GASB)
401 Merritt 7
PO Box 5116
Norwalk, Connecticut
06856-5116, USA
Phone: +1 (203) 847 0700
Fax: +1 (203) 849 9714.
Email: techinquiry@gasb.org

# Index*



*Index applies to Parts One and Two.